Commercial Property

Jurisdictional comparisons   **First edition 2010**

General Editor: Graham Lloyd-Brunt, Berwin Leighton Paisner

General Editor
Graham Lloyd-Brunt

Publisher
Mark Wyatt

International Director
Michele O'Sullivan

Publishing Services Director
Ben Martin

Publishing and Production Manager
Emily Kyriacou

Production Editor
Caroline Pearce

Sub Editor
Lisa Naylor

Design and Production
Dawn McGovern

Published by
The European Lawyer
Futurelex Limited
23-24 Smithfield Street
London EC1A 9LF
T: +44 (0) 20 7332 2582
F: +44 (0) 20 7332 2599
www.europeanlawyer.co.uk

Printed in the UK by CPI William Clowes Beccles NR34 7TL
ISBN: 978-0-9565440-7-0
© *Futurelex Limited 2010*

While all reasonable care has been taken to ensure the accuracy of the publication, the publishers cannot accept responsibility for any errors or omissions.
This publication is protected by international copyright law:
All rights reserved. No paragraph or other part of this document may be reproduced or transmitted in any form by any means, including photocopying and recording, without the written permission of Futurelex Limited or in accordance with the provisions of the Copyright Act 1988 (as amended).
Such written permission must also be obtained before any paragraph or other part of this publication is stored in a retrieval system of any kind.

Commercial Property

Contents

Introduction	Graham Lloyd-Brunt, Berwin Leighton Paisner	v
Foreword	Giles Wintle, GIC Real Estate Government of Singapore Investment Corporation	vi
Overview	Peter Damesick, CB Richard Ellis	vii
Australia	David Sharpe & David Turner, DibbsBarker	1
Belgium	Yves Delacroix & Henk Verstraete, Liederkerke Wolters Waelbroeck Kirkpatrick	19
Bulgaria	Nickolay Nickolov & Iva Miteva, Borislav Boyanov & Co	31
Canada	Heather McKean, Jack Silverson & Brian Donnelly, Osler Hoskin & Harcourt LLP	47
Czech Republic	Jan Holásek & Daniela Kozáková, Havel & Holásek	63
Denmark	Henrik Groos & Kristoffer Westberg, Accura Advokatpartnerselskab	79
France	Véronique Lagarde & Antonia Raccat, Lefèvre Pelletier & Associés	95
Germany	Dr Nicole Kadel & Dr Axel Schilder, Beiten Burkhardt Rechtanwaltsgesellschaft mbH	119
Greece	Eliana Paschalides, Spyros Foulias & Alexandra Mitsokali, V&P Law Firm	137
Guernsey	Aimee Curzon & Paul Nettleship, Collas Day	153
Hungary	Péter Berethalmi & Balázs Karsai, Nagy és Trócsányi	167
India	Sudip Mullick & Sirish Vardhan, Khaitan & Co	179
Italy	Umberto Borzi & Giuseppe Andrea Giannantonio, Chiomenti Studio Legale	185
Jersey	Christopher Philpott & Will Whitehead, Carey Olsen	199
Luxembourg	Eric Fort & Claude Niedner, Arendt & Medernach	213
The Netherlands	Aart Barkey Wolf & Wouter Ekkelkamp, Houthoff Buruma	231
Northern Ireland	David McDonnell & Phyllis Agnew, Tughans	245
Republic of Ireland	Ronan McLoughlin, Matheson Ormsby Prentice	253
Russia	Elena Barinova, Andrey Shpak, Matvey Kaploukhiy & Svetlana Savina, Goltsblat BLP	263
Scotland	Dale Strachan & Alistair Campbell, Brodies LLP	277
Slovak Republic	Jan Holásek & Pavol Polácek, Havel & Holásek	295
Spain	Jordi Sagrera, Bernat Mullerat, Iñigo Rubio, Meritxell Yus, Iñigo de Luisa, Victoria González & Silvia Alcoverro, Cuatrecasas Gonçalves Pereira	311
Sweden	Bob Johanson, Carolina Hertzen & Sara Edström, Gernandt & Danielsson Advokatbyrå KB	327
UK	Graham Lloyd-Brunt & Annabel Pyke, Berwin Leighton Paisner	341
Contact details		359

Introduction

Graham Lloyd-Brunt, Berwin Leighton Paisner

Welcome to the first edition of Commercial Property, which is edited by the leading real estate practitioners in England and Wales with contributions from some of the most highly regarded real estate practices across Europe and a number of other countries.

This book provides a comparison of the position in different countries on key issues which arise in real estate transactions. It also includes expert commentary from leading real estate lawyers on the applicable laws and regulations in their jurisdictions.

Our aim has been to include a high quality of content so that Commercial Property will be seen as an essential reference work in the field.
London, November 2010

Foreword

Giles Wintle, senior vice president, GIC Real Estate Government of Singapore Investment Corporation

Surprises are not generally considered to be good things among the investment community. The diverse range of language, law, tax regime and market practice that segregate the European property markets means that there is plenty of scope for them. It also provides for much opportunity and adventure. Despite attempts to master Europe's complexity, it is not long before one draws the conclusion that the best we can hope for is to learn how to ask the right questions, rather than to know all the answers. Of course it helps to address the right questions to the right professional and so the choice of legal counsel is key. Choosing one is not as straightforward as it might appear.

Thankfully the legal professional appears to have evolved along with the needs of its clients, from a good source of reference and occasional lunch companion into a rounded and nimble adviser, often versed in several disciplines and able to pre-empt those surprises that worry us investors so. Perhaps then, the most useful quality of a commercial legal counsel is an ability to understand their client's assumptions or, more to the point, their presumptions.

With diversity of market has come diversity of investor, culture, strategy, traditions and negotiation style. Sometimes the part of a transaction that is most confusing is the counterparty. Negotiations with certain counterparts might take place over lunch, while others require a lengthy and formal meeting. Some sessions I have attended included so many people at the negotiation table that it became tough to understand who was speaking for whom. The role of legal counsel in these occasions seems to be more akin to that of a diplomat than an interpreter of legal tome. The second most useful quality of commercial legal counsel might therefore be patience.

Finally despite, what I am sure is an interesting and rewarding business, there are still few very excellent international legal counsel. It is therefore often the case that one finds oneself negotiating with a counterparty who is equipped with one's own preferred counsel. As if by magic, said counsel will seemingly forget all it knows that could be to their client's advantage and to one's detriment during negotiations. So, it is either kindness or perhaps a poor memory that is the third key quality of commercial legal counsel, in my view at least.

The market environment for real estate investment in Europe: an overview

Peter Damesick, EMEA chief economist, CB Richard Ellis

Two themes dominate the real estate investment scene in European markets in late 2010: first, the uneven pattern of recovery from the crash triggered by the financial crisis; second, heightened uncertainty about future prospects. The two are connected: both the progress of recovery so far and future prospects are strongly coloured by the legacy of the crisis in terms of the massive overhang of debt in both the public and the private sectors.

Investment turnover in European real estate markets slumped by 70 per cent from a peak of €254 billion in 2007 to €73 billion in 2009. Activity has picked up since mid-2009 and our expectation at CB Richard Ellis is that the outturn for 2010 will see transaction volumes up by between 45-50 per cent on last year. Increased purchasing has been driven mainly by investors buying assets within their own national market, but there has also been a rise in the volume of cross-border transactions, from a very low level at the start of 2009. These have included European investors such as German and Dutch funds and also a significant increase in acquisitions by investors from the Middle East and the Far East. Cross-border investment, especially from outside Europe, is heavily concentrated in a few major European cities, with London in particular attracting a disproportionate share.

Transaction volumes are still well below the exceptional levels of 2006-2007 when debt-based buying was at its height. The market has become largely reliant upon equity-based, institutional-type investors, both local and foreign. Availability of debt finance has improved relative to the depths of the crunch, but bank lending remains highly selective on conservative criteria. The real estate market is operating in the shadow of a huge re-financing requirement for loans originated in the last decade's credit boom, with a large volume due to mature over the next three years. There is a strong concentration of outstanding debt in Britain, Germany and Spain. In absolute terms, Ireland represents the most extreme example of market trauma wrought by explosive growth in real estate debt.

The pick-up in transaction volumes was accompanied by an improvement in investment property pricing in European markets, but this has been highly uneven, both by country and type of real estate asset. The UK has been at the forefront of commercial market recovery. Having seen values among the hardest hit in the downturn, the UK showed the earliest and strongest upturn over the second half of 2009 although momentum has

Overview

flagged over the course of 2010. CB Richard Ellis' European Valuation Monitor shows values in France and the Nordic countries strengthening during 2010, while markets in Benelux, Southern Europe and Ireland have continued to see average values losing ground.

A further striking disparity in pricing recovery has centred on asset quality. High quality real estate offering secure income has seen by far the greatest value uplift across European markets. Lesser quality assets with weaker income security have languished. The yield spread between prime and secondary property has widened sharply, reflecting the preferences of the institutional-type investors dominating the market. Banks prepared to extend new lending to the sector have minimal appetite for lending on secondary quality assets. Demand for high quality 'core' assets, on the other hand, has driven sharp pricing improvements in certain favoured markets such as London, Paris and the Nordic capitals.

Occupational markets for commercial property are improving across Europe to varying degrees. Leasing demand has picked up, with overall vacancy levels in office markets stabilised and in some cities now on a downward trend. The credit crunch had an early impact in checking new development activity. Access to development finance dried up before the recession took hold, so relatively few new developments have started since early 2008. Many markets therefore now have comparatively little space due to be completed in the next couple of years, leaving them free from the overhang of excess new supply seen in the aftermath of previous downturns. With finance likely to remain constrained, a significant upturn in development activity looks some way off in many European markets. London looks likely to be a leader in the next development cycle, but even here it will be 2013 or 2014 before significant amounts of new space can be delivered.

Tight supply pipelines create upside potential for rental growth. Already, rents for Grade A office space are rising in London, Paris, Oslo, Warsaw, Stockholm, Brussels and Berlin. A larger number of other cities have seen prime office rents stabilise with the next movement likely to be upwards. Of the major centres these include Amsterdam, Vienna, Munich, Frankfurt and Moscow. Retail rents are also rising in prime shopping locations in a range of leading European cities where international retailers compete over the limited number of available retail units. Major shopping centres serving as dominant retail destinations continue to sustain high occupancy levels.

The impetus for rental growth in European property markets remains largely confined to core markets and prime quality space where supply is tightening, with little sign of a generalised upturn in rental values driven by expansionary demand from higher employment, consumer spending and business investment. Uncertainty over the prospects for broader rental recovery on the back of economic expansion is now a key factor weighing on investor sentiment in European markets.

Concern over the growth outlook for Europe has been heightened by the state of government finances in a range of countries. Yawning public sector deficits, with threats of a sovereign debt crisis in the Eurozone periphery, have prompted a broad-based switch from stimulus policies to austerity programmes.

Overview

The uncertain outlook naturally induces greater investor caution. However, real estate retains a fundamental attraction as an investment asset in view of the wide margin between property yields and the returns on government bonds or cash. Tight supply pipelines in occupational markets are favourable for rental prospects, although there will be significant variation in potential by sector and location.

Recent investment demand for European real estate has been strongly focused on assets offering secure income in core markets. Limited availability of such assets for sale means they have become more keenly priced. The current environment suggests there is scope for investors to seek a wider range of opportunities, including the creation of core assets. This could be through development or the refurbishment and asset management of existing properties to transform good secondary assets with potential into higher quality real estate. The highly variable pattern of prospects and opportunities across European markets mean that investment activity of this type must be based on deployment of suitable specialist skills and, most importantly, expert local knowledge.

Australia

DibbsBarker David Sharpe & David Turner

1. INVESTMENT PURCHASE OVERVIEW
Before purchasing real estate in Australia, a non-Australian resident should consider the Australian government's foreign investment policy (see 3.2 below), structuring issues (see 3.1), financing issues (see 4), and tax and duty aspects (see 2.1, 2.2 and 2.3).

Steps involved in an acquisition are outlined in 5.2, and related aspects (costs, warranties, liabilities, risk etc) are found in 5.3 to 5.11.

2. A TYPICAL INVESTMENT PURCHASE IN AUSTRALIA
See flow chart on page 18.

2.1 Goods and services tax (GST)
Goods and services tax (GST) is a federal tax imposed on 'taxable supplies'. A taxable supply is made when a right is granted, assigned or surrendered in the furtherance of an enterprise, the supply is made in connection with Australia, and the entity making the supply is registered or required to be registered for GST.

The breadth of the definitions of the elements making up a taxable supply mean that a transfer of commercial real estate (such as offices, factories or shops), commercial residential property (hotels, motels, inns, hostels or boarding houses) and new residential property will generally attract GST.

The tax is calculated as 10 per cent of the GST-exclusive sale price. The seller is liable to pay the GST, but would commonly pass it on to the buyer by including it in the price or, as a term of the contract, requiring the buyer to pay the GST in addition to the GST-exclusive price.

A buyer can offset the GST it pays to the seller against GST it is otherwise liable to pay on taxable supplies it makes. That is, it is entitled to an input tax credit.

2.1.1 Exemptions
- GST is not payable on the sale of second-hand residential property.
- Subject to certain conditions, transfers of farmland and grants of vacant land by government are GST-free.
- The sale of all the elements of an enterprise (the sale of a going concern) is GST-free so that land transferred as part of that enterprise will not attract GST. Leasing out land is regarded as an enterprise, and so the sale of leased land could amount to a sale of a going concern and benefit from this GST-free exemption.

Australia

- GST is not payable in relation to the transfer of shares or units in a trust.

2.1.2 Reduction

GST can be reduced if the seller and buyer agree to use the 'margin scheme'. Under this scheme, GST is paid only on the difference between the price received when the property is sold and the price paid when the property was acquired. If the real estate was acquired prior to 1 July 2000, the purchase price is generally deemed to be the value of the property as at that date. The margin scheme can only be used on the sale of property where the purchase was GST-free or the margin scheme was applied when the property was acquired.

If the margin scheme is applied, the buyer cannot claim input tax credits for the GST it pays. This results in the margin scheme generally only being used where the real estate is to be ultimately redeveloped and sold as new residential premises.

2.2 Stamp duty/transfer tax

Duty is charged by each state and territory (not by the federal government) on the transfer of real estate.

- Duty is calculated on a sliding scale, with rate increases cutting in when particular threshold prices are reached. The amount of the increases, the highest rates and the thresholds vary between the jurisdictions. For instance in the Australian Capital Territory, the rate is 6.75 per cent above a threshold of $1 million. In New South Wales, the rate is 5.5 per cent above a price threshold of $1 million, but if the land is residential and its purchase price exceeds $3 million, a premium rate of seven per cent is payable on the excess over that amount.
- In some states, the legislation makes the buyer liable and in others both seller and buyer are liable. The accepted practice is for the buyer to pay the duty.
- As will be seen below, registration of a land transfer is vital. A transfer cannot be registered unless the duty has been paid.
- No duty or reduced duty may be payable on the transfer of shares in a company or units in a trust. To prevent duty on a land transfer being avoided by transferring shares or units in a 'land rich' entity, in certain circumstances the various states and territories impose duty at land rates on the transfer of shares or units in the entity which owns the land. The criteria for whether duty is payable in relation to the land holding entity vary markedly from state to state.
- Concessions are limited. For example:
- some states provide concessions for property intended for use as a home;
- in certain circumstances, duty is not payable on the transfer of dutiable property between members of a corporate group undertaking a corporate reconstruction.

In addition, in some states, a transfer registration fee is charged, based on the value of the land transferred and calculated on a sliding scale. Rates vary between jurisdictions.

2.3 Tax issues for overseas investors
2.3.1 General
- Liability. Non-residents are taxed on their Australian sourced income, and withholding tax at specific rates applies to dividends, interest and royalties.
- As well, there are particular withholding rates where income arises from managed investment funds including Australian real estate investment trusts.
- Australia has agreements with a number of countries in order to prevent double taxation of income. The provisions of these agreements are not uniform and must be looked at individually to assess their impact on any particular taxpayer.
- International transfer pricing rules are found in Australian law and double tax agreements. These rules permit the Australian Taxation Office to substitute a price for tax purposes as though the parties involved were independent persons entering into a transaction at market value.
- For income purposes, and for taxing foreign exchange gains and losses, there are extensive rules for translating foreign currency amounts into Australian currency.

2.3.2 Capital gains tax
Assessable income will include any capital gains and losses arising on the disposal of taxable Australian real estate. Taxable Australian property includes:
- real estate situated in Australia, including mining or prospecting rights;
- a direct membership interest in resident or non-resident entities which directly or indirectly own real property in Australia which constitutes 50 per cent or more of their asset base, calculated using a prescriptive test; and
- assets used in carrying on a business in Australia via a permanent establishment.

Concessions
- Individuals who dispose of their principal residence are generally not taxed on any resulting gain.
- If the seller is an individual, a trust or an Australian complying superannuation fund and the real estate has been held for at least one year, only 50 per cent (33 per cent for a superannuation fund) of any capital gain will be taxed.

2.3.3 Land tax
Land tax is a state tax levied annually and payable by owners on land located in the relevant jurisdiction. Generally, land tax is not payable on a principal residence or a property used for primary production, for example, a farm.

The amount of land tax is calculated on the unimproved value of taxable land, usually, but not always, above a tax free threshold. The rates and thresholds vary between jurisdictions. In New South Wales for example, for 2010 the tax is calculated on the combined value of all taxable land in NSW owned by the landholder above a threshold of $376,000. The rate of land tax in NSW is $100 plus 1.6 per cent of the unimproved land value between the threshold and the premium rate threshold of $2,299,000, and 2 per cent thereafter.

3. INVESTMENT VEHICLE CHOICE
3.1 Structures used to purchase property
Various structures are available to make direct or indirect investment in Australian real estate. The choice will depend on a number of factors, including the nature of the subject property and taxation and liability issues:
- Direct investment by individuals: more usually found in off the plan acquisitions of residential real estate. The individual would not have available the limited liability or potential for effective taxation structuring which other vehicles may offer.
- Registering a foreign company: except where operating through an Australian subsidiary, a foreign company conducting business in Australia must register as a foreign company with the Australian Securities and Investments Commission and thereafter comply with various requirements under the Commonwealth Corporations Act.
- Forming a company in Australia: an Australian subsidiary of a foreign corporation may be incorporated under the Corporations Act and would most commonly be a company limited by shares. The company must comply with the requirements of the Act and would be subject to the taxation regime applying to incorporated companies.
- Unit trusts: in this type of trust, the beneficiaries' interests are divided into units. The trustee, normally a company, would own the legal title to the assets. A business of investing in and owning units in a private unit trust would be governed by trust law. The obligations under the Corporations Act would apply to the corporate trustee if incorporated in Australia. Tax treatment of unit trusts is a mixture of the treatment of companies and partnerships.
- Incorporated joint ventures: here the venture would be operated by a special purpose joint venture company in which the joint venture participants hold shares.
- Unincorporated joint ventures: here the parties agree to cooperate in relation to a real estate investment, but hold their entitlements in the venture separately rather than jointly. There is the potential for taxation advantages for each venturing party. A participant's liability can be limited as they will not be jointly liable.
- Partnerships: another form of unincorporated joint venture. The arrangement between the parties will be governed by their contract and also by legislation and common law. There are taxation advantages as the partnership itself is not taxable, but income and losses are distributed to each partner. However each partner will have unlimited liability for all of the partnership's debts. Each Australian jurisdiction allows for forms of limited partnership to operate. The limited partners, the passive investor participants, have their liability limited, but lose the tax advantages of an

ordinary partnership and are taxed at the corporate rate.

3.2 Restrictions on foreign ownership or occupation of property
3.2.1 Foreign investment policy
The Australian government's foreign investment policy encourages foreign investment, but at the same time subjects proposals for foreign investment to strict controls.

The Foreign Acquisitions and Takeovers Act 1975 (FATA) and its regulations provide the statutory mechanism to ensure that the policy is complied with.

The following is a simplified guide only. Full details can be obtained from the Australian government's Foreign Investment Review Board (*www.firb.gov.au*).

3.2.2 Foreign person
FATA and the policy apply to certain acquisitions by foreign persons. A foreign person is:
- a natural person not ordinarily resident in Australia; or
- a corporation, or the trustee of a trust estate, in which natural person/s not ordinarily resident in Australia or a foreign corporation holds what are defined as substantial interests.

3.2.3 What must be notified
Certain acquisitions by foreign persons of Australian real estate (including interests that arise via leases, financing and profit sharing arrangements) are subject to FATA and should be notified to the Government for prior approval namely, proposals to acquire:
- developed non-residential commercial real estate, valued at $50 million or more ($1,004 million for a US investor – indexed annually) where the property is not subject to heritage listing; or $5 million or more where the property is subject to heritage listing and the acquirer is not a US investor;
- vacant non-residential land, irrespective of value;
- residential real estate, irrespective of value (although some exemptions apply); or
- shares or units in Australian urban land corporations or trust estates, irrespective of value; or
- proposals where any doubt exists as to whether they are notifiable. (Funding arrangements that include debt instruments having quasi equity characteristics will be treated as direct foreign investment.); or
- direct investments by foreign governments and their agencies irrespective of size.

More detail about a number of these categories is given below.

3.2.4 Conditional contracts
FATA requires all contracts by foreign persons to acquire interests in Australian real estate to be conditional upon foreign investment approval,

Australia

unless approval was obtained before the contract was entered into, or the acquisition does not require notification. Breach of FATA requirements may give rise to significant criminal and civil penalties.

3.2.5 Residential real estate
Some acquisitions are exempt from notification. For example:
- acquisitions by Australian citizens living abroad, or foreign nationals holding permanent resident visas; and
- acquisitions of certain types of property, such as an interest in a time share scheme where the entitlement is less than four weeks in any year, or an interest in a resort which the government designated as an integrated tourism resort prior to September 1999.

Other acquisitions must be notified, but approval is available if certain conditions are met. For example:
- vacant land proposed for residential development, subject to construction and expense requirements.
- new dwellings, if marketed locally as well as overseas.
- second-hand dwellings, but not if they are to be used as rental or holiday properties. Foreign-owned companies may acquire second-hand dwellings to provide housing for their Australian-based staff, subject to divestment conditions.
- established dwellings may be acquired for the purpose of development if the proposal provides for an increase in the number of dwellings.
- acquisitions of residential land by temporary residents, subject to conditions including that the property be sold when the purchaser leaves the country.
- time share schemes where the entitlement is greater than four weeks in any year and other conditions are met.
- certain interests in resorts which the government designated as integrated tourism resorts after September 1999, if conditions such as the tenure of the resort operator are satisfied.

Where a proposal must be notified but the eligibility requirements are not met, the proposal will not normally be approved.

3.2.6 Commercial real estate
Commercial real estate means vacant and developed property which is not approved for residential purposes, or which is not rural land (as referred to below).

Some acquisitions are exempt from notification. For example:
- acquisitions by Australian citizens living abroad;
- an interest acquired from a commonwealth, state, territory or local government;
- an interest in developed commercial property (not heritage listed) valued at less than $50 million or $1,004 million (indexed annually) for US investors, or $5 million for heritage listed properties where the acquirer is not a US investor;
- an interest in developed commercial property where the property is

to be used immediately for non-residential purposes and as part of the purchaser's proposed or existing business.

Other acquisitions must be notified, but approval is available if certain conditions are met. If an acquisition is not exempt, the government must be notified in advance. Proposals involving the following are usually approved unless the government decides they are contrary to the national interest:
- developed commercial property (including acquisitions of hotels, motels, hostels and guesthouses);
- vacant land, subject to compliance with conditions such as construction commencing within five years and minimum amounts being spent on the development;
- a lease or licence giving rights to occupy Australian urban land for a period which is likely to exceed five years, or arrangements involving the sharing of profits or income from the use of Australian urban land, including mining tenements;
- proposals to acquire land to establish a forestry business, subject to compliance with conditions such as development/planting commencing within 12 months, minimum amounts being spent on the development of the business, compliance with relevant state industry practice codes, and divestment requirements.

3.2.7 Rural land
Rural land is land used wholly for carrying on a substantial business of primary production. Rural properties not so used will be classified as commercial or residential property.

The acquisition of an interest in a primary production business where the total assets do not exceed $231 million (or $1,004 million for US investors) is exempt from the need for foreign investment approval.

3.3 Are real estate investment trusts (REITs) available? Are they often used?
Australia has a large, well developed and transparent REIT market. These real estate funds now control a significant percentage of the high grade commercial real estate throughout the country and extend across most types of real estate.

Australian REITs have their basis in the general law of trusts, but are also subject to comprehensive regulation under Australian company law. Like other managed investment schemes, they are required to be registered, to issue product disclosure statements to prospective investors and, where listed, to comply with the rules of the Australian Securities Exchange. The trust structuring allows for favourable tax treatment of income generated.

Investment by non residents in Australian REITs will not normally be impacted by Australia's foreign investment restrictions having regard to the notification and approval criteria. Those restrictions may apply, however, where foreign control over Australian real estate funds or fund managers is at issue.

4. FINANCING AN ACQUISITION

4.1 Financing of real estate transactions
Real estate financing is usually a combination of equity and debt.

Various Australian lending institutions offer loans to foreign buyers, particularly those who are currently resident in Australia. Alternatively, a foreign person could seek finance outside Australia, although such borrowing could involve the risk of exchange rate fluctuations. Wherever the loan originates, it is most likely that the Australian property will need to be purchased in Australian dollars.

The financier's lending criteria must be checked. Most will impose a maximum ratio of loan value to property value. Lending criteria and loan-to-value ratios have contracted markedly since the onset of the global financial crisis.

It is prudent to obtain approval for the proposed borrowing from the lending institution before any contract for the purchase of a property becomes binding.

4.2 Real estate as a means of raising finance
Real estate is a fundamental resource in raising finance. In making financial accommodation available, lenders will seek real estate as a basic security. More detail concerning mortgage financing is set out in 4.3 below.

Real estate financing can take other forms. For instance, a landowner, seeking to release the capital value of its land for use in its business, may seek to sell to a third party and then take a long-term lease back from that third party. The seller enjoys the sale proceeds, while the buyer gains a real estate asset and a rental income stream. And see 4.4 below.

4.3 Common forms of security granted over real estate
Before advancing funds, the lending institution will seek security from the borrower by way of instruments such as:
- a legal mortgage over the property on which the finance is to be raised;
- where the borrower is a company, and the lender requires security over all assets, a fixed and floating charge over all the borrower's assets. A 'fixed charge' secures the assets specified in the charge document on the date it is taken, and will generally include all real estate owned or subsequently acquired by the borrower. A floating charge is a security interest over the changing assets of a company, which 'floats' until conversion to a fixed charge, at which point the charge attaches to specific assets. Until then, the borrower is free to deal with its assets. The conversion can be triggered by a number of events, most commonly, default by the borrower under its borrowing covenants.
- an assignment of the right to receive rents from tenants at the mortgaged property. From the lender's standpoint, the rental income is vital as it will be used to service the debt repayments;
- if the borrower is a special purpose vehicle, a equitable mortgage over the shares in the company or over the units in the unit trust (as the case may be);

- an assignment of the benefit of any major contracts, for instance, in relation to recent developments of the subject property.

In addition, as part of the funding process, the lender will require:
- a valuation of the real estate for the purpose of implementing loan to value ratios;
- satisfactory results of due diligence enquiries regarding the land, its title, permitted uses, environmental issues, the borrower, the guarantors and any project proposed by the borrower;
- a loan/facility agreement covering the particular terms of the subject transaction, and other ancillary documents;
- its legal mortgage to have priority over other borrowings and to be registered in the applicable land titles office;
- any fixed and floating charge to be registered with the Australian Securities and Investments Commission within 45 days after it is created. Otherwise it will be void as a security against a liquidator or administrator;
- the buildings on the land to be covered by an insurance policy which notes the lender's interest; and
- personal guarantees from the directors and/or shareholders of private company borrowers.

4.4 Real estate mortgage securitisation

The Australian residential mortgage-backed securities market has provided an alternative source of capital. As in other countries, there was a sustained period of steady growth in this sector through to early 2007. The turmoil in global credit markets which then occurred had a significant impact on the local mortgage-backed securities market and issuance of those securities has been significantly limited in the following months. Fortunately, Australia has not experienced the significant level of defaulting loans seen in some other parts of the world.

5. MANAGING THE ACQUISITION PROCESS

5.1 Minimum formalities for the sale and purchase of property

With limited exceptions, all transfers of land in Australia are required to be in writing in order to be enforceable. To transfer property:
- for Torrens title land (see 6.3 below), a transfer in the form required by the relevant state or territory titles office, duly signed by the parties, and on which duty has been paid, needs to be registered. In most states the transfer cannot be lodged for registration unless the Certificate of Title for the property is also obtained from the seller; and
- for Old System land (see 6.3 below), a deed of conveyance, duly signed by the seller, needs to be delivered to the buyer. Duty must be paid on the deed. Such a deed may be registered to give it priority over possible competing interests. The buyer would also require delivery of the sequence of prior deeds which evidences title to the property.

5.2 Main legal documents required to transfer a property or grant a lease

5.2.1 Transfer of property

To reach completion of the sale, where the buyer will pay for the property and the seller will hand over the documents referred to in 5.1, it is usual for the transaction to proceed in the following manner.

- Sellers usually use a real estate agent to market the property. Buyers may engage the services of a buyer's agent if the buyer wishes to have specialised help in seeking out a property with particular features.
- The buyer should determine which structure to use to acquire the property and seek confirmation from the chosen financial institution that any necessary funding will be available.
- Although some warranties must be given by the seller at law, in general terms the principle of 'buyer beware' applies. It is necessary for the buyer to conduct various searches and enquiries prior to entering into a binding contract, as a buyer will not be able to cancel a contract if there is a defect in the property which the buyer should have discovered through its own enquiries. Accordingly, the buyer needs to investigate matters of survey, the buildings on the property, utilities servicing the property, land use, and environmental aspects including contamination. For this purpose the prudent buyer engages qualified consultants to assist with enquiries in each of these areas.
- It is usual for both parties to engage professional lawyers or conveyancers to both prepare the necessary documentation and oversee the whole transaction.
- The seller's lawyer normally prepares the contract for sale and, where state legislation requires, ancillary documents such as a vendor's statement providing information relating to the property. The contract for sale is generally based on a standard form contract (although each state and territory has its own standard form). The standard contract will be modified to a greater or lesser extent depending upon the seller's particular requirements.
- When the buyer has completed its pre-contract enquiries, and the terms of the contract have been agreed between the seller and buyer, both parties would normally sign a counterpart of the contract and the counterparts are 'exchanged'. Upon exchange (subject to statutory cooling-off rights in some states), the contract becomes binding on the parties.
- On exchange of contracts, the buyer pays a deposit, which is usually 10 per cent of the purchase price, but may be negotiated at a lesser figure. The deposit is usually held by the selling agent or the seller's lawyer until the sale is completed.
- After exchange of contracts, the buyer will carry out further enquiries to verify the seller's title and any seller's warranties, and will fulfil the requirements of its lending institution to ensure that the necessary funds will be available on completion.
- The contract will state when completion or closure of the sale is to take

place. There are standard periods, but they differ between the various jurisdictions from 28 to 42 days. The parties may agree on a shorter or longer period depending upon, for instance, whether additional time is needed to satisfy certain conditions or to meet the financier's requirements.

5.2.2 Lease of property
A lease granted to a commercial tenant for a term of years should be in writing. The document will state the parties, the premises, the term, the rent and other terms concerning the use and occupation of the premises by the tenant.
- For land under Torrens title, the tenant can obtain the protection of a guaranteed title by having the lease registered. However some leases for particular terms are protected even if not registered. The rules vary between the states and territories and regard must be had to the local practice.
- In order to reach the point where a written lease is entered into, regard should be had to the type of lease and the applicable law in the relevant jurisdiction. Leases of residential property may be required to contain prescribed terms. Leases of retail shops will require landlords to make certain disclosures and provide additional documents apart from the lease itself. Leases of rural properties are often subject to particular legislation.
- Although a registered lease of Torrens title land will give a tenant a guaranteed title, enforceable legal rights will arise between the landlord and tenant when written documentation is entered into. This will commonly take the form of a preliminary agreement for lease which sets out the terms of the lease which are to come into effect at an agreed future time.

5.3 Property transaction costs
5.3.1 Transaction costs paid by sellers
- The real estate agent who has marketed the property is the agent of the seller. The seller will be responsible for paying the agent's commission. The amount of commission is negotiable, but is usually a percentage of the price.
- The seller usually bears its own legal costs in relation to the preparation of documentation and the administration by its lawyers of the sale transaction. To the extent that the sale contract requires disclosure documents or reports to be attached, the seller will be responsible for the costs of obtaining those documents or reports.

5.3.2 Transaction costs paid by buyers
- If the buyer has utilised the services of a buyer's real estate agent to find a suitable property for purchase, then the buyer will be liable for the agent's negotiated fee.
- The buyer bears the legal costs of its lawyers in relation to the transaction.

Australia

- The buyer will become liable for the expenses or outgoings of the property (for instance, council rates, water rates, land tax or *strata levies*) from the date of completion of the purchase.
- As mentioned in 5.2, it is necessary for the buyer to carry out certain enquiries and searches and obtain reports prior to and during the course of the transaction. The costs associated with this due diligence will be met by the buyer.

The buyer and seller must also have regard to taxes and duties.

5.3.3 Transaction costs paid by landlords and tenants for leases

- The landlord's lawyers usually prepare the lease documents. Traditionally the landlord's lawyers' fees for preparing documents and administering the lease transaction were borne by the tenant. In recent times, payment of the landlord's costs has been negotiable and it is quite common for the landlord to bear its own costs. For leases of some retail premises, legislation prevents the landlord from recovering its lease preparation costs from the tenant.
- It is usually the case that the tenant pays for any legal assistance it obtains in relation to the lease transaction.
- Landlords will often engage leasing agents to find tenants for commercial premises. Negotiated fees and commissions due to such leasing agents will be payable by the landlord.
- The lease documents normally provide that any applicable government duty and registration fees will be payable by the tenant.

5.4 Does the seller warrant its ownership of the property?

Such a warranty would be rarely given. Instead a buyer will rely on the conclusiveness of the official land register (see Torrens title under 6.3 below) and/or on the enquiries and checks made to verify the seller's title in the period of time between exchange of contracts and completion of the transaction.

5.5 Warranties a seller usually gives to a buyer

In earlier times, the risk lay almost entirely with the buyer who had to rely on its own searches and enquiries to gain assurance that it was getting a good title. Now, in some jurisdictions, the buyer's position has been improved by legislated seller disclosure and seller warranties.

- Seller disclosure: in several states, before the contract is entered into a seller must attach to the contract detailed information on its title, planning and land use restrictions and other matters.
- Statutory warranties: in some jurisdictions the seller gives certain warranties by law. For instance, that there is no proposal that a government instrumentality will compulsorily acquire the property, there is no proposal to widen adjacent roads, and there are no outstanding orders requiring demolition or repair of buildings.

The buyer should still make its own enquiries and checks, but these can be more safely done after the contract is entered into by way of verifying the seller's disclosure and warranties.

In portfolio sales, it is common for the buyer to seek to have warranties included in the sale contract. For tenanted properties, warranties would be sought stating that the leases are on foot, and that all details of tenancies have been disclosed and are correct. For properties which have been used for industrial purposes or may have been polluted or contaminated, warranties are often sought as to the condition of the property and the existence or extent of contamination.

5.6 Purpose of warranties in the purchase agreement
Information. Statutory disclosure and warranties and contractual warranties serve to provide important information to the buyer. They allow the buyer to enter into the contract more safely, even though the buyer has not been in a position to independently verify the matters disclosed or warranted.

Risk. The disclosures and warranties also serve to apportion risk. The buyer has the benefit of certain remedies if disclosures are incorrect or warranties are false. In some instances the buyer can withdraw from the contract without penalty. In others the buyer will be entitled to damages for any loss suffered.

Under the Commonwealth Trade Practices Act and similar legislation in each state and territory, it is an offence if a seller makes false or misleading statements in the course of trade and commerce, including in the sale of land. A buyer who suffers loss from a false or misleading representation will be entitled to compensation.

5.7 Owners/occupiers' liability for matters relating to the property which occurred before they bought or occupied
A buyer could be affected by various pre-existing conditions concerning the subject property. Proper due diligence prior to purchase would seek to identify and minimise risks, which include:
- Use: types or conditions of use imposed by local planning authorities prior to purchase will apply afterwards.
- Improvements: the buyer may become responsible for rectifying any unauthorised or non-complying structures, even if they pre-date the purchase.
- Encroachments: neighbours will have rights if buildings on a buyer's property encroach on the neighbours' land, even if the encroachment existed prior to the purchase.
- Contamination: if land is polluted or contaminated and the polluter cannot be located or cannot rectify the problem, responsibility for any remediation may fall on the current owner, no matter when the contamination occurred.
- Work orders: the new owner may be responsible for works or repairs required by the relevant planning authority, even though the requirements arose before the purchase.
- Statutory charges: charges imposed by governmental authorities (such as land tax and council and water rates) and which have accrued under previous owners, must be paid when the purchase is completed, or the

buyer will become responsible for them.

When a buyer acquires a leased property, it will generally seek indemnities from the seller against obligations of the landlord to tenants which arose prior to the buyer taking over the property.
- Leasehold: a tenant should check carefully whether its intended use of the property is permitted by the local planning authority. Permission should be obtained before the tenant enters into the lease. Actions by a local planning authority to stop a tenant from carrying on an unauthorised use or a breach of conditions of use will generally not release a tenant from obligations under its lease.

5.8 Notarisation

There is no legal requirement for a contract for sale to be notarised.

Although the general principles of the Torrens system (see 6.3 below) apply throughout Australia, the registries in each state and territory employ their own forms and apply differing procedures. Each has formalities as to the signing and witnessing of documents. In general terms, having documents signed by an authorised notary is not a requirement.

5.9 Formalities for a contract to become a legally binding obligation

For a contract for sale of land to be enforceable against a party, the contract must be signed by the party or a person authorised by the party. As referred to at 5.2 above, the parties normally sign separate counterparts, and then those counterparts are exchanged. The counterparts need to be identical; otherwise the contract may not be legally binding.

Exchange of contracts marks the point at which a legally binding agreement comes into existence.

5.10 Transfer of title

Documents entitling the buyer to a full title are received upon completion in return for payment of the purchase price. For Old System land, the property transfers upon completion. Following completion, the relevant documents are lodged for registration at the applicable land registry. Under the Torrens system, documents received upon completion will enable a registered title to be obtained. The Torrens title is formally transferred upon registration of the transfer document.

5.11 Insurance of the property if there is delay between agreeing terms and actual sale

The position in the various states and territories varies as to when the risk of any damage to the property passes from the seller to the buyer. It is important to check the local law.

Where risk passes when the contract becomes binding, the buyer must have its insurance in place by then. Where risk only passes on completion of the sale, the buyer need not insure until then, but in either case it is important for the seller to maintain its insurance until the conclusion of the transaction.

6. REAL ESTATE BASICS
6.1 Main sources of laws that govern real estate
Australia is a federation of states and territories. The federal or Commonwealth parliament enacts legislation in specific areas listed in the Australian constitution. Separate parliaments in the states and territories enact laws on all other matters.

The law relating to real estate arises from legislation and the 'common law'. Common law refers to decisions by Australian courts based on or evolving from decisions of previous cases. Decided cases also provide interpretation of statutes and other legislation.

Legislation relating to real estate is mainly the responsibility of the states and territories. It is accordingly necessary to have regard to the law of the jurisdiction where the relevant real estate is located.

The Commonwealth constitution does not specifically allow the Commonwealth parliament to legislate on matters of land law. However, in legislating over various matters which fall within its constitutional responsibilities, such as bankruptcy law, native title or compulsory acquisition of land for federal use, the Commonwealth can affect rights and interests in land.

6.2 How property can be held
Under the applicable law in Australia, the two main types of property ownership are freehold and leasehold.
- The most common form of ownership of land in Australia is a 'fee simple' freehold estate. The owner is free to hold such an estate for an unlimited time but is also free to transfer it at any time. In general terms only planning restrictions limit how the land can be used and the buildings or structures which can be constructed on it.
- Freehold title may be held under Old System title, Torrens title (see 6.3) or Crown lands title. Crown lands title refers almost exclusively to rural land.
- Strata title is a form of freehold by which a parcel of land can be split into individual units or lots. This enables the owner to hold a separate title for part of a larger parcel of land, for instance, a warehouse in an industrial park, a floor or suite in a multi-level building, or a shop in a shopping centre, with the title being treated in much the same way as the freehold of the whole parcel – for instance, it may be mortgaged, leased or transferred.

    Most residential apartments are held under strata title; so too are many industrial or commercial units or suites.

    Strata legislation has been extended to provide separate titles for different elements in mixed developments, and separate holdings of units and lots where the underlying interest is a long-term leasehold of Torrens title land.

A leasehold interest is carved out of a freehold interest. It gives the occupier (tenant) the right to possess the land the subject of the lease in return for payment of rent to the freehold owner. The right is granted for a specified time and usually for a stipulated purpose.

6.3 Must land be registered?
From the time the British colonised Australia, freehold and leasehold land was held under 'Old System' title. Under that system, a chain of deeds, each claiming ownership over a specific piece of land, made up the title. Any person asserting a claim over land simply had to be in possession of the relevant title deeds. Proof and transfer of ownership was complex and expensive. There was no requirement to register the deeds making up the title. However, if registered, they gained priority over unregistered deeds.

To overcome the problems and complexity of Old System title, Torrens title, named after Sir Robert Torrens, began in Australia in the 1850s.

The Torrens system reformed the practice of Old System title to the effect that, when a dealing was registered, the registered owner became the indisputable owner of the title. There was no need to possess the old title deeds. This form of ownership now applies to the vast majority of parcels of land in Australia. Dealings must be registered to obtain the benefit of Torrens title.

The Torrens system operates throughout Australia, but forms and processes differ from state to state. There are mechanisms in each state to gradually convert all remaining Old System parcels to Torrens title.

6.4 Public land register
Each state and territory government administers its own register for land within its bounds.

Transactions are registered and, for Torrens title land, give rise to a registered title. In general terms and subject to certain statutory exceptions, the registered title is a guarantee by the relevant state or territory that the owner recorded on the title owns the property free from all interests which are not registered.

In order to obtain the protection of registration, dealings such as land transfers, mortgages, easements and restrictions on use must be registered. The holder of an unregistered interest will be defeated by the registration of a subsequent dealing.

6.5 Land not covered by a public land register
As with a freehold interest, a leasehold interest over Torrens title land can be protected by registration. However, some leases for particular periods do not need to be registered. It is necessary to check the requirements in each jurisdiction, as the applicable periods vary from state to state.

Some rights, for instance, an option to purchase, cannot be registered on Torrens title land. Courts have recognised the validity of unregistered interests in Torrens title property, but an unregistered interest will be extinguished by a registered interest unless it is an exception to the rule of indefeasibility.

An unregistered interest of a proprietary interest in land can be protected by lodging a caveat on the register. A caveat prevents an interest contrary to

Australia

the interest it records being registered on the title.

Other rights between parties are not interests in land but merely contractual. For instance, a licence to occupy land for a certain purpose or use, or a right of first refusal to acquire property. Such rights cannot be registered or protected under the Torrens system.

6.6 Native title

Certain rights to land held by indigenous groups in Australia may constitute native title.

It was only in 1992 that native title was recognised by the Australian High Court. Since that time the federal government and the state and territory governments have passed native title legislation. The legislation establishes processes to claim native title on certain lands and also deals with land dealings affecting that title.

Native title could affect Commonwealth land or land owned by or on behalf of state or territory governments, and so should be taken into account when dealing with those lands. In general terms, native title does not affect land held by non-government owners of freehold title.

Please see page 18 for appendix diagram.

Australia

Appendix: Diagram of a typical investment purchase in Australia

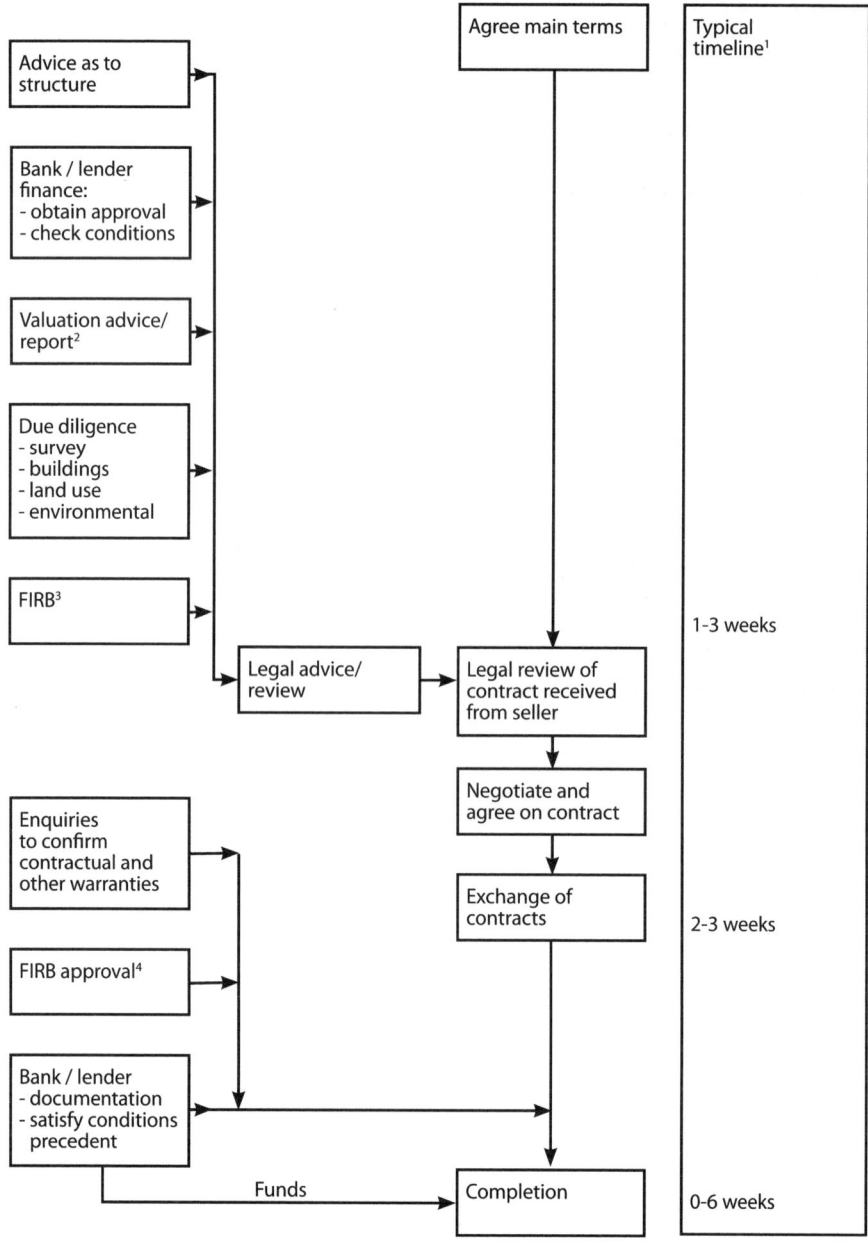

[1] Timelines may differ markedly, either longer or considerably shorter. Exchange and completion may be simultaneous.
[2] Valuation usually required by the lender. The buyer may seek valuation advice, or decide it is unnecessary.
[3] The buyer should seek advice before entering into the contract as to whether it is necessary to notify or to obtain approval from the Foreign Investment Review Board (FIRB) – see 3.2.
[4] If FIRB approval is necessary, approval must be obtained before the purchase contract becomes unconditional.

Belgium

Liedekerke Wolters Waelbroeck Kirkpatrick
Yves Delacroix & Henk Verstraete

1 INVESTMENT PURCHASE OVERVIEW

Typical investment purchase in Belgium

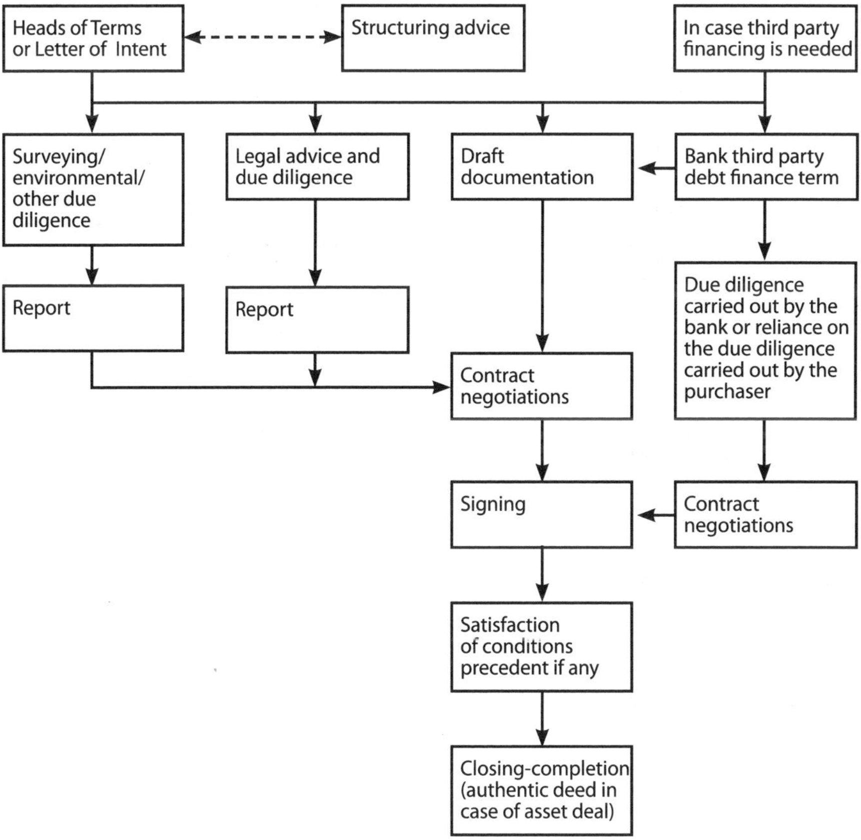

2 TAX CONSIDERATIONS
2.1 Value added tax (VAT)
See answer to question 2.2.

2.2 Stamp duty/transfer tax

Under Belgian law, the sale of real estate is subject to a registration tax of 12.5 per cent (if the property is located in the Walloon region or the Brussels region) or 10 per cent (if the property is located in the Flemish region). The registration tax is calculated on the purchase price. However if the fair market value is higher than the purchase price, the registration tax is calculated on the fair market value. Seller and purchaser are jointly liable to pay the registration tax. However, in practice, registration tax is usually borne by the purchaser.

The sale of a 'new' building may be subject to VAT at a rate of 21 per cent. In that case no proportional registration tax is due. For VAT purposes, a building is new until 31 December of the second year following the year in which the building was first occupied or taken into possession. If the seller is a professional builder, the transfer of a new building is automatically subject to VAT. Any other seller should opt to sell a new building with VAT. VAT is due on the purchase price of the new building. The transfer of the land to which the building is attached remains subject to the abovementioned registration tax of 12.5 per cent or 10 per cent (the rate depends on where the property is located). Hence, the purchase price of a new building transferred with VAT should be split into the price of the building (subject to VAT) and the price of the land (subject to registration tax). Pursuant to a new measure, which will enter into force at the latest on 1 January 2011, if a new building is transferred with VAT, VAT will also be due on the transfer of the land. An earlier date of entry into force of this new measure may be fixed by Royal Decree.

Transfer tax exemptions might be available if real estate is transferred in the framework of the transfer of an undertaking or in the framework of reorganisation.

2.3 Tax issues for overseas investors investing in real estate

A non-Belgian investor investing in Belgian real estate will as a rule be liable to income tax in connection with the Belgian real estate.

Since 2006, the tax base of any Belgian company or foreign company with a permanent establishment in Belgium is reduced, for each year, by a deduction for risk capital, corresponding to a notional interest calculated on the entity's total equity (ie, share capital plus retained earnings as they appear on the balance sheet, subject to a couple of fiscal corrections aimed at countering abuse and double dip) at the close of the previous financial year. The applicable interest rate is the average rate of the 10-year government bond for the previous year, (which for 2010 leads to an applicable rate of 3.8 per cent).

This provision aims at promoting equity funding of companies and has triggered increased foreign direct investment into Belgium. Whereas the nominal corporate tax rate remains at just below 34 per cent, it has been calculated that the provision reduces the effective tax rate to an average of 26 per cent. However, the effective rate is considerably lower (sometimes as low as zero per cent) for capital-intensive activities such as financing.

Belgium

3 INVESTMENT VEHICLE CHOICE
3.1 Structures used to purchase property
Direct purchase (asset deal) of real property is of course very common. However, mainly due to tax considerations (like high transfer tax – see answer to question 2.2), most of the large transactions are done through company acquisition (share deal) or by means of a so-called 'split sale'.

3.1.1 Share deal (sale of shares of company owning real estate)
Transfer taxes are in principle not due in a share deal.

As a rule, except in case of simulation (for instance if the property is contributed to a new company after agreement has been reached on the object of the sale and the shares of the company are sold instead of the asset) no registration tax is due on the sale of shares. Even if the sole asset of the company is the real estate, in principle, no registration tax is due. Since in practice the transfer tax due in an asset deal is usually borne by the purchaser, a share deal may imply for the purchaser a substantial amount of transfer tax saving.

From a direct tax viewpoint, in a share deal, since the property does not change hands, the transferred company continues to depreciate the real estate during the remaining depreciation period and on the remaining depreciation basis. When the company later sells the real estate a taxable capital gain is usually realised. The capital gain is equal to the difference between the sale price and the tax value of the real estate in the books of the company, meaning the historical cost less depreciation (the sale price is usually higher than the tax value of the real estate in the books of the company). Hence, at the time of the sale of the shares, the valuation of the shares should take into account the tax latency, ie the present value of the future potential tax burden in connection with the sale of the real estate by the company. The calculation of the tax latency should also take into account that the share price or goodwill cannot be depreciated under Belgian tax law. The burden of said tax latency is usually shared between seller and buyer.

Corporate income tax is levied in Belgium at a rate of 33.99 per cent (see, however, the impact of the notional interest deduction at question 2.3). The tax on capital gains on fixed assets held for at least five years can be deferred subject to reinvestment of the full proceeds of the sale price in depreciable assets. The tax is recaptured over the duration of the new depreciation.

Tax losses can be carried forward indefinitely. However, in a change of control not justified by so-called 'legitimate financial or economic needs', tax losses are barred. An advance ruling can be applied for with respect to the existence of 'legitimate financial or economic needs'. However, the ruling commission often considers that a change of control of a real estate company is not justified by legitimate financial or economic needs. Hence, carried forward tax losses are generally not taken into account for the calculation of the sale price of the shares.

3.1.2 Split sale
An asset deal can be split into two legal acts, a so-called 'split sale'. If strict

Belgium

conditions are complied with, a split sale may involve a significant transfer tax saving. Legal certainty with respect to the transfer tax due in connection with the split sale can be obtained by way of an advance ruling of the Belgian ruling commission.

A split sale involves the vesting of a long lease right (against payment of a lump-sum price) to the benefit of one party and the transfer of the ownership encumbered with the long lease to another – related – party. At the end of the long lease, the latter party obtains the full ownership of the real estate. The transfer tax due in connection with the long lease is equal to 0.2 per cent of the amounts paid under the long lease. The transfer tax due in connection with the transfer of the encumbered ownership equals 10 per cent or 12.5 per cent (depending on the location of the real estate) of the value of the real estate (such value being considerably reduced due to the encumbrance).

3.2 Restrictions on foreign ownership or occupation of property

Although tax consequences may be different for non-Belgium ownership, there are generally no restrictions on ownership or occupation by foreign entities.

Neither are there in principle any restrictions on obtaining loans from both Belgian or foreign banks, it being understood that the source country of finance is important from a tax point of view (since the tax treaty, if any, may determine to what extent withholding tax is charged on interest payments).

With regard to security rights, no restrictions exist save for the general pledge over the business (similar to UK-law floating charge), which can only be vested to the benefit of an EU-licensed credit institution.

3.3 Real estate investment trusts (REITs)

In 1995, Belgium enacted legislation permitting the creation of a REIT-like structure, the SICAFI/BEVAK. The SICAFI/BEVAK is a listed property fund with a fixed amount of corporate share capital whose role is to provide tax neutrality for collecting and distributing rental income. SICAFIs/BEVAKs must be approved for public offering by the Belgian Banking, Finance and Insurance Commission. They must be established in corporate form and, with limited exceptions, may only invest in real estate assets (including not only buildings, but also options, leasehold interests and other rights in buildings, voting shares of real estate companies related to the SICAFI/BEVAK, and real estate certificates).

Although SICAFIs/BEVAKs are, in principle, subject to Belgian corporate income tax like other investment companies, their taxable income is limited to the amount of any non arm's-length benefits transferred to them by related parties and the amount of certain miscellaneous items which are not tax deductible. Hence, in practice, SICAFIs/BEVAKs are often fully exempt from Belgian corporate income tax.

Dividends paid by a SICAFI/BEVAK to its shareholders are exempt from withholding tax provided at least 60 per cent of the SICAFI's/BEVAK's portfolio consists of Belgian residential real estate and are otherwise subject to a withholding tax of 15 per cent. Dividends paid to foreign investors can also qualify for a reduced rate of withholding tax under certain double tax treaties.

There are currently 15 Belgian listed SICAFIs/BEVAKs with a combined market capitalisation of approximately €4 billion.

4 FINANCING AN ACQUISITION

4.1 Financing of corporate real estate transactions

Corporate real estate financing is usually a mix of debt and equity, where a bank loans a proportion of the price by way of debt. The debt is contracted by the company acquiring the real estate (or the company acquiring the shares in case of a share deal). LMA-based loan documentation is standard market practice (even for Belgian law governed facility agreements).

A large proportion of commercial transactions are done via a sale of shares. This leads to financial assistance issues, ie, a company granting security/ advantage/loans for helping to purchase its own shares. Financial assistance problems are possible to overcome, but it may not be easy even under the recently modified regime (new version of Article 629 of the Belgian Company Code), permitting financial assistance under strict conditions.

The provision of financial assistance under the new strict procedures and conditions is still very difficult to apply and, most notably, is subject to the booking of a blocked reserve in the accounts of the grantor of the security and certain publicity measures. Therefore, market practice to date seems to continue to avoid the giving of financial assistance through the use of various other alternative techniques (eg, permitted capital reductions).

The regime of notional interest deduction (see answer to question 2.3 above) has the effect that debt and equity funding are no longer subject to different tax treatment.

4.2 Real estate as a means of raising finance

Real estate may be used to raise finance through a secured lending (see answer to question 4.3.) or through real estate securitisation (see answer to question 4.4.).

Although it is not always a means to finance real estate, it is worth noting that over the past few years many corporate occupiers (and also public entities, like the Belgian state) have entered into sale and lease back transactions, whereby property is sold to a third party, followed immediately by a lease back to the original owner. The third party is usually a professional property investor, but it can also be a financial institution, especially when the occupier reserves the right to recover the ownership of the property at some point in the future.

The tax aspects of sale and lease back transactions need to be carefully addressed, since the sale of an existing building will normally entail transfer tax (at the rate of 10 or 12.5 per cent) and a taxation of the capital gain realised on the occasion of the sale (it being understood that the taxation of the capital gain may, under certain conditions, be spread over time, eg, if the lease qualifies as a finance lease under accounting law). Alternatives may be applied, for instance through the mechanism of split sale (see answer to question 3.1).

4.3 Common forms of security granted over real estate

The only form of security taken in relation to immovable property is a mortgage (*hypothèque/hypotheek*). A standard security package required by third party lenders generally consists of a mortgage and/or a mortgage mandate.

In large transactions, the lender would also take security over other assets, for example: a pledge over the receivables (rental income); a pledge over the shares of the borrower if the parent company is involved in the loan or a pledge over shares held by the borrower in other companies; or a business pledge (similar to a floating charge in the UK).

A mortgage deed has to be signed before a notary public. Substantial costs can be involved in the vesting of the mortgage, mostly in connection with registration duties and inscription duties at the mortgage registry (the cost amounts approximately to 1.4 per cent on the amounts for which the mortgage has been taken). As a result of this, borrowers will try to have the mortgage granted for an amount less than the value of the loan, and then grant a proxy to mortgage – by which the debtor irrevocably authorises the lender to establish a mortgage on the property – in addition to the mortgage (the borrower will then only pay duties on this second mortgage if and when it is actually established). Note that a proxy to mortgage does not grant any priority rights as such – it is only once the proxy has been exercised (and the mortgage subsequently registered) that the mortgage becomes effective and binding *erga omnes*. As such, a proxy to mortgage does not prevent third parties (acting in good faith) from obtaining rights *in rem* over the property, even if the proxy to mortgage is subject to a negative covenant (negative pledge). Proxies to mortgage minimise costs but increase the risks for the lender – they are fairly common in real estate transactions and when used, the lender usually takes a first ranked mortgage for a lower amount, coupled with a proxy for a more substantial amount. Proxies to mortgage must also be executed before a notary public.

Most mortgages are created 'for all sums due'. This implies that the bank initially grants a facility to be used by way of a single repayable loan under which no new loans can be drawn, but that the facility and mortgage will contain an 'all sums' clause, meaning that the mortgage will secure 'all sums' that the mortgagee owes or will owe to the bank, thus, to the extent the bank from time to time authorises, new funds can be drawn by way of a new loan advance under the 'existing' facility, and further costs for securing this 'new loan' can be avoided.

In addition, certain lenders take an *in rem* security right over the entire 'business' of the debtor by way of a pledge over the business (*pand handelszaak/gage sur fonds de commerce*). The creditor (lender/agent), beneficiary of this security, must be a licensed credit institution.

The assets that can serve as collateral are all movable assets, such as machinery and equipment, but also receivables (monies held, intellectual property rights, etc). Usually, the collateral is broadly described. However, such pledge over the business can only pertain to 50 per cent of the stock of movable assets of the debtor (Article 2 of the Act of 25 October 1919). The pledge over the business can, but does not have to, be vested by

Belgium

notarial deed (usually, a notarial deed is used when this right is granted in combination with a mortgage).

A business pledge must be registered at the land registry and an amount of 0.5 per cent of the amount for which the inscription is taken will be due.

When a business pledge is combined with a mortgage, it has to be decided whether such business pledge will be 'cumulative' or 'non-cumulative'. In the first case a registration fee of 0.5 per cent is due on the amount secured by the business pledge (on top of the duties for the mortgage) and the business pledge can be enforced for its amount in addition to the amount of the mortgage. In the latter only a flat fee of €25 is due for the business pledge, but both the mortgage and the business pledge can only be enforced for an amount equal to the higher of the mortgage and the business pledge.

Finally, in view of the general nature of the business pledge, being a floating charge on all of the business of the debtor, it is often accompanied by guarantees by other group entities and/or more specific pledges on certain assets, such as a pledge over receivables, rental flow income and bank accounts (in that case, it is advisable to determine a priority ranking with the debtor for enforcing the different security rights). Most commonly used are the pledges over shares, over receivables and over bank accounts.

The pledge over financial instruments (such as shares) as well as over cash held on account and the fiduciary transfer of ownership of financial instruments can obtain – under the Collateral Act (the Act of 15 December 15 2004 on collateral agreements – *Loi relative aux sûretés financières/ Wet betreffende de financiële zekerheden*) – a much stronger position (eg, in insolvency proceedings or upon enforcement). In practice, these stronger security rights have mainly played a role in financial market transactions.

For a pledge over receivables (eg, on rental flows) no specific requirements or formalities exist, save that it will only be perfected towards the respective individual debtors of the claims to be pledged – thereby only by due notification of such pledge to such debtors (or acknowledgment of such pledge by such debtors). Also a pledge over insurance claims is common, but subject to additional formal requirements under insurance law.

In respect of inter-company guarantees we add that up-stream and cross-stream guarantees can cause issues under corporate law (being the proof of sufficient corporate benefit for the grantor to incur indebtedness for other (group) entities).

4.4 Real estate mortgage securitisation

Asset-backed securitisation exists under Belgian law, under the impetus of the EU undertakings for collective investments in transferable securities (UCITS) regulations. In respect of real estate a number of larger specialised funds dominate the market. It is atypical to have this type of funding set up for one single project.

For their part, larger Belgian banks have also initiated securitisation projects of their residential and commercial mortgage portfolios.

In all instances regulatory oversight from the Belgian Banking, Finance and Insurance Commission will apply.

Belgium

5 MANAGING THE ACQUISITION PROCESS
5.1 Minimum formalities for the sale and purchase of property
For a contract for the sale of an ownership right or another right *in rem* (eg, usufruct, long term lease), no formal requirements apply but to make it enforceable and opposable against third parties a written deed must be notarised and then transcribed at the Mortgage Register. The parties usually execute a preliminary contract (private deed), even though they can also directly execute a notarial deed.

Depending on the location of the real estate asset (Flemish Walloon or Brussels region) certain formalities related to the management of soil pollution need to be complied with before the sale or the granting of certain rights on a property.

In a share deal, no specific formalities apply and the intervention of a notary is not required, but the transfer of the shares must be operated physically (bearer shares) or by registration in the shareholder's register (registered shares) or in the appropriate accounts (dematerialised shares).

5.2 Main legal documents required to transfer a property or grant a lease
For a freehold transfer, the main legal documents are: the preliminary contract (*compromis de vente/verkoopcompromis*) under the form of a private deed (the execution of such a preliminary contract is not strictly necessary, but is usual) which sets out the terms and conditions of the sale, including the conditions precedent if any; the notarial deed, by which the parties confirm and restate the conditions of the preliminary contract – the notarial deed is necessary for the transcription at the Mortgage Register, which makes the sale opposable against third parties; and some environmental reports and certificates. Before passing the deed, the notary will also have to make certain enquiries and searches with the municipality, the Mortgage Register and the tax administration.

For the grant of a lease, a private deed is sufficient (it being understood that some environmental reports and certificates may also be required). Although a private deed will be legally binding on the parties, leases of more than nine years need to be confirmed by a notarial deed and then transcribed at the Mortgage Register in order to be opposable against third parties for any duration above nine years. Long leases (*emphytéose/erfpacht*), rights of surface (*droit de superficie/opstal*) and usufructs (*usufruit/vruchtgebruik*) also need to be notarised and registered in order to ensure opposability against third parties.

5.3 Property transaction costs
The buyer typically pays:
- its own surveyor's fees and legal costs; and
- in an asset deal: the notary fees (+/- one per cent of the purchase price), the transfer tax (12.5 per cent or 10 per cent depending in which region the property is located) and/or VAT (for a new building).

The seller typically pays:
- its own surveyor's fees and legal costs.

The seller may also need to bear capital gains tax, if any.

In certain transactions, the transfer tax is borne by the seller, in which case it is then comprised in the sale price (*acte en main*).

In a share deal, no transfer tax is due. The purchase of shares therefore results in a substantial tax saving for the buyer, the benefit of which is usually split between the parties. Usually, there is also a split of the economic benefit arising from the fact that no capital gains tax on the property value is made in a share deal (although there is still a latent capital gain burdening the asset).

5.4 Does the seller warrant its ownership of the property?
On the sale of a freehold or leasehold property, the seller usually gives a statutory warranty as to title.

Such a warranty is provided for in the sale agreement and the notary checks the rights of the seller, on the basis of the information available in the Mortgage Register and the Land Register.

5.5 Warranties a seller usually gives to a buyer
The seller must guarantee undisturbed possession of the property. The Belgian Civil code also provides that the seller holds the buyer harmless against hidden defects, but parties may derogate from this provision and quite often do so (such derogation is, however, considered not valid if the seller is a real estate professional).

The extent of the warranties will generally depend on negotiation as to which party is going to bear risks and meet the cost of conducting the due diligence.

In a share deal, legal warranty against hidden defects only covers the nature and the existence of the shares – all other kinds of warranties (about the business or the assets of the company) need to be expressly stipulated in the agreement.

The warranties typically given by the seller (either in an asset deal or in a share deal) relate to: town planning and environmental issues (including soil pollution, absence of asbestos and other hazardous materials, compliance of the building with legislation and regulation etc); absence of real rights affecting the property (such as easements and encumbrances); tenancy issues (including absence of default or litigation under the existing lease agreements); and accuracy of the pre-contractual information. In a share deal, the seller will need to give additional warranties relating to the debts and other liabilities of the company, the accuracy of the accounts, etc.

The scope of the warranties is linked to the level of due diligence which the buyer was authorised and able to carry out. The level of warranties obviously also depends on other factors such as the market and other economic circumstances.

5.6 Purpose of warranties in the purchase agreement
The function of the warranties in a sale/purchase agreement is to apportion risks between the parties. Specific representations are used to provide information to the buyer.

5.7 Owners/occupiers' liability for matters relating to the property which occurred before they bought or occupied
There is generally none, except in environmental liability where the person who caused the contamination cannot be identified, then the current owner can, under certain conditions, become liable.

In a share deal, all liabilities of the target company will be inherited, including tax and environmental liabilities.

5.8 Notarisation
A contract is binding on the parties even if it is not notarised. However, to be effective against third parties, transfers of property ownership must be evidenced by a notarial deed that needs to be transcribed at the Mortgage Register, which implies that in practice all sales contracts are notarised. This obviously does not apply for share deals since the ownership remains with the target company.

5.9 Formalities for a contract to become a legally binding obligation
No formalities are required for a contract to become a legally binding obligation upon the parties. Even in the case of a real estate asset, a sale can be agreed verbally (save of course for the issue of proof).

This implies that the parties need to be very careful when negotiating a contract. Depending on their content and irrespective of their heading, heads of terms or even a letter of intent or any other document, may be legally binding. As indicated above, a notarial deed is, however, necessary in order for the transfer of ownership to be effective against third parties. Under Belgian law a sale contract is deemed to be legally binding when there is an agreement on object and price.

5.10 Transfer of title
According to Belgian law, title passes to the buyer upon agreement on the substantial elements of the sale (object and price). However, for enforceability reasons, the vast majority of preliminary contracts provide that the transfer is postponed until completion – being the notarial deed – provided the price has been fully paid.

5.11 Insurance of the property if there is delay between agreeing terms and actual sale
In an asset deal, there is a maximum delay of four months between the signing of the private deed (or realisation of the conditions precedent, if any) and the passing of the notarial deed. Since the transfer of ownership is in most cases postponed until the passing of the notarial deed, it is up to the seller to insure the property until completion. Usually, the sale agreement provides that the seller undertakes to maintain the insurance until eight days after the passing of the notarial deed.

Belgium

6. REAL ESTATE BASICS
6.1 Main sources of laws that govern real estate
Belgian property law is essentially contained in the Belgian Civil Code, which contains the rules applicable to sales, leases, mortgages, construction, etc. The Code also contains specific rules for, among others, retail leases, residential leases and farm leases. Specific legislation exists for long leases and rights of surface.

Interpretation of the Civil Code by the courts, especially the Supreme court (*Cour de cassation/Hof van Cassatie*), plays an important role.

Planning and environmental regulations are governed by Flemish, Walloon or Brussels regional legislation.

6.2 How property can be held
Two types of rights in real estate exist:
- rights *in rem* relating to a certain direct control over the real property (ownership right, long term lease, right of surface, usufruct, mortgage, easement); and
- rights *in personam* ie, claims allowing the request of a certain performance from another party (leases).

Most property is owned freehold (full ownership, unlimited in time). Many industrial lands are owned by public entities and have been granted on leasehold to the operators (eg, long lease limited to up to 99 years). Mainly due to tax considerations, ownership of the land and ownership of the building is often split on the basis of either a long term lease (27 to 99 years) or a right of surface of up to 50 years.

Except for easements, and obviously for ownership rights (which can be perpetual) no right of use may be granted for more than 99 years. For some rights, the maximum duration is even less – 50 years for a right of surface and 30 years for a usufruct except if granted to a natural person.

Ownership can also take the form of common hold (condominium ownership). Under common hold, the property is split into individual units. The owner of a unit is a unit holder and common parts are held by a common hold association which is made up of the unit holders.

6.3 Must land be registered?
Land and buildings must be registered in the Mortgage Register (*Bureau de conservation des Hypothèques/Hypotheekregister*) to be effective against third parties. They are also described in the Land Register (*cadastre/kadaster*), which has, however, other purposes (the Land Register sets out the categories to which each land parcel or building belongs and indicates the related estimated annual income, which is used for the calculation of the real estate withholding tax).

6.4 Public land register
Ownership of a property is evidenced in the Mortgage Register, in which all registered transfers of property – rights *in rem*, mortgage deeds, easements (with the exception of the legal easements) and leasehold interest of a

duration of more than nine years, need to be made to be effective against third parties.

6.5 State guarantee of title and categories of documents and information that are registered

There is no state guarantee as such and the Mortgage Register cannot be held liable for the registration of inaccurate information provided to them, it being understood that the Mortgage Register may be held liable if the provided information is inaccurately processed.

Belgian notaries may be held liable for the validity and binding force of the deeds passed before them.

Following categories of documents and information are registered:
- ownership titles;
- other rights *in rem* (eg, easements and mortgages); and
- leasehold interests with a duration of more than nine years.

Information available at the Mortgage Register includes: the identity of current and past owners; the acquisition date of the property; the price and other conditions of the transaction; any procedure for the forced sale of a property; or litigation on an ownership right or on other rights *in rem* over a property asset. Any person may obtain a full copy of the deeds that have been transcribed.

Bulgaria

Borislav Boyanov & Co Nickolay Nickolov & Iva Miteva

1. INVESTMENT PURCHASE OVERVIEW
1.1 Typical investment purchase of real estate in Bulgaria

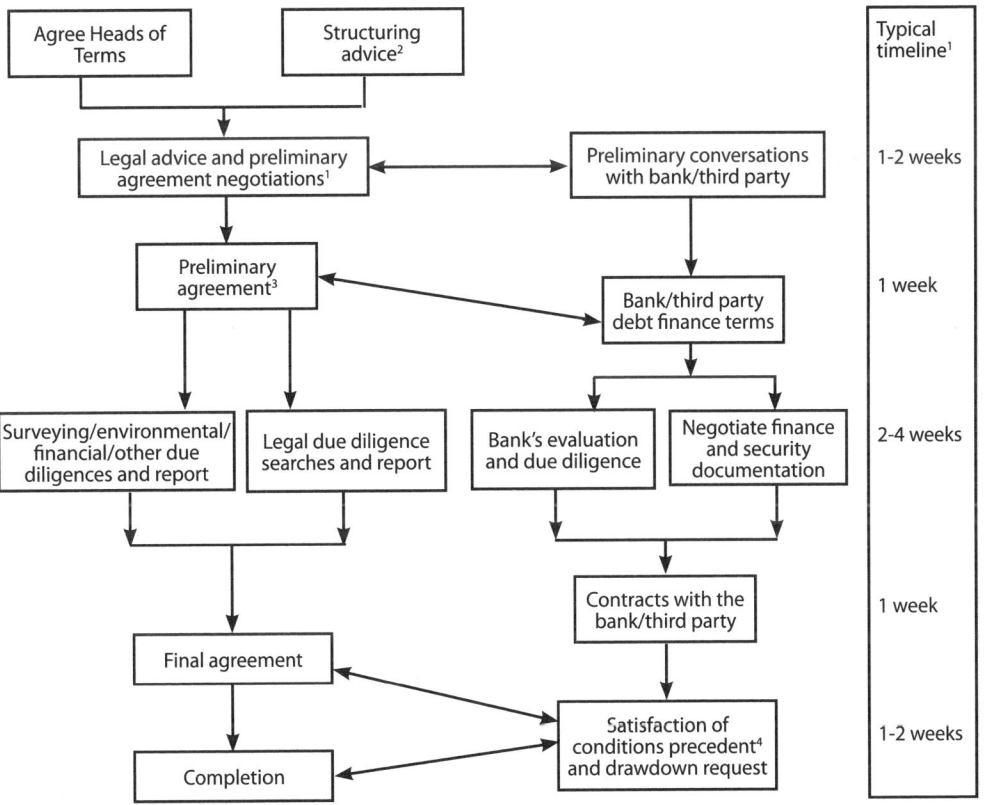

[1] Depending in the particular transaction, the timescale may differ considerably.
[2] Establishing a deal structure is an important early stage which may considerably influence the next stages.
[3] Preliminary agreement negotiations and preliminary agreement may go simultaneously with the due diligence process, may precede or follow it.
[4] Security documents may precede or follow final agreement depending on the type of the security.

2. TAX CONSIDERATIONS
2.1 Value added tax (VAT)
VAT is payable on the sale and purchase of a real estate if:
- the seller is VAT registered; and
- the estate subject to the transaction is a regulated real estate and/or a

new building, and/or specific premises from a new building, and/or the terrain adjacent to the new building.

2.1.1 Under the meaning of Bulgarian law:
'Regulated real estate' is land for which there is an effective zoning plan. 'New building' is a building which, as of the day of accrual of the VAT, was completed at least at 'rough construction ready' stage, or the usage of which was permitted no later than 60 months prior to the date on which the tax was charged.

'Terrain adjacent to a new building' is the aggregate surface of the built-up area and the area which is within three meters from the outside contour of the external walls of the first over-ground floor or the semi-underground floor, and is within the boundaries of the regulated plot.

The VAT rate is 20 per cent. The VAT is accrued by the seller and is due by the buyer.

The VAT tax base is the aggregate amount of the agreed price increased by related taxes and fees as indicated in section 2.2 and section 5.3 below. The tax base of the transaction may not be lower than the tax base upon the initial acquisition of the estate, or less than its cost price. The tax base shall be the market-based value of the property if the deal is made between related parties.

VAT is not applicable to transactions where:
- the seller is not VAT registered; or
- the subject of the deal is agricultural land, or a building that is not new, or has separate premises, as well as terrain adjacent to such a building; or
- the subject of the deal is a transfer or establishment of a limited real right.

It should be noted that in the case of a VAT exempted transaction, the VAT registered seller is entitled to choose whether the transaction is to be charged with VAT.

2.2 Stamp duty/transfer tax
A local tax is payable for any transaction of a real estate or limited real right. The local tax is due to the respective municipality where the estate is located. Each municipal council determines annually the amount of this local tax within the limits from 0.1 per cent to three per cent of the tax base. The tax base is: (i) the sale price; or (ii) the tax evaluation of the property, whichever is higher. The tax evaluations are determined by the municipal administration according to a formula set out by the law. Currently they are still lower than the market values of the properties.

A local tax is not due for certain types of real estate acquisition as follows:
- if the acquirer is the state, municipality or some organisations engaged in social, cultural or charity activity, medical institutions, etc;
- property acquired in a process of privatisation;
- acquisition by way of an in-kind contribution of property in the capital of a company; or
- sale of an agricultural land restituted to the seller under the Ownership

and Usage of Agricultural Lands Act, provided that the sale is made within five years as of the restitution of the land and the parties have agreed that the seller is to pay the expenses of it.

The local tax is paid by the buyer, unless the parties agree otherwise. If the parties agree to pay it in a certain proportion, they are jointly liable for its payment. If the parties agree the tax is to be paid by the seller, the buyer is considered to be its guarantor.

The local tax has to be paid prior to the notary transfer of the property.

There is no local tax due for transfer of property through a share deal.

2.3 Tax issues for overseas investors investing in real estate

The general rule is that all income derived from a real estate located in Bulgaria is taxable in Bulgaria. There could be exceptions, depending on the occurrence of certain conditions.

The respective tax regime applicable to the income depends primarily on the capacity of the income's beneficiary (local or foreign individual or a company).

Considering the fact that the chapter is focused on commercial property investment, the tax implications below are outlined based on the assumption that the overseas investment is effected either through a foreign company, or through a Bulgarian company owned or otherwise controlled by foreign companies and/or individuals.

2.3.1 Tax regime for investment through a foreign company

If the foreign company exercises economic activity through a place of permanent establishment (most commonly through a registered branch), then the income derived from real estate shall not be subject to a separate tax, but shall form part of the annual financial result of the permanent establishment. This result (if positive) is subject to 10 per cent corporate income tax and the approach is identical to the one for Bulgarian legal entities.

If the foreign entity does not exercise such economic activity as specified above, the income shall be subject to one-off withholding tax (WHT). The WHT rate applicable to income derived from a property is 10 per cent. The tax base for property's transfer is the positive difference between the sale price and the documented acquisition price. The tax base for the property's lease is the gross amount of the rent received.

The WHT over income from a property's transfer is to be calculated and paid to the Bulgarian state budget by the income's beneficiary, ie by the foreign entity. The WHT over lease income is to be accrued and paid by the income's payer (the tenant), provided that the latter is a legal entity, sole trader or place of permanent establishment. Otherwise, it shall be paid by the income's beneficiary.

The party who is obliged to accrue and pay the WHT has to file a tax declaration. The tax declaration is to be filed and the tax is to be paid to the National Revenue Agency's Regional Directorate where the income's payer is or shall be registered. If the income's payer is not obliged to be registered, the competent authority shall be the National Revenue Agency's Sofia Directorate.

In a sale of the shares of a Bulgarian company owned by foreign investors, they would generally be subject to 10 per cent local WHT. The taxable base is the positive difference between the sale price of the shares and the documented acquisition price of the shares.

If the income's beneficiary is a resident of a country with which Bulgaria has a double tax treaty (DTT), the tax is to be paid within three months from the beginning of the month following the month of the tax accrual. Otherwise, the payment should be effected by the end of the month following the month of the accrual.

If a DTT is applicable, its provisions shall override the above general local provisions provided that the respective requirements of the DTT are duly met. In such a case, the foreign investor has to apply for issuance of a DTT clearance statement by the local tax revenue authorities. The DTT application is subject to a specific administrative procedure.

Any foreign investor (a company or a physical person) who has acquired a property in Bulgaria is obliged to apply for a BULSTAT registration (registration for statistical purposes). The application should be filed within seven days of the acquisition of the property.

2.3.2 Tax regime for investment through a Bulgarian company owned or otherwise controlled by foreign companies and/or individuals

The capital gain from a real estate derived by a Bulgarian company is included in the company's annual financial result. The reporting and payment of corporate income tax is made annually until end of March of the respective year following the year in which the income was accrued.

The current rate of corporate income tax is 10 per cent.

Bulgarian law normally treats the ownership of land, construction rights over land and ownership of finished buildings as long-term tangible assets (fixed assets). Accordingly, the costs for their acquisition, including the costs of investment in the process of construction, would not normally be treated as immediately deductible. Instead, they would be treated as part of the cost of the acquisition of the fixed asset and deducted as a depreciation expense along the lifetime of the fixed asset. However, land is not subject to depreciation.

2.3.3 Mandatory VAT registration

Any entity with a taxable turnover of BGN 50,000 (€25,600) or more for a period of no longer than the last 12 consecutive months shall be obliged to submit an application for registration under the VAT Act. This should be done within 14 days after the end of the tax period during which this turnover has been reached. 'Taxable turnover' is the aggregate of the tax bases under taxable deliveries made by the person including those chargeable with zero per cent VAT (eg, exports).

2.3.4 Voluntary VAT registration

Any person may register for VAT voluntarily, even if the requirements for registration are not present.

VAT-registered persons are entitled to recover the VAT paid on certain deliveries (related to the acquisition of property, construction of buildings, etc) according to the general rules of the VAT Act.

3. INVESTMENT VEHICLE CHOICE
3.1 Structures used to purchase property
Both direct and indirect structures for property acquisition are commonly used. If a real estate is acquired indirectly (through company acquisition), there is always a risk that the vehicle may have pre-existing or other liabilities. Appropriate due diligence should be carried out so that any such risk can be identified and accounted for the intended transaction. The specific approach depends on the intentions and requirements of the parties as well as on the tax implications and consequences of the transaction. The preferred option depends on the peculiarities of the deal and there is no standard advice on which option should be used.

3.2 Restrictions on foreign ownership or occupation of property
Currently, Bulgarian law does not permit foreigners or foreign legal entities to directly acquire ownership rights over land.

It is permitted, however, for foreigners or foreign legal entities to acquire ownership rights over land by virtue of an international treaty, ratified, published and entered into force in the Republic of Bulgaria. Foreign physical persons are also permitted to acquire ownership rights over land through inheritance by operation of law. However, if the land is classified as an agricultural area, such foreigner has to transfer its ownership rights to another person within three years from the date of the inheritance.

Citizens and legal entities from European Union (EU) member states or from states that are parties to the European Economic Area Agreement (EEAA) can acquire ownership rights over land under the conditions provided for by local laws and in compliance with the Treaty of Accession of Bulgaria to the EU (the Treaty). As a consequence:
- Citizens from EU member states or from EEAA states, who are not residing permanently in the territory of Bulgaria, can acquire ownership rights over a zoned land for a second home after 1 January 2012. The same terms apply to legal entities from EU member states or from EEAA states. This restriction does not apply to persons permanently residing in the territory of Bulgaria.
- Citizens and legal entities from EU member states or from states that are parties to the EEAA can acquire ownership rights over agricultural land, forestry and forestry fund land after 1 January 2014. This restriction does not apply to self-employed agricultural farmers who are citizens of a member state willing to settle and legally reside in Bulgaria.

The above restrictions could be legally bypassed through registration of a Bulgarian company, even if it is fully owned by foreign investors. Such Bulgarian company is entitled to own land.

The above restrictions refer only and solely to ownership rights over land. No restrictions exist for acquisition of ownership rights to buildings, detached parts of buildings or other limited real rights. Foreign investors are not restricted when it comes to occupying a property or guaranteeing or granting a security.

3.3 Real estate investment trusts (REITs)
REITs have existed in Bulgaria from 2004. REITs are subject to special requirements and restrictions provided for the protection of investors. REITs have to be licensed by the Financial Supervision Commission. REITs are obliged to annually distribute as a dividend at least 90 per cent of their profit.

A REIT might be established with a capital of no less than BGN 500,000 (€256,000) and its capital must be increased by at least 30 per cent after its licensing. REITs are generally used for major projects. Currently, there are approximately 60 REITs established in Bulgaria.

4. FINANCING AN ACQUISITION
4.1 Financing of corporate real estate transactions
Corporate real estate transactions are usually financed by equity or equity and loan (bank loan, loan from shareholders or from third parties). The banks usually finance a certain percentage of the acquisition price or the costs of construction. Local bank financing depends upon the bank, the type of the loan, its term, location of the property, etc but is usually up to 70 per cent of the real estate's market value. Market value is determined by the bank itself and may differ from the value of the deal.

4.2 Real estate as a means of raising finance
The typical forms of loan security are the following:
- mortgage over the real estate subject to the purchase. If its value is not enough to secure the loan, the creditor may require additional properties to be mortgaged in its favour;
- special pledge over the ongoing business of the company which is the owner or will become the owner of the property;
- special pledge over the receivables of the debtor from the debtor's bank accounts;
- special pledge over rents received by the owner upon lease of the respective property; or
- special pledge over the shares of the company.

The special pledge securities have to be registered with the Special Pledges Registry. Certain types of special pledges require subsequent registrations. The special pledges over the ongoing business or over the company's shares have to be registered with the Commercial Registry kept by the Registry Agency at the Ministry of Justice. If there is a real estate among the pledged assets of the company, the special pledge over the ongoing business should also be reflected in the Property Register.

4.3 Common forms of security granted over real estate
The mortgage is the most commonly-used form of security. The mortgage

may secure the real estate owner's debt or a third party's debt.

The mortgage may be contractual or statutory. A contractual mortgage is established by virtue of a contract between the owner of the real estate, the debtor (if different from the owner) and the creditor. The contract is to be executed in front of a notary public and in the form of a notary deed. It has to be further registered with the Property Register. In order to be valid, the contract has to specify the creditor, the owner of the real estate, the debtor, the real estate, the secured receivable, the maturity date, the interest (if any) and the amount for which the mortgage has been established.

A statutory mortgage may be established in cases explicitly provided for by the law. Such cases are: by the bank over the real estate fully or partly acquired through the bank loan; or, by the seller if the buyer has not paid the purchase price in full. The statutory mortgage is also subject to mandatory registration with the Property Register.

The registration of the mortgage with the Property Register is valid for 10 years. The term may be extended if the mortgage is to be re-registered before expiry of the initial term. The mortgage expires upon repayment of the debt. It may be released upon consent of the creditor or based on a court decision.

The receivables secured by mortgage have priority among other creditors' receivables. The priority ranks immediately after: (i) receivables for the expenses for securitisation and/or enforcement over the same property and for some specific court claims set forth in the law; and (ii) receivables of the state for taxes due for the mortgaged real estate.

4.4 Real estate mortgage securitisation
Mortgage is the most common real estate securitisation used in Bulgaria.

5. MANAGING THE ACQUISITION PROCESS
5.1 Minimum formalities for the sale and purchase of property
Any direct sale and purchase of the property must be made in the form of a notary deed. However, if the seller of the real estate is the state or a municipality, a simple written form of contract is sufficient.

A joint owner may sell its share in the immovable property to a third party only if the latter has firstly offered it under the same or more favourable conditions to the other joint owners and none of them has accepted the offer.

Notwithstanding the form of the contract, all real estate transferring deeds must be registered with the local Property Register office where the property is located.

Although it is not mandatory, it is common practice for the parties to sign a preliminary contract for sale and purchase of a property prior to signing the notary deed. This agreement does not transfer the title. It only obliges the parties to act in accordance with the agreement. Within the term of the preliminary agreement, the seller collects the documents for the deal and follows its other obligations (if any) as might be agreed between the parties. The buyer makes due diligence as to title and ensures the financing of the deal. The time between the signing of the preliminary agreement and the notary deed is usually between 30 to 60 days. A much longer period may be also agreed depending on the conditions precedent for closing the deal. Theoretically the preliminary agreement may provide for a term up to five years.

The minimum formalities refer to collecting mandatory documents and making required due diligence of the real estate and/or the company in case of a share deal.

In a share deal (sale of shares of a company – owner of a real estate), the formalities depend on the legal form of the company.

The sale of shares of a limited liability company (LLC) is completed by signing a written contract with notarised signatures. In addition, the share transfer has to be registered with the Commercial Registry. The share transfer between shareholders can be made freely whereas the transfer of shares to a third party has to be approved by a general meeting of the shareholders.

The sale of shares of a joint stock company (JSC) depends on the type of the shares. The transfer of bearer's shares is effected with their delivery. The registered shares are transferred by endorsement and delivery and the transfer has to be registered in the Book of Shareholders. Unless otherwise provided for by the statutes of the company, the shares in a JSC may be transferred freely without the approval of any company body.

In all cases of share deals, a set of supplementary corporate documents and resolutions are also required.

5.2 Main legal documents required to transfer a property or grant a lease

The main legal documents required for a transfer of a property depend on the subject of the transaction.

In a real estate direct sale, the main documents are: a seller's title deed (notary deed, resolution for restitution of the property, contract for purchase from the state or a municipality, etc); tax evaluation of the property; layout of the estate; and a set of standard declarations (for lack of outstanding public obligations; of citizenship and marital status – if the sellers are physical persons). If the seller is a company, it should also provide a certificate of good standing, a certificate evidencing who the representatives of the company are, and a resolution of the competent corporate body on the property's sale.

The buyer should present a declaration of funds origin. If the buyer is an individual, it should also provide a declaration of citizenship and marital status. If the buyer is a company, a certificate of good standing, a certificate evidencing who represents the company and a resolution of the competent corporate body on the property's purchase are also required.

If some of the parties are acting by proxy, there should be a notarised power of attorney in a special form. In this case, the respective declarations should be also signed by the parties and notarised.

In the sale of a new building or certain of its premises, the seller should further provide the construction permit, the architectural designs, some other supplementary documents and a document evidencing the stage of construction of that building. If the building has been fully completed, the seller is obliged to present an occupancy permit for the building.

A significant number of additional documents might be also required depending on the peculiarities of the deal. A thorough legal due diligence of the ownership of the real estate must be also made. The due diligence must trace the validity of the previous transactions for a period of at least five years where a check for the last 10 years is recommended. It is recommended that the parties obtain competent professional advice for every single transaction.

In any real estate sale and purchase, the seller has to provide a certificate evidencing lack of encumbrances over the estate issued by the Property Register. This document is not required under the law. It is, however, of great importance for the buyer and should be considered as mandatory from a buyer's perspective.

The main legal document to be presented when granting a lease is the title deed evidencing the landlord's title rights. For a lease of more than three years, a resolution of the General Meeting of Shareholders (for an LLC) or of the Board of Directors is also required (for a JSC).

5.3 Property transaction costs

The property transaction costs are calculated based on the sale price or the tax evaluation of the property, whichever is higher.
- local tax – for the amount of the local tax please see question 2.2 above;
- state fee for registration of the deal in the Property Register – 0.1 per cent of the price of the deal; and
- notary fees to be calculated in accordance with the table below.

Price of the deal	Notary fee (excluding VAT)
From BGN 50,001 to BGN 100,000	BGN 480.50 + 0.5 per cent of the amount exceeding BGN 50,000
From BGN 100,001 to BGN 500,000	BGN 730.50 + 0.2 per cent of the amount exceeding BGN 100,000
More than BGN 500,000	BGN 1,530.50 + 0.1 per cent of the amount exceeding BGN 500,000 but not more than BGN 6,000

The transaction costs are generally due from the buyer, unless the parties agree otherwise. Most commonly, the buyer pays all the costs, and rarely the costs are split between the parties.

In a share deal, the costs include notary fees and state fees for registration of the corporate changes to the Commercial Registry. The notary fee is 30 per cent of the notary fees applicable to the property transfer, whereas the base is the share's sale price. The registration costs are insignificant.

5.4 Does the seller warrant its ownership of the property?
The seller usually warrants its ownership of the property.

Even if the contract does not contain explicit warranties, the seller will still be responsible under the general provisions of Bulgarian law. The seller will be responsible if third parties turn out to have any rights over the property which may infringe the buyer's title rights, provided that such third parties' rights have not been registered with the Property Register as of the date of acquisition. The seller shall be responsible even if it had not known of the existence of the third parties' rights.

The buyer is entitled to cancel the sale through a court proceeding if the property is owned by a third party, and not by the seller. In such a case, the seller is obliged to reimburse the buyer for the sale price, the title transfer costs and the court expenses. The seller shall indemnify the buyer for such other damages that are direct and immediate consequences of the contact termination. The buyer has to prove such damages. The buyer may also be entitled to liquidated damages if agreed between the parties.

The buyer is entitled to cancel the contract if only part of the property is owned by a third party or is encumbered with third party's rights. The right of cancellation may be enforced if, according to the circumstances, it may be concluded that the buyer would not have entered into the sale contract had it known about the third party's rights. Otherwise, the buyer is entitled to claim only reduction of the sale price and indemnification for the other damages.

The seller shall be obliged to refund only the sale price without other compensation if the buyer had been aware of the third parties' rights. This is also valid even if the parties have agreed that the seller shall not be held liable. Any agreement that the seller will not be liable will not be valid if the seller has kept silent about a third party's rights known to it. The buyer shall be deemed to be aware of any third parties' rights if they were registered in the Property Register as of the date of the acquisition.

The buyer might be evicted from the property or part of it only upon a court decision in favour of the third party. The seller shall not be liable if it has not participated in the court case and if it proves that there was enough evidence for the claim to be rejected.

The buyer may agree with the third party to monetary compensation in exchange for cancelling the claim. In this case, the seller will have to reimburse the buyer for the money paid, together with interest and expenses.

5.5 Warranties a seller usually gives to a buyer
The seller usually warrants that it is the exclusive owner of the property and there are no third parties' rights whatsoever (encumbrances, mortgages, injunctions, interdicts, limited real rights, leases, pending court claims or out of court disputes, restitution claims, state or municipal property deeds for the property, etc).

The parties may agree on any other warranties eg, environmental, zoning plan provisions, quality of the materials, etc.

Parties may agree on liquidated damages in case of the buyer's eviction from the property. The amount usually varies from 20 to 35 per cent of the agreed price. The liquidated damages are due in excess of the statutory obligation of the seller to reimburse the sale price to the buyer and the transfer costs for the acquisition of the property.

5.6 Purpose of warranties in the purchase agreement
The warranties are mostly designed to provide information to the buyer and partially to apportion the risk. The seller may limit its responsibility but may not fully exempt its liability based on the warranties.

5.7 Owners/occupiers' liability for matters relating to the property which occurred before they bought or occupied
All encumbrances over a property (mortgage, injunction, limited real rights, pending court procedures, lease agreements, etc) registered with the Property Register are linked to the property, but not to the owner. In case of subsequent transfer of a property or its lease, the buyers/occupiers shall be bound by such encumbrances and shall bear the legal consequences of them.

The buyers/occupants might be held liable for other matters relating to the property which occurred before they bought or occupied it. This, however, is not a general rule and depends very much on the peculiarities of the case.

5.8 Notarisation
Some of the documents for a real estate transaction need to be notarised. For more details, please see questions 5.1 and 5.2 above. A precise estimate of which documents need to be notarised has to be made on a case-by-case basis.

5.9 Formalities for a contract becoming a legally binding obligation
The preliminary contract for a real estate sale and purchase must be in writing. Its notarisation is not mandatory but is recommended. It must specify at least all material terms and conditions of the final notary deed (parties, estate, price, method of payment). Not specifying some of those will make the contract void. The preliminary contract may not be registered on the Property Register.

The final contract for sale and purchase of a real estate becomes legally binding when it is signed in writing by the seller, the buyer and the notary public. It should specify at least the full identification information details of the parties, a detailed description of the property, the purchase price and its payment.

The contract for sale of shares of an LLC becomes binding once signed by the parties and their signatures are notarised.

Certain other formalities might be also required depending on the case, for example a notarised power of attorney in a special form, notarised set of declarations, etc. A precise estimate what other formalities have to be met should be made on a case-by-case basis.

5.10 Point at which parties become legally bound
The parties become legally bound with the conclusion of the respective contract in the form required by law.

5.11 Transfer of title
The title to the property is transferred when the notary deed is signed by the seller, the buyer and the notary public. The title of a property sold by the state or a municipality is transferred by signing a simple contract by the seller and the buyer only.

In any case, the transfer must be registered on the Property Register.

5.12 Insurance of the property if there is delay between agreeing terms and actual sale
Bulgarian law provides that the risk of accidental damage and/or demolition of the property is for the owner to bear. The risk passes from the seller to the buyer as of the date of title transfer. The insurance of a property is not required under Bulgarian law. The property owner decides whether, when and how to insure it. The owner is permitted to not insure the property at all. The insurance of the property in the period between completion of the negotiations and the actual sale is subject to agreement between the parties and should be considered within the negotiations.

6. REAL ESTATE BASICS
6.1 Main sources of law that govern real estate
Statutory legislation is the main source of law which governs real estate rights in Bulgaria. The Constitution of the Republic of Bulgaria is the supreme law. It establishes the fundamental principles of inviolability of private property, the equality of all types of property and equal opportunity for development and protection of the different types of property. The Constitution classifies property as either private or public.

Real estate is further governed by laws and regulations, and the Ownership Act is the main one. Other key real estate regulation laws are inter alia the Ownership and Usage of Agricultural Lands Act, the State Property Act, the Municipal Property Act and the Cadastre and Property Register Act. The Civil Procedure Code also governs some aspects of the title transfer process.

Statutory legislation applies throughout the entire territory of Bulgaria.

Court precedents are also important with respect to interpretation of the law. Certain types of court decisions issued by the Supreme Court of Cassation are deemed mandatory for all other courts when interpreting the law. Other court decisions are indicative but not mandatory.

6.2 Types of tenure
Bulgarian law provides that property can be owned by the state, municipalities, individuals or legal entities. Property is classified as either private or public.

Public property may be owned by the state or municipalities only. Private property may be owned by anyone including the state and municipalities.

Public property is explicitly listed in the law and is subject to special regulations. It cannot be transferred to third parties and may be used only

Bulgaria

based on a concession for not more than 35 years. State and municipal private property can be transferred to and acquired by third parties.

The ownership right is the most comprehensive real estate right. The owner is entitled to use the property, to dispose of it and to possess it in any way permitted by the law. The ownership right may belong to only one owner or to two or more co-owners. The shares of the co-owners are deemed equal unless otherwise stipulated in the title deed. Each co-owner may use the common property according to its purpose and in a manner not likely to disturb the other owners' use according to their rights. Each co-owner may ask for a partition of the common property at any time.

Bulgarian law also recognises the concept of 'limited real rights' over real estate owned by a third party. Those rights are: construction; the right to use; and easement.

These three rights are established, registered and protected in the same way as ownership rights.

A construction right is the right by virtue of which, on land owned by one person, another person can erect a building and become its owner, or an owner of a part of it (eg, an apartment). The holder of the construction right is entitled to use the land beneath the building as far as it is necessary for the use of the building itself. It is also entitled to transfer the title to the building separately from the land. A construction right may be established with or without a term, but more usually without.

If a construction right is granted for a fixed term, the ownership of the building as constructed shall pass to the owner of the land by virtue of law and free of charge. If the construction right is granted with no term, the ownership of the building as constructed shall last until the useful life of the building.

A construction right must be exercised by its holder within five years of its acquisition. The construction right shall lapse in the land owner's favour by virtue of law if not exercised within this period of time. The construction right is considered exercised once the respective building is roofed.

If the building is demolished for whatever reason, the owner of the building or detached part of it is entitled to construct it again in its previous state and size by virtue of the construction right granted earlier. This possibility is also restricted by a five-year term from the date of the building's demolition. Based on these specifics, it is more beneficial for the investor to purchase an ownership right over the land rather than a construction right.

A right of use is the right by virtue of which one person is entitled to use a property owned by another person in compliance with its purpose and to gain profits from it without the property being significantly modified. This right is granted *intuitu personae* and its holder cannot transfer it to any third party.

An easement is the right by virtue of which an owner of one real estate is entitled to benefit from another real estate (usually an adjacent one) in a definite way – for example, the right of passage, the right to build an aqueduct in a property owned by somebody else, etc. Easements can either be granted by law or by agreement (voluntarily agreed by the owners of the real estate).

A condominium ownership is the ownership where floors or parts of them (apartments, offices or other type of detached premises) are owned by different owners but the parts of the building designated for common usage (the foundations, the staircases, the elevators, the roof, the main installations, etc) and the land beneath (if any) are commonly owned by all these owners. These common parts may not be divided. The owners' general meeting governs the common parts of the building. The owners' general meeting should appoint a manager. All owners are obliged to participate in the expenses for maintenance of the common parts in proportion to their share. The shares of the individual owners in the common parts are proportional to the ratio between the area of the detached premises which they own, as calculated at the establishment of the condominium ownership.

Both full and limited ownership rights can be acquired through legal transaction, prescription or other means provided by law. The acquisition of ownership rights and limited real rights over real estate through prescription requires the expiration of a fixed term and continuity and incessancy of possession during that time. The period of time is either five years in case of *bona fide* possession, or 10 years in case of *mala fide* (bad faith) possession. The possession is deemed to be *bona fide* when the entitled person possesses the property on a legal basis fit to make it an owner (eg, a notary deed for sale and purchase of a real estate), without knowing that the transferor was not an owner or that there was a defect in the form of the transaction (eg, that the notary was not regionally competent to certify the deed).

6.3 Must land be registered?
Real estate and any related transactions must be registered on the Property Register.

6.4 Public land register
The Property Register is a register of transactions and other documents explicitly specified by the law (court decisions and orders). It is publicly available and anyone can make checks of it. A copy of any registered title deed might be obtained upon request.

6.5 Land not covered by a public land register
Any acts of disposals with properties are subject to registration with the Property Register save for the acquisition of properties by virtue of the law or through inheritance by operation of law.

State property deeds, municipal property deeds and resolutions for restitution of agricultural lands in favour of third parties were not subject to registration in the Property Register until 2000. In such cases, the title was established by simple deeds, respectively resolutions. As of the beginning of 2001, it became mandatory for such deeds to be registered.

6.6 State guarantee of title and categories of documents and information
Registration on the Property Register does not provide a state guarantee of title. Any third party is fully entitled to claim title rights to a property

registered to someone else. Such claims have to be proved in a court case and to be affirmed by a court decision.

Registration on the Property Register makes the transaction publicly known. All registered circumstances might be opposed by third parties who subsequently acquire any rights over the same property.

The main documents subject to registration with the Property Register are:
- all deeds acknowledging or transferring ownership rights or limited real rights to a real estate in the territory of Bulgaria;
- all deeds establishing, transferring, changing or terminating ownership rights and limited real rights to immovable property in the territory of Bulgaria;
- court decisions which substitute the deeds under the preceding two paragraphs;
- contracts for the transfer of inheritance (if the heritage includes a real estate);
- deeds for waiver of real rights over immovable property;
- the agreements on a property's partition;
- lease agreements with a term longer than one year. Such registration is not mandatory and depends on the agreement between the parties. Registered lease agreements are more beneficial for the tenants with respect to the protection of their tenant's rights;
- copies of the announced wills and the subject immovable property; and
- court claims for cancellation or invalidation of the deeds subject to registration under the preceding paragraphs and the effective court resolutions of them.

The information subject to registration is:
- the full personal information of the parties involved (name, address, unified personal number); if any of them is a company – the name, the seat and address of management and the unified identification code;
- the date and place of issuance of the deed;
- the full description of the property;
- the price of the property.

Canada

Osler Hoskin & Harcourt LLP
Heather McKean, Jack Silverson & Brian Donnelly

1. INVESTMENT PURCHASE OVERVIEW
1.1 Overview
The Canadian real estate market has remained stable during the recent worldwide economic turmoil with negligible distressed real estate coming to market. Canada continues to offer a stable environment for real estate investments.

An indicative process is illustrated in the following diagram:

Typical investment purchase in Canada

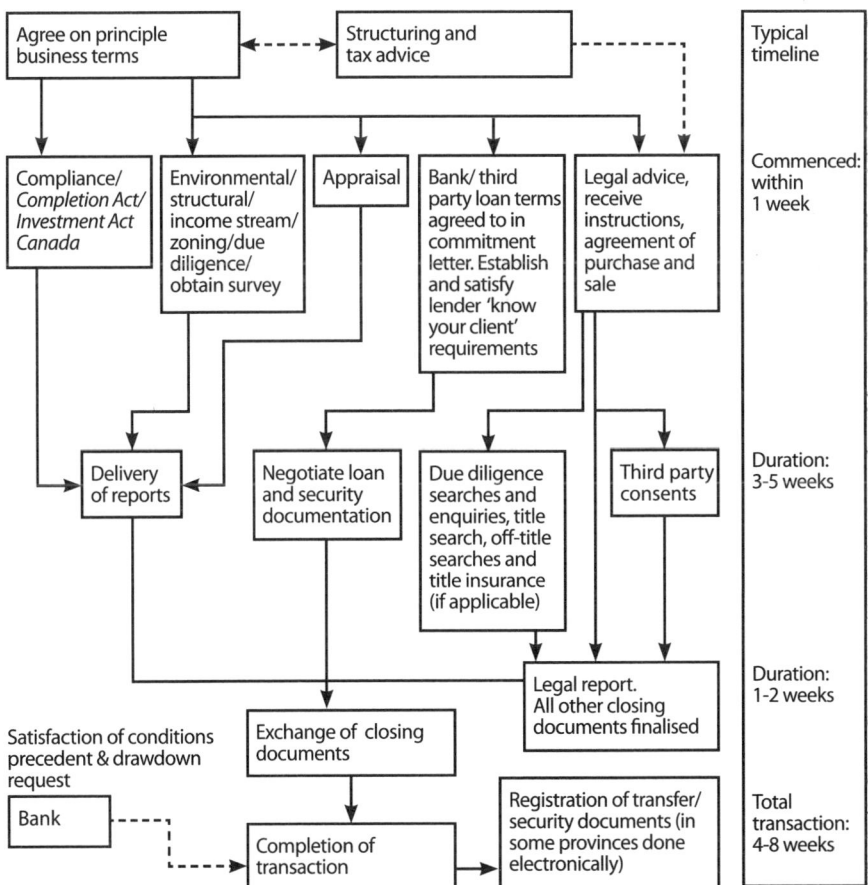

2. TAX CONSIDERATIONS
2.1 The Federal Income Tax Act (Canada)
2.1.1 Income tax
Canada's tax regime is governed by the federal Income Tax Act (Canada) (the ITA) and its regulations, as well as sales tax, corporate tax and other tax laws of the provinces and territories. The ITA levies income tax for each taxation year on the taxable worldwide income of every 'person' resident in Canada in that taxation year, which includes a corporation. At common law, a corporation will generally be resident in Canada if its 'central management and control' is located in Canada. Under the ITA, corporations which may be formed under federal, provincial or territorial law are deemed to be resident for this purpose. The ITA also levies taxes on persons not resident in Canada who carry on business in Canada, and imposes withholding taxes on certain types of passive income, including rent, interest and dividends. In addition, the disposition of 'taxable Canadian property' (as defined in the ITA) may result in a non-resident being subject to tax in Canada. Therefore, the tax treatment of an investment made by a non-resident in Canadian real estate will depend upon whether the investor makes the investment directly or through a Canadian entity, such as a corporation. If the investment is made directly by the foreign investor, the tax treatment will vary based on whether the Canadian real estate generates business income or property income.

2.1.2 Tax treaties
Canada is a party to more than 85 income tax treaties with other jurisdictions. These tax treaties often reduce the withholding tax rate imposed under the ITA and the branch tax rate described below.

2.1.3 Indirect investment through a Canadian corporation
Tax on business profits and deduction of interest. If a non-resident invests through a Canadian corporation, the corporation will be subject to tax on its business profits as determined in accordance with ordinary commercial principles. For this purpose (subject to the thin capitalisation rules discussed below), interest expense is generally deductible if:
(i) it is reasonable in amount;
(ii) it is incurred pursuant to a legal obligation to pay interest on borrowed money or unpaid purchase price; and
(iii) the underlying debt is used for the purpose of earning income from business or property.

In lieu of book depreciation, the ITA sets out a capital cost allowance that provides taxpayers with discretionary deductions.

Thin capitalisation rules. The thin capitalisation rules disallow the deduction of interest payable by a Canadian corporation on debts owing to 'specified non-resident persons' (being various non-arms length parties) to the extent that the ratio of such debts to the corporation's equity exceeds a ratio of 2:1.

Withholding tax. Subject to treaty relief that may reduce or eliminate withholding tax, a Canadian subsidiary must withhold tax at a rate of 25 per cent on several types of payments to non-residents, including dividends, interest paid to non-arms length parties, participating interest, certain management or administration fees, rents and royalties.

2.1.4 Carrying on business directly in Canada

Tax on business profits. If a non-resident invests directly in Canadian real estate and such investment constitutes the carrying on of a business (such as developing property for resale or investing in a hotel, assisted living facility or any rental property where the level of service goes beyond that typically associated with a rental property (for instance, the cleaning of individual suites)), the non-resident will be required to file a Canadian tax return and will be subject to tax based upon the non-resident's taxable income earned in Canada.

Taxable income earned in Canada is generally calculated on the non-resident's business profits from its operations in Canada and based on rules similar to those set out above with respect to Canadian corporations; however, the thin capitalisation rules applicable to Canadian corporations would not apply.

Withholding tax and branch tax. A non-resident is required to remit withholding tax in respect of payments made to other non-residents if such payments are deductible in computing its taxable income earned in Canada. Examples include participating interest or interest paid to non-arm's length parties. In addition, if the non-resident is a corporation, it may be subject to branch tax which is designed to approximate the withholding tax that would have been owed on dividends if paid by a Canadian subsidiary. If the non-resident is not a corporation, it will generally not be subject to branch tax; however, it will be required to pay tax on its business profits at individual tax rates, which are typically higher than corporate tax rates.

2.1.5 Earning property income directly from Canada

If a non-resident investor earns income from property (for example, rental income where the investor did not provide a level of service beyond that normally associated with a rental property), the gross amount of rental income will be subject to a 25 per cent withholding tax (subject to reduction by tax treaty). Non-residents have the option, however, to elect to file a Canadian tax return and pay tax based on the profits from the Canadian rental property. Such tax would be calculated in a manner similar to the calculation obtained when an investor carries on business directly in Canada.

2.1.6 Gain on disposition of investment

Canadian real estate and shares of corporations that primarily derive their value from Canadian real estate, except for certain shares of public corporations, are taxable Canadian property such that tax is payable under the ITA on the disposition of such property. In the case of property held for resale or as an adventure in the nature of trade, the full amount of the gain is subject to tax at normal rates under the ITA.

Where an investor directly holds land and buildings which are not held for resale or as an adventure in the nature of trade, the gain on the sale of the land is generally taxed as a capital gain such that only 50 per cent of the gain is included as income. On a sale of a building, the amount of capital cost allowance previously claimed by the seller is included in the seller's income to the extent that the sale proceeds are greater than the undepreciated capital cost of the building and less than the original cost of the building. To the extent that the sale price exceeds the original cost of the building, only 50 per cent of the gain is included in income. On a sale of shares, a gain is typically treated as a capital gain such that only 50 per cent of the gain is included in income unless the shares were held for resale or as an adventure in the nature of trade.

Typically, a purchaser will not buy taxable Canadian property from a non-resident until the non-resident obtains a certificate from the Canada Revenue Agency certifying that all relevant taxes have been paid or that the seller has furnished security for such taxes. If the purchaser is not provided with such a certificate, it would be liable for tax equal to 25 per cent of the purchase price in the case of land or shares held as capital property, and 50 per cent in the case of buildings or property held for resale or as an adventure in the nature of trade. Under these circumstances, the purchaser is entitled to withhold from the purchase price and pay to the Canada Revenue Agency the amount required to satisfy the tax liability of the purchaser under the ITA.

2.2 Transfer taxes assessed upon disposition of real estate
2.2.1 Provincial land transfer tax
In Canada, a transfer of real estate triggers provincial land transfer tax which the purchaser must pay when a real estate transaction closes. The tax rate differs from province to province and is stratified depending on the total value of consideration paid, which normally includes the cash paid for the land, in addition to the debt assumed and all other benefits transferred to the seller. For instance, in Ontario, land transfer tax for commercial property ranges from 0.5 per cent on the first $55,000 to 1.5 per cent on the amount exceeding $250,000. Certain provinces also charge this tax on long-term leases. In Ontario, a lease that can exceed 50 years is subject to the land transfer tax. This tax is payable on the fair market value of the real property. Exemptions from land transfer tax are also available; for instance, certain inter-corporate transfers between affiliated corporations are exempt provided the transfer is not registered.

2.2.2 Municipal land transfer tax
Pursuant to municipal by-laws, the cities of Montreal and Toronto have implemented municipal land transfer taxes to be paid by a purchaser in addition to the provincial land transfer taxes discussed above. The municipal land transfer tax applies to all purchases of real property within the city limits and is charged on a graduated basis depending on the value of consideration paid for the property.

In Toronto, the tax for commercial property currently ranges from 0.5 per cent on the first $55,000 paid as consideration for the real property, 1.0

per cent from $55,000.01 to $400,000, 1.5 per cent from $400,000.01 to $40,000,000 and 1.0 per cent on anything over $40,000,000. In Montreal, the tax currently ranges from 0.5 per cent on the first $50,000 paid as consideration for the real property, 1.0 per cent from $50,000 to $250,000, 1.5 per cent on the next $250,000 to $500,000 and 2.0 per cent on any amount exceeding $500,000.

2.2.3 Value added tax (VAT)
Goods and Services Tax (GST)
A purchaser of real estate in Canada may be required to pay GST or Harmonized Sales Tax (HST) (described below), subject to certain exceptions. In the provinces and territories where GST is levied, the rate is five per cent. Sales of used residential housing and certain sales of farm land are generally exempt from GST. Further, a purchaser is generally not required to pay GST if registered for GST purposes under the Excise Tax Act (Canada) and the purchaser intends to use the real estate for commercial activities. Commercial rents are also subject to GST in Canada and a collector of such rents (including a non-resident collector) must generally remit GST to the applicable taxation authority. Many businesses can recover GST that is related to commercial activities through a system of input tax credits.

In Canada, a seller has an obligation to remit GST that it has collected from a purchaser. If a seller is a non-resident, is not a GST registrant in Canada, and is not carrying on a business in Canada, the purchaser may be required to self-assess for GST payable on the transaction. Non-residents must register under Canada's GST legislation and charge and collect GST if they make taxable supplies in the course of a business carried on in Canada. A foreign firm with a permanent establishment in Canada is deemed to be a resident of Canada for GST purposes with respect to activities carried on by that establishment in Canada. A business with a Canadian branch may be required to register for GST and collect GST on supplies made through the permanent establishment. Non-resident registrants that do not have a permanent establishment in Canada are required to post security with the Canada Revenue Agency to meet collection and remittance obligations.

Harmonized Sales Tax (HST)
In some provinces, provincial sales taxes have been 'harmonised' with the GST and are collected by the federal government as a single tax known as HST. In provinces where the HST exists, HST (which includes the five per cent GST) is applied to the purchase of real property, rather than GST alone. The application of HST generally parallels that of the GST; for instance, HST does not generally apply to the sale of used residential housing, but HST will apply to the sale or lease of commercial properties subject to the ability of the payee to recover portions of the HST through input tax credits. As of 1 July 2010, five provinces will charge HST at the following rates: Nova Scotia at 15 per cent; Ontario, New Brunswick and Newfoundland and Labrador at 13 per cent; and British Columbia at 12 per cent. In the provinces where the HST does not exist, provincial sales tax does not apply to the purchase of real property.

Canada

2.2.4 Municipal tax

In Ontario, the Municipal Act allows municipalities to charge an annual tax on real property. This tax (known as realty tax) is calculated by multiplying the assessed value of the real property by the 'mill rate', which is established yearly based on the financial needs of the municipality. Any arrears of realty tax have priority as a lien over other interests in the real property including the interest acquired by a purchaser. On the sale of real property, the seller and the purchaser divide the realty tax for the current year. The seller will be responsible for the realty tax attributable to the period before the sale and the purchaser will be responsible for the realty tax attributable to the period following closing.

3. INVESTMENT VEHICLE CHOICE

3.1 Foreign ownership

There are generally no restrictions on foreign ownership of Canadian real estate; however, most provinces require foreign corporations to be extra-provincially registered in their province before being entitled to own real property located within that province. Some provinces also require foreign corporations to register in order to hold a security interest in, or mortgage on, real property. The latter requirement may apply either because holding an interest in real property qualifies as carrying on business under provincial legislation or because, without registration, a foreign corporation will be unable to enforce its security.

3.2 Vehicles for foreign ownership

There are several structures used for ownership of Canadian real estate. Such structures include a corporation, a co-ownership, a general partnership, a limited partnership, a trust, personal ownership or any combination of the foregoing. The choice of legal structure will be governed by factors such as tax planning requirements, liability issues, cost, size and number of assets, the financing structure, liquidity concerns and each foreign investor's rules and regulations.

3.2.1 Corporation

A corporation is a legal entity endowed with a separate legal existence that can carry on business, own real property, possess rights and incur liabilities. Shareholders, through shares of the corporation, have an equity interest in the corporation, but do not directly own the business or the real property belonging to the corporation. As a result, shareholders generally have no direct liability for obligations of the corporation. The creation of a corporation occurs upon a filing with the appropriate government authority and payment of the requisite fee. Incorporation may occur under the federal Canada Business Corporations Act or under the corporate statute of a province or territory. Such incorporation is, generally speaking, a very simple process and does not require any substantive government approvals. A simple filing is necessary and the corporation must register with various tax and other government bodies. Share capital and other financial information about the corporation need not be publicly disclosed unless the corporation is a publicly-listed company or part of a regulated industry.

For most federally incorporated corporations, the Canadian residency requirement is that 25 per cent of the individuals constituting the board of directors be resident in Canada. For boards with fewer than four directors, there must be at least one resident Canadian on the board. Note that some foreign investors choose to incorporate in New Brunswick, the Yukon or Nova Scotia as the applicable business corporation statute in each of these provinces does not have director residency requirements.

3.2.2 Co-ownership
True co-ownership arrangements, commonly involving one or more corporations, avoid the unlimited joint and several liability applicable to partners in a general partnership. Co-ownerships also permit co-owners to be taxed separately, thereby avoiding some potentially adverse tax consequences attributable to a general partnership.

3.2.3 General partnership and limited partnership
Investments may also be held through a general partnership, which is a relationship that exists between two or more entities carrying on business in common with a view to profit. Each partner of a general partnership has unlimited liability in relation to the business carried on by the partnership.

Limited partnerships are commonly used for investment purposes to permit tax deductions for limited partners while retaining their limited liability. The rules governing a limited partnership are found in provincial statutes. A limited partnership consists of one or more limited partners (who will not have liability for the acts of the partnership so long as the limited partners are passive investors) and the limited partnership must have a general partner. The general partner carries on the business of the limited partnership and has unlimited liability for the obligations of the limited partnership; however, a general partner may be a corporation, which generally ensures that the owners will not incur liability.

If any type of partnership consists of one or more non-resident partners, it will be considered a non-resident for certain purposes of the ITA. For instance, if the partnership earns any rental income, that rental income will be subject to withholding tax. Consequently, when a partnership structure is used, the non-resident investors will often invest through a Canadian corporation.

Although the income of a partnership (including the deduction of capital cost allowance) is generally calculated as if the partnership were a separate taxpayer, it is allocated among the partners according to the terms of the partnership agreement and is taxed in the hands of the partners. Special rules apply in determining the adjusted cost base of a partnership interest. The ITA limits certain deductions that may be claimed against a limited partner's 'at-risk' amount for the partnership. In certain cases, a partner that is a general partner for non-tax purposes may be deemed to be a limited partner for tax purposes.

3.2.4 Real Estate Investment Trust (REIT)
REITs are very common in Canada. A REIT is a publicly-traded trust vehicle where the primary source of income is real estate. Investors can purchase units of the trust as they would purchase shares of a corporation and legislation has extended limited liability protection to investors in many Canadian REITs. REITs are designed to be a 'flow-through entity' investment meaning that the trust pays little or no Canadian income tax provided that the REIT distributes its income to the unit holders. In the case of REIT units held by a non-resident, distributions of income to the non-resident unit holder by the REIT are generally subject to withholding tax at a rate of 25 per cent (subject to reduction by tax treaty); however, the gain realised on a disposition of REIT units is generally not subject to tax provided that the unit holder and those persons not dealing at arm's length with the unit holder, hold less than 25 per cent of the units of the REIT.

4. FINANCING AN ACQUISITION
4.1 Purchase and sale
4.1.1 Financing overview
In Canada, most real estate financing is arranged through institutional lenders such as banks, trust companies, pension funds, credit unions and insurance companies. 'Vendor take-back' financing is sometimes available but is not common. Credit terms vary from institution to institution and depend on the nature of the transaction and the risks involved. Statutory and common law restrictions on the ability of an entity to borrow money or to provide guarantees may arise in some circumstances; for instance, where the entity does not meet specified solvency tests.

4.1.2 Interest rate
In Canada, interest rates are usually linked to a 'prime rate' announced by a financial institution, plus a margin of profit on top of the prime rate. The prime rate includes an increment above the cost of borrowing of the financial institution based on the rate announced weekly by the Bank of Canada.

Interest rates can be either fixed for a specified period of time or variable based on the prime rate plus a margin. Section 347 of the Criminal Code of Canada makes it illegal for someone to accept the payment of interest (including fees) at an aggregate rate of more than 60 per cent per annum.

A borrower may consider borrowing in other currencies and has a choice of other interest rate pricing, including applicable Government of Canada bond rates, the London Interbank Offered Rate (LIBOR), the US Federal Funds rate and bankers' acceptances. Commitment and processing fees are normally charged by lenders. Typically, it will be the borrower's responsibility to pay for all of the lender's legal and other costs in arranging real property financing.

4.1.3 Real property security
Mortgage/charge
In Canada, a loan made to acquire real property is typically secured by a

mortgage, charge or debenture on the real property and the loan is typically made 'with recourse' to the assets of the borrower. The repayment of the mortgage can be through blended payments of principal and interest, where the portion of each payment attributable to interest decreases as the principal is reduced or through interest only payments with a balloon payment of principal at maturity. Early prepayment of a mortgage has unfavourable financial consequences for the lender and is usually restricted or subject to a 'make whole' payment.

Bond mortgage/trust deed
Where it is necessary for a borrower to borrow large sums of money, it may be difficult to find a single lender to provide the full amount. In this situation, a borrower may find it easier to secure financing from several parties who will each lend a portion of the total amount of the loan. In return, the borrower will provide a bond mortgage, debenture or trust deed to a trustee who holds the security in trust for each of the lenders. In a bond financing, the trustee then issues bonds to each of those lenders as security for their loan in the amount equal to their respective contributions.

Syndicated loan
Another option is to obtain a syndicated loan where the real property security is held for all the lenders by one financial institution acting as the security agent for all lenders under the loan.

Sale/leaseback
Another financing mechanism is a 'sale/leaseback', whereby the owner of a real property sells the real property to a financial institution for its current market value, and in turn, the financial institution leases the real property back to the original owner in exchange for monthly rental payments over a multi-year term. This allows the original owner to free up the capital tied up in the real property and pay for the use of the real property over a period of time.

Remedies
A lender's most common remedies in Canada for default under a mortgage, charge or debenture are power of sale and judicial sale or foreclosure. The procedure for implementing these remedies varies across the provinces, and some provinces do not offer all options to lenders. Power of sale is the main debt recovery vehicle in Canada. In Ontario, the power of sale remedy permits the lender to sell the real property upon notice provided that the lender must distribute all surplus funds that exceed the total debt secured by the property (plus costs) first to any subsequent secured creditor(s) and finally to the borrower. If there is a deficit upon exercise of this remedy, the lender may sue the borrower for the balance and have recourse to other assets of the borrower.

Foreclosure or judicial sale commences on the lender's application to the court. In a foreclosure in the province of Ontario, the court orders the borrower to remedy the default within a specified period of time, failing which the title to the mortgaged real property passes to the lender with no obligation imposed on the lender to sell the real property or distribute excess proceeds. In a foreclosure, there is no ability of the lender to recover any deficit from the borrower.

4.1.4 Security over personal property
Personal property
An assignment of rents, general security agreement, pledge of shares or stocks and personal or parent guarantees are used as collateral security. General security agreements charging personal property (including rents) must be registered under the personal property security regime existing within the applicable province, which is a different registry system separate from the land registry system. As a result, prior to financing, a lender should search the relevant personal property registries to ensure that there are no prior registrations over such property. The personal property registry in each province does not record ownership; rather, it only records liens on personal property. As there is no public registry that one can search to confirm title to personal property, one must rely on representations and warranties or other evidence from the seller as to title to personal property.

Shares and stocks
Security in shares and stocks may be subject to yet another legislative regime separate from the personal property registry. In order to ensure their priority over pledged securities, lenders should be aware of the control and priority rules existing within the applicable securities transfer legislation existing in each province. In Ontario, the legislation governing this process is the Securities Transfer Act.

4.1.5 Foreign lenders
Most interest payments and commitment fees payable under a traditional loan from a foreign arms-length lender are now exempt from withholding tax. However, loans with participating interest and loans between non-arms length parties are still subject to withholding taxes in Canada.

4.1.6 Know Your Client Rules (KYC Rules)
The KYC Rules act as a screening device for potential money-laundering and terrorist financing schemes and apply to a wide range of activities. Once a lawyer or financial institution is engaged to act on behalf of a client, the KYC Rules apply and require the lawyer or financial institution to collect personal information about the client. In addition, real estate brokers are required to collect personal information under the KYC Rules. The responsibilities under the KYC Rules include identifying and verifying the identity of the client and maintaining records proving the client's identity. As compliance with KYC rules typically requires a significant amount of personal information, it is important to address these requirements early to avoid delaying the transaction.

Canada

5. MANAGING THE ACQUISITION PROCESS
5.1 Overview of timelines
The typical real property transaction takes four to eight weeks depending on the complexity of the deal. Negotiation of the agreement of purchase and sale, advice on tax planning, securing financing, negotiating security documents, conducting diligence review (including environmental and structural reports, tenant estoppel certificates and title and off-title searches) and obtaining title insurance and legal advice will span from four to six weeks in total, while finalising the closing documents and transferring title will require one to two weeks after the aforementioned steps are complete. A transaction can be completed more quickly when the diligence is curtailed.

5.2 Purchasing real property
5.2.1 Agreement of purchase and sale
The main document is the agreement of purchase and sale between the purchaser and the seller. This agreement will contain all necessary business terms, including the description of the real property, purchase price, deposit, closing date and allocation of risk (for example, with respect to environmental liability). This agreement may also contain conditions precedent for the benefit of the purchaser and/or seller, as well as representations and warranties by the seller and, to a lesser extent, the purchaser. On occasion, the agreement of purchase and sale may be preceded by a binding or non-binding letter of intent outlining the key business terms. Sometimes, real property is sold 'as is where is' with minimal representations and warranties from the seller, and in such a case, the purchaser must satisfy itself with respect to the title and condition of the real property.

The agreement of purchase and sale must be in writing and must be signed by all parties. When signing an agreement of purchase and sale in Canada, it is important to be aware of what is not covered by the agreement. For example, a conveyance of land in Ontario does not include unopened road allowances or title to the bed of a navigable body of water or stream as such title remains with the Crown.

5.2.2 Due diligence
Overview
Within the agreement of purchase and sale, a purchaser is often granted a 'due diligence' or conditional period to investigate the real property. The purchaser generally bears the responsibility of conducting due diligence. Diligence review includes title, off-title and zoning searches, a review of an up-to-date survey of the real property, environmental, structural and zoning audits and a review of leases and rent rolls. An independent engineering review of the real property (particularly real property with older buildings) is common practice. If the expectations of the purchaser are not satisfied, the agreement of purchase and sale may allow the purchaser to cancel the transaction and obtain a refund of any deposit. Conversely, the agreement may provide that if the seller receives another offer during the conditional

period, the seller can force the purchaser to either terminate the agreement or waive the conditions within a short period of time.

Title and title insurance
The purchaser will want to obtain comfort that:
(i) the seller is the actual owner of the real property;
(ii) the real property is free from easements and covenants that could restrain the intended use of the real property; and
(iii) there are no outstanding debts against the real property.

The complexity of the title search will depend on the registry system under which the real property is registered. In Canada, some real property is registered in a 'land titles' system, which is a much easier system to search. However, some real property is registered in a 'registry system', which requires that one prove a history of title for a period of years prior to the purchase date (40 years in Ontario, although much of Ontario has now been converted to a land titles system).

Title insurance has become increasingly popular in Canada and is often obtained in commercial real estate transactions. With title insurance, the purchaser obtains a policy from a third-party insurer that guarantees the quality of title to the real property. In Canada, title insurance has become a frequent requirement of lenders. Care must be taken to negotiate the exceptions to the policy as there are a number of items that may not be covered such as environmental risks and expropriation proceedings.

Possessory interests
One of the issues that might not be discovered during a title search is the existence of possessory title, which could vest title in a person other than the owner of the real property if that person has been in open and notorious possession of the real property for at least 10 consecutive years without the owner's objection. Similarly, easements can be acquired by prescription without consent of the owner of the real property provided the enjoyment of the easement is uninterrupted during the prescribed period, which in Ontario is 20 years. Title insurance can provide coverage against such claims of possessory title.

Overlap with interests in personal property
There are different registration systems in Canada for real property and personal property. A thorough search is necessary to reveal not only registrations on title to the real property, but also personal property registrations (which may include security interests in rents, fixtures and chattels).

Off-title matters
There are also liens established by statute that are not disclosed on the register of title. These liens include unregistered hydro easements, realty taxes, and work orders for non-compliance with zoning laws, fire codes and health regulations. These off-title matters can be identified through requests

for clearance certificates from the appropriate government authorities. In addition, zoning laws may limit the permitted uses of the property or the location of improvements on the site. While some zoning information may be obtained through a clearance certificate, an up-to-date survey and report from an urban planner may be required.

Construction liens

It is not uncommon to find a construction lien on a real property in Canada. A construction lien is created in favour of an entity that supplies materials, labour or services in connection with any construction on or improvement to a property for which that entity has not been paid. A construction lien will take priority over the interest of a purchaser and over a lender's charge on the property and should be removed prior to closing. Construction liens may be removed through a discharge via registration of a release signed by the lien claimant or by payment into court of the amount claimed under the lien, plus security for costs.

Environmental audits

In Canada, a real property owner has an obligation to comply with certain duties in connection with the discharge of contaminants and hazardous materials into the environment from its real property. Environmental liabilities can be inherited by subsequent owners or occupants of the real property, even in the absence of their prior knowledge. Unless express representations and warranties concerning the state of the real property are included in the agreement of purchase and sale, recourse against the seller for contamination is unlikely to be successful unless there is a latent defect.

Since the search of title will not of itself reveal the presence of environmental hazards, a purchaser should assess the environmental risks associated with the real property being purchased. In Canada, government officials do not 'certify' that a real property is free from such risks. In almost all cases, a purchaser of commercial property will want a firm specialising in environmental inspections of property to conduct a Phase I environmental audit and if deemed necessary, a more detailed Phase II environmental audit. Lenders often require such audits before advancing any funds.

Governmental restrictions on use of land

In certain cases, governments can limit potential transfers and usage of real property. For instance, Ontario's Planning Act imposes a restriction on the division of real property. An owner cannot transfer or mortgage real property if the owner retains an interest in the abutting real property, subject to statutory exceptions.

Real property development and the use of land is regulated primarily at the municipal level. Municipalities typically control land use and the density of development through official plans and zoning by-laws. Zoning by-laws regulate the size, height, location, density and use of buildings in a specified zone.

New project construction is also subject to provincial and municipal legislation. For instance, building codes set specific standards for the construction of new buildings and regulate the maintenance of existing structures. Before construction commences, most municipalities require building permits and regulatory approvals to be obtained.

5.2.3 Competition Act pre-merger notification thresholds
If certain thresholds of book value or gross revenues of either party are exceeded, the Competition Bureau examines various factors to determine whether an acquisition will result in a substantial lessening or prevention of competition in the relevant market. A purchaser and/or seller may be required to provide prior written notice to the Competition Bureau of a proposed transaction.

5.2.4 Investment Canada Act (ICA) pre-merger ministerial approval threshold
The direct acquisition of control of a business in Canada by a non-Canadian may require the prior approval of the Minister of Industry under the ICA depending on the book value of the assets or whether the business is in a sensitive sector.

If the transaction results in the acquisition of control of a Canadian business by a non-Canadian but does not require prior approval (ie, the value of the assets is below the applicable threshold), a notice of investment must be filed within 30 days after closing.

5.3 Closing details
Obligation to close
The seller and purchaser each have an obligation to close the transaction unless conditions precedent were not met or a party can prove that any of the fundamental elements of a binding agreement were missing. These elements include: intention; capacity; consideration; and offer and acceptance. Under Canadian law, a condition should not be confused with a warranty since a breach of warranty does not typically allow the innocent party to terminate the transaction, but only entitles the innocent party to damages.

In the case of a refusal to close, the remedies of an innocent party include restitution, specific performance of the contract, or damages in lieu of, or in addition to, the performance of the contract. If the breaching party is the purchaser, the seller generally has the option of retaining the deposit without limiting the seller's other remedies. The closing procedure itself involves an exchange of all closing documents, keys and funds along with registration of title and security documents.

Registration of documents
In Ontario, only four types of documents can be registered on title: the Transfer/Deed of Land; Charge/Mortgage of Land; Discharge of Charge/Mortgage of Land; and Document General, which serves as the cover page to any other document that is not a transfer, charge or discharge of charge.

Title documents are registered electronically in many jurisdictions, and otherwise, are registered in paper form.

5.4 Leasing real property
5.4.1 Leases
Overview
Leasing real property is another option for those who are interested in doing business in Canada. Understanding the allocation of costs and risks in a lease is critical to a landlord and tenant alike. In a default scenario, a landlord has multiple options, including the right to enforce the tenant's obligations, to terminate the lease, to accelerate future lease payments, and to collect damages. In Canada, there is a duty to mitigate damages.

Ground leases
One form of leasing arrangement is a long term ground lease, in which an investor leases vacant land and develops it or leases an entire building on a long term basis. Once the development is complete, the investor in its capacity as ground tenant sublets space to retail, office or industrial tenants, depending on the type of development. Ground leasehold interests may be bought and sold in a manner similar to fee simple real property interests, but may be subject to certain conditions imposed by the landlord or its lender. Long-term leases may trigger land transfer tax and may require a severance if the landlord has an interest in adjoining real property.

Commercial leasing
Most commercial lease transactions start with an 'offer to lease'. An offer to lease is typically a binding agreement that contains the business terms of the deal, including the location and size of the leased premises, the term of the lease, basic rent and additional rent, and any tenant inducements. Commercial leases in Canada are typically on a triple net basis, which requires a tenant to pay basic or net rent (which constitutes the landlord's profit) plus all of the landlord's operating costs, including repair costs, realty taxes, insurance, utility and other operating costs. In a retail lease, a tenant may also be required to pay percentage rent based on a percentage of its annual sales in addition to the basic rent.

Residential leasing
Residential leases are regulated by provincial legislation. In some cases, the applicable legislation will override the terms of the lease, regardless of the intention of the parties. For example, the ability of the landlord to increase residential rents may be limited by provincial legislation.

5.5 Brokers in the acquisition process
5.5.1 Real estate brokers legislation
A person who wishes to dispose of, acquire or lease real estate may engage a real estate broker who is paid a commission. Real estate brokers are subject to special regulation in Canada. For example, brokerages, brokers, salespersons

and persons involved in the trade of real estate in Ontario must be registered and adhere to a Code of Ethics.

Commission payable to the broker is generally paid by the seller or landlord; the broker then shares this commission with the purchaser's or tenant's agent, if any. The rate of commission is negotiable. Typically the rate represents a percentage of the sale price or rental income, respectively.

5.5.2 Mortgage broker legislation
Mortgage brokers, lenders and mortgage administrators are subject to specific regulation in Canada at the provincial and territorial level. For example, all mortgage brokerages, administrators, brokers and agents in Ontario must obtain a licence to do business unless they fall within certain exceptions for financial institutions that are otherwise regulated by another governmental authority. Similar legislation either exists or is under consideration in most of the other provinces or territories.

6. REAL ESTATE BASICS
6.1 Sources of law
In Canada, there are 10 provinces and three territories, and all except Québec are based upon English common law principles. In Québec, real property law is governed by the Civil Code of Québec, which is derived from French civil law. Québec law requires all real property transaction documents to be produced in the French language, which is not a requirement in any of the laws of other provinces or territories in Canada. For ease of reference, laws of the provinces and territories are described in this chapter as provincial laws or the laws of the provinces.

There is no constitutional protection for real property rights in Canada. Consequently, real property can be expropriated or taken by eminent domain by governmental and quasi-governmental authorities; however, appropriate compensation must be paid.

6.2 Interests in land
Interests in land are generally held directly in fee simple or as leasehold interests. Condominium or strata title ownership is also common throughout Canada. All provinces maintain a system of public land titles registration through which interests in land are registered and ownership of real property can be verified.

Czech Republic

Havel & Holásek   Jan Holásek & Daniela Kozáková

1. INVESTMENT PURCHASE OVERVIEW
The acquisition of commercial property in the Czech Republic typically includes the following recommended legal steps:
- execution of a letter of intent;
- execution of a future purchase agreement (may be agreed prior to the commencement of due diligence, instead of a letter of intent, or after the due diligence process is completed);
- review of the site (land plots to be purchased) as to future use and taking into consideration the current valid municipal zoning plan;
- ownership title due diligence investigation;
- due diligence investigation of encumbrances over the property as registered in the Real Estate Register;
- due diligence investigation of other agreements and contracts and possible encumbrances (rights and obligations) relating to the property that are not registered in the Real Estate Register;
- legal review of the statutory provisions that govern the purchase and development of the property binding on the seller, the purchaser and attached to the property;
- tax and legal structuring of the acquisition respecting the purchaser's and seller's specifications, character of the property and legal and other defects detected during the due diligence process;
- property (or special purpose vehicle (SPV)'s shareholding) purchase agreement which includes: (i) the purchase price; (ii) warranties to be provided by the seller to the purchaser and vice versa; (iii) termination of the currently valid and effective contracts concluded with suppliers or tenants; (iv) payment of the real estate transfer tax; (v) payment of the fee to be paid for registration in the Real Estate Register;
- executing an application for registration of the new owner in the Real Estate Register (if asset deal) and filing the application and purchase agreements (with attachments required by Czech laws) with the relevant Czech Real Estate Registry;
- payment of the purchase price only after the purchaser receives approval from the Real Estate Registry that the purchaser has become the legal and beneficial owner of the property – the reason for delaying the payment of the purchase price is that title is formally transferred after registration which typically takes between two and four weeks.
- payment of the real estate transfer tax to the relevant Czech tax authority by the seller (or by the purchaser if the parties so agree) within

three months from the month of registration of the transaction (if an asset deal).

2. TAX CONSIDERATIONS
2.1 Acquisition of a Czech company
There are no connected taxes with respect to the acquisition of a Czech company. The acquisition of a share in the company is VAT exempt.

2.2 Acquisition of real estate
2.2.1 General
A building is not part of a land plot and *vice versa*. Land and buildings have separate legal statuses and consequently their own tax regimes.

This, *inter alia*, suggests that if a total price is agreed for land and a building, the price should be split.

2.2.2 Real estate transfer tax
A transfer of real estate is subject to a real estate transfer tax. A tax rate of three per cent applies and is levied on the expert valuation or the purchase price, whichever is higher. The seller is obliged to pay the tax, and the purchaser acts as a guarantor.

There are several exemptions, but these are primarily applicable with respect to transactions where the public sector is involved. In 'standard' commercial transactions you can qualify for a 'first sale of new building' exemption; this exemption is not applicable to a land sale.

2.3 Value added tax (VAT)
2.3.1 VAT – acquisition of land
The acquisition of land from a person registered for VAT may be subject to VAT. However, only the transfer of land approved for construction (qualified building parcel) is subject to 20 per cent VAT. According to the Czech Act on VAT, a qualified building parcel is a plot of land: (i) for which an effective construction permit was issued; and (ii) on which no building has been constructed yet. In all other cases the transfer of land is VAT exempt.

If someone acquires a qualified building parcel (and VAT is applied) with the intention of selling it together with the constructed building, they are not entitled to recover input VAT, because the later sale of the land together with the building would be VAT exempt (the sale is exempt because condition (ii) is not met).

2.3.2 VAT – acquisition of a building
The transfer of a building is exempt from VAT if the building is transferred after three years from the date of issuance of the first approval of use (*kolaudace*) or three years from the date of first use, if this date is earlier.

If the building is subject to approval for another type of use, the exemption period starts again.

2.4 Construction of a building
2.4.1 VAT deduction from construction costs
A VAT payer who receives goods and services may deduct the input VAT, provided that it uses them for business purposes. The full input VAT deduction is allowed when the received supplies are used for taxable or other specified supplies. Otherwise, the tax payer cannot deduct the input VAT or may only deduct it partially.

If a building is sold within three years from issuing the first approval of use or three years from the date of the first use if this date is earlier, the sale is a taxable supply and VAT should be applied. In other cases the sale of a building is VAT exempt.

Full VAT deduction is also possible if the building is leased and VAT is applied to the rent. If the building or its part is leased without VAT in the period of five years following completion of the building, it would be necessary to return the VAT deduction (fully or partially). If the building is sold with five years following the completion of the building and the sale is VAT exempt, it would be necessary to return the VAT deduction (fully or partially).

2.4.2 VAT rates at construction
The standard VAT rate amounts to 20 per cent. A reduced 10 per cent rate is applicable to residential projects if the floor area of a house for residential purposes does not exceed 350 square metres; a reduced rate is also used if the area of an apartment does not exceed 120 square metres.

2.4.3 Corporate income tax – tax loss
A tax loss incurred during construction can be utilised in five consecutive tax periods if the general conditions of the Income Taxes Act are met. This is a general loss carry-forward period; no loss carry-back is possible in the Czech Republic.

2.5 Holding real estate
2.5.1 Corporate income tax
Depreciation
Nowadays, buildings (administrative) are depreciated for tax purposes over 50 years. However, if a building was registered for accounting purposes by the end of a taxable period that started in 2003, the old rules are applicable and the building is depreciated over 30 years, even after 2003. This advantage can be applied only to a share deal where a company is acquired together with a building that falls under the old depreciation rules. In the case of an asset deal, the former depreciation is interrupted and depreciation from the new acquisition price restarts under the new owner.

Other buildings are depreciated over 30 years. Movable assets are depreciated over three, five, or 10 years.

One can opt for an accelerated or straight-line method.

Fit-outs and other improvements

Fit-outs and other improvements not having the character of repairs and maintenance (fit-outs) increase the acquisition price of the building and also the base for tax depreciation.

The taxpayer may ask the fiscal authorities for a binding tax ruling on whether investment in the property is considered to be a fit-out or repairs and maintenance – which don't increase the acquisition price and which can be directly included in the tax base of the current year.

Dividends

According to the Czech Commercial Code, a company can pay dividends if the retained profit exceeds the retained losses and if a statutory reserve fund was created.

According to the Czech Income Taxes Act, a 15 per cent withholding tax is applicable to dividends.

However, this provision may be overruled by an applicable tax treaty or a subsidiary may qualify for an exemption under the EU parent-subsidiary directive (Council Directive of 23 July 1990 on the common system of taxation applicable in the case of parent companies and subsidiaries of different Member States (90i435/EEC), as subsequently amended) as enacted in the Czech Income Tax Act. The exemption applies if a parent company has a share of more than 10 per cent and the share is held for at least 12 months. The time requirement can be met subsequently. There are further conditions to be met (eg, both the parent company and the subsidiary must have a legal form in the EU parent-subsidiary directive and both companies must be subject to corporate income tax). This participation exemption applies to companies located in countries that are members of the EU, Norway, Iceland and Switzerland.

2.5.2 VAT
VAT on rent

Rent is generally VAT exempt. However, if a tenant is registered for VAT and uses the premises for business purposes, the landlord may apply VAT to the rent. In such a case, the standard rate of 20 per cent is applicable.

Short-term rental of buildings, non-residential spaces, rental of parking spaces, and rent of safe deposit or permanently installed equipment or machines is not exempt from VAT. Short-term rental of buildings or non-residential spaces means a rental period, including movable indoor equipment plus supply of electricity, heat, cold, gas or water, which doesn't exceed 48 hours.

Condition for VAT deduction

Generally, a person registered for VAT in the Czech Republic (VAT payer) is allowed to deduct an input VAT if it uses the supply of goods or services for taxable output or a supply that is exempt from VAT with the right of deduction.

If a VAT payer uses the supplies of goods and services only for an output that is VAT exempt without the right of deduction (for example the lease of premises to non-VAT payers or to VAT payers when VAT is not applied to the lease), it has no right to deduct the VAT related to the inputs.

If the inputs are used for both taxable and exempt outputs, a partial deduction can be claimed.

2.5.3 Real estate tax
The rate of real estate tax depends of the type and use of the land/building, location, number of stories and the local coefficient. Real estate tax is not significant.

2.6 Limitations on acquisitions
2.6.1 Acquisition of real estate by EU citizens and citizens of other countries
Since 1 May 2009, citizens from EU and other countries have not been limited in the nature and scope of acquiring real estate (except for land that is part of an agricultural land fund or forest) in the Czech Republic. The original 'legal obstacles' requiring that foreigners hold a Czech residence permit or visa were lifted. Thus, in principle they may acquire real estate under the same conditions as Czech citizens (except for some residual limitations with respect to certain plots of land). The same process of real estate acquisition by Czech citizens applies to foreigners, and is, in principle, based on two fundamental steps: firstly, a contract such as a purchase, donation or barter contract must be entered into between contracting parties; secondly, the acquisition process must be completed by registration of the ownership in the Cadastral Register.

2.6.2 Acquisition of public land: tendering requirements
Acquisition from the Czech Republic
The Czech Republic may transfer its real estate only if the country does not need it for performance of its functions anymore and it must, as a rule, be approved by the Ministry of Finance.

Acquisition from municipalities or regions
Municipal or regional authorities may transfer their real estate only after the intent of the transfer has been published on the official board of the municipal authority for at least 15 days and on the official board of the regional authority for at least 30 days. The transfer must also be approved by the Assembly of the Municipality or the Regional assembly.

Acquisition from the Land Fund
The sale of real estate by the state or other public authorities (such as municipalities and regions) does not fall within the scope of public procurement in accordance with the EC directives or other specific tender procedures, with the exception of the sale of state real estate administered by the Land Office of the Czech Republic.

This real estate is sold in public commercial auctions. The tender procedures differ depending on the status of the real estate sold (ie, agricultural land, buildings). There are several categories of persons who can execute preferential bids, such as entitled persons under restitution laws, municipalities, or tenants on the agricultural land that is the subject of the sale.

3. INVESTMENT VEHICLE CHOICE
3.1 Most commonly used structures to purchase property
The two most common methods for conducting real estate acquisition transactions are asset deals and share deals. However, there are several modifications to these schemes, for example, a merger; a second SPV; or the sale of the business or its part. Therefore, the structure of the transaction should always be set out with respect to the particular project and the investor's needs and should also reflect the results of due diligence investigations.

3.1.1 Asset deal
If the real property is transferred by an asset deal, the agreement on purchase of the real estate is concluded. However, the applicable tax consequences arising from such purchase must always be considered. (For example, the position of the seller with respect to the sale of an asset may not be advantageous because:
(i) a three per cent property transfer tax on the agreed purchase price or price specified in the expert opinion, whichever is higher, is payable;
(ii) corporate/personal income tax shall be paid with respect to the sale of the asset; and
(iii) 20 per cent value added tax (VAT) might be applicable.
For more details please refer to section 3 of this chapter.

3.1.2 Share deal
In general practice, SPVs are established for the development of projects in the form of either a limited liability company or a joint stock company. Since the majority of SPVs are established in the form of a limited liability company, we will summarise briefly below the way of transferring the ownership interest in such a company through a share deal.

The shares in a Czech limited liability company (ie, ownership interests (*obchodní podíly*)) can be acquired on the basis of an ownership interest transfer agreement. Such agreement must be in writing and signed by all participants and a notary must verify the signatures. As a rule, the general meeting of the company (provided that the company has more than one shareholder) shall approve the transfer prior to concluding the agreement on transfer of the entire ownership interest.

The change of the shareholders must be registered in the Commercial Register of the company in question. However, the registration does not affect the effectiveness of the ownership interest transfer, which becomes effective upon signing the ownership interest transfer agreement, or later upon the fulfilment of the conditions precedent, if applicable.

3.2 Other possibilities after acquisition
3.2.1 Financial leasing
Financial leasing is a *sui generis* contract, not regulated in the Civil Code or Commercial Code. The applicable rules are based on civil law, commercial law, banking law, and tax law. Financial leasing is a lease under the terms of which a leasing company acquires, pursuant to an investor's request, real property in order to lease the real property to an investor for a certain term. The investor pays for all the expenses incurred in the acquisition and lease transaction in exchange for the use and undisturbed enjoyment of the real property. Upon expiry of the lease, the investor has the option to acquire the real property.

3.2.2 Operating a lease without the option to purchase
Operating leases are also *sui generis* contracts, similar to financial leasing. The main difference is that a tenant of an operating lease agreement will not purchase the real property at the end of the lease period. The real property needs to be physically returned to the landlord who owns the real property during the entire lease period.

3.3 Sale
3.3.1 Sale of an SPV
The sale of an SPV does not have any VAT consequences and no real estate transfer tax must be paid.

Gains from the sale of shares are taxed within the general corporate income tax base at the rate of 19 per cent.

However, this provision may be overruled by an applicable tax treaty or by Czech participation. Income from the sale of shares may be exempt under the same conditions as the dividends exemption. The exemption applies if a parent company has a share of more than 10 per cent and the share is held for at least 12 months and if the additional conditions are met (eg, both the parent company and the subsidiary must have a legal form in the EU parent subsidiary directive and both companies must be subject to corporate income tax). This participation exemption applies to companies located in countries that are members of the EU, Norway, Iceland and Switzerland.

The participation exemption also applies to Czech subsidiaries, at least 50 per cent of the assets of which consist of property.

3.3.2 Sale of a real estate
Corporate income tax
Gains from the sale of assets including real estate are taxed within the general corporate income tax base, ie, there is no separate tax basket for capital gains. For more details please see section 3. A general corporate income tax base is calculated from the accounting profit based on Czech accounting standards.

At sale the acquisition value of the land or tax residual value (for real estate disclosed as a fixed asset) or the acquisition value (for real estate disclosed as stock) can be applied as a cost. Please note that a loss realised on

the sale of land is not deductible for corporate income tax purposes.
The current corporate income tax rate is 19 per cent.

VAT
The sale of land with construction/real estate standing is VAT exempt.

The sale of a building is subject to VAT if the sale is realised within three years from issuing the first approval of use or within three years from the date when the building started to be used if this date is earlier; otherwise it is exempt.

If not exempt, the applicable VAT rate depends on the size and purpose of the building. If the floor area of a house does not exceed 350 square metres or the floor area of an apartment does not exceed 120 square metres and the house or apartment is used for residential purposes, the VAT reduced rate of 10 per cent should be applied at sale.

Otherwise, the standard rate of 20 per cent is applicable.

Real estate transfer tax
In general, a sale of real estate is subject to a three per cent real estate transfer tax. However, the sale of buildings or apartments would be exempt based on the 'first sale of new building' exemption; this exemption is not applicable to a land sale.

3.4 Obligation to report to the Czech National Bank
Please note that a Czech company has to report certain transactions (eg, a loan granted from foreign entities) to the Czech National Bank (CNB) for statistical purposes.

3.5 Alternative structures
There are alternative business structures that might lead to lower taxation. One example is an investment fund, which has a special corporate income rate of five per cent and which is used by some investors for real estate projects. However, such fund is bound by several conditions (supervision by the CNB, by a depositary bank, diversification in several unrelated projects, etc).

Shareholder loans within the scope of the Czech thin capitalisation rules may reduce a company's (corporate) income tax base. A debt push-down structure is used to ensure the tax deductibility of acquisition loans.

4. FINANCING AN ACQUISITION
4.1 Common forms of security
Since an investor often requires a credit facility from the bank to finance the purchase of land for the project or the completed projects, summarised below are the most common forms of security provided to ensure repayment of the provided credit.

The Credit Facility Agreement must be carefully drafted and must contain:
(i) the amount of the loan and its currency;
(ii) the terms of drawing the credit;

Czech Republic

(iii) terms of repayment of the credit;
(iv) the interest and fees to be paid to the bank;
(v) the security provided; and
(vi) the terms and conditions of termination of the agreement.

The practice of banks usually does not differ very much, and apart from the abovementioned elementary terms of the bank loan, the established practice for providing bank loans includes:
(i) the bank's rights and the lender's obligations;
(ii) specification of the event of default;
(iii) the obligation of the lender to replenish the security if the provided security loses its value,
(iv) change of control clause, or
(v) contractual penalties.

Therefore, the Credit Facility Agreement should be carefully negotiated with the bank if possible.

4.2 Pledge

Under Czech law, *zástavní právo* is used as a term to describe security rights referring to a 'mortgage' as an encumbrance over real estate and a 'pledge' as an encumbrance over any other type of asset. All mortgages and pledges are governed by general rules contained in the Civil Code, as well as by specific laws.

Both mortgages and pledges are used to secure monetary or non-monetary receivables. Czech law allows one receivable to be secured by several mortgages or pledges and a secured receivable to be used for securing another receivable.

4.2.1 Mortgage

In general, a mortgage right is a real right that encumbers the mortgaged real estate property and applies to any subsequent owner of the real property that is encumbered by the mortgage. A mortgage has two important functions: (i) as a security of the receivable; and (ii) in case the receivable is not duly fulfilled, the creditor is entitled to satisfaction from the receivable by means of encashment of yield of the mortgaged real property.

Under Czech law the mortgage applies not only to the relevant real property but also to accessories, accruements, and proceeds from the real property that have not yet been separated from the real property. Czech law also enables securing of the credit by mortgage over several individual real properties (ie, a collective mortgage). The law allows more than one mortgage to be established on the same real property. For satisfaction, the rank of such mortgage rights is crucial. The secured receivables shall be satisfied in sequence according to the time when the mortgage was established.

The mortgage may be established upon:
(i) a written agreement (the Mortgage Agreement);
(ii) the decision of a court approving an inheritance settlement agreement;
(iii) under conditions provided by law, a decision of the court or an

administrative authority; or
(iv) by law.

A mortgage over real property established under the Mortgage Agreement that is subject to registration in the Cadastral Register and over apartments and non-residential premises is established by the registration of a mortgage right in the Cadastral Register.

A mortgage over real property established under the Mortgage Agreement that is not subject to registration in the Cadastral Register is established as of the date of its registration in the Register of Pledges maintained by the Notary Chamber of the Czech Republic (except if the mortgage was established by the decision of a court or administrative authority).

4.2.2 Pledges

A pledge is an encumbrance over any type of asset other than real estate. A pledge over a movable asset (eg, a production unit) is effective either: (i) upon delivery of the asset to the pledgee or to a third party on its behalf; or (ii) upon registration of the pledge in the Register of Pledges administered by the Chamber of Czech Notaries, which is a public register accessible only to notaries.

If the pledge is established by registration in the Register of Pledges, the pledge agreement must be executed in the form of a notarial deed. Czech law distinguishes different pledges as such:
- Pledge over receivables – under Czech law, current and future receivables may also be subject to a pledge, provided that they are clearly specified. A pledge over receivables is established on the date of conclusion of the pledge agreement if not specified otherwise by the parties.
- Pledges over ownership interests in Czech limited liability companies or over the shares in the joint-stock company.
- Pledges over trade marks – a pledge over a trade mark requires registration with the Industrial Property Office.
- Pledge over enterprise – the enterprise shall be understood as the sum of all property owned by an entrepreneur and used for entrepreneurial activity.

4.2.3 Assignment of receivables as collateral security agreement

The Civil Code allows the securing of obligations by assignment of a right (including ownership rights) and assignment of receivables.

The receivables of the bank may also be secured by the transfer of a right of the borrower. The lender becomes the legal owner of the assets and maintains the legal title until the borrower repays in full its debts owed to the lender, at which time the title is retransferred to the borrower. The contract for the assignment of the right must be in writing.

Receivables may also be secured by a security assignment of receivables of either the debtor or of another party (the security provider) to the holder of the security.

4.2.4 Bank guarantee
The bank guarantee is based upon a written declaration in which the bank (the security provider) undertakes to satisfy the entitled person up to the amount stated therein if the debtor fails to satisfy its obligations or if other conditions are met. The bank guarantee is also often used for the purpose of securing the rent and service charge payments with respect to the lease of non-residential premises.

4.2.5 Notarial deed on direct enforcement
A notarial deed on the approval of direct enforceability is an agreement witnessed by a notary public and concluded in the notarial deed, under which the debtor undertakes to satisfy the creditor's receivable and provides consent for direct execution of payment of the receivable in case the debtor does not fulfil its obligation – in such case the receivable may be directly enforced without taking any further action.

4.2.6 Promissory notes
Promissory notes are securities binding the issuer (either the debtor or another person) to pay a certain amount to a creditor. Promissory notes are usually issued blank. The creditor and the issuer conclude an agreement on the creditor's right to fill in the promissory note in case of the debtor's default.

4.2.7 Guarantee
This security is created by a declaration of the guarantor in which the guarantor undertakes to be bound to fulfil an obligation after the debtor in case the debtor fails to do so, though having been so requested by the creditor. The guarantee must be provided in written form. The creditor is obliged to inform the guarantor, upon request and without undue delay, of the current amount of the secured receivable. If the secured receivable is assigned, the guarantor must fulfil its obligations towards the new creditor only if it was notified about the assignment by the assignor or the assignment has been evidenced to it by the assignee. Once the guarantor repaid the debtor's obligation towards the creditor, the guarantor has a right to recourse against the debtor.

5. MANAGING THE ACQUISITION PROCESS
5.1 Minimum formalities for the sale and purchase of property
Before the investor signs a contract to purchase plots of land, there are various enquiries that should be made regarding the target property and its owners. First of all, the property should be inspected to establish whether the property suits the investor's business plans. An inspection can also serve to identify potential legal problems. The investor or investor's advisors should also contact local authorities to examine issues such as the ownership of roads, sewers, and other infrastructure affecting the property; tree preservation orders; historical architecture orders; and planning issues.

Please note that under Czech law, a construction/building is not a part of the land. Therefore, the owner of the land is not automatically the owner of any construction that is built on the land.

5.2 Legal documents required for transfer
5.2.1 Letter of intent
There are several documents that are usually signed before any transfer of property. The first document that can be concluded by the parties is a letter of intent, which is a proposal of the main elements and aims of the contract that will be concluded subsequently. The letter of intent specifies the parties of the contract, the subject of the contract, the price and conditions for sale. It is up to the parties whether they wish to be legally bound by the letter of intent and what sanctions they set for not meeting the stipulated requirements. However, the letter of intent is most commonly considered as a non-binding document.

5.2.2 Agreement to conclude the future agreement
According to Czech law, it is possible to conclude an agreement to conclude a future agreement (the AFA) that is to be understood as an agreement between the parties, ie, the future seller and the future purchaser, to conclude, within a specified period of time, a future agreement with specific content. The AFA is usually used in cases in which the future seller is not the owner of the relevant real estate at the date of signing the agreement on the future purchase agreement.

5.2.3 An AFA for business purposes must be concluded in writing.
If the obliged party fails to meet its obligation to conclude the future agreement, the other party may demand that the court (or a person specified in the agreement) determine the content of the agreement, or it may claim compensation for damages caused by a breach of the obligation to conclude the agreement.

5.2.4 Purchase agreement
If the real property is transferred by an asset deal, the agreement on purchase of the real estate is concluded. Any agreement relating to the transfer of real property must be concluded in writing.

In addition to the plots of lands and the buildings, the buildings in construction may also be transferred. Such buildings can be registered in the Cadastral Register as buildings in construction. Since Czech law recognises buildings separately from land, the owner of the building may differ from the owner of the land.

The purchase agreement for purchase of an apartment can be concluded if the apartment is completed, ie, was approved for use by the relevant Building Office. The agreement on purchase of the apartment shall be concluded if the purchase agreement is governed by the provisions of the Act on the Ownership of Apartments. The law requires that more essential elements be fulfilled in the case of an agreement on purchase of an apartment than the purchase agreement on other real estate.

5.3 Property transaction costs
5.3.1 Purchase price
The price is one of the essential elements of any purchase contract. The purchase price must be agreed by parties in accordance with generally binding legal regulations, otherwise the purchase contract will be declared null and void.

5.3.2 Registration fee for Cadastral Register
The fee for the registration of the ownership and other rights in the Cadastral Register is CZK 500 (ie, €20) for each filing of registration. The fee is paid by the party that submits the petition for registration.

5.4 Creating a legally binding obligation
The parties become legally bound when the contract becomes effective. The effectiveness of the contract arises at the moment when the contract is signed by the parties. Agreements on transfer of real estate property must be concluded in writing. The obligatory written form of an agreement is kept if a written offer is accepted in writing. As for an agreement on transfer of real estate property, the expressions of the participants must be on the same document. The signatures of the parties or their authorised representatives have to be notarised.

5.5 Transfer of ownership
Ownership of real property that is subject to registration in the Cadastral Register is acquired (if transferred by agreement) upon its registration in the Cadastral Register. The act of registration is retrospective, as the ownership transfer is deemed effective from the date of filing the registration application with the relevant Cadastral Office.

Ownership of certain real property (typically minor constructions) is not subject to registration in the Cadastral Register, its ownership (if it is transferred by agreement) is acquired on the effective date of the relevant agreement.

6. REAL ESTATE BASICS
6.1 Sources of law
Different types of real estate are governed by different acts. Our purpose here is to give a general overview of the legal framework and therefore we do not intend to include all acts related to real estate in this summary.

The transfer and lease of buildings are governed by the Civil Code. Referring to the lease and purchase of apartments, the Act on Ownership of Apartments is used. When the subject of the lease is a non-residential premises, the Act on Lease and Sublease of Non-residential Premises will be applied.

The Commercial Code governs relations between businessmen in the course of their business.

The Building Code regulates the procedures for zone planning, regulatory plans, building permits, occupancy permits, and all the procedures connected with these decisions.

The Cadastral Registration Act and the Cadastral Act relate to the real estate enlisted in the Cadastral Register. They govern the procedures of registration of property transfer or registration of newly-built real estate.

Last but not least is the Real Estate Tax Act. The rate of real estate tax depends of the size of the land/building, location, and the local coefficient. Real estate tax is not significant.

6.2 Types of tenure
Under Czech law there are several typical types of property ownership. The most common are the freehold and leasehold of the property.

6.2.1 Freehold
Within the limits of law, the owner shall be entitled to hold the subject of its ownership, use it, consume its proceeds and dispose of it. The ownership is protected by law, however, it is not absolute. The owner of a thing (real estate) must eliminate anything that disturbs another person or that seriously jeopardises the exercise of its rights. Another limitation is that the owner of a thing must permit use of such thing in a state of distress or in an urgent situation regarding public interest for the necessary time and to the necessary extent and for reimbursement unless the purpose of the use cannot be achieved otherwise.

6.2.2 Leasehold
Leasehold is limited in time. It gives the right to the occupier (the tenant) to possession against payment of a rent to the holder of the freehold interest (the landlord). A leasehold interest may be made in respect of land and buildings or the lease of only part of a building, for example a single floor.

6.2.3 Co-ownership
The property may be co-owned by multiple owners. The share specifies the extent to which an individual co-owner may take part in the rights and duties following from the co-ownership of the common thing. If not agreed by the co-owners or stipulated otherwise by law, the shares are equal. All co-owners shall be jointly and severally entitled and obliged to legal acts concerning the common property. If the share is transferred, the co-owners shall have a pre-emptive right unless the share is transferred to a close person.

6.2.4 Joint property of spouses
Joint property may arise only between spouses. It consists of property acquired by any of the spouses or by both of them during the marriage and obligations arise on one spouse or jointly on them both during the marriage. The Civil Code defines exceptions from the property and obligations that are not included in the joint property of spouses.

6.2.5 Ownership of a unit
In buildings with at least two apartments or two non-residential premises or one apartment and one non-residential premises and subject to further

conditions, it is possible to divide ownership of the apartments or non-residential premises into units. In such a case, a co-ownership share of the common part is automatically connected with the ownership of the relevant unit. The co-ownership share is calculated as the share of the area of the unit against the total area of all the units. The co-ownership share is transferred automatically once the ownership right to the unit is transferred. If the owner of the unit is also the co-owner of the land on which the building of units is situated, the unit may be transferred only together with the transfer of the ownership share to the land.

6.2.6 Easement
Easements represent a specific set of real rights permitting their beneficiary a repeated or lasting use of another person's real property, and thus are distinguished from other real rights, such as the right of pre-emption or mortgage. Easements limit the use of such property by its rightful owner, who is obliged, under the easement to suffer the specified usage of its property by the beneficiary, to refrain from a specified use of the property itself and/or from acting in a certain way in relation to the real property.

6.3 The Cadastral Register
6.3.1 Acquisition of ownership
Real property registered in the Cadastral Register
The Czech Republic does not dispose of the register of transactions. The Cadastral Register only contains information about property by title. The subject of registration in the Cadastral Register is always land in the form of plots of land and buildings built directly on the land. Minor constructions as well as underground constructions are not subject to registration.

Ownership of real property that is subject to registration in the Cadastral Register is acquired (if transferred by agreement) upon its registration in the Cadastral Register. The act of registration is retrospective, since the ownership transfer is deemed effective from the date of filing the registration application.

Even though the Cadastral Register as a public register enjoys a state guarantee of title, the ownership rights may be challenged. If previous transfers were not valid for any reason, later purchasers of the real property will not become the legal owners even though they are evidenced as the owners in the Cadastral Register. In such case, the ownership title to real property may only be acquired by positive prescription, ie, good faith possession of the property for a period of at least 10 years. Good faith possession of the real property by previous owners is included in the calculation of the 10-year period. As such, it is recommended to investigate the acquisition titles, which basically involves tracing the chain of ownership back 10 or more years to help guarantee that there are no hidden problems and establish that the current owner has legally acquired the real estate.

The registration process itself may take a long time. Although the Cadastral Offices are required to complete the registration procedure within 30 days (in difficult cases within 60 days), in practice it may take even longer to register the ownership transfer. Therefore, for purchase of real property, it is recommended to credit the purchase price to an escrow account and instruct the escrow agent to release it to the seller only after the Cadastral Register has issued the extract evidencing the transfer. However, when acquiring apartments for private use, this practice has often not been respected by developers due to high demand in the real estate market. However, this business principle may again be established in the market if demand decreases.

Real property not registered in the Cadastral Register
If the real property is not subject to registration in the Cadastral Register, the ownership is acquired on the effective date of the relevant agreement, if it is transferred by agreement.

6.3.2 Extract from the Cadastral Register
The key information related to particular real estate registered in the Cadastral Register is shown in the extract from the Cadastral Register. Such extract specifies who owns the land or building, as well as most of the third party rights that may encumber the land (eg, easements, mortgages, pre-emption rights of a real nature).

As stated above, Czech law distinguishes between the land and the buildings or other constructions on the land. This distinction can cause problems because while all land must be registered, not all constructions require registration with the Cadastral Register. It is important to emphasise that the Cadastral Register records are only presumed to be correct and evidence to the contrary can still override the records.

Denmark

Accura Advokatpartnerselskab
Henrik Groos & Kristoffer Westberg

1. INVESTMENT PURCHASE OVERVIEW

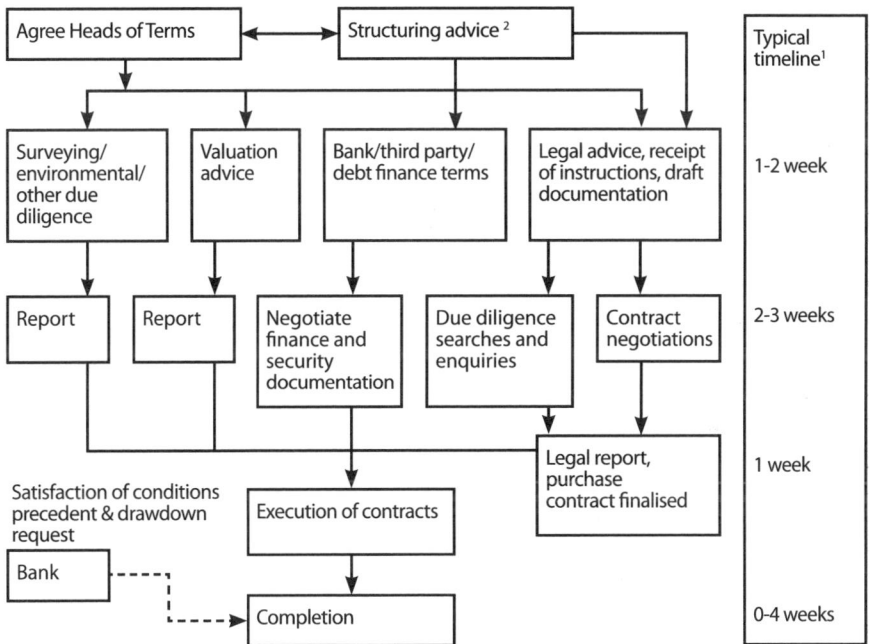

1. Often subject to compression, timescale may differ considerably, exchange and completion may be simultaneous.
2. Establishing an acquistion structure for tax and financial planning is an important early stage which may significantly influence other stages such as the banking arrangements and the purchase structure.

2. TAX CONSIDERATIONS
The Danish tax system and the interplay with international tax treaty law is complex and the acquisition of Danish real estate or non-Danish real estate through Danish investment vehicles should always be carried out using appropriate professional advice. When acquiring Danish real estate, a number of legal (tax) issues need to be examined and the most significant issues are described below.

2.1 Danish tax rates
In Denmark, a flat tax rate of 25 per cent applies for corporate income tax (CIT) and capital gains.

2.2 No Danish transfer tax
In Denmark, transfer of real estate is not subject to transfer tax (except for stamp duty land tax as described below).

If the real estate has been held by an investment vehicle, the shares in the vehicle can be sold without triggering Danish transfer tax on the disposal of the shares.

2.3 No value added tax (VAT)
Currently, there is no VAT added to transfers of real estate in Denmark. However, as per 1 January 2011, VAT will be added to transfers of green field properties and properties which have been erected or substantially refurbished after 1 January 2011. Danish VAT is currently 25 per cent.

Rental of real estate in Denmark is a VAT exempt activity. This implies that expenses related to, *inter alia*, renovation, maintenance, operation and administration of real estate cannot be deducted as input VAT. Furthermore, it implies that no output VAT is to be added in respect of the rental income, etc. However, for certain properties, it is possible to obtain a voluntary VAT registration on the rental of real estate, depending on the actual use of the property. In this case, non-Danish residents will be VAT exempt for the said expenses.

2.4 Stamp duty land tax (SDLT)
Direct transfers of real estate trigger a Danish SDLT, which is computed as 0.6 per cent of the higher of the purchase price and the public tax value of the property plus a base fee of DKK1,400. SDLT is collected upon registration of the transfer of real estate in the electronic Land Register. Usually, the buyer pays the SDLT. However, in the western part of Denmark it is customary that the SDLT is split 50/50 between the seller and the buyer, although the parties are absolutely free to agree any split they may see fit.

2.5 Transfer of shares in Propco holding real estate
If the seller of the shares in a Danish Propco is a non-Danish legal entity, no Danish tax is triggered on any capital gains.

If the seller of the shares in a Danish Propco is a Danish legal entity then any capital gains are tax exempt as long as the seller holds more than 10 per cent of the shares in question.

The following points must be borne in mind when acquiring property in Denmark.

2.5.1 Foreign nationals' acquisition of real property
As a main principle, non-Danish residents must obtain the permission of the Danish Ministry of Justice in order to acquire Danish real estate, and the Ministry of Justice tends to be somewhat reluctant to grant permissions in this respect. However, non-Danish residents who are EU/EEA undertakings established in accordance with the legislation of another EU member state or in a state that has acceded to the agreement on the European Economic Area and which establishes a branch or an agency in Denmark, may acquire

Danish real estate without the permission of the Danish authorities.

Further, if non-Danish residents acquire Danish real estate through a Danish investment vehicle, no permission is required from the Ministry of Justice. Due to the various tax advantages, this set-up is the most commonly used for a non-Danish resident to acquire Danish real estate.

2.5.2 The Danish Weekend Cottage Act
Pursuant to Consolidated Act no. 920 of 22 December 1989 on weekend cottages and camping, etc, as amended (the Weekend Cottage Act), undertakings may not acquire real estate in Denmark without the permission of the National Forest and Nature Agency, unless the property is intended for all-year residence or for commercial use.

3. INVESTMENT VEHICLE CHOICE
3.1 Issues affecting the type of vehicle/structure when making an indirect investment
3.1.1 Control and decision making
When making investments in either Danish real estate or non-Danish real estate through Danish investment vehicles, the management of the Danish vehicle will independently control the real estate held by the Danish vehicle.

3.1.2 Cost
Acquiring real estate through a Danish investment vehicle imposes various costs, including costs of setting up the Danish investment vehicle (dependent on the type of vehicle as outlined below), running costs to pay for management, auditors and lawyers as well as various regulatory costs. These costs are not a factor when acquiring real estate directly (which, however, triggers SDLT as outlined above). For non-Danish residents, the tax advantages when acquiring real estate through a Danish investment vehicle can be significant compared to the costs for the set up and running of the Danish investment vehicle and possible SDLT. This should be examined carefully on a case-by-case basis.

3.1.3 Size and number of assets
Whether a non-Danish resident investor is looking to hold only a few or a number of real estate assets, using a Danish investment vehicle will generally prove to be most beneficial and efficient from a general management perspective.

3.1.4 Location of the management team
The Danish legal system is complex and management of Danish real estate will almost always require local management with knowledge of Danish regulation on Danish real estate. Further, local management in Denmark may in some cases ensure that non-Danish investors maintain their status as a foreign entity.

3.1.5 Long term objectives
If the investor is looking to achieve an immediate tax deduction, the partnership vehicle is generally preferable due to tax transparent treatment, but if the objective of the investor is a long term investment purpose, a limited liability company is generally more favourable.

3.1.6 Other investor requirements
Cross-border tax considerations are especially essential to consider when determining the nature of which Danish investment vehicle to apply. Certain vehicles are independent legal entities, but subject to tax transparent treatment (certain partnerships), while other vehicles are also fully taxable in Denmark (limited liability companies). The choice of investment vehicle may also be determined by restrictions within the jurisdiction of the non-Danish investor or the jurisdictions in which the real estate is located.

3.1.7 Regulatory compliance
Danish limited liability companies are regulated intensely compared with limited partnerships. This is particularly the case in relation to annual accounting, management and publicity, which needs to be considered.

3.1.8 Multiple vehicles
If different investment strategies are applied to different real estate assets, separate Danish investment vehicles should be considered to ensure maximum efficiency and the exit options of the investors when disposing of the assets (or the shares of the Danish investment vehicle, as the case may be). This is particularly the case when investing in real estate in certain non-Danish jurisdictions. In this respect a Danish Holdco/Propco structure could also be considered.

3.1.9 Investment strategy
The number of assets an investor is looking to acquire and the exit strategy are the most predominant factors when determining which vehicle(s) to apply.

3.1.10 Taxation of the vehicle
Determining the SDLT and the ongoing tax position is essential when determining the nature of the investment vehicle. A cross-border combination of investment vehicles will often be most beneficial to the investor.

3.1.11 Term, exit and liquidity
The exit strategy and the term for which a non-Danish resident investor is looking to hold the investment needs to be considered closely as this will have an impact on whether a Danish investment vehicle should be applied or whether investment should be made directly.

3.2 Types of vehicle
3.2.1 Danish Public Limited Liability Company (DPLLC)
Except for one-man-businesses, the DPLLC (A/S), together with the

DPRLLC (ApS) (as outlined below), are the most commonly used vehicles for conducting business in Denmark, and the DPLLC and the DPRLLC are essential vehicles for non-Danish residents' indirect acquisition of real estate in Denmark or in foreign jurisdictions.

Subscription of capital

When setting up a DPLLC the Danish Companies Act requires that a subscription of shares for an amount of at least DKK 500,000 is made. The subscription can be made both as a cash contribution and as an in-kind contribution. The Danish Companies Act contains a possibility to postpone the payment of the share capital, however at least 25 per cent of the share capital needs to be paid up at any time. If, however, the price of the shares is agreed at a premium, the premium has to be paid up in full. The remainder of the share capital can be called with a deadline of minimum two weeks by the central management body.

Types of shares

The shares of a DPPLC can be issued either as bearer shares or as registered shares. If the company wishes to impose any restrictions on the transferability of the shares, eg right of first refusal or requirement of consent to sale, it is important to note that such restrictions can only be imposed on registered shares. A restriction on transfer of shares has to be adopted in the articles of association of the company.

All shares in a DPPLC have equal rights, both with respect to the financial rights, eg to demand dividends and liquidation dividends, and with respect to the so-called administrative rights, eg to attend, speak and vote at the general meetings. This equality principle can only be deviated from by dividing the shares into classes with varying rights. Furthermore, shares can be issued with no voting rights.

Distribution of capital

The capital in a DPPLC can be distributed to the shareholders in a number of ways. The most common way of distributing the capital is through payment of dividends or interim dividends. When paying out dividends or interim dividends, it is important to note that dividends can only be paid from the distributable reserves and that the management or the board of directors as the case may be is responsible for the company's ongoing liabilities after the payment of the dividend. The decision to pay a dividend is taken in the general meeting by a simple majority.

Another way of distributing capital is through a reduction of capital. The decision to implement a reduction of capital has to be taken in the general meeting with the same majority required to amend the articles of association. Generally, this means that the majority needed is two-thirds of the votes given and two-thirds of the shares represented at the general meeting. It is, however, important to note that shares with no voting rights are not added to the calculation of the vote. This principle of double majority can be changed by an amendment to the articles of association.

Liability
The DPLLC offers full limited liability to non-Danish resident investors provided that they are not involved in the management of the company.

Tax
The DPLLC is potentially liable to tax at 25 per cent on its income and chargeable gains. As outlined above, the transfer of the shares of the DPLLC will not trigger any transfer tax and if certain conditions are met, any capital gain on shares in a DPLLC, irrespective of whether the DPLLC holds Danish or foreign real estate, will not trigger Danish taxes.

3.2.2 Danish Private Limited Liability Company (DPRLLC)
The required contribution for setting up a DPRLLC is lower than the required contribution for a DPLLC. Furthermore, the legislative restrictions imposed on private limited companies are fewer than the legislative restrictions imposed on public limited companies, making the DPRLLC a very popular investment vehicle. As outlined above, the DPRLLC can also be used for non-Danish residents' indirect acquisition of real estate in Denmark, or real estate situated in foreign jurisdictions.

Subscription of capital
With the new Danish Companies Act, the minimum subscription of shares in a DPRLLC has been reduced from DKK 125,000 to DKK 80,000. Parallel to the DPLLCs, the subscription can be paid as cash contributions and as in-kind contributions. Likewise, it is also possible for DPRLLCs to postpone the payment of part of the share capital. However, at least DKK 80,000 has to be paid-up.

Types of shares
With the new Danish Companies Act, the rules governing the types of shares in a DPRLLC are the same as the rules governing DPLLCs, see above.

Distribution of capital
The distribution of capital in a DPRLLC has the same rules as those governing DPLLCs, see above. However, it is important to note that a DPRLLC can authorise the central management body to carry out a reduction of capital by amending the articles of association of the company.

Liability
The DPRLLC offers full limited liability to investors provided that they are not involved in the management of the company.

Tax
The DPRLLC is also potentially liable to tax at 25 per cent on its income and chargeable gains. The transfer of the shares of the DPRLLC will not trigger any transfer tax and if certain conditions are met, and any capital gain on shares in a DPLLC, no matter if the DPLLC is holding Danish real estate or

foreign real estate, will not trigger Danish taxes for non-Danish residents.

As is the case for the DPLLC, the DPRLLC is not subject to a flow-through tax treatment, and the DPRLLC is also generally applied by investors applying a long-term investment strategy whereby real estate is held by the company for at least three years.

3.2.3 Danish Limited Partnership (DLP)
The DLP as an investment vehicle is also very popular for non-Danish resident investors when acquiring Danish or non-Danish real estate, because the limited partnership enjoys the regulated structure of the DPLLC and the DPRLLC, but is, however, subject to a flow-through tax treatment for Danish income and capital gains.

In a DLP there are two kinds of partners. The general partner, who is personally liable, and the limited partner(s), who are only liable up to the capital they have contributed. In exchange for the personal liability undertaken by the general partner, the general partner enjoys certain administrative and economic rights, eg a right to veto amendments to the articles of association or a fair share of the profit of the DLP.

When setting up a DLP, it is a requirement that one of the limited partners is either a DPLLC or a DPRLLC. Further, the entire capital of the DPLLC or the DPRLLC has to be subscribed to the DLP. The minimum capital requirement of the DLP is DKK 500,000.

The DLP is especially suitable for investors applying a short term investment strategy with the purpose of optimising their tax position with immediate effect.

3.2.4 Danish Partnership (DP)
In a DP, the basic structure is the same as the DLP, including the two categories of partners. However, there is no required minimum capital for a DP.

Furthermore, there are no requirements as to the structure of the DP, making the DP a very flexible investment vehicle and easy to structure to make fit the transaction on a case-by-case basis. Accordingly, the DP can be structured as a public liability company or a very lightly regulated vehicle (often if the number of investors is limited), enabling the vehicle to distribute the funds of the company back to the investors without having to comply with the strict procedures of the Danish Company Act.

The DP vehicle is also subject to tax transparent treatment for Danish income and capital gains as outlined for the DLP.

Parallel to the DLP, the DP is especially suitable for investors applying a short term investment strategy with the purpose of optimising their tax position with immediate effect.

4. FINANCING AN ACQUISITION
4.1 Mortgage credit financing
Traditionally, the vast majority of the Danish real estate market was financed by Danish mortgage credit institutions, which use a financing structure based on mortgage-backed bonds. This way of financing property has proven

to be highly efficient and competitive and has passed the severe tests of the recent 'credit crunch' climate.

Financing by mortgage credit institution is governed by the Consolidated Mortgage Credit Act.

Based on an assessment of the property and the creditworthiness of the borrower, a mortgage credit institution may finance up to 80 per cent of the value of a property with respect to residential properties, up to 70 per cent of the value of a property with respect to agricultural properties and up to 60 per cent of the value of a property with respect to commercial properties and weekend cottages.

The rules apply without exception to Danish resident and non-Danish resident investors and/or between individual persons and corporate entities.

Usually, the mortgage debt is combined with equity whereby the remaining part of the purchase price (between 20 per cent and 40 per cent) will either be paid in cash by the buyer or be financed through a bank or another finance institution.

When dealing with financing through mortgage credit institutions, the requirements in terms of the loan documentation are heavily regulated, but also very standardised, meaning for all practical purposes that their terms and conditions are more or less non-negotiable. No similar formalities apply to ordinary bank financing.

It should be noted that none of the above-mentioned restrictions are applicable to usual debt/equity financing.

With regard to other creditors of the borrower, the lender is protected by having a first priority mortgage registered on the property. However, the registration of such mortgage does not prevent other creditors from pursuing their claims against the borrower or the real property, unless they have become party to a standstill agreement with the lender. Accordingly, in the absence of such agreement, the property may be subject to a forced sale on the request of lower ranking secured and even unsecured creditors.

4.2 Simple debt/equity financing

As an alternative to the financing offered by Danish mortgage credit institutions, a number of Danish investment banks offer real estate financing based on a mix of debt and equity. This field has within the past decade been joined by a number of foreign credit institutions and investment banks. UK and German credit institutions and investment banks now hold a share of the Danish market for real estate financing.

This increase in foreign credit institutions and investment banks on the Danish market for real estate financing follows from an increase in the number of non-Danish residents investing in Danish real estate, or in non-Danish real estate through Danish investment vehicles within the past decade. As non-Danish resident investors generally already have connections to non-Danish credit institutions and investment banks when entering the Danish real estate market, the non-Danish credit institutions and investment banks will usually follow the non-Danish investor into the Danish real estate market. It may also be a factor that non-Danish resident investors are not familiar with the Danish mortgage credit institutions and the financing that they can offer, and when operating in an international environment, a global financing package can prove more favourable.

This type of real estate financing usually consists of a loan governed by a loan/credit agreement and ancillary finance documents, covering a proportion of the purchase costs by way of debt in return for a number of securities (so-called 'ring fencing', covering all assets and a package of grants).

Usually the security package comprises one or more of the following securities:

- fixed security over the real estate to be purchased. This is usually a mortgage deed registered against the property in the electronic Land Register in favour of the lender (if the loan has been granted on a recourse basis, the lender could also seek enforcement over the borrower's other assets);
- negative pledge registered against the property in the electronic Land Register in favour of the lender. This will prevent other parties from registering mortgages against the property and the borrower to dispose of the property without the lender's prior consent;
- pledge over shares in the Danish investment vehicle in favour of the lender. The security is perfected by way of registration in the register of shareholders;
- parent company guarantees in favour of the lender;
- assignment of rights to receive rent payments from tenants and tenant deposits (effectively by way of the lender taking out a pledge over the accounts into which rent payments and deposits are made). The security is perfected by way of notification to the tenants; and
- assignment of and right of subrogation in all major contracts (eg construction contracts, construction guarantees, purchase agreements, insurance agreements, management agreements, etc). The security is perfected by way of notification to the obligors pursuant to the various contracts.

4.3 Stamp duty
To the extent that mortgage deeds are to be registered as collateral for the repayment of the loan (which is required by statute if the loan is obtained from a mortgage credit institution), stamp duty is payable in the amount of 1.5 per cent of the nominal value of the mortgage deed plus a base fee of DKK 1,400. Certain reductions in the amount payable may be possible in case of the new mortgage replacing earlier mortgages.

5. MANAGING THE ACQUISITION PROCESS
5.1 Introduction
Acquisition of Danish commercial real estate generally follows a standardised procedure from the time negotiations are initiated to the point the purchaser is granted title to the property. In this section, the general process and the usual terms regarding direct sale and purchase of Danish commercial real estate will be outlined. However, if a non-Danish resident

investor is considering acquiring Danish commercial real estate indirectly or foreign real estate through a Danish investment vehicle, this will mainly be considered a corporate transaction governed by different terms which will not be dealt with in this section.

5.2 Agreeing terms and binding contracts
The seller will usually ask a real estate agent to promote the sale of the real estate. The potential buyer's lawyer and in some cases also the buyer's technical advisers will typically carry out legal due diligence investigations regarding the real estate in question. On this basis, the buyer's lawyer will negotiate the terms and conditions with the seller and the seller's lawyer.

When the terms and conditions are agreed between the seller and the buyer, a real estate transaction in Denmark is usually completed in two steps. The terms and conditions of the transaction will be recorded in a sale and purchase agreement, which constitutes a legally binding document between the parties. The sale and purchase agreement as such is not subject to any formalities.

Secondly, an electronic conveyance (*Skøde*) is prepared with the electronic Land Register, which is basically an extract of the most important terms and conditions of the sale and purchase agreement. The electronic conveyance needs to be drafted in Danish and must meet various requirements in terms of layout and content.

Usually, the buyer's lawyer will be the one responsible for completing the sale, including preparing the electronic conveyance, registering the electronic conveyance against the property in the electronic Land Register, releasing the purchase price from the deposit and preparing the completion statement.

5.3 The contract documents
The sale and purchase agreement regarding sale and purchase of Danish (commercial) real estate is an individual document drafted on a case-by-case basis. However, certain usages as to the structure and the content of the sale and purchase agreement have developed over the past centuries. The sale and purchase agreement can be expected to be between 10 and 20 pages long.

As outlined above, the electronic conveyance will have to meet certain requirements in terms of layout and content. Title passes to the buyer upon the signing of the sale and purchase agreement, unless the seller has retained title pending fulfilment of certain conditions (which is often the case), such as payment of the purchase price, etc. However, formal registration of the conveyance without any remarks in the Land Register will protect the buyer against unregistered third party rights against the property (including title).

In addition to the sale and purchase agreement, there may be ancillary documents to be prepared between the parties, for example, rental guarantees, assignment of construction guarantees, etc.

5.4 Typical contract terms
5.4.1 Completion
As a general rule, there will be a period between exchange and completion,

but exchange and completion can take place simultaneously. Typically, the completion date will not be scheduled in the sale and purchase agreement, and completion simply takes place when all conditions precedent have been fulfilled and the electronic conveyance has been duly registered against the property in the Land Register without remarks.

At completion, the process will usually be that the lawyer responsible for the completion of the sale will make sure that all conditions precedent pursuant to the sale and purchase agreement are fulfilled and that the electronic conveyance has been duly registered against the property in the electronic Land Register without remarks. The lawyer responsible for the sale will immediately thereafter release the completion monies to the seller from an escrow account (typically an account with a registered Danish bank) into which the buyer has deposited the purchase price.

5.4.2 Deposit
The buyer will usually pay part of the purchase price as a deposit to an account with the seller's real estate agent (usually between 0.5 and two per cent of the purchase price) as security for the real estate agent's fee. The remainder of the purchase price will usually be paid into an escrow account, which is typically an account with a registered Danish bank as outlined above. However, other arrangements can be made in relation to non-Danish resident investors, for example that the purchase price is deposited with the investor's lawyer who will also be responsible for completing the sale subject to various undertakings.

Generally, the deposits will have to be paid by the buyer between three and seven working days after signing the sale and purchase agreement. Interest, typically, accrues to the buyer prior to exchange and to the seller from the exchange date. The deposits will be released when completion occurs. If the buyer fails to complete, the monies will in whole be repaid to the buyer.

5.4.3 Price
At completion, the monies sitting in the escrow account will be released to the seller by the lawyer responsible for completing the sale. The actual amount to be released to the seller will be the agreed purchase price (at exchange) with the following adjustments to be made at the date of completion:
- property taxes paid in advance by the seller;
- tenant deposits collected by the seller;
- rent payments in advance collected by the seller;
- on account payments by the tenants for utility costs collected by the seller for an account period for which the buyer is responsible for making account statements;
- actual utility costs paid by the seller for an account period for which the buyer is responsible for making account statements;
- accrued interest on the purchase price;
- payment of fee to real estate agent;

- redemption of the seller's existing loans (so that debt secured against the property is discharged); and
- other.

5.4.4 Warranties
Usually, the seller provides a catalogue of warranties to the buyer in the sale and purchase agreement. The catalogue is subject to negotiations, but the seller would as a minimum typically accept warranties against:
- certain types of defects;
- illegal use of the property:
- debt assumption in excess of the purchase price;
- wrongful calculation of rental income; and
- disputes.

The seller rarely gives an express warranty on its ownership, as the seller may be held liable in any event in this respect and regardless of whether the seller has acted negligently.

Warranties are often softened to a certain degree, and the purpose of the warranties is basically to apportion risks, as the seller may be held liable in the case of breach of a warranty. Warranties cannot be seen as substitutes for the buyer carrying out their own due diligence and the principle of 'buyer-beware' (*caveat emptor*) still applies.

5.4.5 Conditions precedent and due diligence
The buyer's lawyer, and possibly other advisers, will typically carry out due diligence investigations regarding the real estate in question as outlined above. If the deal does not materialise, the costs for the due diligence investigations will usually rest with the buyer. In some cases, the parties do agree that the seller must refund such costs to the potential buyer (wholly or partly).

In Denmark, it is common that a sale and purchase agreement contains conditions precedent and in this respect it is usual that one of the conditions precedent is satisfactory due diligence (legal, technical and financial). Usually, this clause is combined with a deadline for the buyer to cancel the transaction in case the due diligence uncovers deal breakers. Often, the 'satisfactory due diligence' condition is so widely drafted that the buyer effectively is not bound to close even if the buyer cannot in effect demonstrate that the due diligence has uncovered any deal breakers. It is usual that exchange of contracts takes place very early in the process, and that the terms are renegotiated when the buyer's due diligence has been conducted. The amended terms will be recorded in an addendum to the sale and purchase agreement. This provides the buyer with a certain comfort early in the process that the seller will not dispose of the property to a third party, unless the buyer decides not to go through with the deal.

5.5 Managing the property between exchange and completion
Until the date of possession, the seller has full responsibility for the property. The sale and purchase agreement will usually contain a clause whereby the seller undertakes not to make any material changes to the property and/or the

administration of the property, including actions towards existing tenants or entering into new lease agreements without the buyer's prior consent.

However, if the property burns down prior to completion, the buyer will still have to take possession of the property, and the buyer subrogates the insurance cover payment under the seller's property insurance. For this reason, the seller usually undertakes to keep the property fully insured until completion.

5.6 Confidentiality
There are no restrictions regarding public access to the electronic Land Register and in so far as rights over a property have been duly registered, these rights are available to the public. However, the sale and purchase agreement will not as such be registered in the electronic Land Register, only an electronic conveyance containing certain information. In principle, the parties could agree that certain information which is not mandatory to disclose when filing the electronic conveyance with the electronic Land Register must not be disclosed. However, this would be highly unusual. In any case, the purchase price, rights registered against the property and encumbrances are always accessible to the public.

5.7 Assignment of contract
The sale and purchase agreement can be assigned if the buyer has made a reservation prior to signing by adding the wording 'or order' after the buyer's name in the agreement.

This is not uncommon in Denmark and highly relevant for non-Danish resident investors looking to acquire Danish real estate through an investment vehicle at a point in time where the final corporate Danish set-up has not yet been decided or is not yet in place. In this situation, the investor can secure a favourable real estate purchase, even if the corporate Danish set-up is not fully in place, and the investor can minimise risks by combining an assignment clause with conditions precedent which enable the investor to pull out of the deal in case the Danish corporate set-up or the investment case in itself proves unfavourable to the investor.

6. REAL ESTATE BASICS
In Denmark, no specific act regarding the sale and purchase of Danish (commercial) real estate has been enacted which means that the seller and the buyer are free to negotiate the terms of the transfer of such real estate.

Basically, there are four ways to create ownership (freehold) over land under Danish law:
- a contractual relationship between the owner of the land (the seller) and the buyer;
- a third party may be granted a prescriptive right over the land if such a right has existed for more than 20 years;
- rights over land may be created pursuant to the Danish heritage rules; and
- governmental acts and orders, particularly with respect to planning, zoning and environmental issues.

Freehold ownership gives the owner absolute ownership to land and buildings and structures on it and is unlimited in time.

A number of condominium properties in Denmark are owned as commonhold which is basically a joint condominium ownership where the building on the property is split into individual units where each unit holds individual ownership registered in the electronic Land Register. The unit-holders are part of a so-called 'commonhold association' which will be the legal entity responsible for the operation of the building as such.

There is no state guarantee as to title to ownership, but if a person, acting in good faith, has relied on a public registration that turns out to be wrong, the state of Denmark may be held liable for the foreseeable loss suffered.

A person can rent a property (wholly or partly). However, leasehold ownership and registration of the tenant's title to a property does not exist under Danish law, ie a tenant cannot register title to a property in the electronic Land Register.

Commercial leaseholds are governed by the Danish Business Rent Act, which came into force on 1 January 2000. The Act heavily regulates the Danish commercial lease market.

Usually commercial leaseholds are made for an indefinite period of time until the lease is terminated by either party (certain strict conditions apply if the landlord wishes to terminate a lease). Fixed term leases are rare, but can be agreed.

6.1 Electronic land registration

Real estate in Denmark is generally divided into so-called title numbers and is registered in the electronic Land Register as such. However, real estate can also include unregistered areas in so far as they can be clearly identified.

On 8 September 2009, the former Danish Land Registration was replaced by an electronic land registration (e-registration), ie an almost completely paperless system providing electronic registration of conveyance documents, mortgages, etc.

With the new system, the processing of applications and the registration of rights in land will become quicker in most cases, providing a very volatile and smooth real estate market. All registrations are electronic, and physical documents will therefore no longer be issued as documentation.

6.1.1 E-registration system

All individuals, businesses (including non-Danish resident businesses) and public authorities are entitled to register documents in the e-registration system provided that they have a valid digital signature authorised by the Danish authorities. In the case of foreign investors, it will often be practical to grant a (standard official format) power of attorney to their Danish lawyer, who will then make the electronic signing on behalf of the foreign investor.

As soon as the system has carried out a check of the application for e-registration, the system will inform the applicant of the processing result. The possible outcomes, of which the applicant is informed, are that:

Denmark

- the document will be registered immediately;
- the document will be registered subject to compliance with a time limit within which the applicant must submit additional information or documentation;
- registration of the document is refused (with a detailed explanation); or
- registration of the document will be processed manually.

6.1.2 Registration of documents
With the new e-registration system, it is no longer possible to sign documents by hand. The relevant documents must be signed by a digital signature, either by the applicant itself or by another person being authorised to sign by digital signature.

There are various types of digital signatures and powers of attorney/notification schemes in this respect.

6.1.3 Digitalisation of documents
To prepare for the introduction of the e-registration system, the Land Registration Court scanned all existing non-negotiable mortgages with the effect that these mortgages now only exist in electronic form.

Since 8 September 2009, it has only been possible to change existing mortgages if they are converted into electronic format. The Land Registration Court will carry out the conversion when it receives the documents.

Owner's mortgages must be converted within five years. Otherwise, they will be removed from the land register. Owner's mortgages with a maximum principal amount of DKK 45,000 may, however, be converted without presentation of the original owner's mortgage if such conversion is requested by the applicant whose entitlement to notification has been endorsed on the owner's mortgage and registered. Such a request must, however, be made before the expiry of the time limit.

France

Lefèvre Pelletier & Associés
Véronique Lagarde & Antonia Raccat

1. INVESTMENT PURCHASE OVERVIEW
Subject to merger control provisions (if the property to be acquired either directly or through the acquisition of an operating company generates revenues that exceed certain thresholds, particular attention shall be given to whether merger control regulations apply to such transaction) and certain authorisations for sensitive markets in connection with public order (such as gambling, weapons, national defence etc), French law does not impose restrictions in connection with the acquisition of real estate located in France. Individuals and legal persons, whether French or foreign, are free to purchase real estate in France directly or through a special purpose vehicle. However, certain operations may require filing formalities when setting up a company by a non-resident or the acquisition by a non-resident of a French company.

Basically, small-scale property acquisitions are often made directly by the purchaser or through a French entity (as a *Société civile immobilière* – SCI) that will own the property and subscribe to a financing agreement, if need be (see section 3.1 below).

With a view to mitigating tax, larger real estate investments can be structured through a non-French company when the applicable tax treaty precludes the levying of French capital gains tax (eg tax treaty between France and Luxembourg). The non-French company will hold a French entity that in turn will own the property. The foreign holding company must have substance in order for this kind of 'two tier' holding structure to be effective.

Another tax optimisation route commonly used for the acquisition of (substantial) real estate asset portfolios consists in using a real estate investment trust (REIT) that is exempt from corporate income tax in France, in particular an 'OPCI' *'Organisme de Placement Collectif Immobilier'* (see section 3.3 below).

2. TAX CONSIDERATIONS
The acquisition of a property is, in principle, subject to registration duties but, in certain cases, value added tax (VAT) applies.

2.1 Registration duties
2.1.1 Purchase of properties
The purchase of property located in France is subject to registration duties at a rate of 5.09 per cent and to a land registration fee of 0.1 per cent. The

purchase of property requires the services of a notary and gives rise to the payment of a negotiable fee on the basis of 0.825 per cent (plus VAT at 19.60 per cent). The overall rate of these tax and legal costs is around 6.18 per cent.

Registration duties are based on the purchase price or fair market value of the property if higher.

Transfer duties are paid by the purchaser unless the parties agree otherwise. If the purchaser defaults on the payment of transfer duties, the seller is jointly liable.

2.1.2 Purchase of shares in real estate companies
Registration duties levied on the purchase of companies' shares are as follows:
Companies whose assets mainly consist of real estate property
These are defined as companies that own real estate properties or rights to such properties or shares in companies that hold such properties accounting for more than 50 per cent of their assets.

The sale of shares in such companies, whatever their legal form (eg SCI, SNC, SARL, SA or SAS), are subject to registration duties of five per cent on the sale price or fair market value of the shares if higher.

Companies other than those which mainly hold real estate

Sales of shares in companies other than SAs (ie joint-stock companies) or SASs (ie simplified stock companies) are subject to a three per cent registration duty on the sale price of the shares, or fair market value if higher.

Sales of shares in SAs or SASs are also subject to the three per cent registration duty, but within a maximum of €5,000.

Miscellaneous
The purchase of the shares of a company that owns a property, rather than the purchase of the property, may be advantageous for the seller, given the company share capital gains tax regime (see section 2.3 below).

On the other hand, purchasers would rather purchase the property itself. The drawbacks of a share deal are threefold:
- the purchaser cannot normally provide a mortgage on the property held by the company;
- the purchaser will endorse the risks relating to an acquisition of shares, thereby incurring liability for the company's debts. A legal and tax audit of the company will have to be carried out and warranties obtained; and
- there is often a deferred capital gain on the company being disposed of, consisting of the difference between the market value of the real property and its net book value in the company's balance sheet. This deferred capital gain may entail one of two disadvantages:
  - in the event of a subsequent disposal of the property by the company, the capital gain will be taxed, including the deferred capital gain which has not yet been realised in economic terms; or
  - in the event of the property being retained, the purchaser cannot benefit from any tax-deductible depreciation calculated on a basis corresponding to the market price of the property and used in

determining the share price. However, when the entity whose shares are purchased is a company that is not subject to corporate income tax (such as an SCI) the real property can be revalued without a tax charge according to a step-up mechanism ('*Quemener case law*').

As a result, there is usually a financial negotiation between the purchaser and the vendor on the impact of this deferred capital gain.

In order to convince the purchaser to purchase the shares of the company instead of the property, the seller can point out that the registration duties are lower if the company shares are purchased. Indeed, the registration duties are assessed on the price of the shares, ie the value of the property, less the amount of company debts, if any.

In the case of the acquisition of a company subject to corporate income tax (CIT), the purchaser may deduct the financial expenses relating to the acquisition from the profits of the target company. To that end, the fiscal unity system (*intégration fiscale*) will have to be chosen, whereby the profits and losses of group members are subject to CIT at the standard rate of 34.44 per cent, on a consolidated tax basis.

2.2 Value added tax (VAT)
Transfers of title of the following real estate assets are subject to VAT:
- plots of developable land;
- buildings that are to be reconstructed or undergo major works that substantially modify the structure;
- all successive transfers of title of new buildings within five years of the completion date; and
- forward sales, ie sales prior to completion of the construction works (*Vente en l'Etat Futur d'Achèvement*).

VAT is levied at 19.6 per cent and recoverable if the building is used for an activity that is subject to VAT, eg, business activity of the purchaser or letting of commercial and industrial premises and offices, if certain conditions are met. When VAT is levied registration duties are not due (see section 2.2.1 above), except for land registration tax of 0.715 per cent (not due on plots of developable land).

2.3 Capital gains tax
Capital gains will be payable by the seller following the sale of a property or of the shares of a company. The capital gains tax regime applicable in France is as follows:

2.3.1 Sale of an asset
Capital gains on the disposal of properties located in France are subject to French capital gains tax. Two different rules apply depending on whether the company making the disposal is resident in France for tax purposes.

Company resident in France for tax purposes
The taxable capital gain is made up of the difference between (i) the disposal price and; (ii) the net book value of the property being disposed of.

The capital gain is subject to CIT at the standard rate of 34.44 per cent or at the rate of 19.63 per cent if the SIIC 3 regime can be enforced (see section 3.3.3).

Company not resident in France for tax purposes
The capital gain is taxed twice:
- on the day of the sale, a tax of 33.33 per cent is levied on the capital gain calculated on the basis of the difference between the disposal price and the historical cost of the property. If the selling company's tax residence is outside the European Union or in Iceland or Norway, the purchase price is reduced by two per cent per annum to reflect theoretical depreciation; and
- following the closure of the financial year, CIT is levied and mitigated by the amount of capital gains tax already paid. The balance, if any, can be claimed back from the French tax authorities if the selling company is tax resident in a jurisdiction that has signed a tax treaty with France. When the rate of 19.63 per cent of the SIIC 3 regime can be enforced, the refundable balance is significant (ie this mitigated rate can be claimed by EU tax residents and tax residents of Iceland and Norway).

2.3.2 Sale of shares
Company resident in France for tax purposes
The capital gain on the shares (ie disposal price less historical cost) incurs CIT at the standard rate or at the rate of 19.63 per cent if the SIIC 3 regime can be enforced (see section 3.3.3).

The participation exemption regime whereby capital gains on the disposal of shares are exempt does not apply to capital gains on disposals of shares in companies whose assets are mainly made up of real properties.

Company not resident in France for tax purposes
The applicable tax treaty, if any, usually gives France the right to tax the gain according to the OECD Model tax treaty. The tax of 33.33 per cent will apply to the gain. This tax is payable within 30 days of the disposal, following the registration of the deed of sale. CIT will also be levied; however the tax of 33.33 per cent can be offset against CIT at the standard rate or at the rate of 19.63 per cent if applicable (see section 2.3.1 above).

However, certain rare tax treaties make it possible to tax the capital gain in the country of disposal only (eg tax treaties with Luxembourg, and the Netherlands if two layers of companies are inserted). In this case, no capital gains tax is due in France. The gain is taxable in the jurisdiction of the selling company where a regime exempting capital gains may be enforced.

2.4 Taxation of wealth
2.4.1 French wealth tax
Non-French tax resident individuals are liable for French wealth tax on their wealth located in France except for their financial investments (eg securities except for shareholdings of more than 10 per cent held for more than two years or subscribed upon issuance).

When there is no tax treaty on wealth enforceable, as is the case for United Kingdom tax residents, real estate assets located in France are held directly or indirectly through a French or foreign entity to a level of more than 50 per cent, even if this entity does not mainly own French real estate assets.

French tax residents are liable for French wealth tax on their worldwide wealth, subject to exceptions (eg shareholdings of at least 25 per cent in the company managed by the taxpayer, works of art, etc). However, the tax treaty on income in force between the United Kingdom and France provides that UK nationals who set up residence in France are exempt from French wealth tax on their assets located outside of France for a period of five calendar years from their setting up residence in France. This exemption is not available for UK nationals who also have the French citizenship.

The net value of the assets liable for French wealth tax is subject to this annual tax if the threshold of €790,000 is passed (for 2010). Progressive rates apply from 0.55 per cent to 1.80 per cent (eg 1.3 per cent for the share of net wealth between €3,980,000 and €7,600,000 and 1.65 per cent for the share of net wealth between €7,600,000 and €16,540,000).

2.4.2 French three per cent tax on real estate assets

To prevent individuals from concealing French real estate assets through foreign companies in order to avoid French wealth tax, disclosure obligations have been set down. A yearly three per cent tax is incurred if these disclosure obligations are not complied with. In theory, any French or foreign entity with assets mainly consisting of French real estate not used for a professional activity may be subject to this tax equal to three per cent of the market value of its real estate assets. This tax is payable on the basis of the situation on 1 January each year, and must be settled on 15 May.

However, all French entities and entities located in the EU or in countries that have concluded tax treaties with France containing either administrative assistance or non-discrimination clauses will be exempt from this tax provided the entity discloses the identity of its partners. This obligation to disclose the identity of the partners is implemented at each link in the shareholding chain, unless the shareholder whose identity is disclosed is exempted without any requirement to file a declaration (or pays the tax).

The following entities are tax exempt without having to disclose their shareholders' identity:
- listed companies on a regulated stock exchange;
- certain mutual-type non-profit making organisations or foundations;
- companies whose French assets are not mainly made up of real estate;
- shareholdings considered to be insignificant (less than one per cent);
- certain entities whose rights relate to less than five per cent (or €100,000) of the market value of the real estate assets located in France;
- Certain types of REIT 'open to the public'.

French or foreign investment funds that hold the majority of their assets in real estate (even if they are not legal persons, such as Luxembourg FCPs (fonds commun de placement), trusts, etc) are subject to the three per cent tax. The tax authorities hold that, if no such step is taken, the management company may in all cases be held liable for payment of the tax in its capacity as representative of the fund. This situation means that the cost of the three per cent tax, if payable, will be mutualised at fund level, especially when the fund's regulations do not authorise it to charge the economic burden of the three per cent tax to the defaulting investor.

If the tax is due by one of the interposed entities in the chain of ownership of a real estate asset, all the entities located between the real estate asset and the person liable for the tax are jointly liable for payment. The French tax authorities can thus attach a legal treasury mortgage to the real estate asset in order to obtain payment of the tax.

3. INVESTMENT VEHICLE CHOICE
3.1 Most commonly used structures to purchase property

An investor who wishes to conduct business in France through the establishment of a direct national presence can choose from among a number of corporate entities. The principal forms of these entities are summarised below. It is important to note that the ultimate choice of an appropriate vehicle will require careful planning, including an analysis of tax and labour issues as well as an evaluation of the particular objectives sought to be achieved through the establishment of French operations. Because such an analysis must necessarily be conducted on a case by case basis, the following is intended only to provide a general overview and does not attempt to examine whether a particular entity will be suited to the needs of specific investment operations.

The most important types of commercial companies in France are the *Société Anonyme* (SA), the *Société par Actions Simplifiée* (SAS) the *Société à Responsabilité Limitée* (SARL) and the *Société en Nom Collectif* (SNC). In the real estate business, and since properties are considered civil activities, the structuring of an investment usually include a *Société Civile* (SC). Whereas the shareholders of the SA, SAS and SARL enjoy limited liability, members of SNC and SC do not. Shareholders of an SNC liability is not only unlimited but is joint and several, ie if there are two members, a creditor may take action against any one of them for the total amount of the debt it owes against the company. Members of an SC have an unlimited liability but only severally, meaning that a member will be liable only for the proportion of its holding in the company.

French SARLs, SAs and SASs are subject to French CIT on their profits at the standard rate of 34.44 per cent. The deduction of interest is subject to limitations for intercompany loans and shareholder loans. These limitations do not apply when the loan is granted directly by a bank. A reduced CIT rate of 15 per cent is available to small and medium-sized businesses for the portion of taxable profits that is less than €38,120 per annum.

French SCs and SNCs are pass-through entities whose profits are taxed in the hands of their shareholders according to their respective financial rights. This system allows the profits or losses of the company to be set off against the profits or losses of the shareholders. Such companies may waive this pass-through regime and opt for CIT.

3.1.1 Société Civile Immobilière (SCI)

An SCI is a civil (as opposed to commercial activity) property company organised to own, manage and lease real estate. It is frequently used for real estate investments.

An SCI must have at least two shareholders, and no minimum share capital is required. The SCI is managed by one or more managers who need not be shareholders.

As a general rule, shares of an SCI may not be transferred without the unanimous prior approval of all of the shareholders. The articles of association may, however, provide that shares may be transferred following the approval of a majority of shareholders or of the manager(s).

3.1.2 Société en Nom Collectif (SNC)

The SNC consists of at least two partners (*associés*) who have the capacity of 'merchants' (*commerçants*) under French company law. Partners need not be individuals and may be citizens or residents of a foreign country (individual partners, unless they are EU, EEA or OECD nationals, must hold a commercial card or a long term residence permit). A partner of an SNC is jointly and severally liable for all debts and obligations incurred during its tenure by any of the partners on behalf of the partnership. In essence, this means that creditors of the SNC may seize the personal assets of a partner where partnership funds are insufficient to satisfy obligations of the SNC. The SNC is managed by one or more managers (*gérants*), who may be designated in the by-laws or in a separate partnership agreement. The manager need not also be a partner and may be a French or foreign individual or entity (if the manager is an entity, the managers or directors of that entity are civilly and criminally liable for mismanagement or violations of law to the same extent as if they were individual managers). An SNC can rent furnished property and purchase several properties with a view to reselling them.

Transfers of shares whether between partners or to third parties, require the (discretionary) and unanimous consent of all shareholders.

3.1.3 Société Anonyme (SA)

This company form is seldom used for real estate transactions as it is more suitable to more complex transactions or where a joint venture is contemplated. Save for the *Société en Commandite par Actions*, it is the only kind of company which may offer its shares to the public and obtain a quotation on the Stock Exchange. Two types of SA exist under French company law: the publicly held SA, whose shares are listed on a French stock exchange and the non publicly held SA, both should have a minimum share capital of €37,000.

An SA must have at least seven shareholders. The SA is managed either by a sole board of directors, or by a two-tier structure involving a Supervisory Board (*Conseil de Surveillance* – between three and 18 directors appointed by and among the shareholders) and an executive management committee (*Directoire*) depending on which structure is provided for in the by-laws. The

SA must appoint at least one statutory auditor whose duty is to examine and certify, but not prepare, the accounts of the company. Its report shall be submitted to shareholders for approval.

3.1.4 Société par actions simplifiée (SAS)
An SAS is a fairly recent form of joint-stock limited liability company. The principal purpose for creating this new form of corporation has been to bring some flexibility to the rather formalistic French corporate law in general, and to the law of SAs in particular, the statutory requirements of which regarding management and administration are especially cumbersome. Overall, it is a very flexible form of company and, for that reason, it is often used to create joint ventures.

No minimum share capital is required. No minimum number of shareholders is imposed by law. Therefore, an SAS may have a single shareholder. An individual or a foreign corporation can be shareholders of an SAS. The by-laws may freely organise the conditions under which an SAS is managed. It can thus be managed by one or several officers who can be individuals or legal entities. There may be a board of directors or any other body created by the by-laws. However, to protect third parties in their dealings with the SAS, the law provides that the by-laws must appoint a president (who can be an individual or a legal entity) who has power to represent the SAS *vis-à-vis* third parties and has full power and authority to act on behalf of the SAS, notwithstanding any internal limitation of powers.

SAs and SASs are subject to CIT. They can be consolidated for tax purposes with their shareholder if the latter holds at least 95 per cent of the share capital.

3.1.5 Société à Responsabilité Limitée (SARL)
Like an SA, an SARL is a limited liability company. It is also seldom used for real estate investments.

Compared with the SA, the SARL has fewer requirements with respect to minimum number of shareholders (two or even a single shareholder, in which case it is called an EURL – *enterprise unipersonnelle à responsabilité limitée*). There is no minimum share capital requirement. An SARL is managed by one or more managers (*gérants*), who must be individuals but need not be shareholders, and who may be either French or foreign citizens or residents (a foreign businessman's card is required for managers who are not EU, EEA or OECD nationals or do not hold a long term residence permit). The number of managers is fixed by the by-laws of the company.

Transfer of shares to third parties (except amongst members and to certain family members) is subject to prior majority approval of the other shareholders and is binding on third parties only after completion of certain formalities of notification of such transfer to the company and filing with the Registry of Commerce and Companies.

3.2 Foreign investors
According to the Decree dated 7 March 2003, real estate investments

in France made by foreign (ie: non-resident) investors that exceed: (i) €15,000,000 must be declared to the Banque de France; and (ii) €1,500,000 or in relation to the purchase of rural lands used in connection with wine growing/producing without any threshold, to the Finance Ministryfor statistical purposes, failing which, heavy sanctions provided in the Customs French Code may apply.

Foreign entities with an establishment in France are deemed residents.

3.3 Real estate investment trusts (REITS)
3.3.1 SIIC (Sociétés d'Investissements Immobiliers Cotées)
In essence, the SIIC regime offers tax exemption for listed property companies provided that they comply with an obligation to distribute 85 per cent of their net rental income and 50 per cent of their net capital gains to shareholders. The SIIC regime is available for companies which:
- are stock companies;
- are quoted on a French Stock Exchange;
- have a share capital amounting to at least €15 million; and
- whose main corporate purpose is the acquisition or construction of buildings with a view to letting and or the direct or indirect holding of participations in companies having the same object.

Subject to the provisions of any applicable double tax treaty, distributions of dividends to non-resident shareholders are subject to a 25 per cent withholding tax.

Capital holdings in an SIIC by one shareholder or a group of persons acting jointly (*de concert*) are limited to a total of 60 per cent (this limitation does not apply to shareholders that are SIICs themselves). The breach of the 60 per cent test would result in the SIIC being subject to corporate income tax at the ordinary rate for the year during which the test is not met. As a consequence, this type of vehicle is used less frequently than OPCIs (see paragraph below) for the creation of real estate investment funds.

3.3.2 OPCIs (Organismes de Placement Collectif Immobilier)
OPCIs are collective investment bodies whose securities are not listed on the stock exchange and whose purpose is the investment in real estate. Setting up an OPCI is subject to prior agreement of the AMF (*Autorité des Marchés Financiers* – the Financial Markets Authority). The OPCI are represented by a French portfolio management company (*société de gestion*) approved by the AMF.

In legal terms, these entities are subject to three specific restrictions:
- division of the investment according to certain quotas between the direct ownership of the real estate asset, by companies owning the building, listed real estate companies and liquidity (the assets taken into account for these ratios differ according to the legal form elected);
- a liquidity obligation to shareholders, who must be able to sell their shares at any time; and
- an indebtedness limit of 40 per cent of the asset value.

These obligations are generally waived if the OPCI elects the reduced operating rules regime (RFA) available to qualified investors only.

There are two legal forms of OPCIs: (i) the FPI, which has no legal personality and constitutes a kind of undivided co-ownership of the real estate assets; and (ii) the SPPICAV which is a limited company with a legal personality and is exempt from tax.

The SPPICAV RFA is a vehicle that is being more often used to structure French real estate funds. The SPPICAV is fully exempt from CIT on rental income and on any capital gains on disposals of real estate assets. On the other hand, the SPPICAV is obliged to distribute 85 per cent of its rental income and 50 per cent of the capital gains on disposal.

French tax resident shareholders liable for CIT are subject to CIT on the income distributed by the SPPICAV. Therefore, the OPCI's exemption from CIT is not an advantage, but rather a transfer of taxation to the shareholders for the income and gains subject to the distribution obligation.

Non-French tax resident shareholders are liable for a withholding tax of 25 per cent subject to treaty provisions. However, it should be pointed out that there is doubt over whether this withholding tax can actually be reduced or eliminated pursuant to double tax treaties in the case of a SPPICAV, except for the tax treaty between France and the United States which expressly provides for a reduced rate of 15 per cent in some cases.

Exemption from CIT has one material advantage. Income and gains that are not distributed by the SPPICAV but are reinvested in real estate assets or used to repay debt will not be taxed at the level of the SPPICAV or at the level of the shareholders.

Sales of shares in OPCIs are subject to registration duties at a rate of 5 per cent if the purchaser is a legal entity that holds or will hold 20 per cent or more of the rights in the OPCI upon acquisition. Conversely, if this threshold is not exceeded, no registration duties are due on the disposal of shares in the OPCI.

3.3.3 SIIC 3 regime
Until 31 December 2011, SPPICAVs (like SIICs) may allow companies subject to CIT that sell buildings or securities in real estate companies to benefit from the SIIC 3 regime. The capital gain is subject to CIT at the reduced rate of 19.63 per cent subject to the following conditions:
- disposals for valuable consideration (contributions or sales);
- of real estate assets and securities in companies mainly owning real estate assets;
- by a company subject to CIT;
- to a property company making a public issue, or approved by the AMF, ie mainly SIICs, SPPICAVs and SCPIs, as well as subsidiaries of SIICs and SPPICAVs under the articles of association of a SIIC, henceforth 'qualified purchasers'; and
- subject to the purchaser's undertaking to hold the asset for five years. If this commitment is breached, the purchaser will be liable to a penalty of 25 per cent of the acquisition price of the asset.

France

4. FINANCING AN ACQUISITION
In view of the scale of the operation, real estate acquisitions often have to be financed by borrowing. To guarantee repayment of all the monies owed, in terms of capital, interest, penalty payments, expenses and incidental items, the lender requires guarantees to ensure that it will get its money back, at low cost and as soon as possible. Loan agreements may either be executed under a private deed or a notarised deed if mortgages or lender's privilege are required. French law contains mandatory rules providing that the global effective interest rate (*taux effectif global*) shall be set out in all written agreements. Failure to comply or miscalculation of such rate will result in the French legal rate applied to the loan agreement.

4.1 Security package
The choice of security package will depend on constraints related primarily to the economics of the operation, the corporate interest of the debtor and the guarantor, the guarantor's solvency and the effects of bankruptcy law. Indeed, the lender's situation may be adversely affected by any type of insolvency procedure opened against the debtor or the guarantor, in particular any judicial reorganisation or liquidation procedure.

Lenders will usually request a form of security that offers the highest protection. Lender's pledges and mortgages are therefore commonly used. A real estate lender may also require security over the debtor's other assets and/or a personal or *in rem* guarantee from a third party. In this respect, one must stress the fact that under French law, there are certain restrictions on a company providing financial assistance and a specific prohibition on providing loans or granting security for the purpose of financing the acquisition of its own shares for commercial companies. Unlike in the United Kingdom, there is no 'white wash procedure' in France and upstream or cross-stream guarantees are very difficult to structure.

Please note also that the French consumer code contains mandatory rules for lenders where the borrowers or the guarantors are individual persons in particular those qualifying as consumers.

4.1.1 Lender's pledge (*privilège de prêteur de denier*)
A lender's pledge is an *in rem* security interest that can only be contracted to secure the reimbursement of the loan taken out to finance the acquisition of the property. The lender has a right to the sale proceeds (after costs and expenses of the procedure) over other non-secured creditors or any other mortgagee whose mortgage was registered after its privilege. The loan agreement will have to be executed by notarial deed and the funds borrowed will have to be used to pay the price of the property. This security has the advantage of being cheaper than a contractual mortgage.

4.1.2 Mortgage (*hypothèque conventionnelle*)
Mortgages can be granted on a property at any stage and not just for financing the acquisition – for instance, a mortgage may secure construction works or the acquisition refinancing of a property.

Any property in France may be mortgaged and there is no limit on the number of mortgages which may be created over the same property.

To be binding on third parties, the mortgage has to be registered with the Land Registry. Priority between mortgages applying to the same property is governed by a complex set of rules and generally depends on the chronological rank of registration.

In principle, a mortgage will secure the entire debt as well as the interest accruing on the debt over a period of three years.

The mortgagee cannot automatically take possession of the property and sell it. It must follow a specific enforcement procedure. However, the parties have the option to agree to insert an automatic enforcement clause (*pacte commissoire*) which under certain conditions may allow the lender to take possession of the property without any judicial procedure.

4.1.3 Assignment of receivables: the Dailly schedule

This type of security, which allows existing, forward and even future receivables to be assigned by registering them in a schedule, is one of the most often used security interests to assign to the benefit of the lender the rents generated by the building financed (which may be derived from current or future leases), any insurance pay-outs resulting from non-compulsory insurance, such as insurance against loss of rents, any sums due under the hedging agreements if any, any monies owed under representations and warranties etc. To date and notwithstanding criticism of some authors and legal professions, the Dailly assignment remains the most effective security interest as it is not affected by the opening of bankruptcy proceedings.

4.1.4 Pledge over accounts covering financial instruments

Shares of SAs and SASs, investment certificates, non-voting shares in public sector enterprises, bonds, treasury bills and shares in undertakings for collective investment in transferable securities (UCITS) (OPCVM) are dematerialised financial instruments. Consequently, in order to pledge such financial instruments, their owner must first register them in a financial instruments account which is secured to the creditor's benefit. The collateral is created when the account holder signs a pledge declaration, specifying the nature and number of the financial instruments registered. The financial instruments account holder issues a pledge certificate to the other party, the 'pledgee', who retains possession of the account until the debt is paid off. This type of collateral is normally pledged by the borrower's partners (if the borrower is a joint-stock company), who agree to stand security and use their shares in the borrowing company.

4.1.5 Pledge over company shares

Shares in a civil law partnership or a commercial company (SNC, SARL) are used as collateral by way of a notarial deed or a private agreement.

4.1.6 Pledge over bank accounts
The lending bank will often ask for this type of security where the balance on a bank account belonging to the borrower will be secured in its favour.

The amount of the receivables pledged does not have to be specified (this would in any case be impossible due to variations in the account balance). It is frequently stipulated that all of the borrower's income (rents, etc) will be pooled in a so-called centralising account.

4.1.7 Cash collateral
Under a cash collateral agreement, the borrower grants its creditor full ownership of certain monies as a security for the fulfilment of certain obligations. These monies are then registered in an account opened in the creditor's name. This type of security interest may be granted where certain circumstances in the structuring or in the economics of the property will require a cash trap mechanism of rents or proceeds of sale of the property.

5. MANAGING THE ACQUISITION PROCESS
5.1 Introduction
In France, the process for acquiring real estate assets is relatively standardised. This section describes the terms which would apply to the purchase of a single real estate asset.

Different terms would apply in case of purchase of a corporate vehicle owning the property. A share deal may be carried out according to a private sale and transfer agreement, without the participation of a public notary. In addition to real estate issues, in share deals, other important aspects have to be considered (management of past liabilities, calculation of purchase price), which are not described in this document.

5.2 Letter of intent – right of exclusivity – offer letter
5.2.1 Letter of intent
Frequently, the first step will be for the purchaser to send a letter of intent to the seller. If this letter is carefully drafted so that it may not be deemed to be an offer, the parties will only be bound once a call option or a bilateral undertaking to sell and purchase has been signed by both parties to the same contract or by the exchange of an offer and an acceptance.

5.2.2 Right of exclusivity
During the short interval (from four weeks to three months depending on the size and complexity of the investment) between the time when a purchaser informs the seller of its intention to buy a property and the date on which the purchaser is required to enter into a preliminary contract, the purchaser may obtain from the seller a right of exclusivity in order to carry out a survey of the real estate project.

This right of exclusivity is generally granted freely and, during its period of validity, the seller undertakes not to negotiate with a third party.

5.2.3 Offer letter
Under French law, the binding offer letter, once accepted by the seller, constitutes a binding sale and purchase agreement since there is no equivalent of the concept 'subject to contract'.

Accordingly, the letter must be drafted with great care especially if, at that time, no searches or title investigations have been carried out.

5.3 Preliminary contract
If the parties have agreed to the main conditions of the sale, the next step is to secure an option over the property in order to enable due diligence to be carried out or authorisations (such as building permits for example) to be obtained. The term of the option will depend of the conditions precedent to be fulfilled but usually it varies between two to six months.

There are two types of preliminary contract:

5.3.1 Call option (*promesse unilatérale de vente*)
With a call option, the seller irrevocably undertakes to sell the property, whereas the purchaser has the option of purchasing the property during the allotted time. In consideration of the option, the purchaser pays a deposit which is usually 10 per cent of the sale price. This deposit is not refundable if the purchaser does not exercise the option, but if it does exercise it, the deposit is deducted from the purchase price. However, the 10 per cent deposit is refunded to the purchaser if any of the conditions precedent stipulated in its favour are not fulfilled.

If not notarised, a call option must be filed with the registration authorities within 10 days of its signature. Failing which, the agreement is deemed null and void.

5.3.2 Bilateral undertaking to sell and purchase (*promesse synallagmatique de vente*)
Under the bilateral undertaking to sell and purchase, both parties are committed, the seller to sell and the purchaser to buy, but most often the transfer of title will be subject to conditions precedent.

It is normal practice for the purchaser to pay a deposit (usually 10 per cent of the price) which will be refunded if the conditions precedent are not satisfied.

A bilateral agreement subject to conditions precedent must also be filed with the tax authorities. Once the conditions precedent are met, the sale is final and the registration duties or taxes must be paid within one month, or the notarial deed of sale must be executed within such a period.

5.4 Deed of sale
Notaries are necessarily involved in the conveyancing procedure relating to direct real estate investments (ie purchase of the property as opposed to purchase of the shares of the company owning the property). This is because the direct purchase of a property must occur by means of a notarial deed of transfer (*acte authentique de vente*) in order to be published at the Land Registry (*Conservation des Hypothèques*) so as to be enforceable against third

parties, and notaries have a monopoly in this respect. The notary will draw up the contract (but a lawyer may be involved as well), witness the signature, collect and pay out the purchase price and publish the transfer. The choice of notary is usually in the hands of the seller (or the lender for a loan).

The notary's fees are payable by the purchaser unless the parties agree otherwise. The notary's fees which are subject to VAT, are payable in accordance with a scale provided by law. Fees amount to a maximum of 0.825 per cent of the price including taxes plus VAT at 19.60 per cent. However, the portion of the notary's fees that exceeds €80,000 before VAT is negotiable, and a reduction may be freely agreed upon. Where, however, two notaries are involved (one for each party) the fee is split between them so that in the case of a negotiated discount, the agreement of the two notaries is required.

In addition to notarial fees, a fee is payable to the Land Registrar at a rate of 0.1 per cent (known as the *salaire du conservateur*) calculated on the higher of either the purchase price or the market value of the property.

Furthermore, when a mortgage is taken on the property (which will almost always be the case when the purchase is financed through a bank loan), notary's fees are payable at the rate of 0.45375 per cent (plus VAT at the rate of 19.60 per cent assessed on the fee) of the amount of the mortgage, together with a Land Registrar's fee of 0.715 per cent (the *Taxe de publicité foncière*) of such amount. However no Land Registrar's fee is due in case of a lender's privilege.

5.5 Typical contract terms

Both types of preliminary contract are generally subject to conditions precedent such as the waiver by the local authorities of their pre-emption right, the obtaining by the purchaser of a loan to finance the acquisition, the issuance of a building permit, etc.

Although the notarial deed is fundamental to the conveyancing procedure in France, the preliminary agreement is of great importance because it contains the conditions that are repeated in the notarial deed. Great care must therefore be taken in the drafting of the preliminary agreement. It is important to note that under French law there are no standard conditions of sale and therefore sale contracts tend to be long as they must expressly contain all the conditions.

If the purchaser is not sufficiently protected in the preliminary contract, it will be difficult to obtain the necessary protection in the notarial deed. A foreign purchaser will need advice and assistance from a lawyer experienced in French property law at the outset before signing a preliminary contract.

Before entering into a preliminary contract, the purchaser shall commission various due diligence reports on the legal, technical and environmental aspects of the property. During this due diligence phase, the purchaser's legal counsel will obtain the following information on the property:
- copy of the title deeds;
- copy of the plans and technical documents relating to the property which contain the exact description of the property;
- *certificat d'urbanisme*, a planning document which shows the administrative easements burdening the property;

France

- copy of the original leases to determine the rental income of the property;
- the administrative classification as to the use of the property: office, residential, etc;
- all documents and information concerning refurbishment works such as building permits, certificates of compliance, insurance etc; and
- confirmation from the Land Registry as to whether the property is mortgaged or burdened by any easements.

5.6 Managing the property between preliminary agreement and deed of sale

During the interval between the preliminary agreement and the deed of sale, the seller of the property remains the owner of the property with all related consequences: the seller will continue to collect rents, carry out any repair works needed, continue the contracts associated with the property, etc.

The transfer of risks to the purchaser only occurs upon signature of the deed of sale. However, if the preliminary agreement was concluded subject to conditions precedent, the Civil Code provides that once the conditions precedent have been satisfied, the sale will be deemed to have been effective on the date of signature of the preliminary agreement. Therefore, in practice, preliminary agreements usually include a waiver of this retroactive effect of the conditions precedent in order to provide for a completion of the sale and a transfer of the risks on the date of signature of the deed of sale.

5.7 Warranties

Under French law, the seller of a property must provide the purchaser with two warranties, different in scope, covering the risks of eviction and hidden defects in the building sold.

In practice, clauses are often inserted into contracts which limit the seller's warranty or even exclude it altogether. Such clauses are invalid if they emanate from a seller who is a professional, unless the purchaser too is a professional, specialising in the same field as the seller. A purchaser should try to refuse such exclusion or limitation clauses, although a seller will almost always refuse to guarantee the state of a property built more than 10 years ago.

Recent laws have imposed a requirement to append various schedules either to the pre-contract or to the notarised deed of sale which relate to the risks attached to the property, such as termites, lead or asbestos. In such cases, if the seller fails to provide these schedules, it is then penalised by being unable to invoke the clause granting exemption from the warranty covering hidden defects, should the risk in question actually materialise. Some documents are required to be attached as exhibits to the preliminary agreement or the deed of sale, failure to comply with such obligation will allow the purchaser to request cancellation of the contract or ask for a discount on the purchase price.

5.7.1 The warranty against eviction

The warranty against eviction is a guarantee granted by law and which

France

covers the risk of eviction by third parties or the seller.

5.7.2 Warranty covering the seller's personal action
The seller is not allowed to interfere with the purchaser's enjoyment or ownership of the property through any material infringement of its rights.

The seller firstly guarantees the purchaser against any direct claims to its property, such as seeking to evict it on the grounds of adverse possession or claiming rights *in rem* to the building, such as usufruct or building lease.

The seller also guarantees the purchaser against any indirect actions against the property, such as selling the property to a third party before the first sale is registered.

This warranty is transferable to subsequent purchasers, and its effects cannot be reduced in scope or removed by a clause in the contract.

In cases involving direct claims to the purchaser's property, the purchaser may invoke the warranty. If the purchaser suffers material infringements of its rights, it may either seek damages or a cancellation of the contract.

5.7.3 Warranty against actions of a third party
This warranty differs from the preceding warranty in that it seeks to protect the purchaser against actions from third parties claiming rights to the property rather than material infringements of its rights.

This may involve a threat of eviction, such as a third party claiming ownership of the property. In this case, there must have been a legal action or a threat of legal action.

This warranty may extend to any charges on the property not declared at the time of sale, such as easements, if they interfere with the purchaser's enjoyment of the property. In this case, the courts must be satisfied that the purchaser was genuinely unaware of this charge at the time of the sale. Another essential condition is that the reason for the eviction must have existed at the time of the sale.

In the event of a total eviction, the seller must refund the original price paid, plus an additional sum if the building has increased in value, as well as any profits it has produced.

In the event of a partial eviction, the purchaser is entitled to a partial refund or to opt for annulment if the right or the part of the building of which it has been deprived were essential.

To avoid eviction, the deed of sale should oblige the seller to report the release of any charges encumbering the asset sold, unless otherwise agreed.

5.7.4 Warranty covering hidden defects
After the sale, the purchaser may discover that the building sold contains a hidden defect: this is defined by the Civil Code as a defect that makes the building sold unfit for the purpose intended by the purchaser, or impairs this to such an extent that the purchaser would not have acquired it, or would have offered a lower price for it, had it known this.

The purchaser is then entitled to apply for annulment of the sale accompanied by a refund of the price paid, or to receive a reduction in this price.

The defect in question may be of a material nature (eg a dilapidated roof on a renovated building). The defect may also be of an intangible or legal nature, such as late disclosure of an obligation to comply with a building line.

The seller is not required to issue warranties covering any apparent defects. The extent to which a defect is deemed not to be apparent depends primarily on the extent of the purchaser's experience in detecting such defects.

The defect must predate the sale. As long as the origins of the defect were present in the building sold, this condition is met, but the onus is on the purchaser to prove it. In practice it will apply to the courts for an expert to be appointed to examine the building.

The purchaser may first seek the annulment of the sale. However, it may also apply to the courts for a reduction in the price of the property. Whichever course of action it chooses, the purchaser must act no later than two years as from the date on which the defect was discovered. Prudence demands that the intending litigants should avoid becoming embroiled in preliminary conciliation proceedings, and should submit their case to the courts as quickly as possible.

5.7 Confidentiality
The sale of real estate assets is recorded in a notarial deed which is then published with the Land Registry. Therefore, the deed of sale may be obtained by third parties. It is however worth noting that, in practice, deeds of sale are divided into two parts: the first part is totally standard and drafted for Land Registry publication purposes. The second part includes specific conditions of the sale and, as the case may be, undertakings or representations of the parties. This second part is not published and its contents can therefore be considered confidential.

The sale of shares of real estate companies is executed through a share purchase agreement. In practice, parties often include a confidentiality provision.

5.9 Assignment of the contract
It is possible to provide for a substitution clause in the preliminary contract. This substitution clause will allow the purchaser to be replaced by another entity for the purposes of signing the deed of sale. In practice, this will allow the foreign investor the time to incorporate the appropriate vehicle in France once the preliminary agreement has been signed. Between professionals, such substitutions must not be onerous. In order to avoid any double transfer tax payment, substitution shall take place before the satisfaction of the last condition precedent.

6. REAL ESTATE BASICS
6.1 Main sources of law
In France, real estate investment is mainly governed by:
- the provisions of the French Civil Code (for transfer of title and provisions relating to civil leases);
- the Commercial Code for business leases and commercial development

France

authorisations;
- the Construction and Housing Code, the Environmental Code and the Public Health Code (especially in respect of the mandatory environmental diagnosis to be carried out before the sale); and
- the Urban Planning Code for planning issues.

If the assistance of a real estate agent is provided for, the agent's contract must comply with law n°70-9 of 2 January 1970 (*Loi Hoguet*). Tax matters and land registration are governed by the provisions of the French Tax Code.

6.2 Various forms of real estate

6.2.1 Freehold ownership (*Pleine propriété*)

In almost all cases, the interest to be acquired in land and buildings will be that of freehold ownership. The freehold ownership of land extends to anything above and below it, including buildings.

An investor having an interest in a property in freehold ownership is entitled to mortgage it, grant easements over it, grant leases of any type and sell it at any time.

There is no limitation under French law on the number of persons who may together own the freehold ownership of a real estate asset. In such a case, they are said to own the property in joint ownership (*indivision*) but this mechanism is not often used in the investment sector as day to day management is cumbersome.

In complex operations, French operators often divide a plot of land vertically, ie, distinct and separate rights of ownership exist on superposed layers or 'volumes' (which is similar to 'flying freehold' under English law) with reciprocal easement rights enabling one owner to erect a building based on the building below. For example, one volume could include particular levels of subsoil (such as car parks) whereas another could include the first basement or another from two to five floors.

6.2.2 Building lease (*bail à construction*)

The owner of a plot of land may grant a building lease for a minimum period of 18 years and a maximum of 99 years. The lessee benefits from a real property right over the property (similar to a 'leasehold estate') and may therefore assign it, mortgage it and create easements over it. The main characteristic of such a lease is the lessee's obligation to build constructions on the land thus rented at its own cost, to maintain and repair them and to pay all taxes and duties relating to such property. The ownership of the constructions is transferred to the lessor upon expiry or termination of the lease without any compensation for the lessee unless otherwise provided.

6.2.3 Long-term lease (*bail emphytéotique*)

The owner of a property may also grant a bail *emphythéotique* which is also a 'leasehold estate' whose minimum duration is 18 years and maximum duration is 99 years. Under such a lease, the lessee benefits from a real property right over the property and may therefore assign it, mortgage it and grant easements as well as sub-leases for the duration of the lease. The lessee

France

must maintain the property and increase its value at its own cost and must pay a fee (*redevance*) to the lessor. At the end of the lease, all improvements made to the property by the lessee are transferred to the lessor without compensation unless expressly provided for.

The main differences between this lease and a 'building lease' is that: (i) there can be no obligation for the lessee to build a building; and (ii) the landlord has only a very limited capacity to restrict the lessee's rights over the property.

6.2.4 Forward sale (*vente en l'état futur d'achèvement*)

Under such a contract, the seller of a plot of land undertakes to build premises within a defined period and on the basis of plans and specifications duly agreed by the purchaser.

Upon execution of the deed of sale, the ownership of the land is transferred to the purchaser whereas the premises are transferred as their construction advances, with the price being paid as the works progress.

The seller is liable towards the purchaser for the visible and latent defects that may affect the premises after their completion.

A performance guarantee is usually delivered by a bank to the purchaser.

6.3 Land registration

All sales and transfer of properties must be registered with the Land Registry depending on the location of the property to be binding against third parties. Any mortgages, charges, easements created by contract, leases granted for a term of over 12 years and any procedure for the forced sale of a property or litigation on a right *in rem* over real estate shall also be registered with the Land Registry.

However, the registration does not in itself create an absolute and unchallenged right. The Land Registrar that carries out the 'registration' and 'public notices formalities' at the Land Registry keeps in its records authenticated copies of all notarial deeds relating to a property and issues copies and extracts of such deeds upon request. Information includes all transfer of ownership, identity of current and past owners, date of acquisition and price paid, easements and encumbrances, charges and any long term leases registered over the property.

7. COMMERCIAL LEASES

The property purchased could be leased to individuals if it is a residential building but usually, investment in property tends to be for commercial or office use. A lease agreement for this use will fall into the scope of the commercial leases (*baux commerciaux*) regulations. Commercial leases are governed by the French Commercial Code. The main purpose of this regulation is to grant the lessee the right to renew its lease in order to ensure the continuation of its business and to secure its clients.

As a preliminary comment, it should be pointed out that the following information/documents shall be provided by the lessor:
- a risk statement (*Etat des risques naturels et technologiques*), which shall be

less than six months old, in areas covered by a risk-prevention plan or an earthquake zone; and
* the list of losses suffered which entailed payment of insurance indemnity in connection with natural disaster risk or technological disaster risk.

If the landlord fails to provide the risk statements and the list of losses mentioned above, the tenant is entitled to either terminate the contract or to ask the judge for a reduction of price.

7.1 Rent
The rent is freely agreed upon between the parties, most often according to the rental value of the premises which is generally the same as the market value. It may include a variable portion calculated according to the lessee's turnover and a fixed portion that corresponds to a guaranteed minimum rent. The rent is generally paid quarterly in advance or in arrears.

Rent may be reviewed during the term of the lease by either of the parties, subject to the provisions of Articles L. 145-38 and L. 145-39 of the French Commercial Code. There are two systems of rent review: Statutory rent review and rent indexation clause.

7.1.1 Statutory rent review
Pursuant to Article L. 145-38 of the French Commercial Code, rent can be reviewed on request of either party every three years as from the date on which the lease came into force. Subsequent rent revision is applied three years after the date of the last fixing of the rent.

The revised rent must correspond to the rental value of the premises, which is – unless agreed by the parties – determined by courts, taking into account the characteristics of the leased premises (their use; respective obligations of parties; current prices charged locally etc).

However, the rent increase (or decrease) upon such triennial revision cannot exceed the variation in the National Construction Cost Index since the last fixing of the rent (either by agreement between the parties or as a result of a court decision) except in the case where, during that period of time, there has been an effective modification of the local commercial factors (*facteurs locaux de commercialité*) resulting in a variation of more than 10 per cent of the rental value of the rented premises.

The provisions of Article L. 145-38 are applicable even though the lease provides for an annual indexation of the rent. However, according to case law, these provisions will not apply where the rent is determined on the basis of a certain percentage of the tenant's turnover.

7.1.2 Rent indexation clause
The parties generally agree on an annual indexation of the rent in accordance with an economic index. In the case of a commercial lease, the index usually chosen for the time being is the National Construction Cost Index published by INSEE (the French State Statistical Institute).

If the lease provides for a rent indexation, a rent review can be applied for each time that, by reason of such indexation, the rent is increased or decreased by more than 25 per cent of that amount previously agreed by the parties or determined by the court.

7.1.3 Rent on renewal
The variation of the rent under an initial lease and the renewed lease cannot exceed the variation in the National Construction Cost Index or if applicable, of the Commercial Rent Index (*Indice des Loyers Commerciaux*) published by INSEE over the period of the lease unless one of the parties can provide the evidence of a significant change in one of the elements that served as basis for the initial setting of the rent.

No rent capping is applicable:
- to a lease entered into for more than nine years;
- to land which has not been built on (*terrains nus*);
- to a lease with a term of more than 12 years;
- to premises which can only be used for a specific activity (*locaux monovalents*) such as premises used for hotels or cinemas;
- to premises used exclusively as offices; or
- where one or more criteria which have been taken into consideration to determine the rental value of the premises, with the exception of current levels of rent in the area, have changed significantly. The judge will assess whether the changes to the parties' respective obligations were significant before deciding whether or not to exclude the rent cap.

In these cases, the rent for the renewed lease must correspond to the rental value of the premises, as determined in accordance with the criteria outlined above.

7.2 Term
The minimum term for a commercial lease agreement is nine years. However the parties can provide for a longer term. Unless otherwise agreed, the tenant may terminate the lease at the end of each three-year period by giving at least a six months' prior notice. The notice is given by notification served by a court bailiff.

A special dispensation from the nine year term is provided under Article L.145-5 of the French Commercial Code in respect of a short term lease which shall not exceed two years. However, should the tenant be authorised to remain in the premises at the expiry of the short term lease agreement, the initial two-year lease would automatically be followed by a new nine-year lease governed by the French Commercial Code.

The parties can provide for a longer term (such as a lease with a 12-year term). The lease agreement shall be prepared as a notarial deed if its term exceeds 12 years. In such a case, the lease shall be registered with the *Conservation des hypothèques* and is subject to the payment of registration duties.

7.3 Termination
7.3.1 From the tenant's perspective
The tenant has an absolute right to complete the entire term of the lease and

France

benefit from a statutory right to receive a renewal offer for a further nine year period.

7.3.2 From the landlord's perspective
In order to terminate the lease, the landlord shall give notice at least six months before the termination date.

In the absence of any notice to quit both from the tenant and the landlord, six months before the end of the term:
- the lease shall not be terminated and shall automatically be continued at the end of the term, for an indefinite period (*called période de tacite prolongation*) running as long as no notice to quit has been served by bailiff either by the landlord or by the tenant, at least six months in advance and for the last day of the quarter (for instance, a notice to quit served during the *période de tacite prolongation* by bailiff on 4 April 2011 would enter into force and terminate the lease only on 31 December 2011); and
- the tenant may ask for the renewal of the lease within this six month period before the end of the term or at any time during the *période de tacite prolongation* – the landlord having then to accept or refuse the renewal within three months.

7.4 Renewal
7.4.1 Right of renewal
An essential feature of the French commercial lease's legal status is the right for the tenant to obtain renewal of the lease upon its expiry.

Renewal occurs when the landlord serves notice of renewal on the tenant or when the tenant serves an application for renewal on the landlord.

Within a three-month period following service by the tenant of its application for renewal, the landlord informs the tenant by court bailiff service whether or not it accepts the renewal. If no response is received from the landlord within the prescribed period, the landlord is deemed to have accepted the renewal.

If the landlord refuses to renew the lease, the tenant must refer the matter to the relevant court within two years either to challenge the landlord's refusal to renew; or to seek the payment of an eviction indemnity

7.4.2 Refusal to renew the lease
The landlord cannot refuse to renew the lease without paying to the tenant an eviction indemnity. This eviction indemnity shall compensate for the losses and expenses incurred by the tenant (value of the business of the lease (except for offices), moving costs, higher rent, etc).

The tenant is entitled to stay in the premises under the terms and conditions of the expired lease until it has been paid an eviction indemnity. In the meantime, the tenant will be liable for occupation compensation.

7.5 Subletting
Subletting is prohibited unless the parties agree to the contrary in the lease agreement or if the landlord expressly authorises it. In practice, the tenant

usually requests having the right to sub-let to companies belonging to its corporate group.

Where sub-letting is permitted by the landlord, the sub-tenant shall benefit from the rules set out in the French Commercial Code in its relationship with the main tenant.

However, the sub-lease does not usually grant to the sub-tenant security of tenure on the premises in its relationship with the landlord, as is commonly stipulated in the head lease that premises are an 'undivided set of premises'.

Thus, upon expiry of the principal lease, the landlord shall renew the sublease, to the sub-tenant's benefit:
- if it has authorised or approved the sub-lease; and
- if the sub-let premises represent only a part of the premises leased under the principal lease and do not constitute a single indivisible whole with the non sub-let premises.

It should be noted that, if the rent by square metre under the sub-lease exceeds the principal rent by a square metre, the landlord is entitled to request a corresponding increase of the principal rent (unless it has waived this right).

7.6 Assignment of the leasehold right

The transfer of the leasehold right is permitted unless otherwise provided.

However, the owner cannot prohibit the assignment of a lease when it is made in favour of a purchaser of the tenant's business concern (*fonds de commerce*).

In addition it is common practice to expressly provide in the lease that the transferor may be jointly liable with the transferee for the performance of the assignee's obligations under the lease (payment of rent and charges). This liability will commonly be maintained throughout the duration of the lease and will end at its renewal or upon delivery of a notice to quit.

7.7 Maintenance and repairs

The term, renewal, termination of the lease, revision of the rent, use of the premises, authorised activities, subletting and transfer of the lease are governed, in whole or in part, by the provisions of the French Commercial Code, whereas the general conditions of the lease such as maintenance and repairs of the premises are governed by the French Civil Code.

Maintenance and repair can either be shared by the parties, the tenant having to bear the ordinary maintenance works and the landlord covering the structural repair works, or the lease can provide that the tenant shall bear the cost of all the works, whether ordinary or structural.

In any case, the lease must expressly and precisely indicate which repairs will be the tenant's responsibility (eg security works, works required by the administration), failing which, according to the Civil Code and to the court precedent, these works shall be borne by the landlord.

Germany

Beiten Burkhardt Rechtanwaltsgesellschaft mbH
Dr Nicole Kadel & Dr Axel Schilder

1. INVESTMENT PURCHASE OVERVIEW

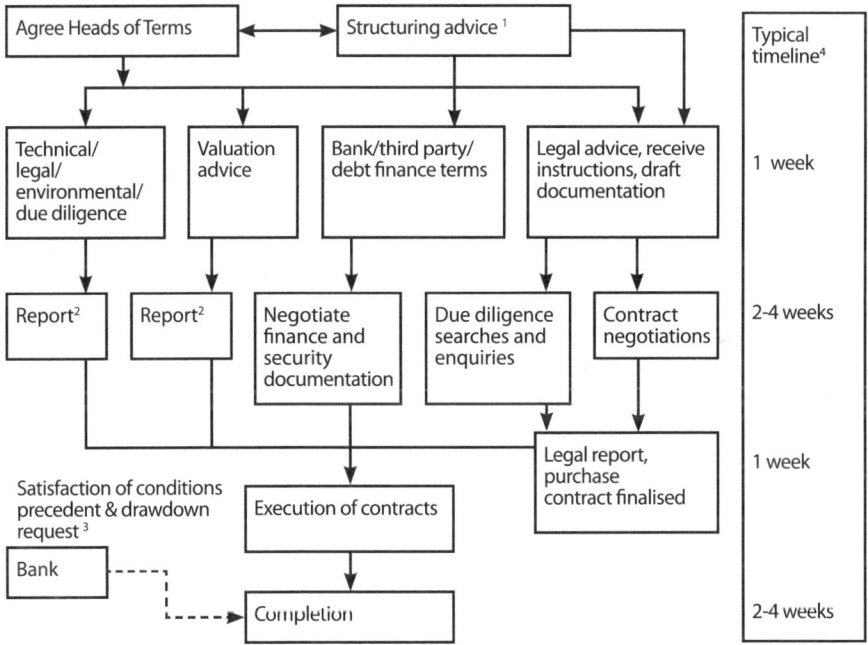

1. Establishing an acquisition structure for tax and financial planning is an important early stage which may significantly influence other stages such as the banking arrangements (eg, using Islamic financing structures) and the purchase contract.
2. Each report will be addressed to the purchaser
3. Before exchanging contracts it is advisable to ensure that all conditions precedent are capable of being satisfied.
4. Often subject to compression, timescales may differ considerably, exchange and completion may be simultaneous.

2. TAX CONSIDERATIONS

2.1 Typical non-resident structure
A non-German company is a very common vehicle for non-German residents to hold German real estate, as it offers the following advantages and restrictions from a taxation point of view.

2.1.1 Rental income taxed at 15 per cent (for companies) or at a floating rate up to 45 per cent (for individuals)
German companies are generally taxed for corporate income tax (CIT) purposes at 15 per cent on their net rental income plus 5.5 per cent solidarity surcharge (*Solidaritätszuschlag* – SolZ) thereon. Non-German tax resident companies holding the property as an investment also pay tax at that tax rate, but only on income from German sources, ie, from letting and renting real estate located in Germany. This rate does not depend upon a double taxation treaty (DTT), so it applies irrespective of where the non-German company is resident.

Germany does not operate a system for withholding tax (WHT) from rent before it is paid to non-residents. Income received from real estate located in Germany has to be declared by the non-German resident company by filing a tax return. Based on this tax return the company will receive a tax assessment note from the competent tax office that shows the tax assessment and the due date for the respective tax payment.

These principles also apply if the non-German resident is an individual. Only the applicable tax rate differs from the tax situation of a non-German resident company. The marginal income tax rate for resident and non-resident taxpayers (individuals) in Germany is 45 per cent (plus 5.5 per cent SolZ).

2.1.2 Limited deductions for interest expenses
Germany has introduced provisions that allow the amount of rent that is taxed to be reduced by the interest paid on third party finance taken out to acquire the German real estate as long as certain restrictions are observed. The so-called interest barrier (*Zinsschranke*) applies to non residents as well as to German residents.

The interest barrier applies to all types of financing irrespective of the creditor (shareholder or third-party bank) and irrespective of the legal form of the financed business (sole entrepreneurship, partnership or corporation). It applies to business and non-business income, such as income from letting German real estate.

A borrowing company holding German real estate is permitted to deduct interest expenses without limit to the extent of its interest income in the same fiscal year. Net interest expense in excess of interest income is deductible only up to 30 per cent of earnings before interest, taxes, depreciation, and amortisation (EBITDA) as calculated pursuant to tax law. Subject to certain restrictions, interest not deductible in a fiscal year may be carried forward. Unutilised EBITDA volume may also be carried forward.

The 30 per cent restriction is not applicable if:

Germany

- the annual net interest expense is less than €3 million;
- the (renting) business (ie the company) is not a member of a consolidated group; or
- the equity ratio of the financed domestic business is higher than or equal to the equity ratio of the global consolidated group. A business is part of a consolidated group as defined for the purposes of the above exception if it is or may be included in consolidated financial statements prepared according to international financial reporting standards (IFRS) (or, where applicable, the accounting rules of an EU member country or US generally accepted accounting principles). A business is also a member of a consolidated group if its financial and business policy may be uniformly determined with one or several businesses (so-called *Gleichordnungskonzern*).

2.1.3 Generally no WHT on interest payments

Interest on shareholder debt may also be deductible, subject to the German transfer pricing rules. Basically, in Germany no withholding tax is due on interest payments if the borrower of the underlying loan is not a bank or if the creditor is a non-resident company or individual.

Nevertheless, subject to the precise structure of the debt, further provisions and/or any available tax treaty relief, a 20 per cent or even 30 per cent WHT (plus 5.5 per cent SolZ) may be levied, for example:
- interest is paid on securitised loans (ie, loans represented by bond certificates for a part of total issue, or represented by a global certificate, or issues that are listed in a domestic or foreign debt register);
- income from a silent partnership or interest paid on loans with a profit-related interest rate; or
- interest paid by a domestic bank as the borrower to a domestic creditor with respect to any loan or deposit that is not represented by a security. This covers all kinds of interest owed by a domestic bank, such as interest on bank checking and savings accounts, or on term deposits with certain minor exceptions.

The WHT rate on interest for domestic creditors is 25 per cent (plus 5.5 per cent SolZ). For individuals generating interest income from privately held assets, a flat-rate tax at the same rate applies.

Interest payments between related enterprises within the EU are exempt from WHT, according to the EU Interest and Royalty Directive.

Interest paid by a domestic borrower to a non-resident creditor with respect to any loan or deposit that is secured by real estate or equivalent rights triggers non-resident taxation for the creditor in Germany, which requires a tax filing unless an applicable DTT provides otherwise.

2.1.4 No German tax on capital gains when shares in a property holding company are sold

Non-German residents holding property are generally subject to German capital gains tax. Therefore, any gain realised when a non-German company sells German real estate should be taxed in Germany. However, if the shares in a non-German company holding German real estate are sold and therefore no asset deal takes place, such share deal will not trigger German corporate income tax on the gain due to treaty relief under an applicable DTT.

2.1.5 Avoidance of a permanent establishment for German trade tax (GTT – *Gewerbesteuer*)

Often non-resident investors use a company managed and controlled outside Germany in order to avoid a permanent establishment for GTT reasons. GTT is an additional tax to CIT or income tax and amounts to up to 15 per cent depending on the tax rate applicable according to the municipality where the real estate property is located. As long as no permanent establishment is created in Germany the non-resident investor will not be subject to GTT.

2.1.6 Structure for avoidance of transfer taxes

The purchase of real estate property is generally subject to a so-called Real Estate Transfer Tax (RETT – *Grunderwerbsteuer*) detailed below.

The tax rate to be applied to the purchase price is 3.5 per cent. If the real estate property is located in Berlin, Hamburg or Sachsen-Anhalt the tax rate is 4.5 per cent. RETT is part of the acquisition cost of the buyer since the purchase agreement in general provides for a contractual mechanism under which the purchaser is liable for the RETT. Therefore, RETT is payable by the buyer to the local tax authorities.

RETT can be avoided by setting up a corporate structure of property holding companies or partnerships. A transfer of shareholding of at least 95 per cent or more of the issued share capital in the company (indirectly or directly) in the hands of one acquirer (or group of acquirers) or the exchange of at least 95 per cent of partners in a partnership within a five-year period (with respect to indirect or direct investment in the partnership's capital) is subject to RETT. As long as not more than 95 per cent of the shares or the partnership interests are transferred, no RETT will be triggered. In terms of shares in a corporation, 100 per cent of the shares can be transferred tax free if one purchaser acquires a 5.1 per cent stake and a second purchaser acquires a 94.9 per cent stake in the corporation. Such an acquisition structure is very common in the German market.

With effect from 2010, a change in law also provides for RETT exemptions in certain intra-group reorganisations.

2.2 Points to bear in mind

The acquisition of German real estate can be complex and there are a number of issues that need to be carefully considered and planned around to reduce exposure to German tax and ensure that the structure is practical to run on a day-to-day basis. Below are just some of the other more significant issues that need to be considered (in addition to the points above) when acquiring German real estate. As always, it is vital to get appropriate professional advice.

2.2.1 Residence and substance requirements
The offshore or non-German entity must be managed and controlled outside Germany to maintain non-German tax resident status. In the case of a company, this generally requires that a majority of the directors (or equivalents) are non-German tax residents and that all board meetings are held outside Germany. This should be manageable, with care. Since German tax authorities have started to challenge such offshore structures, especially in (very common) cases where Luxembourg entities are part of the holding structure. Due to that experience it is very important to observe documentation obligations so that the non-German entity can prove substance requirements and – on a factual basis – that the management decisions have been made abroad. It is necessary – in a best case scenario – to lease office space with an individual address, telephone and fax line, letter box, etc which will be regarded as sufficient substance by the German tax authorities. Alternatively, the non-German entity might enter into a contract with a so-called domiciliation agent in Luxemburg, which provides the required administrative services on a day-to-day basis.

2.2.2 Investment versus trading
The tax treatment outlined above assumes that the non-German resident company will own the German real estate as an investment. If the company is developing or trading in German real estate, then the profits may be taxed differently. The distinction between trading and investment is important – if a non-German resident company is treated as trading in German property, it may become subject to GTT at a maximum of 15 per cent on all of its profits from that trade carried on in Germany, including any gain on the disposal. This can be a particular issue if the real estate is sold soon after acquisition or development. Alternative structuring may be possible if trading is intended.

2.2.3 No lease of business fixtures (*Betriebsvorrichtungen*)
An important issue in terms of the avoidance of a GTT burden is the lease of business fixtures. A property holding company is able to claim so-called extended deduction (*erweiterte Grundstückskürzung*) for GTT purposes. That means that all profits resulting from renting real property can be deducted for the calculation of the trade tax base. In fact due to this deduction no GTT falls due at all. However, if business fixtures (these include, but are not limited to, machinery, equipment, signs, storage bins etc) are leased by the same company leasing the real property, the company would not be allowed to apply the extended deduction for GTT purposes. As a result the whole rental income would be subject to GTT. Therefore, in practice, all business fixtures need ideally to be held by a separate entity. The downside of this structure is that two separate rental agreements need to be entered into.

2.2.4 Value added tax (VAT)
VAT will usually be chargeable on the acquisition of German commercial real estate. The rate is 19 per cent. If the property is let, then a sale may be treated as a transfer of a going concern (*Geschäftsveräußerung im Ganzen*),

provided certain conditions are met. In that situation no VAT will be
payable, reducing funding costs. In the latter case the purchaser will be the
legal successor of the seller for VAT purposes which needs to be observed
in terms of possible VAT repayment claims due to the German VAT
amendments rules (*Vorsteuerberichtungen*) pursuant to section 15a of the
German VAT code. The observation period for such repayment claims, that
can be assessed retroactively, is 10 years.

Similarly, VAT is usually charged on the rents paid by tenants. Owners of
German commercial real estate do not automatically have to charge VAT on
the rents or sale price. It depends upon whether they have opted to charge
VAT. However, if a landlord does not 'opt to tax' in this way, they will not
generally be able to recover any of the VAT payable when acquiring the
property, maintaining or refurbishing it etc, and the VAT will become an
absolute cost. It is generally only worth a landlord not 'opting to tax' if it
can charge more rent as a result and the extra rent makes up for the lost VAT.
In most cases non-recoverable VAT will be calculated as a cost factor and
therefore will increase the gross rental fee to be paid by the lessee. Another
mechanism in order to compensate the 'VAT damage' at the level of the
lessor might be a monthly compensation payment to be paid by the lessee
on top of the regular rent payment.

Different VAT rules apply to property for residential or charitable use. In
this case the landlord will not be allowed to opt for VAT for the rent services.
Specific advice should be obtained on the facts where appropriate, in
particular in situations where a change in the tenant structure takes place.

2.2.5 Due diligence
Where an interest in German real estate is acquired indirectly (via shares
or units) there is always a risk that the vehicle has pre-existing tax or other
liabilities. Appropriate corporate, financial and tax due diligence should be
carried out so that any such liabilities can be identified and quantified and
accounted for in the acquisition transaction.

3. INVESTMENT VEHICLES
This section briefly considers below some of the factors which may influence
the type of vehicle or structure to be used when deciding to invest in
Germany. This section additionally summarises a few of the more popular
vehicles, together with their primary advantages and disadvantages, the
majority of which are tax related. However, this is not an exhaustive list and,
clearly, does not address the requirements of all potential investors, which
would need to be considered on the facts.

3.1 Issues affecting the type of vehicle/structure when making an indirect investment
Control and decision making – certain vehicles, in order to protect
the efficacy of their structure, prohibit investors from controlling the
assets held by the vehicle. This is true of German limited partnerships
(*Kommanditgesellschaft* – KG) where the investor purchases an interest as a

limited partner (*Kommanditist*). However, for German tax purposes a limited partner gets power of representation for the partnership besides the general partner (*Komplementär*) if the general partner is a corporation, eg, a German limited liability corporation (GmbH). This requirement needs to be installed in order to avoid a trade tax liability at the level of the partnership itself.

Cost – investing indirectly is generally more expensive at the point of set up than acquiring an asset directly. There are the ongoing running costs of the vehicle (including particular compliance issues) and in addition potential regulatory costs to factor in.

Size and number of assets – where an investor is only proposing to hold one or two assets it may be more efficient to hold them directly. Where there are multiple assets there is merit in establishing an umbrella vehicle which can allow central management and increase the options on the future sale of the assets. However, for German tax purposes it might be necessary to set up so-called 'single-property companies' to avoid the application of the interest barrier rules. In these cases the tax structure might lead to a complex corporate structure of several companies holding only one real estate property each.

Location of the management team – if the management team is not based in Germany how the asset will be managed on a day-to-day basis within the vehicle needs to be considered. Typically an asset manager is appointed to undertake this task to ensure efficiency and in some cases to ensure that the investors may retain their offshore tax status, which is decisive in particular for the avoidance of a trade tax burden in Germany.

Long-term objectives – consideration needs to be given to whether the assets are to be held for investment purposes or for trading. The answer to this question will affect the type of vehicle chosen. German limited partnerships, for example, are most commonly used for investment type assets whilst limited liability companies (eg the German GmbH) are often used for trading assets, in particular for RETT saving reasons. Such trading companies will always be subject to German trade tax so that an additional tax burden has to be calculated for potential capital gains triggered by the sale of the properties.

Other investor requirements – certain vehicles are more or less attractive to different types of investors. Some investors have restrictions within their own constitutions which prohibit their investment into certain vehicles.

Multiple vehicles – often investors hold their assets through a series of vehicles in order to maximise both the tax efficiency of the structure and also the exit options for the investors. This may involve a combination of vehicles, in particular in most structures with a cross-border approach. Equally, certain investors may require a feeder vehicle through which to invest into the main holding vehicle (often in funds structures).

Investment strategy – if the investor is to retain the investment for any length of time, it will wish to ensure that the tax, control and regulatory aspects of the investment vehicle are compliant with its requirements. Equally, if it is intended to hold the investment for a short time only, it will be necessary to ensure that these characteristics do not prejudice liquidity.

Taxation of the vehicle – the summary below looks at some of the tax issues affecting different structures. In particular, the trade tax and RETT position will need to be considered, as this could be the main set-up or transactional cost. Ongoing tax will also be relevant and may depend on the likely level of the investor's involvement.

Term, exit and liquidity – some types of vehicles have established markets for the trading of interests, others may be more limited.

In some cases a combination of the structures described below may be needed to achieve the requirements of all anticipated investors.

3.2 Types of vehicle
3.2.1 German limited partnership (KG)
KGs have traditionally been popular vehicles for indirect real estate investment, because they are tax transparent for direct tax purposes, enabling different types of investor to invest together, but to be taxed according to their individual status.

KGs offer limited liability to investors provided that they are not involved directly in the management or that the investor takes the position of the general partner (*Komplementär*). Investors in a KG are known as limited partners. All KGs have at least one limited partner and must have one general partner. The general partner has control over the management of the partnership and unlimited liability for the debts and obligations of the partnership.

For German tax purposes often a limited partner gets power of representation for the partnership besides the general partner (*Komplementär*) if the general partner is a corporation, eg, a German limited liability corporation (GmbH). This requirement needs to be installed in order to avoid a trade tax liability at the level of the partnership itself.

3.2.2 German limited liability company (GmbH)
A GmbH is commonly used by investors if/when the asset they are acquiring is already held by a company. However, generally, companies are unattractive as indirect vehicles because they are not tax transparent and do not provide exempt investment returns for individuals and offshore investors. The company is potentially liable to CIT at 15 per cent (plus 5.5 per cent SolZ thereon) on its income and chargeable capitals gains.

The following tax regime applies to the dividend distribution by a GmbH to a foreign shareholder:
Principle
- 25 per cent (plus 5.5 per cent SolZ);
- a (partial or full) exemption or refund is possible, depending on the EU-Parent-Subsidiary Directive or the respective double tax treaty.

Exception – zero per cent WHT if:
- the legal form of the investor and the shareholder is listed in the appendix of the EU parent-subsidiary Directive;
- the foreign shareholder holds a continuous direct participation (> or =

10 per cent minimum for at least 12 months);
- a DTT provides for zero per cent withholding tax; and
- in case of EU parent-subsidiary or treaty relief availability, the foreign shareholder shows business substance and income other than from shareholding in order to quality for relief.

A tax exemption certificate issued by the Federal Tax Office (*Bundesamt für Finanzen*) is always required for payers to be able to desist from withholding. If a dividend is distributed before an exemption certificate is issued, WHT will be due, but refundable under certain conditions.

The following tax regime applies to the sale of real estate property in Germany by a corporate non-resident:

3.2.3 Asset deal
- If there is no permanent establishment in Germany and only a real estate investment, there is no exposure to GTT;
- no treaty relief is available for capital gains on real estate disposals in Germany;
- there is no WHT on capital gains; and
- if applicable, tax exemptions of capital gain or tax credit might be available for taxes in the state of residence of the non-resident investor due to a DTT.

3.2.4 Share deal
- Generally no trade tax exposure exists if the shares of a German real estate holding company are sold by a non-resident.
- WHT of 25 per cent (plus 5.5 per cent SolZ) will generally be levied if the payments are received through a domestic bank and no treaty exemption certificate is presented by the non-resident shareholder.
- If applicable, capital gains may be tax exempt in Germany pursuant to the provisions of an applicable DTT.

3.3 Use of partnerships
Partnerships are frequently used as key components in the structuring of indirect investments. The benefits of partnerships include the following: flow-through tax treatment; flexible remuneration arrangements for general partners; and flexible internal governance and control.

As partnerships are generally treated by fiscal authorities in Germany as tax transparent for purposes of direct taxes, partners are treated as having invested directly in the underlying assets held by the partnership. Direct tax at the partnership level is generally either minimal or non-existent.

3.4 Types of partner
A limited partnership has two categories of partner:
- general partners, who have control over the management of the partnership and unlimited liability for the debts and obligations of the partnership; and
- limited partners, who are passive investors in the activities of the

partnership and whose liability to the partnership is limited to their contributed capital.

The partnership agreement will allocate costs between the limited partners and the general partner. Those expenses related to the initial structuring, the ongoing operation and the investment activities of the partnership will be the responsibility of the limited partnership. The general partner will traditionally cover its own internal costs of operation. However, where fund expenses may have placed an unnecessary drag on fund performance, especially in the early years, a fund manager may cap the amount payable by the fund and cover the remaining amount itself.

A partner's interest in a partnership will be based on its capital account, which rises and falls in two ways: due to contributions and withdrawals of capital by a partner; and due to profits or losses of the partnership allocated to the partner.

The manner in which allocations of realised and unrealised gains and losses, together with income and expenses, are made will be governed by the partnership agreement.

Every limited partnership must have a general partner. In some respects the need to nominate or establish an entity to serve in this role has been a drawback to using partnerships. The rise of limited liability companies in the United States and limited liability partnerships in the United Kingdom reflects an attempt by legislatures to provide a vehicle with the flexibility of a traditional limited partnership, but without the formal requirement for a general partner.

A general partner may be either an individual or, more commonly in funds, a legal entity, which may be specifically organised for this purpose. The domicile, tax status and internal structure of the fund manager will frequently drive the choice of general partner.

Limited partners may lose the benefit of their limited liability if they participate in the management of the partnership and therefore become subject to a special liability not based on the status of a limited partner itself.

3.5 Partnership agreements
The affairs of the partners are governed by the partnership agreement, the scope and contents of which are negotiated by the general and limited partners. This flexibility is one of the principal attractions of partnerships, as opposed to the mandated structure and procedures associated with companies.

4. FINANCING AN ACQUISITION
Real estate financing is usually a combination of debt and equity. However, at present and in context with the financial crisis the debt portion might be limited to 70 per cent whereas before the financial crisis often much higher leverage deals were being made – up to 95 per cent. A bank loans a proportion of the purchase costs by way of debt to the buyer in return for:
- a security *in rem* (land charge) to be created by a notarial land charge deed and to be registered with the Land Register in favour of the

financing bank over the property to be purchased. In connection with the creation of the land charge, the financing bank and the borrower enter into an agreement on the security purpose of the land charge. In addition to the security over the property in general other assets are to be charged by way of security (please see below).
- an assignment of the right to receive rents from occupational tenants in the property to be mortgaged as security for the loan (standard practice for investment property). The assignment of the rental stream is critical from the lender's point of view; it will be used to service the debt repayments;
- a pledge over shares (if a borrower is an SPV for example) whereas the share pledge agreement has to be notarised according to German law;
- a pledge over rent accounts and other accounts held in the name of the borrower;
- assignment of the benefit of any major contracts as well as transfer of provided securities, as the case may be (eg, in connection with recent development of the property to be funded).

There will be a number of finance documents in addition to those mentioned above (not least the loan/facility agreement) to be negotiated.

In the package of rights granted to the lender will be a series of restrictions on the activities a borrower can undertake. In particular, it will be unable to dispose of the assets forming part of the security package without first obtaining the lender's consent. In practice this will only be given where the lender is to receive the payment proceeds, usually, to repay the debt. In addition, the borrower will be prevented from borrowing from or granting security to other parties (the so-called 'negative pledge' provision). In addition, the agreement on appropriate so-called 'change of control' clauses is prevalent in finance documents.

The lender will usually expect first ranking security over the property which is to be secured for the debt due from the borrower. The security *in rem* (land charge) has to be registered with division III (*Abteilung III*) of the Land Register as a valid creation of a land charge requires its registration with the Land Register.

5. MANAGING THE ACQUISITION PROCESS
5.1 Introduction
In Germany the process and terms on which commercial property is bought and sold are relatively standardised. This section explains the usual terms that apply to the sale and purchase of a commercial property. For the purposes of this section, we assume that the transaction is the purchase of a commercial property that is already let to tenants by way of an asset deal. If the property is to be acquired by purchasing the corporate vehicle that currently owns the property (share deal) different terms would apply.

At the beginning of the investment process the buyer usually enforces an evaluation of the property to be purchased accompanied by legal, technical and environmental due diligence in order to identify the risks involved in the intended transaction.

From a legal point of view, such risks may in particular result from lease agreements being in force with respect to the purchase object as these lease agreements are generally automatically transferred to the buyer. Therefore, it is important for the buyer to identify not only the economic parameters such as income from rent and size of leasable area, but also legal issues such as compliance of the lease agreements with written form requirements (*Schriftform*) as well as term, termination rights and other obligations and responsibilities which can arise from the existing lease agreements to the buyer as new landlord.

Another legal risk may result from the potential transfer of employment relationships to the buyer. In the case of a business being sold, employment contracts persist with the buyer. In the context of real estate investment this may in particular apply to the employment contract with a janitor.

Risks affecting the property directly in particular concern restrictions resulting from entries in the Land Register such as easements, but also restrictions resulting from neighbour agreements, building law requirements or public easements.

In general, the buyer might also be liable for matters relating to the property which occurred before its acquisition. In the event that the property is contaminated or the seller is in arrears with charges, taxes and fees, for example, claims might be brought against the buyer by the respective public authority.

The findings that have been disclosed by the enforced technical, environmental and legal due diligence usually influence the terms and conditions of the sale contract.

5.2 Agreeing terms and binding contracts

As a general rule, the seller or its solicitor respectively provides a first draft of the sale contract to the buyer. The buyer and its solicitor review the seller's draft with special attention to those risks which have been disclosed in the due diligence reports. Disclosed risks are generally covered by guarantees given by the seller in order to do justice to the buyer's interests, provided that these risks cannot be cured in line with the acquisition process or have already been reflected in the purchase price.

Repeated exchange of revised drafts before seller and buyer finally agree on the terms and conditions of the sale contract must be expected. The length of this period of the investment process depends on the complexity of the transaction and the features of the property to be acquired.

The sale contract is effective and valid upon its notarisation before a notary public only. For the purpose of notarisation the seller and the buyer – or their authorised representatives – have to appear before the notary public. Subsequently the notary public is mandated to execute the sale contract as only the notary public is authorised to file applications for transcription of ownership and for the entry of land charges in favour of the buyer's financing bank with the Land Register. The buyer acquires title to the property when the transcription of ownership has been executed so that as a result the buyer is recorded as new owner in the Land Register.

Germany

Notarial fees are based on the purchase price; however, they do not increase proportionally, but on a diminishing scale.

As the sale contract is valid upon its notarisation only, in general during the period of due diligence and negotiation of the terms and conditions of the sale contract both the seller and the buyer are entitled to refrain from the transaction and to negotiate with third parties without being liable to the other party. This normally even applies if the parties agreed on a letter of intent or an exclusivity agreement which often includes the obligation for both parties to maintain discretion and confidentiality with respect to the intended transaction, provided information and the conducted negotiation. As this means in general a 'moral' obligation only, claims for damages in connection with a default of the letter of intent or exclusivity agreement are generally enforceable if and to the extent that a contractual penalty has been agreed only.

When real estate investment in Germany was at its peak in 2006/2007 sellers often did not restrict themselves by negotiating with one interested party only. Rather, competitive bidding proceedings of all interested parties took place and the seller was free to accept one – normally the highest – tender.

Even after its notarisation, the sale contract can be non-binding as it can be concluded subject to a condition precedent. At times the seller, for example, demands the submission of confirmation by the buyer's bank stating that the financing of the transaction is backed.

Furthermore, unless otherwise agreed under the sale contract, the parties are entitled to withdraw from the notarised sale contract if statutory provisions provide for this. This can first of all apply in favour of the seller if the buyer delays with the payment of the purchase price.

5.3 The contract documents

Even if the parties are to a large extent free to agree on the terms and conditions of the sale contract these in principle are relatively standardised. The most important issues for negotiation are in particular the guarantees and warranties the seller gives with respect to the property to be purchased.

The parties do not agree on issues in the sale contract, for which statutory stipulations apply. First of all, this is true for matters of warranties, liability, claims for damages and the right to withdraw. If the seller knowingly and intentionally does not disclose material defects of the property to be purchased or provides for false information, the seller might be liable to the buyer as per statutory regulations on fraudulent intent.

Usually the notarised sale contract refers to an also notarised reference deed including scores of documents pertaining to the property to be purchased such as rent rolls, lease agreements, floor plans, site plans, construction documents etc. These documents become, by reference, part of the sale contract.

5.4 Typical contract terms

The following is a summary of typical sale contract terms:

5.4.1 Purchase price

Usually the buyer conducts an evaluation of the property considering, *inter alia*, its location, attainable rent price, its use and constructional condition.

The purchase price is often calculated on the basis of the annual rent income. Risks that have been disclosed by the legal, technical and environmental due diligence often trigger negotiations on purchase price with the seller provided such risks cannot be cured or otherwise remedied within the acquisition process.

5.4.2 Maturity requirements

The purchase price is in general not payable directly after the notarisation of the sale contract. Rather, the sale contract usually provides for the purchase price to fall due subject to the fulfilment of certain maturity requirements.

As per standard terms the purchase price falls due after the notary public has given notice that at least:
(i) a priority notice of conveyance in favour of the buyer has been entered with the Land Register;
(ii) easements not to be taken over by the buyer have been deleted from the Land Register;
(iii) a negative certification has been issued by the authority and other third parties with regard to pre-emption rights; and
(iv) all documents required for the enforcement of the sale contract have been submitted.

A priority notice of conveyance (*Auflassungsvormerkung*) is an encumbrance registered with the Land Register in order to protect the claim for the transfer of ownership, making dispositions which run counter to this transfer invalid *vis-à-vis* the person in whose favour the priority notice of conveyance has been registered.

A person who has a pre-emption right (*Vorkaufsrecht*) concerning a property may exercise this right as soon as the owner has concluded a sale contract relating to the property with a third party. Upon the exercise of the right, a sale contract between the person entitled and the owner will be concluded, the terms of which will be in accordance with the terms agreed between the third party and the owner.

Further maturity requirements depend on the features of the property to be purchased.

If the parties have a special need of securitisation, the purchase price can be paid to the notary public trust account.

5.4.3 Guarantees and warranty

The extent of the seller giving guarantees and warranties under the sale contract is subject to negotiations between the seller and the buyer. Supplementary statutory regulations may apply.

Standard matters of guarantees and warranties are particularly, but not limited to:
(i) the non-existence of contamination of the site;
(ii) the validity of the lease agreements as well as the compliance of the

lease agreements with the written form requirements;
(iii) the compliance of the erected building with building law;
(iv) the existence of all parking spaces as per statutory requirements;
(v) the non-existence or the content of neighbour agreements being in force;
(vi) the non-existence of easements not registered with the Land Register;
(vii) the non-existence of litigation relating to the property;
(viii) the non-existence of arrears with charges, taxes and fees; and
(ix) the non-existence of material defects of the building.

Objective guarantees are deemed to be the guarantees richest in content. By these the seller guarantees that the purchase object possesses the guaranteed qualities. In the case of subjective guarantees, the guarantee is only subject to the seller's knowledge about the property's qualities. The seller, therefore, is not in any case liable for any discrepancies between the actual condition of the property and its given guarantee but only if it provides false information knowingly and intentionally.

As a basic principle the seller is also liable for matters relating to the property which occurred before its own acquisition.

5.4.4 Right to withdraw
The buyer may reserve its right to withdraw from the sale contract provided that maturity requirements are not fulfilled after a determined time period. Further, the seller is entitled to withdraw from the sale contract provided that the public authority or another third party executes its pre-emption right.

As outlined above, the seller is as per statutory regulations entitled to withdraw from the sale contract if the buyer delays with the payment of the purchase price.

5.4.5 Submission to execution proceedings
As a standard term the buyer submits itself to execution proceedings with regard to its obligation to pay the purchase price and all other costs to be borne by it in connection with the transaction, such as the notary's fees. This submission entitles the seller to enforce against the buyer without prior instituting proceedings against it.

5.5 Managing the property between exchange and completion
Transfer of possession of the property is in general subject to the payment of the full purchase price.

Unless otherwise agreed between the parties, the lease agreements are transferred as per statutory regulations upon transcription of ownership in the Land Register only. The prior transfer of the lease agreements can only be agreed effectively with the tenant's consent. However, from an economic point of view the parties in general agree that the rent income belongs to the buyer from transfer of possession (ie, from payment of the full purchase price).

Insurance policies that are in force with regard to the property are automatically transferred to the buyer whereas the buyer is entitled to terminate the insurance extraordinarily.

5.6 Confidentiality
As set out above, parties at times agree to keep the terms and conditions of the acquisition confidential. In such cases, the purchase price is not entered into the Land Register. The Land Register only states the buyer and the date of transfer of ownership; although the height of the registered land charges may give an indication of the purchase price paid.

5.7 Assignment of the contract
Unless otherwise agreed, the buyer can in general assign the benefit of the sale contract including its claim for transfer of ownership. However, the assignment of all rights and obligations of the buyer is subject to the seller's consent as buyer's obligations may be assigned with the seller's consent only.

6. REAL ESTATE BASICS
Property, ie, a piece of land, in Germany is typically either held by a right *in rem* or by a relative right. Under German law the most important right *in rem* is the freehold (*Eigentum*) which means the ownership of land and building. The following types of freehold exist:
- Sole and co-ownership. Sole ownership offers the owner absolute ownership, unlimited in time, both to the land and buildings/structures on it. 'Absolute' does not mean that the land may be used free from any restriction, however, as planning restrictions may apply.
  Co-ownership is a legal concept where two or more co-owners share the legal ownership of a property.
- Part-ownership and condominium. According to the Condominium and Part Ownership Act (WEG, *Wohnungseigentumsgesetz*) separate ownership of a self-contained unit in a building may be acquired. Condominium ownership (where flats are concerned) or part ownership (where the premises in question are not used for residential purposes) is created by means of a partition declaration (*Teilungserklärung*) that usually refers to a partition plan (*Aufteilungsplan*). The owners form a community. Rights and obligations of each owner and the community are governed by the WEG, but can be modified by community rules (*Gemeinschaftsordnung*).

In addition to the aforesaid types of freehold, there is also a special form of ownership, the hereditary building right (*Erbbaurecht*) which grants the ownership of a building, but only a long-term right to use (not to own) the real property. The hereditary building right, therefore, is an encumbrance upon real property consisting of a transferable and heritable right to build or develop the land above or below the surface. The hereditary building right is recorded in the Land Register. The hereditary building right can be encumbered in the same way as freehold, subject to the hereditary building right contract (*Erbbaurechtsvertrag*). Hereditary building rights are granted for set periods; customary terms are between 30 and 99 years. The holder of the hereditary building right usually pays a ground rent (*Erbbauzins*).

When the hereditary building right expires, ownership of the building passes automatically to the owner of the land whereas the former holder of the hereditary building right usually receives compensation for the building.

Under German law, it is also possible to have a relative right to use a land which is generated by an agreement *inter partes*. The most common types of relative rights are commercial or residential leases which give the tenant a temporary right to use the property in return for payment of rent. A special form of lease agreement (*Pachtvertrag*) – typically used for premises such as restaurants – entitles the tenant also to enjoy the fruits and benefits associated with the property.

Leases can be entered into for an indefinite period or a precisely defined term. With regard to commercial leases, the parties in general agree upon fixed terms and the tenant often has an option right to extend the lease when the fixed term expires. Leases with fixed terms of more than 30 years are uncommon because there is a special termination right for both parties to terminate the lease after a 30-year-term.

Under German law, residential leases are governed mainly by legal provisions that protect the tenant including restrictions on termination rights and rent increases.

6.1 Land registration

Freehold is registered with the Land Register, as it is a register of title and rights, whereas leasehold is not registered with the Land Register. However, the leasehold might be secured *in rem* by way of entry of an easement in favour of the tenant (*Mieterdienstbarkeit*) with the Land Register.

Each acquisition of ownership is preconditioned by the registration of the title with the Land Register. There is a delay between the date of the notarisation of the sale contract/payment of purchase price and the date on which the buyer becomes registered with the Land Register as the owner of the land. However, the buyer's interests during this delay are covered by a priority notice of conveyance since it ensures no competing applications as regards the transfer of ownership. The entry of the aforesaid priority notice of conveyance with the Land Register is one maturity requirement which must be fulfilled before payment of purchase price.

The Land Register applies to a specific district and is kept at the respective local court responsible for the district in question. The Land Register is divided into three sections. In the first section the property is described (district, parcel, size and kind of use) and information on the owner and the type of ownership is given. Further, the date of transfer of ownership and usually also the previous owner are stated in the first section of the Land Register.

The second section of the Land Register provides for information on encumbrances of the property, especially easements such as right of way and right to have and maintain supply circuits on the property as well as pre-emption rights or hereditary building rights.

In the third section of the Land Register, land charges and mortgages are registered and the respective land charge/mortgage amount and the creditors are disclosed.

Greece

V&P Law Firm Eliana Paschalides, Spyros Foulias & Alexandra Mitsokali

1. INVESTMENT PURCHASE OVERVIEW

Indicative investment purchase in Greece

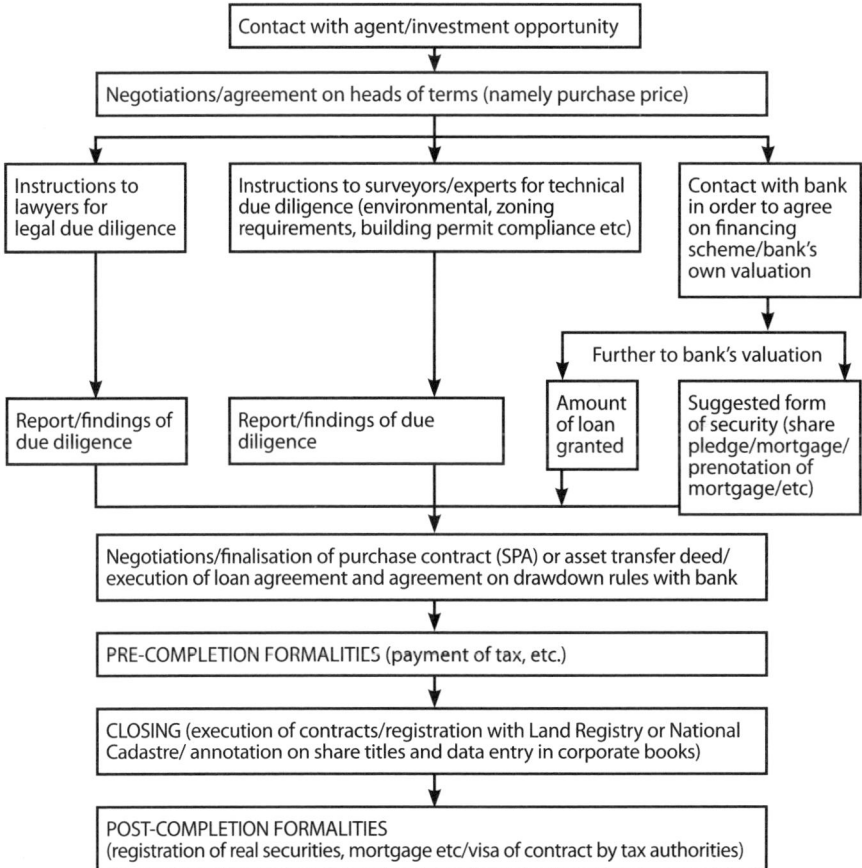

Important note: Time scales for each step differ considerably depending on the particulars of each transaction, thus no typical or indicative timeline can be provided.
Payment of purchase price may be made once off upon closing day or in tranches depending on the satisfaction of conditions precedent

2. TAX CONSIDERATIONS
2.1 Value added tax (VAT)
As of 1 January 2006 a new tax regime has been applicable for the transfer by builders of newly-constructed buildings with a construction permit issued or renewed after 1 January 2006. In particular, such transactions are subject to the applicable VAT (currently at the rate of 21 per cent – likely to be increased to 23 per cent after 1 July 2010). Such tax is due by the constructor (seller) but in practice is always paid by the buyer. The relevant tax obligation is borne and the tax is due at the time of execution of the deed of transfer. There is an exemption for dwellings qualifying as the primary residence of the buyer.

In order for a transfer of real estate to be subject to VAT, the following criteria must be met cumulatively:
- the transferor/seller is a builder (ie, an individual or legal entity that constructs buildings for sale;
- the transfer of the real estate is made for consideration;
- the real estate transferred is a building and not land;
- the relevant construction permit was issued or renewed after 1 January 2006; and
- the building is 'new', ie, transfer takes place before the building has been used for the first time. In case the transfer takes place after the lapse of five years from the date of the issuance of its building permit, then such building is not considered new, thus it is not subject to VAT but to real property transfer tax (transfer tax).

VAT under the above conditions and transfer tax are mutually exclusive.

2.2 Stamp duty/transfer tax
As mentioned above, the transfer of real estate is either subject to VAT or to transfer tax. The latter was reinstated by virtue of recent Law 3842/2010 (passed on April 23), under which the capital gains tax and property transfer duty (imposed on the transfer of property acquired after 1 January 2006) were abolished. Thus, where the acquisition of a property is not subject to VAT, it is subject to transfer tax.

Transfer tax is paid in full before the execution of the relevant notarial deed (transfer deed). The relevant receipt of payment for such tax issued by the tax authority is must be attached to the notarial deed of transfer.

Transfer tax is calculated on the value assessed by the tax authority on the basis of objective criteria or on the transfer value agreed, whichever is higher, and must be paid by the buyer. The tax is levied at the rates of 8 per cent for taxable values up to €20,000 and 10 per cent on any excess.

An additional three per cent municipality tax is also payable, calculated on the amount of the property transfer tax due.

Exemptions from transfer tax (in part or in full) are provided under certain circumstances. It should also be noted that an exemption from the obligation to pay transfer tax may be obtained for the purchase of a 'primary' residence for the first time (there are additional criteria for this exemption, which are aimed at providing tax relief to low income families). Under Law 3842/2010

Greece

the exemption from transfer tax no longer depends on the size of the real estate but on the value of the property. The relevant exemption is available to EU citizens as well as to citizens of non-EU countries under certain conditions.

2.3 Tax issues for overseas investors investing in real estate
2.3.1 Offshore entities
Properties owned by offshore entities are subject to special annual real property tax which under Law 3842/2010 (and effective from 1 January 2010) is levied at the rate 15 per cent on the taxable value of such properties (increased from three per cent under the previous regime). This tax is extended to types of foreign legal entities which are not recognised under Greek law, such as trusts.

Under the above law an exemption from the tax may be obtained (under certain circumstances) by EU companies if disclosure of the shareholders/partners etc of such entity up to individual level is made, provided also that the shareholders/partners/etc obtain a Greek tax identification number.

Furthermore, for transfer of properties owned by offshore legal entities to individuals taxable in Greece made within a specific period (six months from the publication of the law tax incentives) exemption from the special annual real property tax (as well as exemption from 50 per cent of the abovementioned transfer tax) is available.

2.3.2 Annual real property tax
All legal entities or individuals owing real estate in Greece (with the exception of non-urban land and forests) must pay a new annual real property tax on any property right in Greece introduced by Law 3842/2010 (the annual real property duty as provided under the previous tax legislation was abolished), levied as at 1 January of every year.

For individuals, the tax is levied on the basis of a progressive scale commencing with tax at zero per cent for the first €400,000 and up to maximum tax at one per cent on the total property value. Exceptionally, for the three years 2010, 2011 and 2012, the tax rate for property value in excess of EUR 5,000,000 is 2 per cent.

For legal entities there are two tax rates – 0.1 per cent for self-occupied property and 0.6 per cent for other property. The tax cannot be lower than €1 per square metre. The tax is levied on the taxable value used for other property taxes ('objective value'). A tax return must be filed by 15 May (exceptionally for the current year by 15 June). The tax is payable in three instalments.

2.3.3 International conventions for the avoidance of double taxation
Greece is a party to a number of bilateral and multilateral (OECD type) conventions for the avoidance of double taxation. In principle, such conventions provide that if the resident of a contracting state to such conventions acquires income arising out of the direct use, letting or other form of exploitation of real estate in another contracting state, this income may be taxed only in the other state.

Greece

3. INVESTMENT VEHICLE CHOICE
3.1 Structures used to purchase property
Property investors in Greece can purchase property either directly – in which case the acquisition is subject to transfer tax or VAT as above – or through a company – in which case the transaction is subject to income tax as described below.

Institutional investors (such as funds) generally use Greek special purpose vehicles (SPVs) for the acquisition of Greek property. The new trend is for investors to use real estate investment companies (REICs) (see below).

3.1.1 Most common investment vehicles
In practice the forms of Greek companies usually used for investment are the corporation (*société anonyme*, SA) and the limited liability company (LLC, EPE) the main characteristics of which are the following:

Corporation
The minimum share capital of an SA is set at €60,000 divided into shares, which can be either to the bearer or registered.

The transfer of shares not listed on the Athens Exchange is subject to tax at a rate of five per cent on the sale price, normally burdening the seller. The transfer of unlisted shares is made either through written agreement filed at the Tax Office or through a notarial deed.

The corporation is managed by a board of directors of at least three members (that can be either natural persons or legal entities), while the supreme organ is always the general meeting of shareholders, which can appoint and revoke directors at any time.

There are no restrictions on the nationality or residence of shareholders or of directors, except that the managing director is normally required to be a Greek resident, and if they are a non-EU national they will need a work and residence permit.

Corporations are subject to an annual ordinary audit by auditors, the number and capacity of whom depends on the size of the corporation, according to the specific criteria (total amount of balance sheet, net turnover and number of employees) that are set out by the law.

Every voting share gives the right to one vote in the general meetings of shareholders and certain minorities have rights prescribed by law, which cannot be abolished by the articles of incorporation. However, the holder of a majority of 50 per cent plus one vote has control of the management of the corporation, but certain decisions require a higher majority, usually two-thirds of the votes. Such decisions are either provided by law (eg, increase of the share capital) or must be described specifically in the articles of incorporation.

Limited liability company (EPE)
These companies require at least two partners (with the exception of the 'sole-partner EPE'). Their capital, set at a minimum of €4,500 is divided into 'parts' (with a minimum value of €30 each) that cannot be represented by any transferable instrument or certificate. Each partner may have one or

more parts, which form its portion of participation in the company.

Any transfer of parts, as well as any other amendment of the articles, requires a notarial deed. The transfer of parts is subject to capital gains tax at a rate of 20 per cent.

The EPE is managed by one or more administrators and the partners must meet at least once a year or whenever the administrator(s) or a specific minority requests a meeting.

The procedure and requirements for formation, such as the compulsory tax registration in Greece of all partners, whether Greek or foreign, natural persons or legal entities, and their compulsory registration with social security funds, mean that this type of company is not always suitable for large enterprises, especially for foreign investors.

Taxation of the above corporate structures

Under the provisions of Law 3842/2010, profits of Greek companies arising from financial statements drafted from 31 December 2010 onwards will be taxed as follows. Corporations will be subject to corporate tax on their retained (non-distributed) profits, currently at the rate of 24 per cent, which will be gradually reduced until 2014 to reach the rate of 20 per cent, as well as on their distributed profits at the rate of 40 per cent. The above corporate tax does not exhaust the tax liability of the shareholders with respect to their dividends. Retained profits of previous accounting periods can be distributed until 31 December 2010 without this new 40 per cent tax. In addition, the share capital of the corporation is subject to a capital tax of one per cent.

The retained profits of an EPE will be also taxed at the rate of 24 per cent, which will be reduced to 20 per cent until 2014, while distributed profits will be taxed at 40 per cent. Again, retained profits of previous accounting periods can be distributed until 31 December 2010 without this new 40 per cent tax.

3.2 Restrictions on foreign ownership or occupation of property

In principle there are no legal restrictions on foreign acquisition of property, whether acquisition is by an individual or legal entity. However, different permissions and formalities are required in connection with the purchase of property and construction of buildings in designated 'border areas'. Restrictions are far stricter for non-EU nationals, and apply not only to the purchase of property, but also the acquisition of shares in a company owning property in such areas.

In particular, pursuant to Law 1892/1990 (as in force), certain formalities need to be observed prior to transfer of real property in certain areas of Greece (characterised as 'border areas'), either by way of an asset or by way of a share deal. These formalities are not required in the event the acquiring person or entity is an EU national.

Furthermore, the Supreme Court Decision 425/1983 (*in plenum*) has ruled that the nationality of a legal entity, for the purposes of the above provisions, is determined by the nationality of the persons exercising controlling power over the entity concerned, in light of a number of criteria including management, shareholding participation and origin of capital. Presumably the controlling person/entity may have to be identified at a higher tier (especially if the direct shareholders of the owning company and of any intermediate companies are SPVs).

3.3 Real estate investment trusts (REITs)
At the outset, it should be noted that a trust is not a corporate formation recognised under Greek law. The equivalent of REITs in Greece are REICs. The operation of such companies is regulated by Law 2778/1999 (as amended and in force) in combination with the Codified Law on SAs and the Regulations of the Hellenic Capital Market Commission. REICs are special purpose companies under the legal form of an AE (corporation, *Société Anonyme*), which engage exclusively in property investments. REICs constitute a new corporate vehicle which was introduced in 1999 to provide for a new corporate and tax framework through which to develop Greece's property market. The share capital of such companies amounts to a minimum of €29,350,000 and their shares are listed on the Athens Exchange. REICs are obliged under the law to distribute at least 35 per cent of their annual net profits to their shareholders.

REICs are subject to a favourable tax regime. Their tax obligation, in general, is equal to 10 per cent of the rate of the Central European Bank increased by one per cent on the average of its investments, which is considerably low if one considers that the profits of a common corporation letting real estate would be taxed at a much higher rate even under the current regime where retained profits are taxed at 24 per cent (the tax rate is gradually decreased by one per cent per year to reach 20 per cent for accounting periods commencing after 1 January 2014). In addition, the shares in REICs and the real estate acquired by REICs are exempt from any tax, duty, contribution, etc. Such exemption is not applied to the transfer of real estate from REICs to third parties. In addition, REICs are exempt from income tax for income arising from any kind of securities acquired (domestic or foreign).

REICs may acquire real estate which can be immediately used as business premises or for any other commercial or industrial purpose. Real estate acquired by REICs may not be further transferred before the lapse of one year. The commercial value of the property owned by REICs must be evaluated by the Greek body of sworn-in valuers using a specific method of evaluation. Real property belonging to REICs must be evaluated semi-annually. Any acquisition or sale of real property by REICs cannot deviate from such evaluation at a percentage below or in excess of five per cent.

Although REICs are treated favourably from a tax point of view, they were not often used in practice for various reasons including the tax imposed under the previous tax legislation on the contributed real estate.

4. FINANCING AN ACQUISITION
4.1 Financing of corporate real estate transactions and real estate as a means of raising finance
4.1.1 Bank loans
The most common way to finance a real estate transaction is through a bank

loan. Individuals apply for housing loans which finance the acquisition of a dwelling or other real estate either to be used by the owner itself or as an investment. Such financing may cover up to the total amount of the value of the real estate as well as that of the expenses of the acquisition process (transfer taxes, notary's fees, legal fess, etc) and is usually secured by a pre-notation of mortgage.

Corporations may also use bank loans in order to acquire land or buildings for professional use or as an investment. Again the bank will normally request the registration of a pre-notation of mortgage over the property.

Other means of financing corporate real estate transactions are outlined below.

4.1.2 Securitisation under Law 3156/2003
This form of securitisation (real estate securities) is provided for under Article 11 of Law 3156/2003, and enables the transfer of real estate located in Greece to an SPV (seated in Greece) which issues bonds in relation to the securitisation of such real estate.

In this case real estate is sold and transferred by means of a written contract between seller and purchaser in combination with the issuance and distribution (only by private placement) of bonds of any kind (with a par value of at least €100,000 each), the repayment of which is made either from the income generated by their management or sale as per the above or by loans, credit facilities or derivatives. Summary of the written contract regarding the real estate sale agreement must be registered with the competent Land Registry.

In principle, exploitation of the property is made through the letting of the property to the original owner (and seller) of the property, that raises funds from the securitisation but also retains use of the property as lessee. It is evident from the above that this form of securitisation has a lot of similarities with factoring agreements as well as sale and lease back agreements, because in this case the company seeking financing through the securitisation process transfers to an SPV real rights over its real property (either ownership or usufruct). This way the funds corresponding to the purchase price are raised by the bondholders/lenders while the bonds issued will be repaid from the commercial exploitation of the real estate.

4.1.3 Leasing
Leasing was introduced in Greek practice under laws 1665/86 (as amended an in force). Leasing as a form of financing is addressed to professionals and corporations of any kind wishing to acquire real estate or movable assets for professional use. Thus, one can acquire by means of leasing (for professional use only) plots of land with buildings (including horizontal or other ownership, but excluding plots of land without buildings) as well as agricultural plots of land. According to the relevant legislation only special purpose companies ie, leasing companies, or credit institutions may undertake this kind of activity.

In particular the leasing of real estate involves the following steps: the corporation or professional (lessee) indicates to the leasing company the real estate of its choice for the purpose of acquiring the means to finance its acquisition by the seller, in accordance with the terms and conditions it has already agreed. Consequently a notarial deed of transfer is executed between the seller and the leasing company as well as a notarial deed of leasing between the leasing company and the lessee that regulates their relationship including the regular rental payments of the lessee for a period of time agreed in advance (leasing period) which cannot be less than 10 years. At the expiration of the leasing the leasing company transfers to the lessee the ownership over the property against the agreed consideration (usually a small amount), and is exempt from transfer tax.

This form of finance is usually selected for tax reasons (ie, the rentals are considered as expenses deductible from the taxed income, favourable VAT treatment) as well as for practical reasons (eg, for maintaining cash liquidity). Usually professionals selecting to acquire real estate by means of leasing may acquire financing covering the total value of the property.

It should be noted that, with regard to the leasing of real estate, where restrictions are imposed by the applicable legislation on the nationality of the owner of real estate, such restrictions are considered with reference to the nationality of the lessee of the real estate.

4.1.4 Real estate sale and lease back
Real estate sale and lease back is a special type of leasing agreement, by means of which a corporation sells its real estate to a leasing company and then the latter leases this real estate to the same corporation (original seller). After the expiration/repayment of the sale and lease back agreement, the real estate is re-transferred to the ownership of the corporation that sold the real estate in the first place/lessee, without having to pay any transfer tax.

Sale and lease back is subject to the same above legislation regulating leasing agreements in general, but it is addressed only to legal entities and not individuals.

It is in fact a method of refinancing using the fixed assets owned by a corporation. More specifically, a corporation that owns real estate the value of which has been amortised or is considerably low in comparison with its current commercial value, may opt for real estate sale and lease back in order to secure its cash liquidity as well as for many other reasons (mainly accounting), without being deprived of the use of such real estate, which will eventually return to its ownership.

4.2 Common forms of security granted over real estate
The following forms of security over real estate are available under Greek law.

4.2.1 Mortgage
Mortgage is a limited real right over another person's property granted for the purpose of securing an obligation (eg, repayment of a loan), by means of preferential satisfaction of the creditor from the value of such property. Mortgage can be granted also in favour of a future or conditional claim. It

can only be granted over real estate which can be sold out as well as over the usufruct of such real estate.

Mortgage over property is granted by virtue of the following: (i) under the law; (ii) under a court decision; or (iii) by contract.

For the purpose of raising finance, a mortgage will be normally granted by the owner/usufructuary of the property in favour of the lender by virtue of a relevant notarial deed for the granting of such security. A certified copy of the deed must then be registered with the respective Land Registry or Cadastre Office. The granting of a mortgage exists over a real estate from the time that such right has been duly recorded in the special books (Books of Mortgages) kept by the competent Land Registry and are filed with the relevant National Cadastre, as the case may be.

Ranking between mortgages over the same real estate is defined by the chronological order between such mortgages with the earlier prevailing over the latter. This means that the lender can protect itself by having registered a higher ranking mortgage over the borrower's property, namely by registering its mortgage before other creditors. In this way no other creditors can have a prior claim over the property. Mortgages registered on the same day have the same ranking and are satisfied *pro rata*.

If a mortgage has been registered over a plot of land then it is automatically extended to the building (or horizontal properties) erected on such land, unless the borrower and lender agree otherwise in a subsequent notarial deed.

4.2.2 Pre-notation of mortgage (ie, conditional mortgage)
For the protection of a lender who has not yet acquired a court-enforceable title, the law provides for the granting of a 'pre-notation' of a mortgage over real property. A pre-notation of mortgage may be created by virtue of the following:
- issuance of a court decision further to the injunctive measures procedure;
- issuance of a final judgment of the first instance court; or
- issuance of a payment order.

The registration of a pre-notation of a mortgage over real estate grants to the lender an expectation to acquire a mortgage, in other words, it is a conditional mortgage. If the pre-notation of the mortgage is not converted within a specific time period into a mortgage then it does not grant to the lender any preferential rights over the property. The time period for the conversion of a pre-notation of mortgage into a mortgage is 90 days from the final adjudication of the claim.

The pre-notation of a mortgage must be registered in the Books of Mortgages kept by Land Registries, or filed with the National Cadastre, as applicable, in order to perfect the granting of the relevant security.

4.3 Real estate mortgage securitisation
Securitisation appeared in Greece and was consecrated by the Law 3156/2003. It is a new form of financing with many advantages and favourable terms but as every institution, it also has deficiencies that create

Greece

severe problems as it grows. In particular, the securitisation of claims secured by mortgage over property (mortgage-backed securities) usually includes housing loans to consumers but also business loans the repayment of which is secured by a mortgage over real estate.

The law provides that issuance of such securities is made by an SPV which is the issuer of the securities. This intervention of the SPV ensures the separation (from a legal and a financial point of view) of the claims secured on the remainder of the assets of the seller company (usually a bank) and also has as a consequence that the repayment of the securities issued is made only from this distinct group of assets that has been separated and securitised.

This securitisation is distinct from real estate securities, which is a form of securitisation provided for under Law 3156/2003 (Article 11). In this case a sale and transfer of real estate (and not of claims as is the case for mortgage-backed securities) is effected by means of a written contract between seller and purchaser in combination with the issuance and distribution (only by private placement) of bonds of any kind. This securitisation has a lot of similarities with factoring agreements as well as sale and lease back agreements, because in this case the company seeking financing through the securitisation transfers to an SPV real rights over its real property (either ownership or usufruct). This way the funds corresponding to the purchase price are raised by the bondholders/lenders while the bonds issued will be repaid from the commercial exploitation of the real estate. In principle, exploitation of the property is made through the letting of the property to the original owner (and seller) of the property, which raises funds from the securitisation but also retains use of the property as lessee.

5. MANAGING THE ACQUISITION PROCESS
5.1 Minimum formalities for the sale and purchase of property

The process of acquisition differs depending on whether it is made by means of an asset deal (by direct acquisition of the property) or a share deal (purchase of the corporate vehicle which owns the property). The answers below are based on the assumption of an asset deal, namely the acquisition of property.

In Greece, the acquisition process usually commences when agents indicate business opportunities to the parties. Although use of agents is not compulsory by law, agents are being increasingly used, especially for property deals involving commercial/business properties. As soon as the main heads of terms are agreed between the parties, it is common practice that the buyer will undertake and conduct due diligence of the property (while for a share deal, a full 'corporate' legal due diligence will have to be conducted as well).

The types of searches carried out will depend on the location and actual or proposed use of the property.

The main (legal) due diligence of property is carried out by means of an on-the-spot examination of titles of ownership kept at the relevant Land Registry (and/or by examination of the relevant Cadastre issue of the relevant office of the National Cadastre, as applicable). Such legal examination will enable the buyer to ascertain whether the titles of ownership are in order and whether

Greece

any encumbrances (mortgages/seizures) or claims are recorded against the property.

Buyers must also obtain (where applicable) proof that the property has obtained the required construction permits from the local authority (the relevant office of the Urban Planning Authority) and ensure compliance of any constructions with it, confirmation by the local forest authority that the property is not considered a forest area and in general, compliance with urban planning legislation, zoning requirements and requirements governing permitted use of land. Environmental searches (where applicable) are also increasingly important.

Buyers are often assisted by civil engineers/external surveyors in conducting the above 'technical' due diligence and obtaining the above confirmation/information.

Further to the completion of the due diligence process, the parties will instruct their lawyers to proceed and draft the contract of sale of property. In practice, a contract of sale of property is to large extent standardised and mainly prepared by the notary public. The role of lawyers is significantly increased in share deals (purchase of the corporate vehicle that owns the property), in which case lawyers will usually negotiate extensively the relevant contractual clauses and draft the share purchase agreement and other relevant documentation.

Usually before signing, the seller will be required to discharge the property from any burden/encumbrance (eg, mortgage securing a debt) and sell the property to the buyer free of encumbrances.

For a contract for the sale of an interest in property to be valid, Greek law requires that: it must be made in writing and notarised; it must be signed by or on behalf of each party; and it (the notarial deed) must be duly registered with the Land Registry or filed with the National Cadastre, as applicable.

It should be noted that various other subsidiary documents are required to be produced before the Notary Public and attached to the notarial deed (such as the seller's tax clearance, solemn declarations, certificates etc), including the receipt issued by the competent tax office evidencing that transfer tax obligations have been fulfilled prior to the execution of the notarial deed.

5.2 Main legal documents required to transfer a property or grant a lease?

As mentioned above, the main legal documents are:
- (for the purchase of property), the purchase and sale contract, to be executed by the parties before a Notary Public, which must then be registered with the Land Registry or filed with the National Cadastre; or
- (for the grant of a lease), the lease agreement, to be executed by both parties. Usually lease agreements are not notarised. Exceptionally, leases having a term of more than nine years may be notarised and registered with the Land Registry, in order for such leases to be opposable and the lessee to be protected *vis-à-vis* any new owner of the property.

Greece

5.3 Property transaction costs
The buyer typically pays:
- the notarial fees and legal costs (notarial proportional fees amount to approximately one per cent of the value of the property mentioned in the notarised act);
- the Land Registry registration fees or Cadastre filing fees (0.475 per cent and 0.575 per cent of the value of the property respectively);
- the transfer tax obligations (see above); and
- its agent's fees (where applicable).

The seller typically pays:
- its own legal costs;
- costs of preparing certificates of title for the property (if applicable); and
- its agent's fees (where applicable).

Allocation of costs may differ in the case of a share deal, where eg, the share transfer tax is, in principle, to be borne by the seller and not by the buyer (see above).

5.4 Does the seller warrant its ownership of the property?
The seller of ownership usually declares, represents and warrants expressly in the contract of sale that it has valid title of ownership of the property to be transferred and that such property is free of charges, encumbrances and third party claims, defects, leases (otherwise it assigns such rights to the buyer) and liabilities.

5.5 Warranties a seller usually gives to a buyer
In addition to warranties as to the title of ownership and existence or non-existence of third party rights and encumbrances (easements/mortgages/seizures/claims) over the property, the seller might warrant the accuracy of pre-contract information supplied to the buyer during the due diligence process. Warranties may also extend to compliance with specific regulatory requirements and legislation, such as environmental legislation, archaeological legislation, zone planning legislation, and building regulations.

In the case of a portfolio sale, which is most commonly made through a share deal, the seller will usually also provide corporate representations and warranties regarding the legal status of the company (articles of association, certificate of good standing etc) along with title-related warranties.

5.6 Purpose of warranties in the purchase agreement
Warranties in the purchase agreement are mainly intended to apportion the risk. Information will mainly be provided to the buyer in the context of the due diligence process (both legal and technical). Usually two methods of due diligence can be used for acquisitions of large portfolios of properties:
- the buyer may conduct its own full due diligence and receive the standard warranties in the sale agreement; or
- the buyer may conduct limited due diligence and obtain full warranties from the seller.

Greece

The extent of due diligence and respective warranties will generally depend on the commercial agreement as to which party is going to bear risks and meet the cost of conducting the due diligence.

In practice buyers almost always conduct full legal due diligence of the properties and tend to rely less on seller's representations and warranties, at least with regard to the legal status of the properties. Moreover, buyers are always advised to request a complete set of official certificates pertaining to the property in question, issued by the Land Registry and/or the National Cadastre and evidencing its legal status.

5.7 Owners/occupiers' liability for matters relating to the property which occurred before they bought or occupied

Although exceptional, there are circumstances in which buyers may become liable even for matters related to property before they acquired it. By way of example we can mention town planning burdens and tax burdens (*in rem* obligations) which affect the property and burden the owner – each time – of the property in question. The same applies in principle with environmental liabilities which burden the owner – each time – of the property in question.

Moreover (for share deals), in certain circumstances (governed by specific statutes) the managing director and other officers of an SA may be liable for tax obligations or obligations towards the social security fund regardless of the time such obligations arose. Always in the same context (share deals), in the case of corporate mergers, all liabilities of a company are to be inherited by the new entity, including tax, social security and environmental liabilities.

5.8 Notarisation

Under Greek law a deed of sale and purchase of property must be notarised. So must any preliminary agreement with the same subject matter.

5.9 Formalities for a contract becoming a legally binding obligation

In order for a contract to become a legally binding obligation, this must be drawn up in writing, embodied in one single written notarised deed, duly signed by both seller and buyer, by their lawyers and by the notary public.

Thereafter, such notarised deeds must be registered with the National Cadastre or Land Registry, as each time applicable, in order for the transfer of property rights in question to be completed.

5.10 Point at which parties become legally bound

Once the contract is signed by both parties, it creates a binding contract between them, after which neither party will ordinarily be able to withdraw from the transaction without incurring liability for breach of contract.

5.11 Transfer of title

Legal title is passed to the buyer once the notarised deed has been duly registered with the Land Registry/duly filed with the National Cadastre.

5.12 Insurance of the property if there is delay between agreeing terms and actual sale

As mentioned above, legal title to the property is passed to the buyer upon registration of the transfer with the Land Registry or National Cadastre. Therefore, until such registration, which concludes actual sale of the property, the seller bears the risk of the property and is the one to insure such property.

6. REAL ESTATE BASICS

6.1 Main sources of laws that govern real estate

Book III of the Greek Civil Code on Real Property Law (Articles 947 to 1345) sets out the basic principles and governs the majority of Greek property law matters, while more specialist statutes govern specific areas of property law (eg, Law 3741/1929 and Legislative Decree 1024/1971 on horizontal and vertical division of ownership respectively, Laws 2308/1995, 2664/1998, 3481/2006 etc on issues relating to the National Cadastre etc).

Case law plays an increasingly important role both in interpreting the provisions of the Greek Civil Code and the above special legislation.

6.2 Types of tenure

The main type of tenure is ownership. The following types of ownership exist:
- absolute ownership of property;
- co-ownership of property; and
- horizontal/vertical divisions of ownership (having features from both absolute ownership and co-ownership). By way of example, where property belongs to several persons in undivided shares (co-ownership), by virtue of a notarised act of 'establishment of horizontal properties', a development built on co-owned land may be split into independent units (horizontal properties). Each former co-owner of the land becomes the absolute owner of the unit and the common parts are owned by a commonhold association which is made up of the unit holders. Each unit holder has absolute ownership over the unit (horizontal property) and a percentage of co-ownership over the land.

Apart from ownership, other types of tenure include:
- Leasehold: by virtue of a lease contract/tenancy agreement, the lessee/tenant may make use of the leased property. Leases may be either commercial (business) or residential. Specific statutes govern each of the above types of lease. What stands out is the *ex lege* minimum 12-year duration of all commercial/business leases under Greek law.
- Usufruct: the 'usufructuary' may be granted by the owner of property the right to enjoy, use and exploit the property for a period of time. Usually usufruct is granted by one individual to another, most commonly between members of a family, and the relevant right of usufruct ceases upon decease of the usufructuary, whereby full ownership is recovered by the initial owner/grantor of the right of usufruct.

- Right of occupancy: right to reside in someone else's property (of minor practical importance).

6.3 Must land be registered?
All real property must be registered under Greek law. Registration of all real property in Greece has been undertaken by the National Cadastre Organisation. Given that Greece has been subject to a system of land registration only since 1995, a significant portion of land remains unregistered.

6.4 Public land register
Publicity of property rights is currently ensured by two systems, the National Cadastre and the local Land Registry (so-called Mortgage Registry).

As mentioned above, property – as such – is registered in Greece only with the National Cadastre. The National Cadastre aims at providing a registry 'per property' and every plot of land is intended to have its own 'identity', a 12-digit serial number, while the local Land Registries (gradually being replaced by the National Cadastre) provide a registry of 'title of ownership' (ie, a registry per owner) and enable the searcher to trace property only through the name of its owner. Accordingly, where the National Cadastre system is implemented, one can complete a legal check by identifying the property and on the relevant pages the searcher will be able to have a fair idea of all rights, encumbrances, seizures, claims etc that burden such property. On the other hand, a searcher in a Land Registry will have to run the index of persons (owners), trace their share of transactions, then look into the books of mortgages, seizures and claims, in order to be sure of the legal status of one specific property.

6.5 Land not covered by a public land register
Yet, in Greece there still exist significant portions of private land – especially in non-urban areas – which are not covered by either the National Cadastre (not in place in such areas) or by the Land Registries (in case no recordable transaction has occurred or in case transfers of ownership have been made orally/informally, which is common in the Greek countryside). In these cases, ownership may only be evidenced by means of extraordinary usucapio, which is the equivalent of 'acquisitive prescription' (adverse possession), under the proviso that the person is able to show that they have been in possession of the property for an uninterrupted period of 20 years. Following full implementation of the National Cadastre throughout Greece, the practical importance of usucapio will be significantly reduced.

6.6 State guarantee of title and categories of documents and information
Under Greek law there is no *stricto sensu* 'state guarantee of title'. However, one who relied on official certificates issued by the Land Registries or the National Cadastre which have errors and who suffered losses may – in certain circumstances – sue either the registrar (and eventually trigger also

the state's civil liability) or the Greek state respectively and claim damages.

Under Greek law, it is compulsory to register with the Land Registry or file with the National Cadastre, as applicable, all acts which bring about changes (creation, transfer, alteration or abolition) to the rights of ownership and easements over property, such as:
- transfer of ownership of property whether by sale, gift or court order;
- notarised acceptance of inheritance, where this includes real property;
- expropriation of property by the state; and
- grant of a lease of nine years or more, in order for such lease to be opposable and the lessee to be protected *vis-a-vis* the new owner of the property.

Moreover, encumbrances over real property are also subject to registration, such as:
- grants of a mortgage or of a pre-notation of mortgage are recorded in special books kept by the competent Land Registry and are filed with the relevant National Cadastre;
- orders of seizure of property are recorded in the Books of Seizures kept by the competent Land Registry and are filed with the relevant National Cadastre; and
- lawsuits on real property rights and judicial claims over property are also recorded in special books (Books of Claims) kept by the competent Land Registry and are now filed with the relevant National Cadastre.

Guernsey

Collas Day Aimee Curzon & Paul Nettleship

1. INVESTMENT PURCHASE OVERVIEW

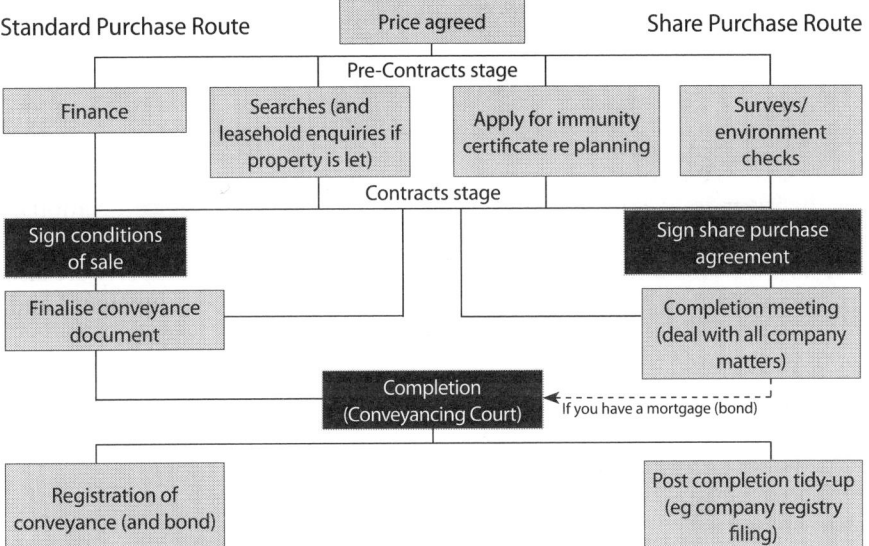

2. TAX CONSIDERATIONS

2.1 Value added tax (VAT)
There is no liability for VAT in Guernsey. Although there is currently no sales tax levied in Guernsey, it is foreseeable that this may be introduced in the future.

Owners of property in Guernsey are liable to pay an annual fee for Tax on Real Property (TRP). This is based on the unit value of the property, related to the property's size. TRP is charged at a higher rate for commercial premises than for residential. As TRP is paid annually, the figure will be apportioned between the parties upon completion. There are currently no exemptions.

2.2 Stamp duty/transfer tax
Stamp Duty (or 'document duty' as it is called in Guernsey) is payable by the purchaser upon a conveyance of a property. The rates are as follows:

For land with dwellings:
£1 to £150,000: two per cent

£150,001 to £250,000: 2.5 per cent
£250,001 and above: three per cent.
For land with no dwellings: three per cent

There are also certain exceptions, for example a conveyance of a life enjoyment will be capped at £5.

If the property is owned by a company, duty can be mitigated 100 per cent if the shares in the company are purchased, rather than the property itself, as there is no document duty applicable on a transfer of shares.

Duty at the rate of 0.5 per cent of the secured sum is payable on a mortgage.

2.3 Tax issues for overseas investors investing in real estate

As an international finance centre, Guernsey has many tax advantages, making it a popular choice for corporate entities and investors alike. There are no capital gains, inheritance or value added taxes.

The year of charge for Guernsey income tax is 1 January to 31 December. Income tax is capped at a 20 per cent rate for individuals and a 'Zero-10' regime is applicable for companies, whereby a zero per cent flat rate charge on a company's income applies, except for several circumstances where a 10 per cent rate is charged, although this is currently being reviewed and may change in the near future.

One of the main exceptions to the Zero-10 regime is that property-holding companies are subject to a 20 per cent tax rate.

Similarly, a company's profits which arise from property development and exploitation of land in Guernsey are also charged at 20 per cent. This includes, for example, income which is derived from the extraction and subsequent sale of solid materials. This is irrespective of the residence status of the company's shareholders.

Indirect investment in UK real estate through a Guernsey vehicle can significantly reduce or indeed remove completely any liability to UK tax and duties. A transfer of shares in a holding company will not attract stamp duty liability. This also applies to transfers of interests in unit trusts.

Non-resident corporate vehicles investing in UK property are only charged a 22 per cent rate for income tax. If the investment vehicle is a limited partnership, the partners themselves will be liable. VAT will only be applicable if, on a sale, the vendor elects the UK property into the VAT regime. Of course, the investment vehicle may be structured so that such costs are borne by the investors.

3. INVESTMENT VEHICLE CHOICE
3.1 Structures used to purchase property

As a leading financial centre, Guernsey attracts a high number of investors. It is both legislatively and fiscally independent, and offers a number of tax advantages.

With an excellent reputation in the regulatory and funds market, Guernsey funds have been promoted in over 38 countries, the Organisation for Economic Co-operation and Development (OECD) declaring Guernsey to be a white-list jurisdiction (in that it has substantially implemented internationally-agreed tax standards).

Due to the many advantages Guernsey offers, and with close links to the UK, political stability and heightened regulation, property investment is a key asset class for the island. Commercial property is a key element of Guernsey's economy, being a large and important area of several industries. As such, Guernsey vehicles are often used for investment purposes.

Most residential property is purchased directly by individuals. However a number of properties on the open market (see below) are owned by special purpose vehicles. By purchasing the shares in a property-holding company, the purchaser does not need to attend court (unless they require a mortgage) to complete the sale, nor will most incur stamp duty. Therefore a practice has evolved whereby a high value property (as open market properties are) is placed into a company, whose only asset will be the property.

The main real estate holding structures used are limited companies, limited partnerships, and unit trusts (although other structures can also be used). These may all be established as investment funds, which can be listed on The Channel Islands Stock Exchange, a recognised and approved exchange, and there are no minimum asset requirements for listing, thus providing a wider investment base and readily accessible choice for investors.

3.1.1 Limited companies

In this context, these are also commonly referred to as special purpose vehicles. This is a popular and commonly used vehicle as the asset or assets which the investors are interested in are already held by the company, for example, a portfolio of properties in a property-holding company.

The Companies (Guernsey) Law 2008 simplifies and consolidates many corporate processes in Guernsey, and governs companies incorporated (and indeed migrated into) Guernsey, and is largely modelled on the English Companies Act. Online formation is available on either a 24 hour, two hour or 15 minute basis. There is a requirement for only one shareholder and a minimum of one director. A company need not have a secretary. However, in the absence of one, a director must fulfil such duties.

It is also possible to incorporate companies limited by guarantee. These do not have share capital. Instead, members guarantee to contribute a set amount into the company upon its winding up. Such additional structures provide investors with a greater choice of vehicle in which to invest.

Guernsey allows for a company to be registered in another jurisdiction and to be re-registered as a Guernsey company. This is known as migration. There have been many companies de-registering from their original jurisdictions and migrating into Guernsey to take advantage of the many benefits Guernsey offers. For example, a UK property-holding company could 'uproot' to Guernsey, thus saving on tax liabilities for both the company itself and its investors.

As well as tax advantages – most Guernsey companies paying a standard zero per cent rate for income tax purposes – an attractive option for investment funds is the ability for companies to issue redeemable shares (although the issue of bearer shares is prohibited), and shares can be issued at a premium. Share capital can be converted into any currency. Also, companies are not required to have, or indeed state, a fixed authorised share capital.

3.1.2 Incorporated cell and protected cell companies

Guernsey's law is also able to facilitate the incorporation of incorporated cell companies (ICC) and protected cell companies (PCC). These too are governed by The Companies (Guernsey) Law 2008.

A PCC is a single legal entity with distinct cells which can have their own assets and liabilities. ICCs are similar. However, each cell of an ICC is in itself a separate legal entity. These can be particularly useful structures for investment, with each cell holding a different asset class. For example, an ICC may have three separate cells holding art, property and gold. This provides investors the opportunity to invest into different asset classes within the same structure, each cell having separate and distinct liability, which offers investors the opportunity to spread their investment risk.

3.1.3 Limited partnerships

Governed by the Limited Partnerships (Guernsey) Law 1995, a limited partnership must have at least one general partner, who is responsible for the management of the partnership, and at least one limited partner (limited partners investing in the partnership but not undertaking a management role). The general partners are jointly and severally liable for all partnership debts. Limited partners, on the other hand, are only liable up to the contribution they have made, or have agreed to make, into the partnership.

There are no restrictions on the number of limited partners, whose identity need not be disclosed on any public registers.

Limited partnerships are a popular choice as a property-holding structure. They are 'see-through' for tax purposes in that the individual partners are liable to tax. In other words, the limited partnership itself will not be subject to a separate assessment for income tax.

There is no requirement for a limited partnership to be audited, unless the general partners elect otherwise (there are several circumstances in which this applies). The partnership is required to have a written partnership agreement, which is binding on all partners, and a registered office in Guernsey. It must also appear on the Register of Limited Partnerships.

It is possible to be both a general partner and a limited partner, and this can be a corporate body. Limited partners are able to lend money to and borrow money from the partnership. It is also possible for limited partners to assign, either in whole or part, their partnership interest, providing investors with the opportunity of a transferable interest.

Limited partnerships offer flexibility on distributions of income and capital, and are given special tax treatment in both the UK and US. They are not required to file their partnership agreement, or submit annual returns. Ease of management and flexibility make limited partnerships an attractive structure for investors.

3.1.4 Limited liability partnerships
Further to the above, as the partners in a limited partnership are liable to tax, the Limited Partnerships (Guernsey) Law 1995 facilitates somewhat of a hybrid between a company and a limited partnership whereby there is the ability to elect that the partnership has a separate legal personality.

This could be an attractive option for investors as the partnership will be viewed for tax purposes as only one investor. However, investors should bear in mind that the partnership may be structured in a way which means that such costs are passed back to the investors.

3.1.5 Unit trusts
A unit trust is classified as either a Guernsey open-ended or closed-ended fund. Unit trusts are regulated by the Guernsey Financial Services Commission (GFSC), in accordance with international standards, providing comfort to investors, in addition to protection to the island's reputation.

The liability of investors (unit-holders) is limited to the amount paid for their unit(s). Unit trusts are generally tax-exempt, and income earned for a Guernsey fund is exempt, even if that income is paid to a non-Guernsey resident. There are no registration fees or duties incurred in the establishment or administration of a unit trust. Unit trusts are also excluded from incurring stamp duty on any UK property transfers.

Not a separate legal entity, a unit trust is a trust arrangement, whereby its assets are held by a trustee, on trust for the unit holders. Although this function can be undertaken by a trustee, unit trusts often appoint a manager who is responsible for the day-to-day management and administration of the trust.

These were arguably more popular before the introduction of real estate investments trusts (REITs) (see below).

3.2 Restrictions on foreign ownership or occupation of property and on foreign guarantees or security
Guernsey does not have any restrictions at all on the ownership of property: an investor can buy any Guernsey property, subject of course to due diligence checks and clearance of anti-money laundering regulations (some jurisdictions will be prohibited).

However, there are strict rules in place in relation to residential property, due to the small size of the island and the density of its population. In the early 1960s a housing control system was established in order to control the island's population.

The island's residential accommodation stock is split into two sectors – the local market and the open market. The open market, comprising about 10 per cent of the housing stock, as the name suggests, is open – anyone (generally UK and EU citizens) can purchase and live in open market property, and work in the island.

Local market housing is for those with local status, (a 'qualified resident'), and those who hold a licence. The open market is for those without a licence, and who do not qualify for local status. Broadly speaking, those with local status are people who were born on the island and have remained here for a certain number of years, or those living here for a minimum period of time, subject to a number of conditions. Licences are granted on a short term (up to three years), five-year (often for employment reasons) and 15-year basis. Such licences allow the holder and their direct family to rent or buy property on the local market.

For employment purposes, every Guernsey occupant will be required to obtain a 'right to work' document by the Housing Department, indicating that they are lawfully housed.

Guarantees and security may be given by foreign entities.

3.3 Real estate investment trusts (REITs)

REITs are used in Guernsey, primarily involving investment into UK real estate. Structuring a REIT as a Guernsey company can have many advantages, such as an expedited regulatory approach (it may take as little as three days for an application to be approved), tax efficiencies, and it benefitting from Guernsey's more flexible companies law, particularly in relation to choice of company structure and capital distributions.

Also, a Guernsey REIT will not be liable to stamp duty on a transfer of shares. REITS can be listed on the Channel Islands Stock Exchange (thereby avoiding the need to have three-year audited accounts).

4. FINANCING AN ACQUISITION

4.1 Financing of corporate real estate transactions

4.1.1 Mortgage

Corporate real estate transactions are financed on terms similar to that in other financial centres sometimes involving a security trustee acting on behalf of a consortium of lenders. The actual form of security in Guernsey is known as a 'bond', being the equivalent of a UK mortgage, and is referred to as a 'bond' throughout this chapter.

A bond can be described as a hybrid between a mortgage and a loan agreement, and is the means by which real property is charged with the repayment of capital borrowing and interest.

A bond can only charge real estate that is owned by the borrower at the time the bond is registered, unless expressly limited by the terms of the bond.

Bonds must be in writing, be consented to in the Royal Court (this is usually done on the same day as the purchase of the property), and registered with the Greffe (Guernsey's registry). It is not necessary for the lending bank to sign the document.

If a company is borrowing, it is likely that the lending bank will also require guarantees from its directors and/or parent or subsidiary companies.

4.1.2 RATS scheme

Retirement Annuity Trust Schemes (RATS), as approved by The Income Tax (Guernsey) Law 1975, are another means by which the purchase of real estate may be financed.

The trustees of this discretionary trust will own the property, which will be let on a commercial basis.

4.2 Real estate as a means of raising finance

In addition to the below, it may be possible to obtain an assignment of the right to receive rent from tenants in a let property.

Similarly, by purchasing property which is then let out (particularly lucrative for flats and for property on the open market), the owner can raise finance. Often in Guernsey when residents move away from the island, they continue to hold their Guernsey property and rent it out, thus providing them with an additional income stream.

In a similar vein, another way of raising finance could be to sub-let the property.

Please also see sections 4.1 and 4.3.

4.3 Forms of security granted over real estate to raise finance
4.3.1 Bonds

Please see section 4.1 above.

Bonds may confer either a general or specific charge. If general, the lending bank has (or purports to have) a charge over the borrower's entire real and personal property (under Guernsey law, bonds do not attach to personal property, yet the wording in the bond is kept). A specific charge is generally over certain real property of the borrower. Although general charges are common, these are actually fixed charges. Guernsey does not have a concept of floating charges, as applies in the UK.

Bonds rank in priority as to their stated sum, according to the date on which the document was registered.

If part only of a charged property is being sold, it will be necessary to release that part of the property from the bond, so that the purchaser gets good, unencumbered title to that part. Also, when a bond has been paid off, it must be cancelled. This is done by taking the original document to the Greffe and signing the vacating book. A nominal charge will be incurred.

4.3.2 Security interest agreements

It may be possible for a lender to take security under the Security Interests (Guernsey) Law 1993 by way of a security interest agreement (SIA). This could be, for example, taking security over a property's rental income, or over shares in a property-holding company.

It is possible for the same property, be it rental income or shares, to be subject to more than one security interest, even if this is in favour of different lenders, and rank in order of priority based on the date of creation (if not agreed by way of an intercreditor agreement).

Under an SIA a lender may exercise a power of sale of the secured property. The proceeds of sale are to be applied in the following order:
- costs and expenses of the sale;
- the discharge of prior security interests (if any);
- the discharge of the security interests of the party exercising the power;
- the discharge of subsequent security interests (if any); and
- in payment of the balance to the debtor.

4.4 Real estate mortgage securitisation
This is used – see above.

5. MANAGING THE ACQUISITION PROCESS
5.1 Minimum formalities for the sale and purchase of property
Discussed in more detail below, the main formalities are:
- a written agreement is in place, incorporating all agreed terms, signed by, or on behalf of, both parties;
  The Conveyancing (Guernsey) Law 1996 sets out the formal requirements, the main one being contained in section 1(1) which provides: *'An Agreement for the sale or other disposition of real property can be made only in writing and only by incorporating all the terms which the parties have expressly agreed in one or more documents, or where conditions of sale are exchanged, in each'* (different requirements apply for a sale by public auction);
- the vendor owns the property and has the right to sell it;
- the purchaser has sufficient funds to buy the property;
- the vendor provides good unencumbered title to the property, and all relevant searches are carried out; and
- the purchaser obtains an immunity certificate (see 5.7 below). Although not a requirement under Guernsey law, in practice banks and lending institutions will insist upon one being obtained prior to lending.

5.2 Main legal documents required to transfer a property or grant a lease?
5.2.1 Property transfer
In respect of a property transfer, the main documents are the sale contract ('conditions of sale') (see below) and the conveyance (the transfer document). The conditions of sale contain standard conditions as approved by the Guernsey Bar. The conveyance sets out details of the parties, date of completion, the property being transferred, the consideration, boundaries with neighbouring properties, any rights and servitudes affecting the property, and details of the previous conveyance.

Conditions of sale are normally prepared by either the vendor's estate agent or advocate. Conversely, the purchaser's advocate will prepare the conveyance.

In Guernsey, conveyancing takes place before the Royal Court ('Conveyancing Court' as it is commonly called) which sits only on Tuesday and Thursday mornings. Therefore, a quirk of Guernsey custom and law is that one cannot buy or sell a property on any other day of the week (unless by share transfer – see section 5).

Prior to completion, the Conditions of Sale will have been signed by both vendor and purchaser and the deposit (usually 10 per cent) paid, thus forming a binding contract. This will provide for the completion date. On the day of completion, the parties attend Conveyancing Court and give their verbal consent. Alternatively, they may appoint a third party to attend by power of attorney. The conveyance document is signed by Jurats and registered.

If the shares in a property-holding company are being purchased then the key document will be the share sale and purchase agreement (SPA), instead of conditions of sale, a contract governing the sale and purchase of company shares, and the obligations on the vendor and purchaser in this regard.

The main body of the SPA contains the operative provisions – how the sale, purchase and transfer of the shares will be effected. A number of schedules set out information about the company, the vendor's warranties and indemnities, pro forma board minutes and shareholder consents confirming agreement to the transaction, and any other documents required for completion.

Warranties are usually set out in a schedule to the SPA, which give comfort to a purchaser that it has been given all information on the company in which they are acquiring shares. Such information will include accounting and taxation issues, employee and pension rights, and insurance. It is common for vendors to limit their liability under warranties, for example capping the amount of a claim, the duration in which a claim can be brought, and excluding small claims (eg, those under £500).

Other key documents will include a tax indemnity, share transfer forms, board and shareholder approvals regarding the sale, and documents dealing with general corporate matters such as changes of directors and secretaries.

5.2.2 Grant of a lease

The key document will of course be the lease, which is the contract between the landlord and the tenant and contains all of the agreed rights and obligations of the parties. Leases are generally prepared by advocates.

Leases take a similar form to those in England. However, the content can differ enormously. There is no concept of security of tenure for commercial tenants (as in the English Landlord and Tenant Act 1954) once a lease has come to an end, meaning that the tenant has no right to remain in occupation of the property after the expiry of the lease term. Nor does Guernsey recognise privity of contract. Liability remains with the initial tenant as there is no equivalent of the English Landlord and Tenant (Covenants) Act 1995, therefore the initial tenant would need to seek a release from the landlord.

Rent reviews are often linked to a retail prices index (usually the Guernsey Retail Prices Index), and there is no requirement for a lease to be registered, regardless of the length of term.

In Guernsey, leases are viewed as personal rather than real property. In other words, they are viewed for Guernsey law purposes as contracts and not as a legal estate. As such, they are not seen as good security for lenders. This also has implications for inheritance, as personal and real property are treated differently.

5.3 Property transaction costs

The vendor will be responsible for paying estate agent's fees and cancellation fees for any cancelled bonds, together with its own legal costs.

The purchaser, in addition to paying the purchase price of the property, will also incur document duty, court and Greffe fees, advocate's fees and costs incurred with any bond granted.

5.4 Does the vendor warrant its ownership of the property?
Guernsey does not have an equivalent to full title guarantee. Different warranties apply depending on whether it is an outright sale of the property or the purchase of shares in a property-holding company.

5.4.1 Standard sale
The conditions of sale, being the written agreement between the parties, will contain a general condition concerning covenants and warranties.
   The vendor will provide covenants that:
- the vendor has not been involved in any disputes relating to the property and/or its contents;
- the vendor is the sole owner of the contents which are free from encumbrances ;
- any development carried out to the property was done so in accordance with the relevant permissions and regulations;
- the property's current use is lawful; and
- if an open market property, that it is inscribed on the Housing Control Register.

The vendor must also give good unencumbered title to the property (subject to existing rights and servitudes), and give an indemnity against defects in title in the conveyance.

Although relatively rare, the vendor will provide additional warranties to a purchaser where a new-build is being purchased; for example, that the works were carried out in accordance with the relevant authorities and permissions.

5.4.2 Share purchase
In the case of a share transfer, where the purchaser is acquiring shares of a property-holding company, there are inevitably more substantial warranties provided by the vendor in the SPA than in standard conditions of sale, concerning not only the property but the company being sold.

5.5 Warranties a vendor usually gives to a buyer
Standard warranties include:
- all information provided in the agreement is true and correct;
- the property and its contents will remain in the same state and condition pending completion (fair wear and tear excepted);
- the vendor is not aware of any facts or circumstances relating to the property of the company that have not been disclosed to the purchaser and might affect its decision to purchase;
- all information provided on the company is true and accurate;
- the purchaser will have vacant possession of the property;
- the company has good title to the property (subject to existing rights and servitudes);
- the company has not agreed to issue any shares, options, guarantees, nor is there a current power of attorney in place;
- the company has complied with all corporate governance/filing requirements;
- no resolution for the winding up of the company has been passed;

Guernsey

- there is no litigation against the company; and
- the company had complied with all relevant laws, and has no outstanding tax liability.

5.6 Purpose of warranties in the purchase agreement
The warranties are primarily designed to apportion risk between the parties.

The agreement will contain a general condition as to risk, confirming that the property and its contents remain at the vendor's risk until completion.

The vendor is required to keep the property and its contents pending completion in the same conditions as last seen by the buyer (excepting any fair wear and tear). The vendor is also obliged to maintain insurance until the completion date.

5.7 Owners/occupiers' liability for matters relating to the property which occurred before they bought or occupied
At the start of any purchase transaction, an Immunity Certificate should be applied for by the purchaser. Once obtained (from the island's Environment Department at a £50 cost) it provides comfort to a purchaser that the Department will not take any action against them for a known or suspected breach of planning control prior to them becoming owner of the property.

The Immunity Certificate has effect from its issue date.

5.8 Notarisation
There is no requirement that such documentation be notarised.

5.9 Formalities for a contract becoming a legally binding obligation
The Conveyancing (Guernsey) Law 1996 provides that an agreement for the sale/purchase of property must be in writing.

5.10 Point at which the parties become legally bound
Under the standard conditions of sale, the contract becomes binding on the parties once signed by the purchaser and vendor and the deposit paid. In addition, if the contract is conditional upon, for example, a survey, then the conditional date ('operative date') must have passed before the contract becomes unconditional.

5.11 Transfer of title
Effective completion occurs once the completed conveyance, after being confirmed and ratified in Conveyancing Court, is registered with the Greffe. This occurs at 4 pm on the date of completion.

Vacant possession will be given upon completion to the buyer (unless there are special conditions to the contrary).

5.12 Insurance of the property if there is delay between agreeing terms and actual sale
The vendor is responsible for insurance of the property (and its contents) up until midnight the day before completion.

Guernsey

6. REAL ESTATE BASICS

6.1 Main sources of laws that govern real estate
Legislation in Guernsey is split into primary legislation (laws) which are known as 'Orders in Council', and secondary legislation, 'Ordinances'.

The conveyancing procedure in Guernsey is predominantly founded on Norman customary law, there being little legislation available. This is particularly the case with landlord and tenant law. In the absence of such, Guernsey is able to look to case law and statute from other jurisdictions.

6.2 Types of tenure
Land in Guernsey can be held either freehold or leasehold.

A leasehold interest arises from a freehold interest, the owner of the freehold (landlord) letting the whole or a part of the property to the leaseholder (tenant) in return for rental income. There are no requirements as to the term of the lease, its length being a matter for negotiation between landlord and tenant. It is usual, however, to see leases of between a three- and 21-year term.

The tenant in turn may be able to sub-let the property or assign its leasehold interest to a third party, subject to the provisions of the lease.

In Guernsey, a leasehold interest is not, in fact, a property interest. It is classed as personal property, being a personal, contractual right. There is no equivalent UK legislation, in fact very little legislation on landlord and tenant, and notably no equivalent to the UK's Landlord and Tenant Covenants Act 1985.

There is no concept of condominium ownership. Partial ownership is possible under a housing association scheme.

6.3 Must land be registered?
Guernsey property law does not have a concept of registered land. Determination of the extent of a property involves boundary research and site visits. Land is transferred by a conveyance.

6.4 Public land register and land is not covered by a public land register. State guarantee of title and categories of documents and information that must be registered
There is no register of title in Guernsey. Rather, there is a system of registration of documents.

Researching title to a property comprises several stages. First, initial searches of ownership on computer databases are undertaken. These will indicate the current owner's name and address, current Tax on Real Property of the property, and recent transfer and assessment history.

Searches against neighbours are also carried out, to check whether the boundaries with the property correspond (if not, the buyer must be informed), and if there are any restrictive covenants or servitudes. Sometimes it can be difficult to ascertain title, in which case it may be necessary to obtain defective title insurance.

It is then necessary to carry out vendor, purchaser and bond searches at the Greffe and obtain copies of title, creating a chain of title as far back as possible. These are manual searches, based on a referencing system.

Conveyances prior to 1969 are written in French, earlier ones being handwritten. Vendor and purchaser searches are required to ascertain whether the property has been added to, or any parts sold off. The vendor search is to provide confirmation that the vendor is the current owner of the property intended to be sold and has the right to sell it.

Bond searches will determine whether there are any mortgages secured against the property, which need to be cancelled.

It is also worth checking whether the property is listed on the register of Ancient Monuments and Protected Buildings, which will determine which, if any, parts of the property are listed and subject to tight controls on development. In that sense, it can be said that the records comprise both title and transactions in one.

There are talks of introducing a Land Registry in Guernsey, to be aided financially by an increase in property tax. Such an introduction will herald a move away from checking boundaries of a property on site and obtaining copies of records held at the Greffe, thus simplifying and modernising the conveyancing process. Whether and when such a system will be put in place remains to be seen.

Hungary

Nagy és Trócsányi Péter Berethalmi & Balázs Karsai

1. INVESTMENT PURCHASE OVERVIEW

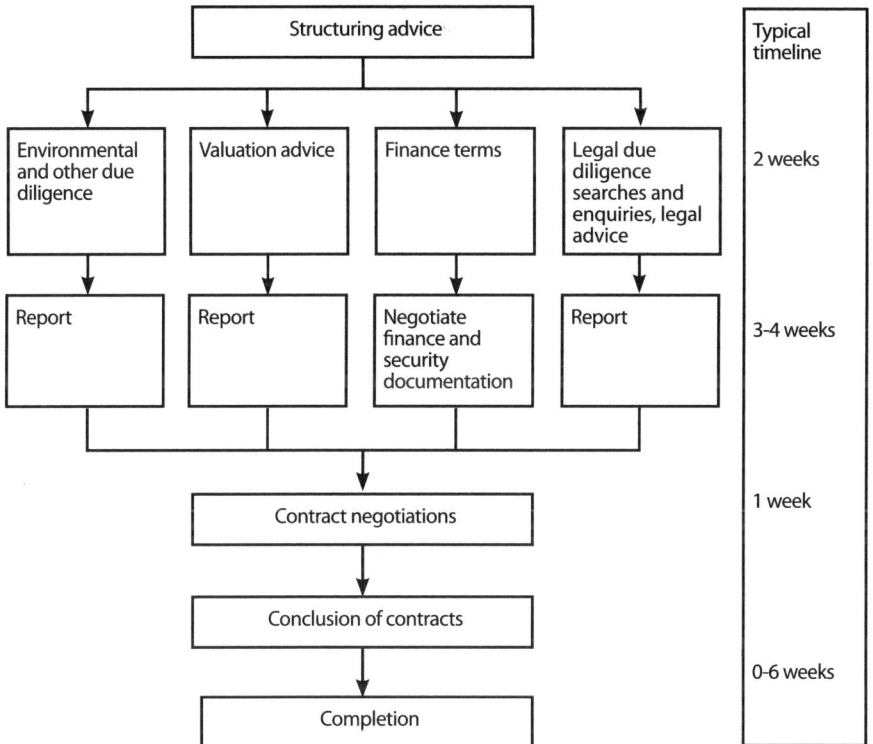

2. TAX CONSIDERATIONS

2.1 Value added tax (VAT)
The purchase of land and new residential property is subject to 25 per cent VAT payable by the purchaser (even if the property is not financed by loan but leased by an investment bank for the benefit of the purchaser, in which case the bank purchases the property and leases it to the actual purchaser who will acquire ownership at a later date only).

2.1.1 Exceptions
The purchase of a building or parts of a building and the land on which it

stands, with the exception of any building or parts of a building and the land on which it stands:
- that is purchased before first occupation;
- where the period elapsing, after first occupation, between the date of the final occupancy permit of the relevant authority and the date of purchase is less than two years.

The purchase of land or part of land which has not been built with the exception of the purchase of a building plot or part of a building plot.

2.2 Stamp duty
2.2.1 Real estate property purchase in general (asset transfer)
Acquisition of real estate property shall be subject to stamp duty payment. The general rate of such stamp duty shall be four per cent of the market value of the real estate property acquired up to HUF 1 billion (approximately €3.6 million), plus two per cent of the portion of the market value above HUF 1 billion not to exceed HUF 200 million.

2.2.2 Company purchase (share transfer)
New transfer duty rules were introduced from 1 January 2010. Acquiring at least 75 per cent of the shares of a Hungarian company which owns real property is subject to stamp duty payment based on the value of the property. The rate of duty shall be four per cent of the market value of each real estate property acquired up to HUF 1 billion, plus two per cent of the portion of the market value above HUF 1 billion not to exceed HUF 200 million per property.

2.2.3 Purchase of residential property
Acquisition of residential property is subject to a gradual stamp duty: two per cent up to HUF 4 million and four per cent of the value above HUF 4 million.

2.2.4 Purchase for the purpose of commercial resale
Companies dealing in the sale and purchase of real estate property as their primary business, shall pay two per cent stamp duty. This discount is only applicable if the purchaser transfers ownership within two years of completion of the building.

2.2.5 Exceptions (a few examples)
- If the person acquiring ownership of land erects a residential property (a house) on it within four years of purchase, the acquisition of the land is free of stamp duty.
- Acquisition of the management right of residential property.
- Acquisition of the management right of water facilities and its components serving public purposes.
- Acquisition by the nature conservation administrator of the right of management of nature conservation areas owned by the state.
- Acquisition of the right to manage state property.

- When a new residential property or a share in such property (with a market value of HUF 15,000,000 or less) is purchased, if it has been built or developed by a company for the purpose of resale, including if developed by the conversion of a building that was not registered in the real estate register, or by expansion (eg addition of a mansard), and was not used as a residential house or dwelling place.

3. INVESTMENT VEHICLE CHOICE

In Hungary, before 1 January 2010, a share transfer was more commonly used than an asset transfer as a form of transaction. With special regard to transfer taxes, a company purchase was less favourable. However, the sale and purchase of a company requires more careful due diligence. Since 1 January 2010 the transfer duty on asset transfers and share transfers no longer differs (see under point 2.2) thus any preference for one over the other is likely to disappear.

In the case of a company purchase the most common vehicle choice in Hungary is the limited liability company (*korlátolt felelősségű társaság*). With the exception of the company's own quotas, quotas may be freely transferred among the members of the company. Quotas may be transferred to third persons only if the member concerned has paid up its capital contribution in full. It is to be noted that, as a general rule, the member, the company or the person assigned by the quotaholders' meeting shall have right of first refusal on quotas to be transferred by means of sale and purchase agreement, provided that this is not precluded or restricted in the deed of foundation. (The separate transfer of the right of first refusal is null and void.)

As of 1 May 2004 citizens of the European Economic Area (EEA), as well as legal persons and organisations without legal personality with their seat in the EEA may acquire ownership of real estate not considered to be arable land as primary domicile under the same conditions as Hungarian persons (ie without administrative consent).

If the EEA citizen has been living in Hungary continuously and lawfully for at least four years, it may purchase the real estate serving as secondary domicile without consent.

In some specific cases the consent must be given, if:
- the acquisition seeks to serve the foreigner's settling in Hungary in an economic sense;
- the aim of the acquisition of real estate is terminating common ownership;
- the foreigner intends to exchange its Hungarian real estate for another one in Hungary; and
- the foreigner has been living lawfully in Hungary for at least five years based on employment, and if the property of the foreigner was expropriated based on Law-Decree 24 of 1976.

No consent is required where the real property has been inherited. In certain cases, a preferable and recommended solution can be to establish a business corporation under Hungarian law so as to avoid this mandatory formal authorisation procedure.

According to the latest survey by Ernst and Young, despite real estate investment trusts (REITs) operating in many European countries (eg France, UK), they are not yet present in the Hungarian market. In Hungary it is still the banks (especially investment banks) that provide loans and manage the assets. Funds as institutions are unfamiliar in the Hungarian legal system and we are not aware of any forthcoming changes.

4. ARABLE LAND
Among the two types of real estate (arable land and commercial properties) arable land is more subject to restrictions.

4.1 Acquisition by domestic persons
Domestic private individuals may acquire arable land up to the limit of 300 hectares in terms of size or 6000 Gold Crowns (*Aranykorona*) in terms of quality rating. Domestic legal entities may not acquire arable land, except for the state, the municipalities and common purpose foundations. Other institutions, such as churches and mortgage institutions may acquire arable land as limited by statute.

A citizen of an EEA member state may acquire non-arable property as a citizen of Hungary. In terms of arable land the EEA citizen shall obtain the following official certificates as proof of their eligibility for acquiring title of ownership:
- an official certificate issued by the immigration authority to verify that they have been legitimately residing in Hungary for three consecutive years;
- an authorisation to reside, or a certificate of proof of having submitted an application for such authorisation for any EEA citizen who does not have a permanent residence permit;
- an official certificate issued by the agricultural administration body, verifying that the applicant had been engaged in agricultural activities in Hungary in their own name and at their own risk for three consecutive years prior to the acquisition of ownership; and
- an environmental study consisting of the examination of the agricultural activities.

4.2 Acquisition by foreign persons
Arable land is subject to an almost absolute prohibition until 1 May 2011 for both foreign legal entities and foreign natural persons to acquire ownership over. Despite the strict restriction, there are exceptions classified by the type of land (farmsteads up to maximum 6000 square metres) and the acquirer. The latter means that EEA member state citizens who: (i) intend to settle in Hungary as individual agricultural professionals; (ii) have been living in Hungary; and (iii) performing agricultural activities continuously and lawfully for at least three years are subject to the same rules as Hungarian citizens.

5. FINANCING AN ACQUISITION
Until recent times real estate financing was restricted to purchase only,

Hungary

however due to high demand from other jurisdictions and customs, so-called 'sale and lease-backs' appeared on the market. Sale and lease-backs describe a business model whereby the real property (which is often a business residence or production premises) is sold to an investor in order to liquidise assets and the seller and the buyer enter into a lease agreement in which the seller becomes the tenant and the buyer the landlord. These lease agreements are specifically made for lengthy periods of time and unlike a regular lease, include provisions which grant more rights and levy more obligations on the tenant (the former owner).

Taking into account both residential and business purpose real estate finance (and the combination of the two), financing will involve a mix of debt and equity. Equity is the part which the developer (buyer) has to provide and its amount (usually a percentage of the overall amount and value of the transaction) depends on various terms. Generally speaking, the credit crunch scared financial institutions who therefore raised the equity percentage on their loans and now require more security than before.

The securities that banks and other financial institutions providing financing may and usually require include:

Mortgage – a mortgage must be registered at the land registry. Mortgage is usually established by mortgage agreement and notarised by a notary public. Most likely, a bank will tend to register a framework mortgage on the property. If it is a newly-built apartment block, for example, then the banks register their mortgage first on the construction area (the land where the building is built) and when that land registry lot number is split into individual lot numbers (the individual apartments to be sold), each sub-lot property will have the total amount of mortgage registered on it, until the apartment is sold. When a specific apartment is sold, the seller must provide that the mortgage by the financing bank is removed (as the buyer may want to encumber its own property, usually when it buys the property using a loan and that bank wants a first rank mortgage).

Charge on quotas – as most investments and developments in the real estate business are carried out by companies, it is possible to place additional securities on the quota and shares of these entities. As it is common to establish a special purpose vehicle (SPV) also known as a project company, the banks are usually very careful with this. A project company's only purpose is to effect the project and once it is completed, it is usually vacated and is left empty. However the mortgages and securities and obligations on the financing bank tend to survive the finishing of the project itself and encumbering an empty company's quota would not be sufficient for any financing institutions. However a project company is never a stand-alone and the parent companies are less likely to become empty and are more likely to be able to secure payment. Therefore it is also common to encumber parent company shares together with parent company guarantees. Apart from the quota and the shares, the assets (including rights, contracts, permits) of both the project company and the parent company may be encumbered, however it is unlikely that the bank will want to encumber the parent company's assets.

Assignment – unfortunately and especially in recent years, many project companies have gone bankrupt. One of the advantages and purposes of a project company is that it will be the company which acquires the necessary building and operational permits, it will be the project company which will be contracting entrepreneurs, therefore in the case of a development effected and carried out by an SPV, the latter will have all the assets, rights, permits and contracts to perform the project. If the SPV becomes insolvent, the financing bank has several avenues which it may take however, a common one is to take over the project either by establishing its own SPV or contract another already existing, operating and insolvent SPV. In this case – as permitted by law – the new SPV will need all the tools (rights, permits, contracts) and assets to complete the project. Therefore it is common that the event of default on the side of the SPV results in the contracts, permits and rights being assigned and transferred to the bank and then the bank may continue and proceed. Moreover assignment could include any rights and claims of the seller that the buyer takes as security (rent, permits, major contracts).

6. MANAGING THE ACQUISITION PROCESS
6.1 Introduction
In Hungary there are generally no fixed terms in a real estate investment, however if it involves a municipality or a state organ then there might be local regulations specific to the land which need to be respected. In terms of commercial property, the only mandatory provisions are those prescribed in the laws mentioned below. As elsewhere, the market has worked out and implemented several provisions that are customary, if not obligatory. These terms and conditions were created by practice and are more or less followed. To avoid restricting the study to greenfield investments, sale and lease-backs or general second hand purchases, the terms described and outlined below are not specific, rather an orientation to show what terms are usually included in a contract for commercial property purchase in Hungary.

6.2 Agreeing terms and binding contracts
6.2.1 Asset transfer
In the case of an asset transfer (direct transfer), in Hungary the sale and purchase agreement regarding the real property shall be countersigned by a Hungarian attorney at law or a notary public and the transfer document shall be filed with the Hungarian Land Registry Office and Hungarian Tax Authority.

6.2.2 Share transfer
As stated above, the most common vehicle choice in Hungary is the limited liability company. Quotas may only be transferred by written agreement, however, the deed of foundation need not be amended as a result of transfer of quotas. The purchaser of the quota shall notify the company of the change of ownership and date to be entered in the register of members within eight days. The notice shall be drawn up in a private document of full probative force or in a public document, and the sale and purchase

agreement shall be attached. (The managing director of the company shall keep records of the members of the company and submit the register of the members to the court of registry.)

Prior to signing, the parties are free to negotiate, conduct due diligence reports, evaluate the property and seek additional advice. Once the purchaser has made up its mind and the execution documents are drafted based on the reports and evaluations and optional expert's advice, the parties may sign.

There is another reason why the attorney-at-law is a necessary player in this transaction: escrow. Some documents are likely to be deposited in escrow and released as the contract terms are fulfilled. This is a safety regulation for both parties and although the escrow agent is usually the attorney-at-law acting on one of the party's behalf, this is a safe procedure. It is also possible to deposit documents with a notary public. Notary publics are authorised to sign and certify sale and purchase contracts too, but this is not a common practice.

Parties must bear in mind that in certain cases the property is encumbered with third party rights of which the most important are: pre-emption rights, easements, mortgages and usufruct rights. These rights are registered on the extract of the property kept at the Land Registry Office. Although some of the legal risks may be detected based on the extract and the pertaining contracts (eg mortgage agreement), due diligence is necessary, especially in case greenfield developments uncover any environmental risks, which may arise following the purchase at an unexpected date and which will be levied upon the buyer.

6.3 Typical contract terms

The following is a summary of typical sale contract terms in Hungary which would be special in any other jurisdiction.

6.3.1 Non-refundable deposit

It is customary for the purchaser to make a non-refundable deposit (*foglaló*). A non-refundable deposit is subject to special provisions. The rule is that the non-refundable deposit must be handed over at the execution (signing and countersigning) of the agreement. Because some purchases involve massive sums of money and thereby the non-refundable deposit could be very large; the practice accepts certificates of wire transfers sent by a bank evidencing that the non-refundable deposit has been transferred to the seller's appointed account.

It must be emphasised that this type of deposit has a penal effect too. If the sale and purchase agreement is frustrated and it is attributable to the seller, then the seller must give to the purchaser double the amount of the non-refundable deposit. If the frustration was attributable to the purchaser, then the latter loses the non-refundable deposit for good. To make sure that these provisions are effected, the contract must state that the parties accept the amount as a non-refundable deposit. The countersigning attorney-at-law must inform the parties of the nature of this instrument.

The non-refundable deposit usually amounts to 10 per cent of the purchase price agreed.

6.3.2 Price
The price is a negotiable item and a necessary item to be agreed upon. The parties negotiate the price freely. The price is usually subject to the evaluation reports and the encumbrances on the commercial property including detectable but unforeseeable risks. If there are any loans, mortgages or debentures, then this must be taken into account as well. In the case of a second hand purchase with a mortgage on the property, the property may be sold with the mortgage (and apart from obtaining the consent of the mortgagor bank). It is common for the duties to be payable by the purchaser.

6.3.3 Financing
If the property purchase involves a financing scheme, this must be included in the agreement. The most common methods of financing are loans secured by mortgages and floating charges. It is yet uncommon to use a leasing structure at property purchase but it is available on the market.

6.3.4 Land registry procedures
This is not to refer to the registration of title procedure but to the process of land-allocation and registration. When a new development is made (regardless whether office, residential or both), the building is erected on the land and when the building is finished, the apartments or offices are given sub-lot numbers and are registered individually. Since this process takes time it is common to enter into a pre-contract first and sign the final agreement when the sub-lot numbers are formed. The pre-contract and the final contract are usually the same, the only difference is that the final contract includes the exact lot number (being a sub-lot number to the original construction area).

In some cases the classification of the land needs to be changed in order to obtain a building permit. This is a process involving negotiations with the local authorities and also an administrative procedure by the Land Registry Office. The failure to reclassify a property to make it fit for the project may mean that the project fails completely and the purchase will not take place.

6.3.5 Conditions precedent and due diligence
It is common practice for the purchaser to undertake all due diligence before exchanging contracts. The main risk for a purchaser is that it will have to cover the whole cost of that due diligence usually without any legally binding agreement for a seller to sell or otherwise refund the cost.

There are usually no conditions precedent so the buyer should have the results of all due diligence reports (legal reports, surveys etc) and all funding arrangements committed prior to execution. The principle of 'buyer-beware' (caveat emptor) applies.

The seller usually gives warranties limited to its ownership of the property and it is the purchaser's interest and responsibility to try to negotiate any additional warranties based on the due diligence. If the report uncovers a severe fault and risk, it may be a deal breaker and the purchaser may refrain from proceeding until the seller gives the special warranties or the seller undertakes to release and free the risks and encumbrances itself prior to the next step in the negotiations.

6.4 Managing the property between exchange and completion
The basic and common rule is that the rights and obligations on the property transfer with the title. Therefore, although the parties may agree otherwise, until the purchaser is registered as the owner, the seller must bear all costs and shall keep the profits of the commercial property. In the case of a sale and lease-back, when possession in fact does not change (the former owner will be the holder of the property as leased back to it by the purchaser), it is reasonable to agree otherwise, especially because the purchaser will not take possession of the property on completion.

6.4.1 Insurance
The seller will usually continue to insure the property, in the case of a sale and lease-back, the terms might include that the property must be insured by the tenant (the same person as the seller).

6.4.2 Rent
Provided that the purchaser was a former tenant of the seller, the parties may agree that some part of the rent will be deductive of the purchase price. This may apply to fittings and construction agreed and carried out by the purchaser. The parties may also agree that in case the completion is delayed, which delay does not constitute a deal breaker, then until the delay is over and completion may be effected, the purchaser can use the property and pay a rent, which again may be deducted from the sale price – up to the parties' negotiations.

6.5 Brief summary of the registration of title procedure
To effect a transfer of property, a written purchase agreement and registration at the land registry are required. In order for the purchase agreement to be valid, it is necessary that the written agreement contains the designation of the parties, the subject of the purchase, the purchase price, and the declaration of the will of the parties aiming to transfer the property.

6.5.1 The legal effect of registration
The title is created solely on the basis of the administrative measure of registration and not by the agreement. The real estate register is considered authentic which means that all titles registered must be presumed real in the absence of proof to the contrary. Title to ownership can be registered for a whole real estate, a whole ownership stake or for a certain value of these. The title can only be registered by the land registry on the basis of documents complying with certain formal requirements. According to the regulations the sale and purchase agreement must either be countersigned by an attorney or created by a notary public. In certain cases, in addition to

a document serving as a basis for registration, an application for registration and permission for registration, special regulatory permit (approval) or verification is required if so prescribed by law. A diagram drawing is also required for registration if the change affects the relevant realty map, or if so prescribed by legal regulation.

6.5.2 The registration
The file number assigned to an application is entered on the land registry title deed (of which the land registry extracts are formed) on the day of submission, and this fact is also indicated on the application. The index contains a brief description of the application to which it pertains. The application can be suspended for a maximum period of six months from the date of submission of the document to the real estate supervisory authority, permitted to the registered right-holder for granting authorisation for registration. If the declaration of the seller aiming to sell the property is not submitted until the mentioned deadline, the application will be rejected since the period cannot be prolonged. With the suspension, the application acquires and keeps a rank during the procedure.

6.5.3 Costs
There are two types of costs which arise in connection with the property transfer: stamp duty and administrative fees for the registration procedure. The costs of the delivery and the settlements of the real estate register are charged to the seller. The costs of the conclusion of the agreement, the duty of the transfer and the registration fees are charged to the buyer.

7. REAL ESTATE BASICS
7.1 The main sources of law

Title	No. of the Act
Act on the Hungarian Civil Code	Act IV of 1959
Act on Real Estate Registration	Act CXLI of 1997
Decree on the Enforcement of Act CXLI of 1997 on Real Estate Registration	Decree No. 109/1999 (XII.29.)
Act on Duties	Act XCIII of 1990
Act on Value Added Tax	Act CXXVII of 2007
Act on Arable Land	Act LV of 1994
Act on the General Rules of Environmental Protection	Act LIII of 1995
Act on the Lease and Alienation of Dwelling Apartments and other Premises	Act LXXVIII of 1993
Act on Condominiums	Act CXXXIII of 2003

7.2 The necessity of registration

The primary and absolute rule is that land (and property) must be registered at the land registry. This is the basis of the authenticity of the land registry. If by any chance the registration is not completed and the party acquiring the land is not registered, then such person (meaning also the beneficiary of other proprietary rights and facts pertaining to the land) cannot enforce its rights (claims) against anyone registered in the land registry, provided that the latter acquired such right prior in rank and in good faith.

7.3 The authority in charge: the land registry office

The public registry of properties is managed by the land registry office. Land registers are kept for each settlement (village, town, districts of Budapest), and in respect of the following cities with county-level rights: Debrecen, Győr, Miskolc, Pécs and Szeged for each district of such cities. Land registries are publicly accessible and provide authentic information. Indeed the information kept and managed by the land registries bears authenticity regarding the information in them.

7.3.1 Official registrations

For the purposes of land registration, rights are created upon being recorded in the title deed. The registration of rights and facts are of constitutive effect. If a right is recorded on the basis of a deed, it shall signify ownership based on transfer, or asset management right, use of land, usufruct and the right of use, easement and mortgage (independent lien) based on contract. The registration of rights and facts shall restrict or render conditional any future acquisition of rights.

7.3.2 Authenticity

Real estate registration records shall be construed as authentic proof of registered rights and facts. If a right or a fact has been registered in the land register, lack of knowledge of such shall not constitute an excuse under any circumstances.

On the basis of registered rights and facts, it is to be presumed that such registered rights and facts pertain, until proven otherwise, to the right-holder of them. In the event of cancellation of any right or fact, it shall be presumed, until proven otherwise, that such abrogated right or fact does not prevail.

A person acquiring a right that is not entered in the land register or the holder of a right that was cancelled from the land register may not enforce such right against a party acquiring in good faith a right which is registered in the real estate register, or who enjoys priority before such person.

7.3.3 Rights to be recorded in the land register

The most important property-related rights, and the holders of such, that may be recorded in land registers are:
- ownership;
- land use on the basis of agreement or court decision;
- usufruct and the right of use;

- easement rights;
- right of pre-emption, repurchase and option;
- mortgage (independent lien); and
- right of execution.

7.3.4 Facts to be recorded in the land register
The most important property-related facts that may be recorded in real estate registers are:
- liquidation or winding-up proceedings started against the right-holder of record;
- commencement of expropriation and lot formation proceedings;
- construction or demolition of a building;
- suspension of real estate registration proceedings;
- ownership restriction(s) based on a court decision;
- scheduling of an auction or public offering;
- maintaining the ranking of a cancelled lien, or waiver of the right of disposition of ranking; and
- advance reservation of ranking for mortgage.

7.3.5 The land registry extract
The land registry extract consists of three parts. Part I contains the data of the property, part II contains the rights and beneficiaries pertaining to the property and finally part III contains the facts pertaining to the property or the rights and their beneficiaries.

Access to the land registry may be effected in three ways and through two avenues. The data may be accessed by providing the lot number (more sufficient) or the address of the property. Access may be obtained:
(i) personally from the land registry office;
(ii) electronically by downloading from the online database called Takarnet (attorneys, notary publics and anyone with a contract may have access); or
(iii) downloading from a publicly available website (*www.magyarorszag.hu*) by using a personal identification ticket obtained from the local municipality.

Downloading and obtaining land registry extracts incur a fee. The fee at the moment is between HUF 1000 and HUF 4000 depending on the type of extract (full; effective; not certified; or certified). Certified land registry extracts may be used in civil and administrative procedures and for a property sale and purchase are obtained by the seller and attached to the completion documents.

India

Khaitan & Co Sudip Mullick & Sirish Vardhan

At a time when most economies are facing recession, the Indian economy is resilient and growing at a steady pace. Various sectors of the economy have witnessed an upward swing in investments which have not only come from domestic investors but also from foreign investors. One of the major sectors in India which has gathered lots of interest among the foreign investors is the real estate sector.

Since the real estate sector is sensitive in India, the government of India has been very cautious about opening it up to foreign investments.

This chapter aims to touch upon the regulations for acquisition of immovable property by foreign investors in India and some of the other applicable laws and aspects relating to transactions for acquisition of immovable property.

1. INVESTMENT PURCHASE OVERVIEW

The following steps are normally followed for purchase of immovable property:

> **Step 1**
> Letter of intent or memorandum of understanding or agreement for sale between the buyer and seller.

> **Step 2**
> Investigation of title of the seller to the property.

> **Step 3**
> On seller making out clear and marketable title, parties execute definitive agreement like sale deed.

When conducting investigation of title, *inter alia,* the following steps are recommended:
- Searching the records maintained in the office of the sub-registrar of

assurances in the jurisdiction where the property is situated in order to ascertain various instruments relating to the property registered with it.
- All documents relating to the title should be perused to determine the devolution of title.
- Requisitions should be raised on the seller to ascertain various facts in respect of the property which the seller is aware of.
- Public notice in two newspapers, one of which should be in the language of the region where property is situated.
- A declaration on oath from the seller should be taken setting out the facts regarding the property.
- One should also make sure that no electricity, municipal or other statutory dues in relation to the property are outstanding.

If the seller is a company, in addition to the above, a search in the records maintained by the Registrar of Companies should be conducted in order to check whether any mortgage or charge in respect of the property has been registered with it.

For the purchase of a residential flat or office in a building the buyer should ensure that a completion certificate in respect of the building has been issued by the competent authority.

In the definitive agreement the seller usually gives a representation as to the title to the property. Apart from the definitive agreements like the sale deed, the purchaser should take custody of the original title deeds relating to the property and also take a power of attorney from the seller to apply to various authorities like the electricity board for transferring the utility into the name of the purchaser and the municipal corporation for updating its records in the name of the purchaser. It is pertinent to note that if part of a larger property is sold and the original title deeds relate to a larger property, a covenant is usually taken in the definitive agreement that the seller will produce the title deeds when called upon to do so by the purchaser.

2. TAX CONSIDERATIONS
2.1 Indirect tax
The government of India has, with effect from May 2010, brought the purchase of premises within the ambit of service tax. The liability to pay service tax is in respect of the purchase of premises in a building which is still under construction and has not obtained a completion certificate from the competent authority. Further, the purchase of premises in a building which is still under construction also attracts value added tax (VAT).

2.2 Income tax
When a commercial property is acquired on an ownership basis, any profits or gains arising from the sale of such property will be taxable in India as capital gains. If no tax depreciation is claimed in respect of such property and the property is held for more than 36 months prior to its sale, the capital gains will be regarded as long term capital gains and will accordingly be taxable at a concessional rate of 20 per cent. If the property is not held for more than 36 months, the capital gains will be regarded as short term and

taxable at the normal tax rate of 40 per cent as applicable to non-residents. Further, the capital gains tax will be increased by a surcharge of 2.5 per cent if the taxable income of the non-resident in India exceeds INR 10 million and by education cess of three per cent. Therefore, the effective tax rate for long term capital gains would be 21.115 per cent whereas for short term capital gains, it would be 42.23 per cent.

If tax depreciation is claimed on the commercial property, then the sale value of the property is to be reduced from the 'written down value' of the property (ie, property value net of tax depreciation claimed) and the resultant amount is regarded as 'short term capital gains' and taxable at 42.23 per cent irrespective of its period of holding before the sale.

If a residential property is acquired by an Indian citizen resident outside India or by a person of Indian origin and the same is held for more than 36 months prior to its sale, the capital gains will be regarded as long term and will accordingly be taxable at a concessional rate of 20 per cent plus applicable surcharge and education cess. If the property is held for less than 36 months the capital gains will be regarded as short term and will accordingly be taxable at the rate of 30 per cent plus applicable surcharge and education cess.

3. REAL ESTATE BASICS

The Transfer of Property Act 1882 (TOP Act) prescribes the law on transfer of immovable property. The TOP Act lays down the general principles relating to the transfer of property, including among other things, the persons competent to transfer property, the validity of restrictions and conditions imposed on the transfer and the creation of contingent and vested interest in the property.

The Registration Act 1908 (Registration Act) has been enacted with the object of providing public notice of execution of documents affecting the transfer of interest in immovable properties. The purpose of the Registration Act is the conservation of registered documents and the prevention of fraud. It details the formalities for registering an instrument effecting transfer of immovable property. Section 17 of the Registration Act identifies documents for which registration is compulsory and includes, among other things, any non-testamentary instrument which purports or operates to create, declare, assign, limit or extinguish (whether in present or in future), any right, title or interest, whether vested or contingent, in immovable property of the value of 100 rupees or more, and a lease of immovable property from year to year or for any term exceeding one year or reserving a yearly rent. A document will not affect the property comprised in it, nor be received as evidence of any transaction affecting such property (except as evidence of a contract in a suit for specific performance or as evidence of any collateral transaction not required to be effected by registered instrument) unless it has been registered. It is pertinent to note that the registration of documents does not guarantee the title to the property and merely acts as a public notice of the transaction covered by the registered document.

Further, various state governments have prescribed stamp duty which is payable on transactions involving immovable property including the sale and lease of immovable property and if a document is unstamped or insufficiently stamped it may not be admissible in evidence and will attract a penalty.

4. ACQUISITION OF COMMERCIAL PROPERTY IN INDIA BY PERSON RESIDENT OUTSIDE INDIA

Investments in India by persons resident outside India (PROI) are governed by the Foreign Exchange Management Act 1999 and various rules, regulations and press notes issued by the government of India and Reserve Bank of India from time to time.

A PROI who desires to acquire commercial property in India will have to abide by the Foreign Exchange Management Act (Acquisition and Transfer of Immovable Property in India) Regulations 2000 (FEMA Regulations).

Under Regulation 5 of the FEMA Regulations a PROI can acquire immovable property provided that:
- in accordance with the Foreign Exchange Management (Establishment in India of Branch or Office or other Place of Business) Regulations 2000, the PROI has established in India a branch office or other place of business excluding liaison office for carrying on any activity in India; and
- the immovable property is required for or incidental to carrying on such activity.

In addition to the aforesaid conditions, the PROI has to ensure that while acquiring the immovable property all applicable laws are complied with and a declaration in the form prescribed by the FEMA Regulations is filed not later than 90 days from the date of such acquisition.

FEMA Regulations also permit a PROI who has acquired immovable property in accordance with FEMA Regulations to mortgage such immovable property to an authorised dealer as a security for any borrowing.

5. ACQUISITION AND TRANSFER OF IMMOVABLE PROPERTY BY AN INDIAN CITIZEN RESIDENT OUTSIDE INDIA

Under Regulation 3 of the FEMA Regulations, a person resident outside India who is a citizen of India can acquire immovable property in India other than an agricultural property, plantation, or a farm house provided such acquisition is made out of funds received in India through normal banking channels by way of inward remittance from any place outside India, or funds held in any non-resident account maintained in accordance with the provisions of the Act and the regulations made by the Reserve Bank of India. Payment of the purchase price for acquisition of immovable property by traveller's cheque or by foreign currency notes is prohibited.

FEMA Regulations permit an Indian citizen resident outside India to transfer any immovable property in India to:
(i) a person resident in India;
(ii) a person of Indian origin resident outside India; and
(iii) a person resident outside India who is a citizen of India.

However there is a restriction on transfer of agricultural or plantation property or farm houses to a person of Indian origin resident outside India and to a person resident outside India who is a citizen of India.

6. ACQUISITION AND TRANSFER OF IMMOVABLE PROPERTY BY A PERSON OF INDIAN ORIGIN

Under Regulation 4 of the FEMA Regulations, a person of Indian origin (PIO) resident outside India can acquire immovable property in India other than an agricultural property, plantation, or a farm house. However, such acquisition must be made out of funds received in India through normal banking channels by way of inward remittance from any place outside India, or funds held in any non-resident account maintained in accordance with the provisions of the Act and the regulations made by the Reserve Bank of India. Payment of the purchase price for acquisition of immovable property by traveller's cheque or by foreign currency notes is prohibited.

A PIO can acquire by way of gift from a person resident in India, or from a person resident outside India who is a citizen of India, or from a person of Indian origin resident outside India, any immovable property in India other than agricultural land/farm house/plantation property.

A PIO can acquire immovable property in India by way of inheritance from a person resident outside India who had acquired such property in accordance with the provisions of the foreign exchange law in force at the time of such acquisition; or in accordance with the provisions of the FEMA Regulations; or from a person resident in India.

A PIO has the right to transfer residential or commercial property in India by way of gift to a person resident in India, or to a person resident outside India who is a citizen of India, or to a person of Indian origin resident outside India.

A PIO can transfer/sell any immovable property in India other than agricultural land/farm house/plantation property, by way of sale to a person resident in India. In the case of transfer of agricultural land/farm house/plantation property by way of gift or sale, the transferee not only has to be a person resident in India but also a citizen of India.

7. PROHIBITION ON TRANSFER OF IMMOVABLE PROPERTY IN INDIA

Under Regulation 8 of FEMA Regulations a citizen of Pakistan, Bangladesh, Sri Lanka, Afghanistan, China, Iran, Nepal or Bhutan can acquire or transfer immovable property only with prior permission of the Reserve Bank of India other than a lease not exceeding five years.

8. OTHER FOREIGN INVESTMENTS

With a view to liberalising foreign direct investment (FDI) in the real estate sector, the government through its Department of Industrial Policy and Promotion (DIPP) has from time to time issued press notes setting out the terms and conditions for FDI in India. Under Press Note 2 of 2005 (Press Note 2) issued by the DIPP, 100 per cent FDI is permitted under the automatic route in townships, housing, built-up infrastructure and construction development projects subject to compliance with the conditions prescribed in Press Note 2. Further, Press Note 3 of 2008 (Press Note 3) issued by DIPP permits 100 per cent FDI in industrial parks under the automatic route subject to compliance with the terms and conditions stated in Press Note 3. Realising the necessity for one consolidated document which reflects the entire FDI policy and with a view to simplifying the process of foreign investments in India, the DIPP has recently issued a circular which consolidates into one document all prior policies, regulations and press notes including Press Note 2, Press Note 3 and clarifications issued by DIPP. The circular reflects the current policy framework on FDI and is effective from 1 April 2010.

Italy

Chiomenti Studio Legale
Umberto Borzi & Giuseppe Andrea Giannantonio

1. INVESTMENT PURCHASE OVERVIEW

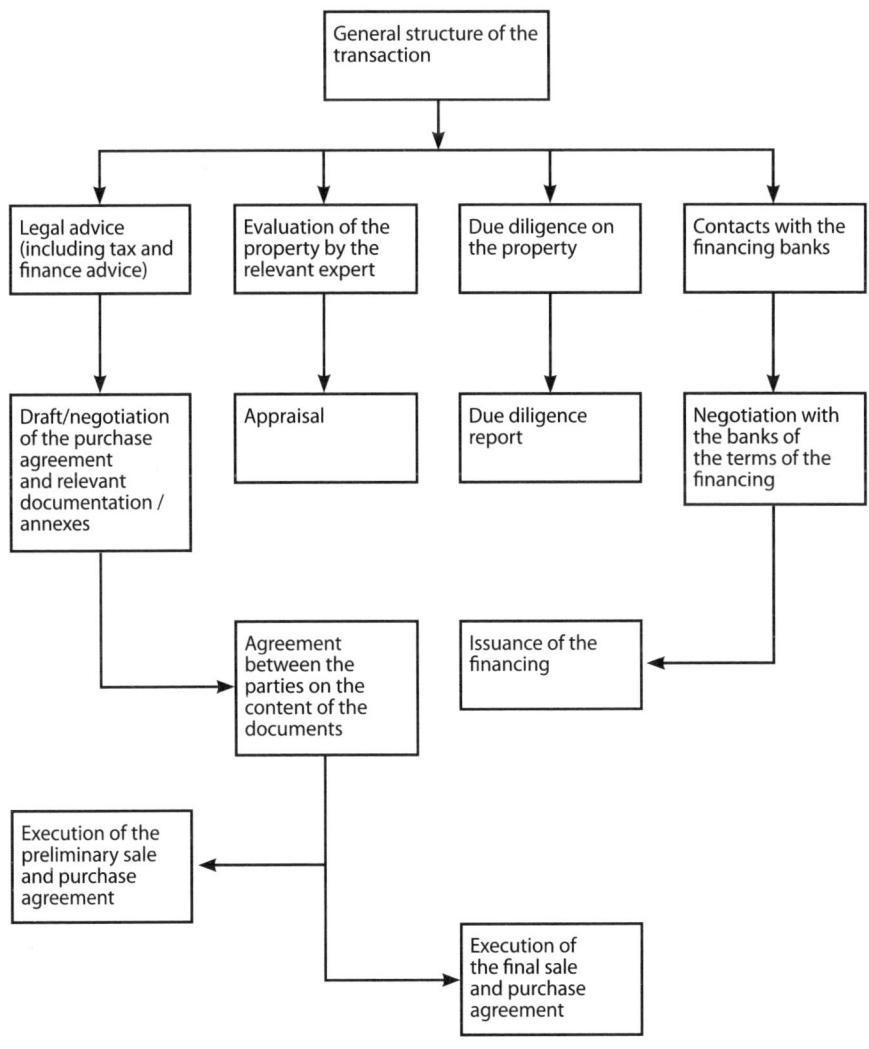

Italy

2. TAX CONSIDERATIONS
2.1 Value added tax (VAT)
As a general rule, for VAT purposes, real estate transfers are considered as ordinary transfers of goods. In order to apply VAT to a certain real estate transfer, the vendor must be a VAT relevant subject (or entrepreneur or a professional) and the real estate to be transferred shall be included among the assets concerning the entrepreneurial or professional activity carried on by the vendor. Accordingly, sale of assets by private individuals which do not carry on a business activity or by non commercial entities (*enti non commerciali*) do not fall within the scope of the VAT regime. Should both the requirements set forth above be met, the relevant transaction will fall within the scope of VAT, unless the transfer concerns land on which building is not allowed. If a real estate transaction falls within the scope of VAT, the following should be considered:
- transfers of residential real estate are exempt from VAT (ie, the transaction is subject to VAT at zero rate) unless the seller is the enterprise that built or renovated the transferred properties and the sale occurs within four years from the end of the construction or the renovation work; should this be the case the sale is subject to the ordinary VAT regime at a rate varying from four to 20 per cent depending on additional circumstances; and
- transfers of commercial assets (ie, real estate properties which do not qualify as residential assets for cadastral purposes) are, in principle, exempt from VAT (the transaction is subject to VAT at zero rate). However, the VAT regime is applicable at an ordinary 20 per cent rate if the commercial real estate properties are transferred: (i) by the enterprise that built (or renovated) the property, provided that the transfer occurs within four years from the end of the building or renovation works; (ii) to a VAT entity with a pro rata of VAT deductibility equal or lower than 25 per cent, (eg, banks and other financial companies); or (iii) to acquiring entities not acting in connection with a business or professional activity. Furthermore, the ordinary VAT regime also applies if the seller elects in the sale deed for the application of such regime.

2.2 Stamp duty/transfer tax
In principle, the proportional registration tax is applied when the relevant real estate transactions are not subject to VAT (eg, the vendor is not an Italian company). Accordingly, the transfer of buildings falling outside the scope of VAT, are subject to registration tax at a rate of seven per cent which may be reduced to three per cent for buildings of historical, artistic and archaeological interest and provided that the purchaser complies with the obligations related to their preservation and protection. The three per cent rate is also applied on the purchase of real estate used by the purchaser as its main residence. As to the taxable basis of the proportional registration tax it should be pointed out that it is equal to the market value of the transferred assets at the date of the relevant transfer. As a consequence, the Italian tax authorities can increase, for tax purposes, the value declared by the parties

in the relevant transfer deed, should such value be lower than the relevant market value. Notwithstanding the above, it should be also considered that, according to provisions set forth by Article 1, paragraph 497 of Law 266/2005, for a transaction between individuals not carrying on a business activity and having as its object the transfer of a building for residential purposes, the parties may elect to apply registration tax on the basis of the cadastral value of the assets sold instead of on the relevant transaction value. If such election is made, the taxable value is not subject to reassessment by the taxation authorities for the purposes of registration tax.

Notwithstanding the above, if the relevant real estate transaction falls within the scope of VAT (eg, the vendor is an Italian company) then the following is relevant:
- transfers of real estate (both residential and commercial) which are subject to the ordinary VAT regime, are subject to registration tax at the €168 fixed rate; and
- transfers of real estate which are exempt from VAT (ie, the transaction is subject to VAT at zero rate) are subject to registration tax: (i) at a proportional rate varying from three per cent to seven per cent in case of residential properties; and (ii) at the €168 fixed rate in the other cases (ie, a transfer of commercial properties).

As to mortgage and cadastral taxes, the following should be considered:
- for sale of residential real estate properties such taxes are due at the ordinary fixed tax rate of €168 each if the transaction falls within the scope of VAT and at the three per cent cumulative tax rate on the value of the transferred assets in the other cases; and
- for sale of commercial properties such taxes are due at the four per cent cumulative tax rate on the value of the transferred assets, to be reduced up to two per cent if one of the relevant counterparties is a real estate fund or a financial intermediary carrying on a leasing activity.

For the sake of completeness it should be also pointed out that the contribution into an Italian real estate fund, of a plurality of properties (*pluralità d'immobili*) that are mainly rented (*prevalentemente locati*) at the moment of contribution, is assimilated, for Italian indirect tax purposes, to a contribution of a going concern. Accordingly, the contribution is outside the scope of VAT, and the contribution deed is subject to registration tax and to mortgage and cadastral taxes only at the fixed flat rates of €168 for each of these taxes. The same indirect tax regime also applies with reference to contribution into an Italian listed real estate company which opted for the special tax regime provided for by Article 1 (paragraphs 119 to 141) of Law no. 296/2006 (*società di investimento immobiliari quotate*, or SIIQ).

2.3 Tax issues for overseas investors investing in real estate

For non-resident companies which do not have a permanent establishment in Italy and invest directly in Italian real estate properties, the gross rental income – less a flat deduction of 15 per cent – is subject to 27.5 per cent corporate income tax (*Ires*) and must be declared in a tax return. No other deductions or expenses are allowed. If the gross rental income, less a flat

Italy

deduction of 15 per cent, is lower than the cadastral value, this latest value is in any case subject to 27.5 per cent *Ires*. The rental income is not subject to regional tax (*Irap*) whose rate varies on a regional basis for direct holding of the Italian real estate properties. Capital gains made by non-resident companies (which do not have a permanent establishment to which the investments in real estate properties may be connected) are taxable at the corporate income tax rate, but only for *Ires* purposes (the rate of 27.5 per cent) and not for *Irap* purposes. Such capital gains consist of the difference between the consideration received for the selling of the real estate property, and its purchase price/construction cost (increased by all expenses directly attributable to it other than dwellings). The capital gains will not be subject to Italian taxation if the real estate transferred has been held for a period of over five years.

3. INVESTMENT VEHICLE CHOICE
3.1 Commonly used structures to purchase property
The choice of the structure to be adopted when investing in real estate assets located in Italy mainly depends on:
(i) tax efficiency evaluations;
(ii) the nature of the investment (eg, merely 'passive' financial investment in which the investor prefers to have a local partner managing the property or 'active' investment, in which the investor prefers to manage the property and its developments directly);
(iii) potential liability issues (eg, 'limited recourse' structures as opposed to having the investor directly and fully liable for potential liabilities or costs; and
(iv) to a more limited extent, legal issues concerning limits on foreign investments in real estate.

The most common structures for real estate investments in Italy (other than a direct acquisition by the foreign investor, which is not very usual) are the following:
- acquisition of the property through a real estate investment fund. From an income tax perspective it should be pointed out that Italian laws provide for a general exemption from income taxes at the level of the fund and for taxation at the level of the relevant fund investors for the proceeds received in respect of the units that they own. Foreign fund investors are subject to a final 20 per cent withholding tax, except for foreign investors which are resident, for tax purposes, in a country which recognises the Italian tax authorities' right to an adequate exchange of information and which is accordingly included in the list (the 'White List') of states and territories to be approved by a forthcoming Ministerial Decree to be enacted according to the provision set forth by Article 168-bis of Presidential Decree 22 December 1986, no. 917 (pending the approval of such ministerial Decree the relevant countries for these purposes are those included in the list approved with Ministerial Decree of 4 September 1996, as amended). Such a structure allows a 'passive' investor to entrust the management of the property

to a specialised fund manager, ensuring that any liabilities arising
from the property remain limited to the fund in a 'limited recourse'
structure. The main drawbacks of such structure concern the rather
limited powers which (pursuant to Italian law) the investor can retain
in the management of the property and the governance of the fund,
and the need to ensure that the fund has a 'plurality' of investors. As to
the tax regime provided for real estate investments through real estate
fund structures, it should be pointed out that Law Decree no. 78/2010,
entered into force as of 31 May 2010, providing austerity measures to
contrast the current financial crisis, abolished the exemption on the
proceeds distributed by Italian real estate investment funds to foreign
investors resident for tax purposes in a White List jurisdiction. In this
respect, please consider that the Law Decree should be converted into
law by the Italian Parliament by 30 July 2010. Should this not be the
case, the Law Decree is cancelled and has so effect, as it never entered
into force. Just for the sake of completeness, it should be also taken
into account that the newly enacted Law Decree no. 78/2010 provides
for a new definition of 'investment fund'. For real estate funds already
set up when Law Decree no. 78/2010 entered into force which are not
complaint with such new definition, the relevant asset management
company (*società di gestione del risparmio*) must consistently adjust the
regulation of such fund. Upon adjustment, a five per cent substitute tax
to be levied on the average net asset value of the real estate investment
fund (REIF) resulting from the half-year reports of the fiscal years 2007,
2008 and 2009 has been provided for. The SGRs that do not resolve
upon the adjustment of the fund regulations must wind up the relevant
fund, paying the substitute tax at a rate raised up to seven per cent. It
is worth to noting that the resolution modifying the REIF regulation
must be adopted within 30 days from the date of issuance of a new
implementing decree, the latter to be issued within 30 days from
the date of conversion into law of the Budget Decree. The new rules
described above are currently causing some uncertainty as to the regime
applicable to real estate funds and might lead to a less widespread use of
such structures in the future.
- acquisition of the property through an Italian company (usually
a limited liability or joint stock company). From an income tax
perspective it should be considered that rental income as well as capital
gains on real estate transfer are subject to corporate income tax at the
27.5 per cent tax rate and to regional tax at a variable rate depending on
location but not exceeding 3.9 per cent. The capital gain arising from
the sale of a real estate asset (which consists of the difference between
the consideration received for the selling of the real estate property, and
its purchase price/construction cost increased by all expenses directly
attributable to it other than dwellings) is charged to taxation either
in the fiscal year in which it is realised or, if the real estate sold has
been held for at least three years, an election can be made to charge it
to taxation in equal instalments over five fiscal periods. The structure

under this item allows for extensive governance powers by the investor and ensures (especially in the case of the joint stock company) that any liabilities arising from the property remain limited to the fund in a 'limited recourse' structure. See also below with respect to SIIQs.
- acquisition of a company which already owns the property. Such structure offers benefits similar to those mentioned in the point above, but requires a more in-depth due diligence to take into account the situation of the target company.

3.2 Restrictions on foreign ownership or occupation of property
The only legal restriction on foreign ownership or occupation of property concerns the 'reciprocity' regime. Under such regime, unless there is a specific international treaty in force (such as with all members of the European Union and other countries which have entered into specific bi- or multilateral treaties with Italy) foreign nationals can acquire or occupy real estate in Italy only if Italian nationals or entities are allowed to acquire or occupy real estate in their country of origin. The Ministry of foreign affairs is charged with verifying the 'reciprocity' requirement, but the relevant checks are infrequently updated and as a consequence there is some uncertainty with respect to the reciprocity requirement with certain countries. This is one of the reasons for which foreign investors sometimes elect to invest through an Italian (or EU) entity.

There are no specific restrictions for foreign guarantees or security, other than the abovementioned 'reciprocity' requirement. Please see below with respect to the kind of security which can be granted.

3.3 Real estate investment trusts (REITs)
Article 1, paragraphs 119 to 141, of Law no. 296 of 27 December 2006 (Budget Law for 2007), provides for the institution in Italy of listed real estate investment companies (SIIQ), a new type of real estate investment vehicle, based on the model of REITs. In particular, the SIIQ will be allowed, upon election, to benefit from a tax exemption regime in respect of the income arising from real property leasing activity. The new provisions only apply to Italian resident companies, or to Italian permanent establishment of an EU real estate company whose shares are listed on a regulated market. The tax exemption regime may be extended, upon joint election, to non-listed subsidiaries of the SIIQ, provided that at least 95 per cent of the voting rights in the ordinary shareholders' meeting, and 95 per cent of the profit participation rights, are owned by an SIIQ (SIINQ). Specific rules are set forth to ensure adequate diffusion of SIIQs' shares among investors. In particular: (i) no single shareholder can hold, directly or indirectly, more than 51 per cent of the voting rights in the ordinary shareholders' meeting and more than 51 per cent of the profit participation rights; and (ii) at least 35 per cent of the shares must be held by shareholders who do not own more than 2 per cent of the voting rights and of the profit participation rights. SIIQs must mainly carry out a real property leasing activity. This condition is fulfilled when: (i) the value of leased real property amounts to at least 80 per cent

of total assets (including the value of shareholdings in SIINQs); and (ii) in each accounting period, at least 80 per cent of the revenues derive from the leasing of real property. To this end, dividends received from SIINQs shall also be taken into account. In order to preserve their status, the SIIQs must distribute to the shareholders, in each accounting period, at least 85 per cent of the lower of the profit deriving from property leasing activities carried out directly or through SIINQ, and the total accounting profit.

The rules and conditions mentioned above significantly restrict the possibility of creating an SIIQ. As a consequence, the use of SIIQs is very limited, and we are not aware of any foreign investors who have structured an SIIQ to manage its investments (but foreign investors may have invested in existing SIIQs).

An alternative structure is one which provides for the setting up of a REIF. Such fund must be managed by a specialised management company, whose activity is regulated by the Bank of Italy (and by the stock market regulator for listed funds). As mentioned above, real estate funds are ideally suited to 'passive' investors, due to the extensive role of the management company in the management of the fund and of the property and to the limited powers which can be granted to the investor. Real estate investment funds are very common and often used by foreign investors.

From a tax perspective, the Italian tax system provides for a general exemption from income taxes both at the level of the fund and at the level of the investors' unit proceeds. In particular, an Italian real estate fund is neither subject to ordinary personal income tax, nor to corporate income tax, nor to the local tax on productive activities. Accordingly, income deriving to the fund from the ownership, management (rentals) and any transfer (capital gain) of properties, is not taxed at fund level. The fund is taxed through a substitutive/withholding taxation regime, for financial income received, with some limited exceptions. On certain conditions, a one per cent wealth tax is applicable to the real estate funds whose units are not to be traded on regulated stock exchange markets and whose net asset value does not exceed €400 million. However, it should be considered that such one per cent wealth tax has been abolished by the abovementioned Law Decree no. 78/2010 which, if not converted into law by 30 July 2010, will be cancelled and its relevant provisions will be considered as never enacted.

As to the income distributions made by the fund, it should be pointed out that if the relevant unitholders qualify as:
(i) individuals carrying out commercial activities for units held as business assets;
(ii) Italian resident partnerships;
(iii) Italian resident companies and public and private entities other than companies, carrying out commercial activity as their main exclusive object; or
(iv) permanent establishments in Italy of non-resident entities;
then such distributions are subject to a 20 per cent withholding tax to be applied as an account income tax. Accordingly, should this be the case, the proceeds arising from the investment in the real estate fund must

be included in the investor's relevant annual income tax return and are therefore subject to general Italian income taxation. On certain conditions such income may be also subject to local tax. In all other cases, the relevant management company applies a 20 per cent final withholding tax. For foreign investors, it should be considered that a special exemption regime should in principle be provided for investors resident for tax purposes in a country included in the White List. However, as already noted, such exemption regime has been recently abolished by the Law Decree no. 78/2010, whose provisions should be confirmed when it will be converted into law by 30 July 2010.

4. FINANCING AN ACQUISITION
4.1 Financing of corporate real estate transactions
Acquisitions of large real estate portfolios or companies holding real estate are generally financed through bank loan facilities or through the independent financial resources of the investor. In some cases (usually if the financing is for a significant amount) the initial bank loan is subsequently securitised.

As mentioned above, in some cases the property can be acquired by means of a financial lease, in which a leasing company purchases the property and then leases it to the investor, with an option for the investor to buy the property at a pre-set price at the end of the lease period. This structure is mostly used for small and medium sized transactions usually involving a single property.

4.2 Real estate as a means of raising finance
Real estate is often given as security (by means of a mortgage and, sometimes, an assignment of rent receivables) against financing to the owner or a third party. In some cases (usually if the financing is for a significant amount) the initial bank loan is subsequently securitised.

An alternative structure, used mostly by Italian investors, is a sale and lease back transaction, whereby the owner sells the property to a leasing company, which in turn leases the property back to the seller, with an option for the seller to repurchase the property after a certain period of time against payment of a pre-set price. In such structures the 'financing' is given by the leasing company in the form of price for the original purchase of the property, and pursuant to the leaseback agreement the lessee pays to the leasing company a rent against the right to use the property during the lease period. Upon expiry of the lease period the lessee has the right to repurchase the property from the leasing company at a price which was set at the beginning of the lease period. Usually such price is lower than the residual market value of the property, as the amount of the rent is usually set at a level sufficient to ensure an adequate remuneration to the leasing company and to gradually reimburse to the leasing company part of the initial financial outlay for the purchase of the property. In such cases the role of the leasing company is purely financial, the management of the property and all associated costs and benefits are borne by the lessee. Financial leasing activity (including sale and lease back transactions) can be carried out only by regulated financial intermediaries.

Italy

Please note that sale and lease back transactions have to be carefully evaluated and structured, with the involvement of regulated leasing companies, in view of the fact that Italian law does not allow in principle the transfer of ownership of assets as a mechanism to grant security to creditors.

4.3 Common forms of security granted over real estate
Pursuant to Italian law only two kinds of *in rem* security can be granted over real estate, mortgage (*ipoteca*) or assignment of rent or other receivables (*cessione di crediti in garanzia*).

Security over real estate can only be taken in the form of a mortgage. The security document must be notarised and the mortgage must be registered with the land registry. Registration of the mortgage with the land registry is a constitutive element of the mortgage, ie, the security interest does not exist until registration is made. The mortgage does not involve the transfer of the ownership of the real estate and therefore the chargor can still occupy the real estate.

As for the timing of granting such security, considering that the perfection of the mortgage requires the registration with the competent land register (ie, of the municipality where the property is located), it depends on the number of land registers involved in the mortgage registration (for example when the properties are located in different municipalities). As a matter of practice, registration with the land register may require up to seven business days from the execution of the security agreement.

Of course additional securities (such as pledges on other assets, personal guarantees, etc) can be granted in order to secure the financing for the acquisition of the property. Please note, however, that if the acquisition is carried out through a real estate fund, security given by the unit holders of the fund (as opposed to security given by the fund itself) may raise some concerns from a regulatory and tax standpoint and should be carefully evaluated.

4.4 Real estate mortgage securitisation
Real estate mortgage securitisation is used both with respect to mortgage financing granted with respect to a single transaction of significant value and with respect to portfolios of small mortgage loans.

5. MANAGING THE ACQUISITION PROCESS
5.1 Minimum formalities for the sale and purchase of property
The agreement for the sale of real estate assets, in order to be valid and effective, shall be in writing and signed by the parties. Furthermore, if the agreement is a definitive agreement which transfers the ownership of the assets (as opposed to a preliminary agreement whereby the parties only undertake to transfer the ownership at a later date) the parties must:
- indicate in the agreement the building permits pursuant to which any buildings being transferred have been built;
- if the transaction concerns land (as opposed to buildings), attach to the agreement a certificate (issued by the municipality) indicating the allowed uses for such land;

- pursuant to the newly-issued Law Decree no. 78/2010, check that the situation of the asset is correctly reflected in the cadaster (which is the real estate registry for tax purposes);
- include in the agreement the cadaster data of the asset and a statement of the seller to the effect that the cadaster correctly reflects the actual situation of the asset;
- indicate in the agreement whether the transaction has been assisted by any agent or intermediary and in such a case how much has been paid in fees to such agent or intermediary; and
- indicate in the agreement how the price has been (or will be) paid.

With respect to assets in some regions of Italy it is also necessary to attach to agreements for the sale of buildings a certificate indicating the energy consumption of the property.

In order to ensure the enforceability of the agreement *vis à vis* third parties (eg, in order to ensure that the purchase agreement prevails over a subsequent sale of the same property by the original seller to another person) the agreement must be registered at the land registry, and in order to obtain such registration the agreement must be notarised or the signatures of the parties must be confirmed by a court. From a practical standpoint all agreements for the sale and purchase of property (except for letters of intent and a few preliminary agreements which do not transfer the ownership of the property) are notarised and registered with the land registry.

In certain regions of Italy (Trentino Alto Adige and certain other areas in north east Italy) (the Special Regions) the transfer of ownership of the real estate asset occurs only upon registration with the land registry, and therefore the notarisation and subsequent registration of the transfer is even more important than in the other regions.

In some cases (eg, properties of historical, artistic and archaeological interest) additional formalities and steps may be necessary.

5.2 Main legal documents required to transfer a property or grant a lease?

- For a property purchase, the transfer agreement is the principal legal document. Its notarisation implies that the public notary is obliged to register the deed at the land registry, and that the deed will be enforceable *vis à vis* third parties (see above with respect to the Special Regions).
- Property purchases are usually preceded by a preliminary sale and purchase agreement, which sets out the undertakings of the parties to execute the definitive sale and purchase agreement. Such preliminary sale and purchase agreements may be notarised and registered at the land registry, thus giving priority in case sale and purchase agreements are executed by the seller with a third party before the definitive sale and purchase agreement is executed between the seller and the buyer.
- For the validity of the purchase of a land parcel (as opposed to buildings) having a surface area exceeding 5,000 square metres, the up-to-date 'zoning allowed use certificate' of the property is required, and must be attached to the relevant sale and purchase agreement.

Italy

- For the grant of a lease, the lease agreement is the principal legal document.

5.3 Property transaction costs
The buyer typically pays:
- for its due diligence (if any) and legal advisors;
- the cost of enquiries of the statutory undertakers and public bodies (carried out as part of the legal due diligence);
- registration, mortgage and cadastral taxes;
- notarial fee for the notarisation of the deed of transfer;
- a share of the agency fees, if any; and
- any valuation or survey report fees.

The seller typically pays:
- for its due diligence (if any) and legal advisors;
- costs of preparing certificates of title for the property (sometimes including the updated notarial report); and
- a share of the agency fees, if any.

5.4 Does the seller warrant its ownership of the property?
By law, the seller must give a full warranty of title. Except for express disclosure, such warranty implies that the seller is disposing of the property free from all charges and from all other third party rights. The warranty can be limited, but the seller is always liable for problems on title arising from its own actions (eg, a previous sale to another buyer).

5.5 Warranties a seller usually gives to a buyer
The seller generally represents and warrants that full ownership of the property:
- is free from any liens, easements and encumbrances or third party claims or rights;
- has been built and used in compliance with applicable law and the building permits disclosed to the buyer; and
- is in compliance with the current town planning provisions with regards to its current use; and
- is in compliance with environmental and health protection laws.

In addition, the seller might also give additional warranties, such as the validity and enforceability of lease agreements concerning the property and the absence of works in progress with respect to the property.

5.6 Purpose of warranties in the purchase agreement
The warranties perform both roles. Their main role is to provide indemnification in favour of the purchaser, thus apportioning the risk between the parties. However, as an indirect effect, they also ensure that the seller carefully discloses potential issues in order to limit its own liability.

5.7 Owners/occupiers' liability for matters relating to the property which occurred before they bought or occupied
Owners or occupiers are not generally responsible for matters which occurred before their purchase or occupation of the property. There are,

Italy

however, some limited exceptions, such as environmental or certain tax matters, with respect to which the authorities may raise claims against the current owner of the property (or cause a forced sale of the property to use the proceeds to pay tax issues) even if the environmental or tax issue has occurred when the property was owned by another person.

5.8 Notarisation
The sale and purchase of a property needs to be notarised. In particular, notarisation ensures registration with the land registry and enforceability *vis à vis* third parties (and, in the Special Regions above, is required for the transfer of ownership).

5.9 Formalities for a contract becoming a legally binding obligation
The contract for the sale and purchase of a property must be in writing and signed by the parties. As mentioned above, notarisation is necessary in order to proceed with the registration with the land registry.

5.10 Point at which the parties become legally bound
Pursuant to Article 1326 of the Italian Civil Code a document becomes a legally binding contract when the party who made the offer is informed of the other party's acceptance.

5.11 Transfer of title
Unless otherwise agreed between the parties, the execution of the sale and purchase agreement by the parties is sufficient for the transfer of ownership.

Payment of the purchase price or delivery are not, unless otherwise agreed, essential to the transfer of title over the goods or property being sold. Please note that in the Special Regions, legal title passes to the buyer once registration with the land registry is performed. In some other cases (eg buildings of historical, artistic and archaeological interest, assets owned by certain entities) additional formalities must be complied with.

5.12 Insurance of the property if there is delay between agreeing terms and actual sale
Usually the owner/seller insures the property until the transfer of ownership.

6. REAL ESTATE BASICS
6.1 Main sources of laws that govern real estate
The Italian Civil Code governs *inter alia*: (i) the ownership of properties or lands and other *in rem* rights (such as usufruct, use, *emphyteusis*, etc); (ii) sale and purchase agreements; and (iii) lease agreements.

Property is increasingly also governed by special laws (such as Italian Law no. 392/1978, which deals with leases of town properties, and Italian Legislative Decree no. 122/2005, which regulates the sale of real estate still under construction, and grants particular guarantees in favour of the purchasers).

In addition to the above, there are some differences in the laws applicable

Italy

to Italian regions, the main difference relating to the Special Regions mentioned above where the acquisition of the ownership (or other *in rem* rights) of property becomes effective only once the acquisition is registered in the land register.

Certain issues concerning real estate (mainly building codes and permits) are regulated by regional and municipal regulations and orders. Regional and municipal regulations and orders vary in some respects as far as building, permits and other administrative law issues relating to the properties are concerned.

6.2 Types of tenure
The following main types of rights to hold property exist:
- Ownership: the owner is granted a right to enjoy, exploit and dispose of assets in a full and exclusive manner. Ownership can be restricted by covenants and/or the rights of others.
- Time-sharing (*multiproprietà*): this is a situation whereby multiple individuals or entities share the ownership of a property and each is allowed to use the property during a certain period of time. The requirements are: (i) the payment of a price for the use of the property; (ii) the duration of the timesharing right being no less than three years; (iii) the buyer having a right or rights of enjoyment over one or more properties; and (iv) use of the property for at least one week per year in a determined time period.
- Commonhold: under commonhold the ownership (or other *in rem* right) is held jointly by two or more individuals or entities.
- Leasehold: this is a contractual title and is an interest granted for a specified period of time which may contain certain restrictions relating to what the leaseholder can do with the property. Italian Law 392/1978 grants tenants of town property (either business or residential) a right to renew on expiry of their lease for a maximum of four years for residential property, six years for business property and nine years in the case of hotels.
- Usufruct: the owner of real estate may grant to a third party the right to enjoy and exploit the land as if that party was the owner of it, subject to the requirement not to alter the land's character or purpose. The right of usufruct terminates: (i) at the expiration of the usufruct contractual term or, if there is no contractual term set; (ii) when the party vested with the usufruct right dies or (if that party is a corporation) at the expiration of the 30th year. Correspondingly, the owner of the property which has granted a right of usufruct holds a 'naked' ownership, which reverts to full ownership upon expiry of the usufruct.
- Right of occupancy.
- Condominium ownership: whereby each member of a condominium has full ownership of a unit in a building (typically a flat) and the common parts of the building (eg, stairs, lobby, external walls) are held in condominium ownership, usually governed by condominium rules.
- Piecrust lease (*superficie*): whereby the person holding such right can

Italy

build and maintain a building over (or below) another person's property. In such a case the building held under the piecrust lease is owned by the holder of such right, until the piecrust lease expires upon which expiration the owner of the underlying property acquires the full ownership of the building.

6.3 Must land be registered?
Land must be registered in the cadaster register (for tax purposes) and with the land registry. The two registries are currently being unified.

6.4 Public land register
The register is of both title and transactions, ie, by searching under the name of the current owner of the property it is possible to find the transaction by which it has acquired the property (a copy of the deed can usually be obtained by the relevant public notary). Then the search can be extended to the previous owner (as indicated in the register) and so on.

6.5 Land not covered by a public land register
Property must be registered and the relevant register land registry shows transactions.

6.6 State guarantee of title and what categories of documents and information are registered
There are two public record offices that cover real estate properties in Italy and they have separate roles.
- The cadastral archives contain, *inter alia*, the indication of the size of the building, the number of rooms and the intended use. Its main purpose is to ensure payment of real estate taxes.
- The land register list *inter alia*:
  - all certified contracts concerning ownership, rights *in rem* and leases (where the duration of the lease exceeds nine years);
  - the mortgages created over properties; and
  - the judicial claims over property and rights *in rem* and the court decisions affecting the same.

As indicated above, in order to be enforceable *vis à vis* third parties, most transfers of real estate must be registered with the land register. As a consequence the land register is usually more up to date and reliable than the cadastral archives.

Jersey

Carey Olsen Christopher Philpott & Will Whitehead

1. INVESTMENT PURCHASE OVERVIEW

The diagram below provides a graphic overview of a freehold purchase transaction involving Jersey real estate. The timing and process of any given transaction will depend on the nature of the investment being acquired and the chosen acquisition structure. If the transaction in question is an acquisition of shares in a corporate entity which owns Jersey real estate (rather than a freehold acquisition) the process will differ to that outlined. This overview would be broadly similar if an investor were looking to enter into a long term contract lease for Jersey real estate (see 2.2 below).

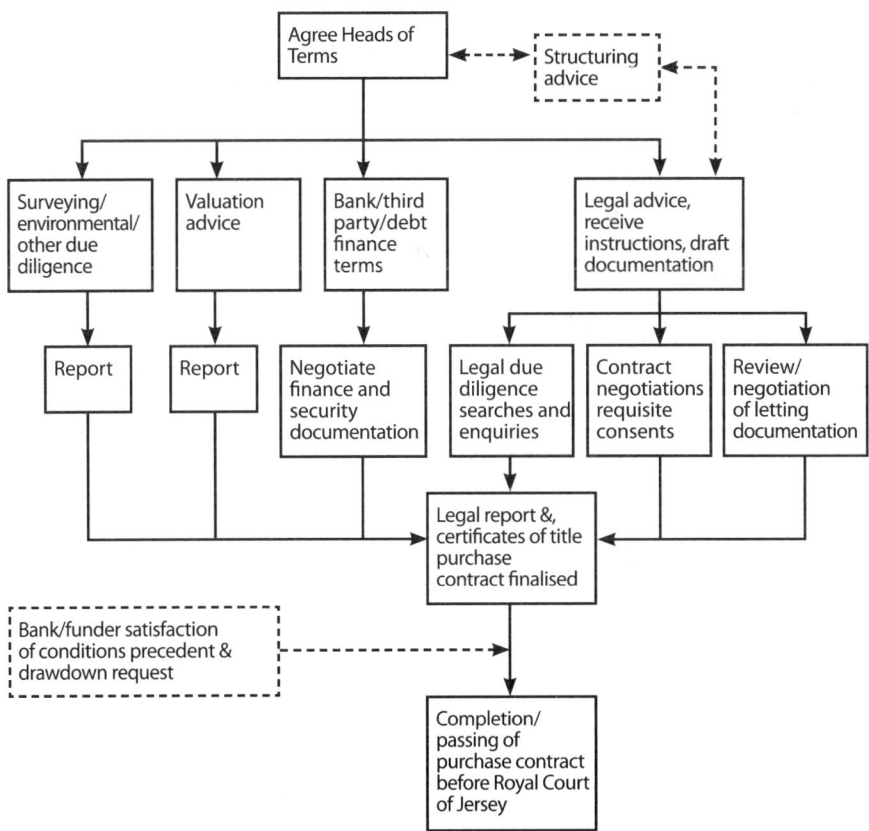

2. TAX CONSIDERATIONS
2.1 Value added tax (VAT)
VAT is not payable in Jersey. A Goods and Services Tax (GST) was introduced in 2008 pursuant to the Goods and Services Tax (Jersey) Law 2007, as amended (the GST Law). Unless specific relief under the GST Law is available, GST will usually be payable by a purchaser on the acquisition of Jersey commercial real estate at the standard rate.

2.1.1 GST on freehold acquisition
The current standard rate of GST in Jersey is three per cent. Whether a given freehold acquisition attracts a GST charge will depend on the nature of the property in question and the GST status of the parties to the transaction.

Jersey residential real estate is generally zero-rated for GST purposes. There are some exceptions to this treatment where the property is registered as either a guest house or lodging house under relevant Jersey legislation. Specific advice should be obtained at an early stage of any proposed acquisition to clarify the permitted use of the property and the GST implications of the relevant transaction. This might involve direct discussions with the Comptroller of Taxes in Jersey whose Department is responsible for administering the GST Law.

Jersey commercial real estate is subject to GST. However, where such real estate is purchased subject to commercial leases, and the property is being acquired as an investment, the acquisition may, where certain conditions are met, be treated as a transfer of a going concern (TOGC) under the GST Law. A TOGC falls outside the scope of GST.

GST is not chargeable on the transfer of shares in a corporate entity which owns Jersey commercial or residential real estate.

2.1.2 GST on rental income
Under the GST Law, a landlord of Jersey commercial real estate is liable to account to the States of Jersey for GST at the standard rate on its rental income if its total annual combined turnover is higher than £300,000 (note that this turnover figure applies to all turnover of the landlord and not simply rental income). If the annual combined turnover of the landlord is higher than £300,000 it is required to register for GST purposes by completing the necessary registration forms and submitting this to the Comptroller of Taxes in Jersey.

Under the GST Law, the legal obligation is on the landlord of Jersey commercial real estate to account for GST on its rental income. The landlord will charge the tenant GST provided the relevant lease contains specific GST provisions. The GST status of the parties is relevant. If either the landlord or the tenant is registered under the GST Law as an International Services Entity (ISE), no GST will be payable.

An ISE is, broadly speaking, treated as being outside the scope of GST. An entity which is entitled to adopt ISE status becomes an ISE when its name is included either on a list of such entities maintained by the Comptroller of Taxes in Jersey or in certain cases on a list maintained by an entity

Jersey

which is authorised to maintain a list of ISEs. An entity will be included on the Comptroller's list if it makes an application to the Comptroller, the Comptroller is satisfied that it meets the relevant requirements and it pays the relevant fee to the Comptroller.

Leases for commercial real estate in Jersey entered into before the GST Law came into force are unlikely to contain adequate recovery provisions and therefore certain 'grandfathering' provisions are included in the GST Law. Leases entered into before 17 August 2007 will be treated as zero-rated supplies for a period of five years from that date (that is to say until 16 August 2012) unless the lease is varied in the meantime.

A potential purchaser of commercial real estate in Jersey will need to get appropriate professional advice to ensure that any commercial leases contain the necessary GST provisions. If not structured correctly, investors could risk incurring additional costs.

2.2 Stamp duty/transfer tax
2.2.1 Stamp duty on freehold acquisitions

Stamp duty in Jersey is governed by the Stamp Duties and Fees (Jersey) Law 1998, as amended, (the Stamp Duty Law). Stamp duty is payable on all acquisitions and transfers of Jersey commercial and residential real estate, on an *ad valorem* basis, unless the transaction in question benefits from specific relief. The amount of stamp duty payable will depend on the purchase price. It is calculated by reference to the higher of: (i) the purchase price; and (ii) the gross value of the property where the property is gifted or transferred for non-monetary consideration.

The current stamp duty rates payable on acquisitions and transfers of Jersey real estate are as follows:

Consideration/ Value of Property	Stamp duty
<£50,000	0.5 per cent per £100 or part thereof (minimum of £10)
>£50,000 but <£300,000	£250 in respect of first £50,000, 1.5 per cent per £100 or part thereof in excess of £50,000
>£300,000 but <£500,000	£4,000 in respect of first £300,000, 2 per cent per £100 or part thereof in excess of £300,000
>£500,000 but <£700,000	£8,000 in respect of first £500,000, 2.5 per cent per £100 or part thereof in excess of £500,000
>£700,000	£13,000 in respect of first £700,000, 3 per cent per £100 or part thereof in excess of £700,000

Unless otherwise agreed between the contracting parties, stamp duty is ordinarily payable by the purchaser/transferee of the property, and must be paid in full prior to the passing of the relevant hereditary contract before the Royal Court of Jersey. The Royal Court of Jersey will refuse to register a contract if the required treasury receipt (showing that stamp duty has been paid) is not attached to the contract.

Stamp duty is not payable on contents, and therefore it is usual for a specific value to be attributable to any contents which are being sold (if any) within the hereditary contract.

There are no stamp duty exemptions available to a purchaser on a freehold acquisition of Jersey commercial real estate. There is also no intra-group relief in Jersey. This means a sale or transfer of Jersey real estate between group companies will ordinarily attract stamp duty at the usual rates as set out above.

Stamp duty is reduced for individuals who are first time buyers of Jersey residential real estate. These reduced rates are only available where the purchase price of the property is £400,000 or less. A person will not qualify for first time buyer rates if they have previously purchased real estate outside Jersey. In order for a purchase contract to be stamped at a reduced rate, a written declaration from the buyer's lawyer is required.

2.2.2 Stamp duty payable on contract leases

Under Jersey law there are two types of lease. Leases having a term of nine years or less are known as paper leases. Those with a term of more than nine years are known as contract leases. Contract leases need to be passed before the Royal Court of Jersey to be legally valid and binding. Paper leases do not need to be passed before the Royal Court of Jersey and can simply be a private agreement between the landlord and the tenant.

Passing a contract lease before the Royal Court of Jersey attracts stamp duty which is broadly calculated as being 0.75 per cent of the commencing annual rental multiplied by the number of years of the term (up to a maximum of 21 years). Any premium paid is also liable to stamp duty at the same rates applicable to freehold transactions.

Paper leases do not attract stamp duty.

2.2.3 Stamp duty on shares

Stamp duty is not payable on the acquisition or transfer of shares in a corporate entity which owns Jersey commercial real estate. However, if the corporate entity owns residential real estate and its articles of association confer specific rights of occupation of that dwelling accommodation onto its shareholders (known in Jersey as share transfer properties (see 6.2 below)), the acquisition or transfer of those shares may be subject to the payment of Land Transaction Tax (LTT) under the Taxation (Land Transactions) (Jersey) Law 2009. This law came into force on 1 January 2010 and was designed to bring the tax treatment of share transfer properties in line with freehold acquisitions. The amount of LTT is broadly the same as the amount of stamp duty that would be payable by a buyer on a freehold purchase.

2.2.4 Stamp duty payable on registration of security

Stamp duty is payable when a lender registers security over Jersey real estate

Jersey

(commonly known as a *hypotheque* or hypothec). Stamp duty is calculated at the rate of 0.5 per cent of the amount of debt secured over the property in favour of the lender, and must be paid in full before the required charge document can be registered in the Jersey Public Registry.

LTT is payable when a lender takes security over a share transfer property and is calculated at a rate of 0.5 per cent of the amount of the debt to be secured.

Stamp duty is generally administered by the Judicial Greffier. Under Article 6 of the Stamp Duty Law, the Judicial Greffier has authority to reduce or remit any stamp duty on a specific transaction where it would, in its opinion, be just to do so. A specific application is required to request the Judicial Greffier to exercise this discretion.

2.3 Tax issues for overseas investors investing in real estate

In addition to those issues surrounding GST, stamp duty and LTT (as set out above) the following tax considerations should be noted by a non-Jersey resident investor looking to acquire Jersey real estate as an investment. As with other jurisdictions, it is advisable for any investor to obtain specific tax advice at an early stage in order to establish the most appropriate and tax efficient purchasing structure.

2.3.1 Income tax

Under the current 'zero/ten' tax regime, a company that is resident in Jersey (subject to certain exceptions) will be liable to income tax at a rate of zero per cent. A key exception is that income earned from land (eg rental income), and any profits from the development of Jersey real estate, will be liable to income tax at the standard rate, currently 20 per cent.

Jersey has rules that allow the amount of rental income that is subject to Jersey income tax, as above, to be reduced by interest paid on third party finance taken out to acquire the Jersey real estate.

Following a recent amendment to the Income Tax (Jersey) Law 1961, non-resident investors who receive rental income from Jersey real estate are liable to have tax, at the standard rate of 20 per cent, withheld from rental payments. The tax is withheld either by the tenant or, if an agent manages the property, the managing agent. A non-resident investor can obtain a certificate of good standing from the Comptroller of Taxes in Jersey, which would allow the rent to be paid without deduction, but subject to the settlement of tax due at the relevant payment date.

2.4 Capital gains

There is no capital gains tax in Jersey. Capital gains are not ordinarily included in ordinary taxable income.

2.5 Capital allowances

Jersey has rules that allow capital allowances to be claimed on certain machinery and plant which will reduce the amount of rent that is subject to Jersey income tax. On any acquisition of Jersey commercial real estate, appropriate apportionment agreements should be considered to ensure maximum benefit is obtained.

3. INVESTMENT VEHICLE CHOICE
3.1 Commonly used structures to purchase property
Much will depend on the preliminary tax advice provided to an investor. Internal restrictions may also dictate how an institutional investor is permitted to acquire an interest in Jersey commercial real estate.

While non-Jersey resident investors often acquire the freehold of Jersey commercial real estate directly into their existing structures, it is more usual for non-resident investors to establish a Jersey company to be used as an SPV for the purposes of acquiring the freehold. Where the freehold is already held by an existing corporate entity, many investors prefer to acquire the asset indirectly (by acquiring the shares) in order to minimise exposure to stamp duty and GST. Acquiring an existing corporate entity carries with it the usual risks associated with pre-existing tax and other liabilities and the additional costs incurred in undertaking the corporate due diligence.

Other vehicles, such as limited partnerships, are rarely used to acquire Jersey real estate.

3.1.1 Jersey investment vehicles commonly used by investors for the purposes of holding non-Jersey real estate
Jersey companies, unit trusts and limited partnerships are all popular vehicles for the holding of non-Jersey real estate. Whereas the precise benefits for investors in each vehicle will usually depend upon the tax treatment obtained in the investor's home jurisdiction (upon which advice should be obtained from an appropriately qualified adviser in the relevant jurisdiction), the vehicles themselves have the following characteristics:
3.1.2 Jersey companies
Jersey companies are broadly equivalent to English companies. However, Jersey companies can have either par value or no par value shares, and can also be structured as 'normal' companies with limited liability shares, guarantee companies (where the liability of members is limited to the amount of a specified guarantee) and unlimited liability companies (where members have unlimited liability). Further, Jersey has pioneered the use of incorporated cell companies (which can create a number of incorporated cells which each have their own legal personality and which are each treated as separate companies for almost all purposes of Jersey companies law) and has also introduced protected cell companies (which can create a number of protected cells which do not have separate legal personality but are otherwise treated as separate companies for almost all purposes of Jersey companies law).

Jersey companies established to hold non-Jersey situate real estate will ordinarily be subject to Jersey income tax at the rate of 0 per cent. Other rates may apply if the company engages in certain categories of financial services business, owns Jersey-situate real property or acts as a utility company (ie, provides water, gas, or electricity in Jersey).

In Jersey, no stamp duty is levied on the issue or transfer *inter vivos* of shares in a Jersey company, save where that company owns Jersey residential real estate. Jersey does not levy taxes upon capital, inheritances, capital gains or gifts nor are there estate duties, except for probate duty upon the death of an individual of up to 0.75 per cent of (in the case of a Jersey resident individual) the value of the individual's estate or (otherwise) the value of the individual's estate in Jersey (which would include the value of any shares in a Jersey company).

3.1.3 Jersey unit trusts
Jersey trust law is largely based upon the law of England and Wales, but with several important differences. The Trusts (Jersey) Law 1984 contains provisions, *inter alia*, which:
- do not require two trustees to be appointed to overreach the interests of beneficiaries;
- do not impose any rule on perpetuities;
- limit the liability of a trustee of a Jersey trust to a third party arising out of any transaction affecting a trust (save for breach of trust) to the relevant trust property (provided the third party was aware that the trustee was acting in such a capacity); and
- enable Jersey trusts to be established for purposes, whether charitable or otherwise, under which there are no named or ascertainable beneficiaries.

Jersey unit trusts cannot currently be used to hold Jersey-situate real estate. The trustees of Jersey unit trusts are, by concession, exempt from Jersey income tax other than on income (except bank deposit interest) arising in Jersey.

In Jersey, no stamp duty is levied on the issue or transfer *inter vivos* of units in a Jersey unit trust. Jersey does not levy taxes upon capital, inheritances, capital gains or gifts nor are there estate duties, except for probate duty upon the death of an individual of up to 0.75 per cent of (in the case of a Jersey resident individual) the value of the individual's estate or (otherwise) the value of the individual's estate in Jersey (which would include the value of any units in a Jersey unit trust).

The Hague Convention on the law applicable to trusts and their recognition was extended to Jersey in 1992.

3.1.4 Jersey limited partnerships
Jersey limited partnerships are broadly equivalent to limited partnerships in England and Wales. They have no legal personality, and must have both at least one general partner (who is responsible for the management of the limited partnership and who has unlimited liability for the debts of the limited partnership) and one limited partner (whose liability is limited to the amount they have agreed to contribute to the limited partnership but who may not take part in the management of the limited partnership without losing such limited liability).

Jersey limited partnerships are transparent for the purposes of Jersey income tax. Accordingly, non Jersey-resident limited partners of Jersey limited partnerships are assessed to Jersey income tax in their own names. Their liability to Jersey income tax is limited to Jersey-source income excluding, by long-standing concession, bank deposit interest. The receipt of any monies in respect of non-Jersey situate assets (such as non-Jersey situate real property) does not constitute Jersey-source income for these purposes.

In Jersey, no stamp duty is levied on the issue or transfer *inter vivos* of limited partnership interests in a Jersey limited partnership. Jersey does not levy taxes upon capital, inheritances, capital gains or gifts nor are there estate duties, except for probate duty upon the death of an individual of up to 0.75 per cent of (in the case of a Jersey resident individual) the value of the individual's estate or (otherwise) the value of the individual's estate in Jersey (which would include the value of any interest in a Jersey limited partnership).

3.2 Restrictions on foreign ownership or occupation of property and on foreign guarantees or security

There are no restrictions on foreign guarantees or security in Jersey.

Land is a scarce resource in Jersey. Due to the high levels of demand, the real estate market is regulated by the States of Jersey. All transactions involving the sale, acquisition or transfer of Jersey real estate (including the registration or assignment of contract leases) require the prior consent of the States of Jersey Housing Minister. Consent must be obtained for each freehold or leasehold property transaction by making the necessary applications.

The residential real estate market in Jersey is highly regulated in order to preserve the housing stock for locally qualified residents. In order to acquire the freehold of a residential property, a purchaser must qualify under the Housing (Jersey) Law 1949 and the Housing (General Provisions) (Jersey) Regulations 1970. There are a number of specific categories under the Regulations and a person must fall within one of those categories in order to be entitled to purchase and occupy Jersey residential real estate. Non-resident investors who do not qualify under the Regulations may nevertheless purchase share transfer properties (see 6.2 below) without the consent of the States of Jersey Housing Minister, but will not ordinarily be able to occupy such properties.

The commercial real estate market in Jersey is more accessible with non-resident investors being able to freely acquire commercial property, but such transactions still require the prior consent of the States of Jersey Housing Minister. When acquiring either commercial, residential or mixed use real estate in Jersey, careful consideration needs to be given to any occupancy restrictions which may affect the property in question.

3.3 Real estate investment trusts (REITs)

In respect of non-Jersey real estate, Jersey entities structured as collective investment funds are either subject to Jersey income tax at a rate of zero per cent or are otherwise not subject to Jersey income tax. Accordingly, there has not been any need for Jersey to introduce REITS. As for Jersey real estate, Jersey law does not recognise a trust of Jersey immovable property. It is,

Jersey

however, possible for the shares in a Jersey company which owns Jersey real estate to be held on trust. A foreign trust shall be unenforceable in Jersey to the extent that it purports to apply directly to real estate in Jersey.

4. FINANCING AN ACQUISITION
4.1 Financing corporate real estate transactions
There are a variety of ways in which commercial real estate transactions may be financed in Jersey. As foreign investors hold Jersey commercial real estate, either individually or as part of a larger portfolio, Jersey is exposed to many of the same financing trends experienced in the UK and elsewhere. Jersey real estate financing is usually a mix of debt and equity. The most common means of financing Jersey real estate transactions is direct financial assistance from a lender to enable an investor to acquire a specific property.

As with many other jurisdictions, the amount of debt that lenders are willing to advance has decreased over the past 18-24 months. Currently levels of debt provided by lenders in respect of Jersey real estate acquisitions are typically in the region of 60-70 per cent of the purchase cost.

4.2 Real estate as a means of raising finance
The availability of debt has been restricted over the past 18-24 months. Jersey real estate owners are finding it increasingly difficult to release equity from their properties in traditional equity release re-financing structures. There have recently been several 'sale and lease-back' transactions involving Jersey commercial real estate, enabling business occupiers to extract capital value from their properties.

4.3 Forms of security granted over real estate to raise finance
The nature of the security package required by a lender will naturally depend on the nature of property, the structure of the transaction and the proposed debt/equity split. The primary security required by a lender would normally be *hypothec* (charge) secured over the Jersey real estate in question.

In order to secure a *hypothec* over Jersey real estate, a borrower will sign a *Billet* (charge document) which is then registered before the Royal Court of Jersey by the lender's lawyers on a Friday afternoon. It is the registration of this document that creates the hypothec (charge) over the property. *Hypothecs* can be specific (ie, over one property) or general (ie, attaching to all Jersey real estate owned by the borrower at the date of registration).

In share transfer transactions (see 6.2), as the purchaser acquires an interest in shares in a Jersey company (rather than an interest in the property) share security will be required by a lender. Share security is created by a Jersey law security interest agreement, in accordance with the terms of the Security Interests (Jersey) Law 1983. Share security over a Jersey registered company can be created at any time (and not only on a Friday afternoon as with registration of security over Jersey real estate).

There is no concept of a floating charge in Jersey.

If a property is subject to either paper leases or contract leases, it is common for a lender to take security over the lease receivables (rents, deposits etc). In order to obtain such security, a Jersey law security interest agreement is required.

Where the borrower/purchasing entity is a special purpose vehicle (SPV), a lender will frequently require share security to be provided by the parent company/beneficial owner. In order to obtain such security, a Jersey law security interest agreement will be required.

If the property in question has recently been developed or is in the course of development at the time of the financing, a lender will in the usual way require security over, or an assignment of, the major contracts, supported by appropriate warranties from the professional team.

The terms of any financing arrangement will be determined on the facts of each case. However, standard conditions imposed by lenders often include prohibiting alienation or granting additional third party (second ranking) security without the lender's consent.

4.4 Real estate mortgage securitisation

Although due to the manner in which security is taken over Jersey-situated real estate (see response to question 4.3), it is not ordinarily straightforward for such security to be used in support of mortgage securitisations, we are aware of a small number of instances where loans secured against Jersey-situate real estate have formed part of larger portfolios of loans which have been securitised.

By contrast, there are many instances where loans secured against non-Jersey situate real estate owned (or held as nominee) by Jersey companies, unit trusts and limited partnerships have been securitised and many instances where Jersey companies, unit trusts and limited partnerships have been used as issuing vehicles in connection with real estate mortgage securitisations.

5. MANAGING THE ACQUISITION PROCESS
5.1 Minimum formalities for the sale and purchase of property

A hereditary contract, pursuant to which a seller sells the property to the buyer, must be passed before the Royal Court of Jersey on a Friday afternoon and registered in the Jersey Public Registry. A hereditary contract must be in writing, and must contain sufficient information to identify the seller, the purchaser, the property, and the hereditary rights and servitudes affecting the property.

Until November 2006, all hereditary contracts (other than contract leases) were written and registered in the French language and consequently researching title to Jersey real estate requires specialist knowledge.

As all hereditary contracts must be passed before the Royal Court of Jersey, there is no requirement for them to be signed or executed by the parties. Each party (either personally or by attorney) must appear before the Royal Court in order for the hereditary contract to be passed.

The prior consent of the States of Jersey Housing Minister is required before a hereditary contract can be passed.

5.2 Main legal documents required to transfer a property or grant a lease

The principal legal documents are:
- for a freehold sale or transfer: a hereditary contract;
- for a paper lease: a lease agreement; and
- for a contract lease: a hereditary contract of lease.

On some transactions the parties will agree to enter into a preliminary agreement preceding the sale of a property or the grant of a lease. Such agreements typically provide that the transaction shall complete on the satisfaction of specific conditions.

5.3 Property transaction costs

For freehold transactions involving Jersey real estate, the seller will typically pay:
- its own legal and other professional costs;
- estate agent fees;
- the costs of any insurances, contracts or other agreements required to remedy defects or inconsistencies in title; and
- lender redemption fees.

The buyer will typically pay:
- its own legal and other professional costs (including surveys and valuations);
- the costs of undertaking searches and enquiries of the statutory bodies (where such searches are undertaken as part of the due diligence process);
- the costs of obtaining any statutory or regulatory consents;
- its lender's legal and other costs; and
- stamp duty.

5.4 Does the seller warrant its ownership of the property?

A seller does not warrant its ownership in Jersey. This is a matter for the buyer's lawyer.

5.5 Warranties a seller usually gives to a buyer

There are very few express contractual warranties contained within a standard hereditary contract of sale or transfer. It is usual for a seller to provide certain pre-contract confirmations in response to a purchaser's enquiries.

Warranties that a seller usually provides to a buyer within a standard hereditary contract of sale or transfer include:
- that the property is sold free of hypothecs and other encumbrances; and
- that any contents included in the sale are the absolute property of the seller.

In the event of a sale of shares in a corporate entity which owns Jersey real estate, specific warranties concerning the company and its ownership of the property will be included within the share purchase agreement. The scope and extent of such warranties will be negotiated between the parties.

5.6 Purpose of warranties in the purchase agreement
The extent and purpose of any warranties given by the seller will depend on the nature of the transaction and the commercial terms agreed between the parties.

5.7 Owners/occupiers' liability for matters relating to the property which occurred before they bought or occupied
There are certain circumstances where the buyer may be liable for matters which occurred before their acquisition of the property, such as:
- if the property encroaches onto a neighbouring property;
- if the property is in breach of any hereditary obligations; or
- if there are historic breaches of local planning or environmental legislation.

Contract leases generally include provisions whereby the tenant is required to comply with legislation affecting the use of the property and any encumbrances that may affect the property.

On acquisitions of corporate entities owning Jersey real estate, a purchaser ordinarily assumes all liabilities of the company in respect of the property, subject to such warranties or indemnities as may be provided in the share purchase agreement

5.8 Notarisation
There is no requirement under Jersey law for a hereditary contract to be notarised, either in respect of a freehold sale or transfer, or of a contract lease.

5.9 Formalities for a contract becoming a legally binding obligation
A hereditary contract of purchase or transfer must be passed before the Royal Court of Jersey to be legally valid and binding. This is also the position for contract leases.

Paper leases are not required to be passed before the Royal Court of Jersey and become legally binding once validly executed and exchanged by the parties.

5.10 Point at which the parties become legally bound
The parties are legally bound once the hereditary contract of purchase or transfer, or contract lease, is passed before the Royal Court of Jersey on a Friday afternoon.

The parties to a paper lease are legally bound on execution of the lease agreement by each party. Completion of a paper lease can occur on any day.

5.11 Transfer of title
Freehold title transfers to a purchaser on the passing of the hereditary contract before the Royal Court of Jersey on a Friday afternoon.

5.12 Insurance of the property if there is delay between agreeing terms and actual sale
It is usual for the seller to insure the property up until transfer of legal title.

6. REAL ESTATE LAW BASICS

6.1 Main sources of laws that govern real estate

Jersey is the largest of the Channel Islands and is a self-governing British Crown Dependency with its own financial and legal systems and its own courts of law.

Jersey property law is derived from a mixture of local statute and customary law. Customary law has evolved from Norman-French law over the past 800 years and is primarily contained in the judgments of the Royal Court of Jersey and the writings of local and French jurists. The Jersey Public Registry (in which all hereditary contracts concerning real estate must be registered) dates from 1604.

6.2 Types of tenure

The following types of property ownership/tenure exist in Jersey:
- Freehold: (*a fin d'heritage*) – ownership in perpetuity.
- Leasehold: being rights of tenure created by paper leases and contract leases. Contract leases must be passed before the Royal Court of Jersey to be legally valid and binding.
- Flying freehold: a form of ownership established by the *Loi (1991) sur la copropriété des immeubles batis* – typically used for multiple dwelling properties, such as apartment blocks. Recently some commercial property developments have been structured as flying freehold developments under this law. An owner of a flying freehold 'lot' has exclusive ownership of the 'lot' and a shared interest in the common parts of the property, all of which are specifically defined within a co-ownership declaration registered before the Royal Court of Jersey.
- Share transfer: share transfer ownership structures are used as a method of dividing property (such as apartments) into separate units. Unlike freehold and flying freehold ownership, the freehold of the property is owned by a Jersey company. Purchasers acquire individual blocks of shares in the underlying property holding company and there are various rights attaching to those shares pursuant to the constitutional documents which allow the shareholder specific rights of exclusive use and occupation of a particular flat or unit at the property. There is no purchase contract required (unlike freehold or flying freehold transactions) but there will be a share purchase agreement agreed and signed between the parties confirming the transfer of the shares.

6.3 Must land be registered?

There is no system of registered title in Jersey. However, all hereditary contracts relating to land must be passed before the Royal Court of Jersey to be legally valid and binding. Once passed, such hereditary contracts are registered and available for inspection in the Jersey Public Registry.

If property is acquired by way of an acquisition of shares in a corporate entity which owns Jersey real estate, there is no requirement to register details of the transfer in the Jersey Public Registry (although the transfer must be registered in the company's register of members). The hereditary contract by

Jersey

which that corporate entity acquired the property in question will previously have been registered in the Jersey Public Registry.

6.4 Land not covered by a public land register
The Jersey Public Registry is a register of land transactions. Title to a property is established by the buyer's lawyer who must investigate and review all relevant hereditary contracts relating to the property which have been registered in the Jersey Public Registry.

6.5 State guarantee of title
There is no state guarantee of title in Jersey. In practice, the risk of establishing good title rests with the buyer's lawyer.

Luxembourg

Arendt & Medernach Eric Fort & Claude Niedner

1. INVESTMENT PURCHASE OVERVIEW

Typical investment purchase in Luxembourg

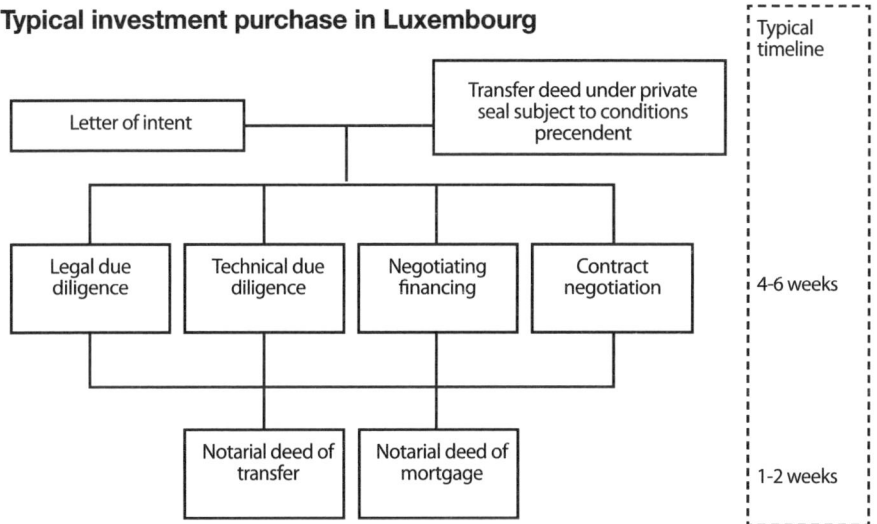

2. TAXATION
2.1 Direct acquisition of real estate
Registration duties

The transfer of real estate located in Luxembourg is subject to registration duties assessed on the purchase price or the effective value of the property, whichever is higher.

The aggregate tax burden for the transfer of immovable property situated in Luxembourg City amounts to 10 per cent (ie, six per cent registration duties plus three per cent municipal surcharge when the property is located in Luxembourg City plus one per cent transcription duty). The registration duties are payable on the registration of the transfer of property with the register of mortgages.

The contribution of real estate situated in Luxembourg benefits from a reduced registration duty of 0.6 per cent (plus a municipal surcharge of 0.3 per cent for real estate located in Luxembourg City) and a reduced transcription duty of 0.5 per cent provided that such contribution is remunerated by shares (*droits sociaux*).

Luxembourg

Taxation of rental income
Non-Luxembourg resident companies are subject to corporate income tax (*impôt sur le revenu des collectivités* or CIT) at a rate of 21.84 per cent in 2010 including the solidarity surcharge while non-resident individuals are subject to the progressive scale of income tax (current marginal rate of 38.95 per cent in 2010, including the employment fund contribution) on their rental income realised in Luxembourg.

Non-resident corporate and individual taxpayers are subject to a minimum rate of 15.37 per cent (including the employment fund contribution) unless they file a request with the Luxembourg tax authorities to be treated as a Luxembourg resident. Please note that according to a bill introduced before Luxembourg Parliament on 28 April 2010, the 15.37 per cent threshold may be reduced in some limited cases.

Taxation of capital gains on real estate
Capital gains realised on the sale of a property by non-resident companies are subject to CIT at the same rate than the one applicable to current income (ie, 21.84 per cent in 2010 including the solidarity surcharge).

Capital gains realised upon the disposal of a Luxembourg real property (forming part of a permanent establishment's net assets for at least five years prior to disposal) are not taxable at the time of disposal if the proceeds of sale are reinvested into another eligible property. Please note that this mechanism does not provide for an exemption but for a tax deferral. In addition, the tax deferral may be obtained if the new real property is acquired prior to the disposal of the real property being sold (the latter needs however to be sold within two years of the acquisition of the new real property).

VAT considerations
Considering Article 135 section 1(j) of Council Directive 2006/112/EC of 28 November 2006 and Article 44 section 1(f) of the Luxembourg VAT law, the supply of a building or parts thereof as well as the real estate rights is exempt from VAT. This VAT exemption does not apply to a building which has not been built at the time the sale is concluded. Such a transfer of a building which is yet to be built is subject to VAT at the standard rate of 15 per cent. Furthermore, the VAT law specifically provides for the transfer to be subject to VAT by means of a VAT option form, which has to be filed with the relevant VAT office. The grand-ducal decree of 7 March 1980, which determines the conditions to opt for the application of the VAT regime, provides inter alia that the building has to be affected by the purchaser mainly to activities allowing the deduction of input VAT. The purpose of this specific option is that the seller has the right to deduct its input VAT on overheads and investment costs (ie, VAT paid on the construction of the property).

2.1.1 Special purpose vehicle acquisition
To avoid direct acquisition of real estate, quite often special purpose vehicles

(SPVs) are set up for tax reasons, whereby the company holding the real estate can be acquired/sold. In such a case, from a legal point of view, the real estate does not change owner and thus no registration or transcription duties would be due as the object of the sale is shares in a company and not real estate.

In order to avoid any issues with regard to a share deal appearing to be a sham transaction a careful review of the legal documentation is required. According to Luxembourg case law, sham transactions require a fraudulent act, which can be avoided if the parties to the contract have the choice between two possible options and in a legitimate way decide to proceed with the more tax efficient option and follow it through the transaction to the eventual outcome.

Luxembourg SPVs are as a general rule subject to CIT and municipal business tax (*impôt commercial communal* – MBT) on their worldwide profits (including recurrent income and capital gains) subject to the provisions of any applicable double tax treaty. CIT is levied at an effective current rate of 21 per cent (21.84 per cent including the four per cent surcharge designated for employment funds) and MBT is levied at a variable rate according to the municipality in which the SPV is located (6.75 per cent for Luxembourg City). The maximum aggregate corporate income tax and municipal business tax rate amounts to 28.59 per cent (Luxembourg City). Luxembourg imposes additional net worth tax (*impôt sur la fortune* – NWT) on Luxembourg SPVs at the rate of 0.5 per cent applied to net assets as determined for net worth tax purposes on 1 January.

The disposal of the shares in an SPV is not subject to Luxembourg registration tax or stamp duty, if the transfer of the shares is not the subject of a Luxembourg notarial deed or otherwise registered in Luxembourg. If the share purchase agreement is voluntarily registered, a fixed registration duty of €12 would apply.

Should the SPV holding the real estate property be a Luxembourg resident company and be held by a non-resident investor, the capital gains realised by the investor will generally only be taxable if the investor: i) holds more than 10 per cent of the share capital of the Luxembourg resident SPV; and ii) sells the interest within six months following its acquisition (only applicable where no double tax treaty is applicable between Luxembourg and the country of residence of the non-resident investor).

2.1.2 Real estate certificates

The acquisition of real estate through a Luxembourg SPV may be financed by the issue of real estate certificates, which are either registered certificates or bearer certificates.

Holders of real estate certificates do not benefit from a fixed profit but they are creditors of: (i) the net income deriving from the real estate (rents less expenses); and (ii) from a part of the capital gains deriving from the future sale of the real estate. Such holders are from a legal and tax perspective not considered as owners of the real estate (the real estate belongs to the issuing company) nor as shareholders of the issuing company (the company belongs to the shareholders and not the real estate certificate holders).

Even though the issue of the real estate certificates requires a public or private placement, according to the current practice of the Luxembourg tax authorities, there is no condition regarding the number, the residency or the fiscal status of the investors.

Contrary to ordinary certificates or bonds, whose return is generally fixed at the date of issue, the return on the real estate certificates depends on the rental income and, as the case may be, on the capital gain realised on the later sale of the real estate.

The company distributes to the certificate holders the difference between the gross rental income from the real estate and the expenses in relation to the real estate. According to current administrative practice, this sum corresponds partially to a reimbursement of the principal amount of the real estate certificates and partially as an interest payment. The principal part corresponds generally to the depreciation rate of the real estate and the related supplemental acquisition costs and does not constitute a deductible expense for the issuing company and generally does not result in taxable income in the hands of the certificate holders. Correspondingly, a depreciation in value of the property or any loss realised on the property, will be mirrored by a partial reimbursement of the principal of the real estate certificates. The other part of the proceeds paid to the real estate certificate holders being considered as interest, results in a tax deductible charge for the company and income from capital at the level of the certificate holder, which can be generally distributed free of withholding tax.

With the sale of the real estate the issuing company will be liquidated. The capital gain realised by the company will be distributed to the certificate holders primarily as a reimbursement of the principal of the certificates. Cash which exceeds the principal will be distributed to the investors as an interest payment. Such interest payments result in a tax deductible charge for the company and income from capital at the level of the certificate holders, which can be generally made free of withholding tax.

3. INVESTMENT VEHICLE CHOICE
3.1 Unregulated real estate investment structures
In order to improve the tax efficiency of a real estate investment, it may be envisaged that instead of directly acquiring the shares of an SPV, to acquire these shares through a Luxembourg holding company named *Société de participation financière* or SOPARFI.

3.1.1 Legal aspects
SOPARFIs are unregulated vehicles governed by the law on commercial companies dated 10 August 1915 as amended (the '1915 Law'), and may therefore adopt any company form available in accordance with the 1915 Law, the most commonly used being the public limited company (*société anonyme* or SA), the private limited company (*société à responsabilité limitée* or Sàrl) and the partnership limited by shares (*société en commandite par Actions* or SCA).

Alternatively, the company may be established as a cooperative company (*société coopérative* or SC), a cooperative company in the form of a public limited company (*société coopérative sous forme de société anonyme* or SCoSA), a limited partnership (*société en commandite simple* or SCS) or a general partnership (*société en nom collectif* or SNC).

Additionally, the financing of the SOPARFIs may be provided through a variety of debt, equity and hybrid instruments (including (convertible) preferred equity certificates (ie CPECs and PECs) and profit participating loans) to ensure a tax efficient real estate investment structure at the level of the real estate investment and the SOPARFI as well as for resident and non-resident investors.

SOPARFIs need to be provided with a registered office but do not have to own or rent premises. However, foreign legislation from a tax perspective generally requires appropriate business substance in the Grand Duchy of Luxembourg.

3.1.2 Tax aspects
SOPARFIs are fully taxable entities and are thus eligible entities under Luxembourg double tax treaties as well as the EC Parent-Subsidiary Directive.

Taxation of SOPARFIs
Upon incorporation, any contribution, whether in cash or in kind (particular rules apply for the contribution of real properties) triggers a fixed registration duty of €75. The same fixed registration duty will apply each time the by-laws of the company will be amended.

SOPARFIs are as a general rule subject to CIT and MBT on their worldwide profits (subject to the provisions of any applicable double tax treaty) at an aggregate rate of 28.59 per cent in 2010.

SOPARFIs are also subject to NWT at the rate of 0.5 per cent applied to net assets as determined for net worth tax purposes on 1 January.

However, under the participation exemption regime, the following exemptions are available:
- dividends, liquidation proceeds and capital gains realised on shareholdings representing at least 10 per cent or an acquisition cost of at least €1.2 million (€6 million as regards capital gains) in eligible subsidiaries are exempted in the hands of the SOPARFI from CIT and MBT, provided such participation is held for at least 12 months;
- dividends distributed by SOPARFIs under participations representing at least 10 per cent of the capital of the distributing company or an acquisition price of at least €1.2 million to eligible parent companies are exempted from dividend withholding tax, provided such participation is held for at least 12 months; and
- qualifying shareholdings are exempted from NWT.

Taxation of investors
Non-resident shareholders of a SOPARFI are not subject to any capital gains or income tax in Luxembourg, except for:

- those who hold more than 10 per cent of the shares of the SOPARFI and who dispose of all or part of their holdings within six months from the date of acquisition (only in case no double tax treaty is applicable); or
- in some limited cases, some former residents of Luxembourg who hold more than 10 per cent of the shares of a SOPARFI (only in case no double tax treaty is applicable).

Distribution of liquidation proceeds (deriving from pre-existing reserves or otherwise) is neither subject to a withholding tax nor generally subject to taxation in the hands of non-resident shareholders.

3.1.3 International aspects
SOPARFIs are fully-taxable entities and as such can generally benefit from local withholding tax exemptions in the countries where investments are realised under the EC Parent-Subsidiary Directive, the Directive on Interest and Royalty Payments as well as under the double tax treaties (DTT) concluded by Luxembourg (Luxembourg has currently concluded 57 double tax treaties).

3.1.4 VAT aspects
In principle, the mere holding of participations in a company and the granting of one single loan are not to be regarded as economic activities conferring on the holder the status of a taxable person. If the scope of the activities includes, for example, granting of several remunerated loans or providing services on a regular and ongoing basis, the company providing these services would acquire the status of a taxable person for VAT purposes with all the consequences in relation to it (VAT registration, VAT returns, place of supply rules, etc).

3.2 Regulated real estate investment structures
Luxembourg regulated investment vehicles are very tax efficient for the acquisition of real estate as they benefit from a favourable tax regime consisting mostly of:
(i) the exemption of vehicles from CIT and MBT on current income and capital gains;
(ii) the exemption of non-resident investors on capital gains realised on the shares of the vehicles except if a) they hold more than 10 per cent of the share capital of the vehicle and b) they sell their participation within six months following its acquisition;
(iii) an exemption from withholding tax on dividends, capital gains and interests (save for limited exceptions); and
(iv) a liability to a 0.05 per cent subscription tax (with reduced rates and exemptions available).

For an overview of the Luxembourg tax treatment of regulated investment structures, please refer to the chart below.

3.2.1 Forms of regulated real estate investment structures
Regulated real estate funds may be created both under the law of 20

December 2002 on undertakings for collective investments (the 2002 Law) or under the law of 13 February 2007 on specialised investment funds (the SIF Law). In practice, the SIF Law, limited to sophisticated investors, offers a more flexible regime and a lighter supervision from the *Commission de surveillance du secteur financier* (the CSSF).

The choice of the most efficient vehicle for a real estate investment structure mostly depends on the investors' tax status, the type of investments made through the structure, the debt finance structure, the desired control aspects and the desired level of investors' protection.

Under both regimes, regulated funds may be set up as Common Funds or as investment funds of the corporate type.

Common funds (*Fonds commun de placement* – FCP)

Due to its flexible regime, the most commonly used vehicle for a regulated real estate investment structure is the FCP. As a contractual vehicle, the FCP is not subject to the requirements of Luxembourg company law or a specific statutory regime. In certain respects, the FCP is similar to the unit trust in the United Kingdom.

An FCP is an unincorporated co-proprietorship of assets. An FCP does not have any legal personality and therefore may not itself enter into contracts or obligations. Neither are the unitholders vested with the power to manage and administer the FCP. Such power is granted to a management company organised under Luxembourg law and governed by the provisions of the 2002 Law.

The management company must manage the FCP in accordance with the management regulations and in the exclusive interests of the unitholders. It decides on the implementation of the investment policy and investment strategies, either by taking the investment decisions itself or delegating this function to an investment manager located either in Luxembourg or abroad. Furthermore, the management company may appoint one or more property managers who generally are in charge of the daily management of the relevant properties.

Investors subscribe for units of the FCP, which entitle them to a proportionate share of the net assets of the FCP. Similarly to the shareholders of a public limited company, the liability of the unitholders of an FCP is limited to the amount contributed by them.

The contractual rights and obligations of the unitholders and of the management company are set forth in management regulations generally signed by the management company and the custodian bank. By execution of a subscription agreement with the management company, the investors are bound by the terms of the management regulations of the FCP.

Since unitholders, unless otherwise provided in the management regulations, do not have any voting rights, the FCP is typically protected from hostile takeovers. If investor co-decision rights are necessary, voting rights may be granted in respect of certain matters to a general meeting of unitholders, or an advisory or investment committee of investors.

The FCP may issue several classes of units, permitting the fund to create classes with features which are adapted to the needs of the different investors. FCPs may either be open-ended, ie open for redemptions at the request of unitholders, or closed-ended. However, due to the lack of liquidity of real estate investments, real estate investment structures often are set-up as closed-ended FCPs.

The FCP may be established as an umbrella structure, ie one single fund with one or more sub-funds, where each sub-fund corresponds to a distinct portfolio of assets and liabilities. Each sub-fund constitutes a separate pool of assets, which is ring-fenced against the liabilities of any other sub-funds. Unless otherwise provided by the management regulations, the rights of the investors are limited to the assets of the relevant sub-fund.

Regarding the financing structure of the FCP, the investors make capital commitments which are successively drawn down against the issue of units which are either partly or fully paid. Units of an FCP must be issued at their net asset value, except for FCPs set up under the SIF Law for which the management regulations may provide otherwise.

Investment companies with variable share capital (*Société d'investissement à capital variable* – SICAV)

A SICAV is an investment company with a variable capital always equal to its net assets. This frequently used form of investment company offers the possibility to increase or to reduce the share capital without requiring the approval of a general meeting of shareholders and upon the sole issue or redemption of shares.

The SICAV is generally the legal form used for open-ended vehicles. However it is also possible to close a SICAV for redemptions; furthermore, a SICAV may be closed for further issues of shares by resolution of the board of directors.

Shares of a SICAV must be fully paid on subscription (except for SIFs, as explained below). Subscriptions in different instalments in a SICAV can only be achieved by subscription commitments, where the shares issued at the different capital calls must normally be issued on the basis of their net asset value. Additional flexibility is granted with respect to shares of a SIF, where shares may be partly paid (paid-up to at least five per cent), and where shares do not have to be issued at the net asset value (the issue price may be freely determined in accordance with the provisions of the articles of incorporation).

Pursuant to the 2002 Law, a SICAV must be set up in the form of a public limited company (*société anonyme*). Other legal forms are available for SICAVs created under the SIF Law. Except as otherwise determined by the 2002 Law or the SIF Law, the provisions of the 1915 Law are applicable to SICAVs.

As for an FCP, a SICAV may be established as an umbrella structure.

Investment companies with fixed share capital (*Société d'investissement à capital fixe* – SICAF)

The capital of a SICAF is fixed and may therefore only vary in accordance with the formalities required by the 1915 Law for capital increases (ie either by approval of the general meeting of shareholders and modification of the articles of incorporation before a notary, or by virtue of the 'authorised capital' procedure set out in the articles of incorporation of the company, where a general meeting of shareholders authorises the board of directors to increase the capital under certain conditions). The SICAF is used for structures which do not offer shares on a continuous basis, but which have one or more offering periods.

The payment of the subscription proceeds in different tranches can be organised either in the form of commitments to subscribe or through the issuance of partly paid shares (to be paid-up to at least 25 per cent). However in comparison with the FCP and the SICAVs subject to the 2002 Law, the SICAF governed by the 2002 Law also offers the option to issue and redeem its shares at a price based on criteria other than the net asset value, such as the stock exchange price or a price agreed for a specific transaction, if justified by the circumstances. The provisions regarding the issue price are laid down in the articles of incorporation.

The SICAF may also be created as an umbrella structure.

Investment companies in risk capital (*Société d'investissement en capital à risque* – SICAR)

Created by the law of 15 June 2004 (the 2004 Law), the SICAR is a corporate structure which allows the investment in risk and venture capital by direct or indirect investment in entities to be launched, developed or listed with the aim of offsetting the high level of risks taken by investors expecting higher than average returns. This vehicle is subject to a degree of regulation equivalent to the regulation of SIFs.

The SICAR is limited to well-informed investors being defined by the 2004 Law as any institutional investor, professional investor and any other investor who:
(i) has confirmed in writing that it adheres to the status of well-informed investor; and
(ii) invests a minimum of €125,000 in the company; or
(iii) has obtained an assessment made by a credit institution, another professional of the financial sector subject to rules of conduct within the meaning of Article 11 of Directive 93/22/EEC, or by a management company within the meaning of Directive 2001/107/EC certifying its expertise, experience and knowledge in adequately appraising an investment in risk capital.

SICARs may invest indirectly in real estate through entities investing in or holding property assets constituting risk capital (private equity real estate). Pursuant to CSSF Circular 06/241 concerning the concept of risk capital as set out in the Law of 15 June 2004 with reference to SICAR, in order to assess whether the property investments constitute 'risk capital', the following factors are taken into account:
- investments with high growth potential because of the specific risks attached to the underlying properties;
- development or value-adding projects on the underlying property assets;
- high level of risk/discounted return;

- identity of the management, their form of remuneration and procedures for selection of property assets;
- the managers' or founders' financial participation in the project;
- active management of the underlying property assets, limited holding/investment period;
- in general, a lack of regular rental income; and
- type of funding: often with significant leverage effect, mezzanine, distressed or non-performing funding, or CBOs.

The CSSF does not at present accept that investments in real estate be made directly by a SICAR. The CSSF requires that a special purpose vehicle be inserted in between the SICAR and the real estate (such as local real estate companies or Luxembourg fully-taxable capital companies).

The share capital of a SICAR may not be less than €1 million. This minimum must be reached within a period of 12 months following the authorisation of the company.

3.2.2 Main features regarding the organisation of regulated real estate investment structures
The obligation to have a Promoter
The Promoter is considered to be the person who or the entity that initiates the creation of the real estate investment structure and that determines the nature of the structure. The Promoter, who needs to be approved by the CSSF, must fulfil certain requirements in respect of background and experience as well as professional reputation.

For the above reasons, only well known financial institutions are in practice eligible to act as promoter of regulated structures such as SICAVs/SICAFs/FCPs governed by the 2002 Law. For SIFs and SICARs, there is no promoter requirement.

The obligation to publish a prospectus
All regulated real estate investment structures are obliged to publish a prospectus, which must include the information necessary for investors to be able to make an informed judgment about the investment proposed and in particular of the risks attached to it. The prospectus must at least include the information provided for in Schedule A of Annex I of the 2002 Law (insofar as the relevant information does not already appear in the constitutional documents). Pursuant to the 2002 Law, the content of the prospectus must be approved by the CSSF. Regarding SIFs and SICARs, the Law on SIFs does not set out any minimum content for the prospectus, but provides that the offering document must include the information necessary for investors to be able to make an informed judgment about the investment proposed to them and in particular of the risks attached to it.

Investment restrictions
In accordance with the principle of risk spreading, no more than 20 per cent of the net assets of the structure may be invested in a single property. This restriction is however not applicable during the start-up period of the

investment structure, ie during the first four years of the structure's existence.

With regard to leverage, which is in practice one of the key elements of real estate finance, borrowings, as a general rule, cannot exceed an average of 50 per cent of the valuation of all properties. However, this rule is subject to derogations granted by the CSSF on a case-by-case basis. The CSSF is more reluctant to depart from the general applicable rules in the case of retail funds than specialised investment funds, since well-informed investors are deemed to be in a better position to assess the risks incurred by higher leverage. In the past, the CSSF has already approved borrowings representing up to 75 per cent of the valuation of all properties in SIFs and up to 60 per cent in retail funds.

The specific rules for retail investment funds investing in real estate are set out in Chapter I of the Circular 91/75.

In relation to SIFs and SICARs, the applicable laws do not set out any detailed risk diversification rules, but only a general principle of risk diversification. There are no specific rules regarding leverage; the CSSF requires that the maximum leverage rules are set out in the prospectus.

Property valuation and independent appraiser

Properties owned by the regulated real estate investment structure or by its affiliated real estate companies must be valued by an independent property appraiser with specific experience in the field of property valuation. The valuation normally takes place at each year-end and at the date of purchase or sale of properties (this appraisal is not required for sales made within six months of the last valuation).

In respect of real estate properties, the valuation made at the year-end may be used throughout the following year for the net asset value calculation unless there is a change in the general economic situation or in the condition of the properties which requires new valuations to be carried out under the same criteria as the annual valuation.

Investment through wholly owned subsidiaries

Regulated real estate investment structures frequently utilise wholly owned Luxembourg subsidiaries. Such subsidiaries, in turn, may either hold subsidiaries, in Luxembourg or abroad, or invest directly in real estate.

Investments through wholly owned subsidiaries are accepted by the CSSF subject to several conditions, the purpose of which is to ensure that investor protection is no lower than that offered to direct investment. These conditions are as follows:
- the investment structure must wholly own the share capital of the subsidiary;
- the subsidiary may not carry on activities other than holding investments on behalf of the investment structure;
- the shares of the subsidiary must remain in registered form;
- a majority of the directors of the subsidiary must be directors of the investment company or, in the case of an FCP, of its management company;

- in the investment structure's semi-annual and annual financial statements, the subsidiary must be regarded as transparent and the accounts of the investment structure must contain a list of final investments made through the subsidiary;
- the accounts of the investment structure and of the subsidiary must be audited by the same auditor;
- the depositary of the investment structure must be in a position to perform its legal duties in respect of the assets held by the subsidiary;
- the use of a subsidiary must be specifically mentioned in the prospectus of the investment structure.

The investment restrictions applicable to the real estate investment structure will be regarded on a consolidated basis.

3.2.3 Consolidation requirements

In addition to the general rules applicable to investments through wholly owned subsidiaries, Chapter I, paragraph III, of the Circular 91/75, provides for consolidation requirements applicable specifically to real estate investment funds.

The accounts of real estate companies which are funded more than 50 per cent by the real estate fund either by way of equity or loans must be audited by the same auditor as the real estate fund. The accounts of these entities must in principle be drawn up as at the same date and must be consolidated with the accounts of the real estate fund at the end of each half-year.

3.2.4 Tax considerations

The Luxembourg tax treatment applicable to investment funds of contractual and corporate type as well as to SICARs (in comparison with the tax treatment of SOPARFIs) is summarised in the following table:

	Companies		Investment funds	
	SOPARFI	**SICAR**	**Funds subject to the 2002 Law**	**Funds subject to the SIF Law**
Corporate income tax	SOPARFIs are liable to CIT at a rate of 21.54 per cent in 2010 (including the solidarity surcharge). Exemptions are available.	SICARs in the form of a corporation are fully liable to CIT at a rate of 21.54 per cent in 2010 (including the solidarity surcharge). However, income derived from (i) portfolio items consisting of securities and capital gains deriving from such securities and (ii) temporary investments in liquid assets held for a maximum period of 12 months before investment in 'risk capital' are excluded.	n/a	n/a
Municipal business tax	SOPARFIs are liable to MBT at a rate of 6.75 per cent in 2010 (Luxembourg City). Exemptions are available under the participation exemption regimes provided by Luxembourg domestic tax law or by double tax treaties concluded by Luxembourg	SICARs in the form of a limited partnership (*société en commandite simple*) are not liable to MBT. SICARs in other corporate forms are liable to MBT at a current rate of 6.75 per cent (Luxembourg City). However, the same exclusions for CIT apply.	n/a	n/a
Net worth tax	Applicable but exemptions are available.	n/a	n/a	n/a
Subscription tax	n/a	n/a	As a general rule, 0.05 per cent of the aggregate net asset value of the investment fund as valued on the last day of each quarter (0.01 per cent reduced rate and exemptions available).	As a general rule, 0.01 per cent of the aggregate net asset value of the investment fund as valued on the last day of each quarter (exemption available).
Withholding on tax dividends	Applicable but exemptions	n/a	n/a	n/a

	Companies		Investment funds	
	SOPARFI	**SICAR**	**Funds subject to the 2002 Law**	**Funds subject to the SIF Law**
Withholding on tax interest	n/a subject to the provisions of the EU Savings Directive	n/a subject to the provisions of the EU Savings Directive	n/a subject to the provisions of the EU Savings Directive	n/a subject to the provisions of the EU Savings Directive
Withholding on tax capital gains	n/a	n/a	n/a except in limited cases	n/a except in limited cases
Double tax treaties	Applicable	Applicable	Several DTTs (32 as of today) are applicable to investment funds structure of the corporate type (SICAVs, SICAFs). FCP are transparent entities for tax purposes and, as such, are not eligible to DTTs.	Several DTTs (32 as of today) are applicable to investment funds structure of the corporate type (SICAVs, SICAFs). FCP are transparent entities for tax purposes and, as such, are not eligible to DTTs.
Registration duty	€75	€75	€75	€75
VAT	SOPARFIs qualify as taxable persons for VAT purposes. VAT exemption for management services not available.	SICARs qualify as taxable persons for VAT purposes. A VAT exemption for management services applies.	Unlike FCP, SICAVs and SICAFs qualify as taxable person for VAT purposes without input VAT deduction right. Management services supplied to the management company of the FCP as well as to the SICAVs and SICAFs benefit from a Luxembourg VAT exemption.	Unlike FCP, SICAVs and SICAFs qualify as taxable person for VAT purposes without input VAT deduction right. Management services supplied to the management company of the FCP as well as to the SICAVs and SICAFs benefit from a Luxembourg VAT exemption.

4. FINANCING AN ACQUISITION
4.1 Facility agreement – choice of law

For the financing of real estate the choice of law and choice of jurisdiction in the loan agreement is free (in accordance with Regulation (EC) 593/2008), but increasingly it is common that at least for local deals the loan documentation is governed by Luxembourg law.

Additionally, Luxembourg laws and regulations are very progressive in as far as they permit a high level of flexibility for lenders and borrowers as there are no restrictions on the choice of currency, and deferred payments and limited recourse clauses are permitted.

4.2 Collateral

Traditionally, financial institutions require collateral to secure credit facilities granted to borrowers who intend to acquire real estate assets.

Typically, loans are secured by a mortgage over the property. Security over real property may also be given by way of a kind of security trust, called security fiduciary agreement, in favour of qualifying entities that hold the property for the beneficiaries.

In addition to a mortgage over the assets, fixed and floating charges (subject to certain conditions) are permitted as well as the following guarantees and *in rem* securities which are common under Luxembourg law: (i) the parent or group entities of the borrower may be required to grant guarantees to secure the obligations of the borrower under the loan; and (ii) other collateral may be given by way of pledges, assignments of rights and claims, delegation or transfer of title for security purposes under the law of 12 July 2005 on financial collateral arrangements (the 'Collateral Law'):

4.2.1 Personal scope

The Collateral Law applies to all natural or legal persons and may not only be granted to the actual creditor but also in favour of a third party, such as a security trustee. This considerably facilitates the granting of security in the context of secured financing and avoids the complex recourse to provisions of parallel debt.

4.2.2 Nature of financial collateral

The Collateral Law applies to a broad range of financial instruments, including securities and warrants, and to all types of claims including, in particular, monetary claims.

The most common form of security arrangement used in Luxembourg – the pledge – may extend to both current and future assets of the pledgor without any need to specifically designate such assets and may secure current and future obligations of the pledgor to the pledgee. This is easily documented, such as the granting of a notice to the debtor in case of a pledge over receivables (or the acknowledgement thereof by such debtor) or the recording of the pledge on a share register in case of a pledge over registered shares of a Luxembourg company.

Voting rights attaching to pledged securities can be contractually granted to the pledgee. The parties to a pledge may also agree that the pledgee has the right to use the pledged assets subject only to the duty of the pledgee to return such assets, or equivalent assets, to the pledgor at termination of the pledge agreement.

Unless provided under the contract, there is no requirement that the pledgee give notice to the pledgor before enforcing the collateral.

Finally, enforcement procedures for pledges are straightforward, especially with respect to unlisted securities, which do not need to be auctioned or be the subject of a court allocation procedure but rather can be appropriated or privately sold on such terms as the parties to the pledge agreement agree.

4.2.3 Protection against insolvency
The most interesting feature of the Collateral Law is the exceptional protection it provides to those holding securities in the case of insolvency of the entity granting security.

In disapplying all national and foreign insolvency law rules, the Collateral Law ring-fences security held in Luxembourg from the insolvency rules and rules of the collateral provider. In practice this means that zero hours rules, stay of action requirements and voidance rules (eg hardening period rules) will not take effect on security held over assets in Luxembourg, thus enabling those holding security to enforce their security notwithstanding the insolvency of the entity granting security.

Luxembourg thus makes use of some of the rules laid down in the EU Insolvency Regulation and similar provisions contained in the Winding Up Directives for credit and insurance undertakings and offers those granting credit a safe and predictable legal environment.

The provisions described above make Luxembourg an attractive hub for real estate finance in or outside of Luxembourg.

5. MANAGING THE ACQUISITION PROCESS
The sale of property takes the form of a transfer deed under private seal. In order to be enforceable against third parties, the transfer deed needs to be notarised and registered with the mortgage register.

A lease can be granted by a deed under private seal, unless the duration of the lease exceeds nine years in which case the lease agreement needs to be notarised and registered with the mortgage register.

The buyer bears the notary's fees and the registration and transcription duties. The seller typically pays the fees of the real estate agent. If lawyers or surveyors are involved, each party will bear the costs of its advisors.

The seller warrants its ownership of the property as provided by law. Further statutory warranties relate to the size of the property and provide that the seller is liable for hidden defects, that the property is free of charges and third party rights. Parties may however derogate from these provisions.

For a sale between professionals, warranties are freely negotiable and often include warranties in relation to environmental issues and compliance with administrative permits. In case of a portfolio sale, warranties tend to be limited.

Warranties usually serve to apportion risk between the parties and to provide information to the buyer.

In general, a new owner cannot be liable for matters relating to the property that occurred before it was purchased. However, a new owner can be bound by an existing lease agreement. In relation to soil pollution, the current owner can be required by the authorities to carry out remedial works. In case the person who caused the pollution cannot be identified or is insolvent, the current owner may be liable to bear these costs.

The parties become legally bound through the unconditional exchange of their consents. However, transfer deeds under private seal often contain conditions precedent.

Between parties, title to the property passes at the time of the agreement on the object and price, even if the property has not been delivered, nor the price paid. In order to be enforceable against third parties, the parties usually agree that transfer of title occurs only at the date of the notarial deed.

6. REAL ESTATE BASICS

Specific laws complement the general provisions contained in the Civil Code on real estate with respect to, among others, long-term leases and building rights (law of 22 October 2008), residential leases (law of 21 September 2006), condominium (law of 16 May 1975) and registration (law of 25 September 1905).

The *droit de propriété* (freehold ownership) is a fundamental right defined by the Civil Code as the right to enjoy and dispose of assets absolutely, provided its exercise does not interfere with a legal provision (such as planning restrictions) or a third party's right. Aside from ownership as such, other rights *in rem* can be granted with regard to real estate. They may take the form of long-term leases between 27 and 99 years (the *droit d'emphytéose*), building rights lasting up to 99 years (the *droit de superficie*) or usufructs. They derive from the ownership and are granted to persons other than the owner. For the beneficiary these rights *in rem* procure more stability than a mere occupational lease agreement, as well as more extensive rights. Condominium ownership is common for residential property.

All land in Luxembourg comes parcelled into plots which are registered in the land register (the cadastre). The mortgage register (*bureau de conservation des hypothèques*) contains all notarial and registered transfers of ownership and other rights *in rem*, such as deeds establishing easements or mortgages and lease agreements exceeding nine years.

In order to be enforceable against third parties, the following rights need to be notarised and registered with the mortgage register: ownership, rights *in rem* and lease agreements exceeding nine years.

There is no state guarantee of title. The notary establishing a deed is required to check the ownership of the seller and may be held liable for the validity and enforceability of the deed.

The Netherlands

Houthoff Buruma Aart Barkey Wolf & Wouter Ekkelkamp

1. INVESTMENT PURCHASE OVERVIEW

Typical investment purchase in the Netherlands

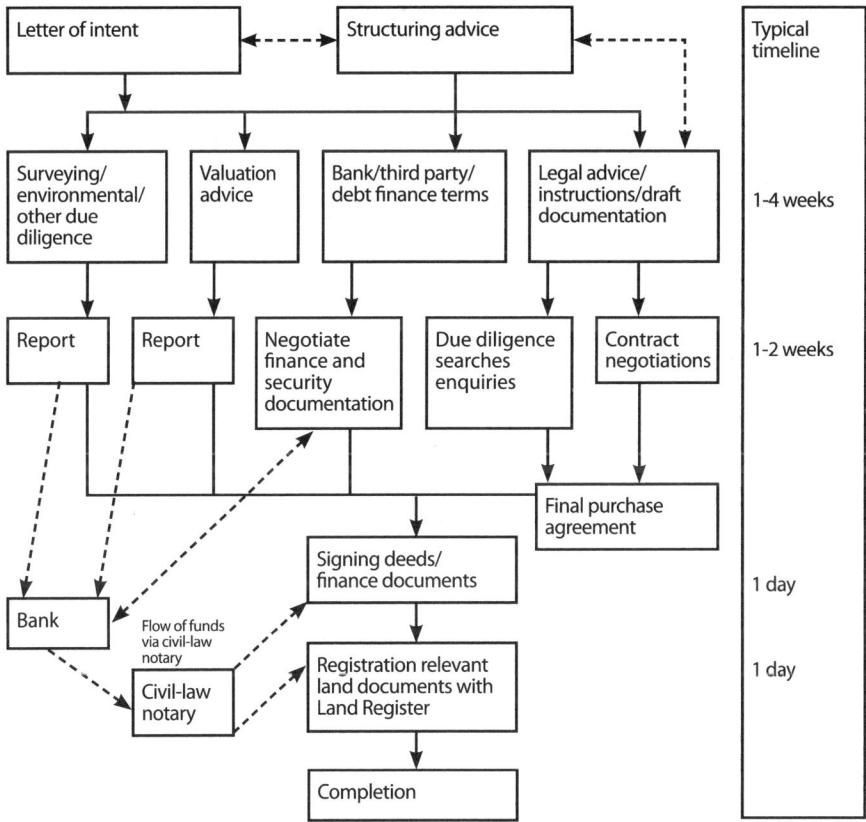

2. TAX CONSIDERATIONS
2.1 Value added tax (VAT)
The Dutch VAT system is based on the Principal VAT Directive (Council Directive 2006/112/EC of 28 November 2006 on the common system of value added tax (last amendment 16 March 2010, 2010/23/EU)). VAT is levied at a general rate of 19 per cent. The other applicable rates are zero per cent and six per cent. In principle, these lower rates do not apply to real

estate transactions.

The main rule is that the transfer of immovable property is not subject to VAT. However, exceptions to this main rule apply to the following:
- the supply of a building (or part thereof) and the land on which the building stands if this supply takes place before the initial occupation, on occupation of the building for the first time, or within two years after the initial occupation;
- the supply of building land; and
- the supply of a building (or parts thereof) and of the land on which it stands, other than as referred to in the first point above, if this was supplied by taxable persons (ie, qualifying entrepreneurs) who were in the preceding stage entitled to deduction of the VAT paid for the building concerned.

If the sale of immovable property is statutorily subject to VAT, the seller is required to forward the VAT received from the buyer to the tax authorities. The invoice to the buyer should therefore be issued with VAT. Qualifying entrepreneurs for VAT purposes may deduct the VAT that has been paid if the property is used for activities that are, for the large part, eligible for VAT deduction.

If the sale of property is not statutorily subject to VAT, the parties may opt for the transaction to be subject to VAT if the buyer intends the property to be at least 90 per cent used for activities that are eligible for VAT deduction. If both parties agree to opt for the transaction to be subject to VAT, the parties may request this option, but must do so jointly and no later than the time of transfer of the property. This request for VAT-taxable transfer is ordinarily indicated in the notarial deed. Furthermore, on opting for a transfer of property subject to VAT, the VAT liability is shifted from the seller to the buyer, ie the invoice sent to the buyer will state that the buyer is charged the VAT.

A 10-year review period, starting on transfer, applies to the transfer of property subject to VAT. During this review period, the use of the property is reviewed on an annual basis. This provision may lead to all or part of the VAT that was deducted at an earlier stage having to be repaid to the tax authorities. Certain conditions that apply to this review process are not discussed further in this overview because of space limitations.

Under certain conditions, property may be transferred as a 'going concern'. The transfer of a going concern is, generally speaking, not regarded as a taxable event for VAT purposes. In that event, the buyer takes over the VAT position of the seller with respect to that property, including the remaining part of the aforementioned 10-year review period. In practice, this mechanism is usually agreed on in advance with the tax authorities.

2.2 Stamp duty/transfer tax

No 'stamp duty' is levied in the Netherlands.

In principle, the transfer of property in the Netherlands is subject to 6 per cent transfer tax. If certain balance-sheet requirements are met, eg, 70 per cent of the assets of the company consist of Dutch real estate, a company is considered to be a 'real-estate company' for transfer tax purposes. The sale of the shares in this company is, in certain circumstances, subject to transfer tax as well. In both cases the tax is based on the value of the real estate.

There are a few general exemptions from transfer tax. For example, transfer tax is not payable in the case of a reorganisation within a group of companies or a legal merger. Because of space limitations, the specific conditions for applying these exemptions are not explained further in this investment overview.

2.2.1 Concurrence of VAT and transfer tax
The obligation to pay VAT on a property transfer may coincide with the obligation to pay transfer tax. Transfer tax legislation provides for certain exemptions from transfer tax if VAT is mandatorily not optionally payable on the transfer of property. This exemption does not apply if: (i) the property has been used for business purposes; and (ii) the buyer is eligible for full or part VAT deduction.

In practice, developers may enter into lease agreements prior to selling and transferring the property to an investor. In that case, the exemption from transfer tax would technically not be applicable on such transfer, as the property has been used for business purposes before the transfer. To meet practical needs, the tax authorities provide a specific facility: no transfer tax is due if: (i) the developer (ie, the seller) never had an intention to develop and exploit the property for the developer's own needs; and (ii) the transfer of the property takes place within six months after the time of the initial use of the property.

2.3 Tax issues for overseas investors investing in property?
2.3.1 VAT, transfer tax and corporate income tax
We refer to our explanation above for an overview of the VAT and transfer tax issues relating to an overseas investor investing in Dutch property.

Corporate income tax is levied on income and capital gains at a maximum rate of 25.5 per cent (2010). The first €200,000 of the taxable result is subject to 20 per cent corporate income tax.

For foreign investors, it is important to note that non-Dutch residents are only subject to Dutch corporate income tax on Dutch-source income, which includes Dutch real estate. The Netherlands has an extensive tax-treaty network. Most tax treaties allow the Netherlands to tax income received from Dutch real estate.

3. INVESTMENT VEHICLE CHOICE
3.1 Structures used to purchase property
The acquisition of property can be structured as an asset deal or as a share deal. The main differences between the two relate to the purpose of the deal, the typical guarantees given in a purchase agreement and the tax consequences. In an asset deal, the guarantees specifically pertain to the property concerned. Transfer tax and VAT are levied on the acquisition of property, if applicable. In a share deal, the guarantees given would not

relate just to the property concerned, but also to the shares purchased and, of course, the company holding the property. The purchase of shares in a company always entails the risk that the company has hidden liabilities, especially in view of possible transfer tax obligations. In Dutch practice, acquisition of property through share deals is not common; but nor is it rare, especially in larger portfolio transactions.

3.1.1 Investment vehicles
The choice of investment structure and vehicle is determined by a number of factors, including the desired control mechanisms, the decision-making processes, taxation, expected costs and compliance issues. Furthermore, the flexibility of the structure may be relevant.

The typical investment vehicles used in the Netherlands are the following:
- a private limited liability company (*besloten vennootschap met beperkte aansprakelijkheid* or BV) or a public limited liability company (*naamloze vennootschap* or NV);
- a co-op (*coöperatie*);
- a partnership (*personenvennootschap*), ie, a limited partnership (*commanditaire vennootschap* or CV) or a general partnership (*vennootschap onder firma* or VOF); and
- other typical fund vehicles, including an 'FGR mutual fund' (*fonds voor gemene rekening*).

(An FGR mutual fund is a type of cooperation agreement between several parties. It is not a partnership and does not constitute a legal entity. The use of an FGR mutual fund is aimed at maintaining tax transparency and flexibility, without the technicalities that arise when a partnership agreement is involved.)

3.1.2 BV and NV
The BV and NV are well-known, respectable investment vehicles in the Netherlands. The statute law applicable to these companies is mandatory in nature and already includes basic corporate governance rules and a system of checks and balances. For example, certain restrictions apply to distributions to shareholders. The standard corporate bodies in a BV or NV are the 'management board' and the 'general meeting of shareholders'. Optionally, a 'supervisory board' may also be installed. A BV's articles of association must include a restriction on the transfer of shares.

A BV or NV is incorporated by means of a notarial deed executed before a Dutch civil law notary and registered in the trade register at the Chamber of Commerce. The incorporation of a BV or NV requires the prior approval of the Dutch Ministry of Justice, which performs a check on the credentials of the incorporator(s), its ultimate beneficial owner and the initial managing director(s). Amendment of the articles of association also requires a notarial deed and the prior approval of the Dutch Ministry of Justice. Furthermore, a minimum amount of capital is currently required for incorporation (ie, €45,000 for an NV and €18,000 for a BV).

In the Netherlands, the BV and NV are the main legal entities with legal personality (*rechtspersoonlijkheid*) used by commercial investors. Because the statutory provisions are mandatory in nature, the rules governing these entities can appear inflexible at times. A bill reforming the incorporation system is currently pending. If enacted, there will be more flexibility in how a BV is structured.

Both the BV and the NV are ordinarily subject to corporate income tax.

3.1.3 Co-op

The co-op (coöperatie) is firmly rooted in Dutch corporate law. The creation of a co-op and the amendment of its articles of association are effected by notarial deed. Although some mandatory statutory provisions do apply to co-ops, there is more room for organisational flexibility and tailor-made solutions. Co-ops are frequently used in Dutch fund structures as a tax-transparent vehicle.

A co-op is ordinarily subject to corporate income tax. In principle, no dividend withholding tax is payable on distribution of a co-op's dividends.

3.1.4 Limited partnership, general partnership and FGR mutual fund

A partnership does not have legal personality. Therefore, a partnership itself cannot be the holder of rights and obligations. In the case of a limited partnership (CV), a general partner (beherend vennoot) in a limited partnership usually holds the legal rights and obligations (including those related to property). The beneficial interests accrue to all the partners in accordance with the partnership agreement. In the case of a general partnership (VOF), the partners usually hold the rights and obligations jointly. Basic information about a partnership and its general partners (but not its limited partners) are registered in the trade register at the Chamber of Commerce.

A CV is considered to be transparent if the limited partners can only be admitted or substituted with the prior consent of all partners.

An FGR mutual fund is considered to be transparent if an interest in the fund may be transferred solely to new or existing participants with the prior consent of all other participants, or may be transferred solely to the fund itself.

A partnership is entered into by agreement. Although a written agreement is not necessary, typically a partnership agreement is in written form. All partners make contributions, with the object being a mutual profit.

In a limited partnership, a limited partner is not liable for partnership obligations that exceed the amount of the limited partner's agreed contribution. In return, the limited partner may not act on behalf of the limited partnership (or decisively influence the limited partnership's affairs). If the limited partner does so, the limited partner may become liable for all partnership obligations. A general partner is jointly and severally liable for partnership obligations in either a general partnership or a limited partnership.

In certain cases, a special purpose vehicle holds the property as custodian (bewaarder). In fund structures, a custodian is frequently used. The custodian holds the property on behalf of the partners as a bankruptcy remote vehicle.

A bill on partnerships has been proposed and is currently pending. If enacted, this new system would be based on a single pattern for the different kinds of partnerships. One new element would be the option of legal personality. Under the proposed bill, a partnership would be able to acquire legal personality if: (i) this was specifically stated in the partnership agreement; and (ii) at least the core of the partnership agreement was recorded in a notarial deed. Partner liability for partnership obligations would not change, but it would become possible for the partnership itself to be liable. A partnership with legal personality would be able to acquire property in its own name. In that case, the construction in which a general partner or a custodian holds the property on behalf of the partnership would not be necessary. Furthermore, there would be transfer tax opportunities on transfer of partnership interests.

Tax transparency and flexibility are the main reasons for an investor to use a partnership as an investment vehicle.

3.2 Restrictions on foreign ownership or occupation of property, and on foreign guarantees or security

There are no commercial restrictions on foreign ownership or occupation of property. Foreign guarantees may be given, although mandatory Dutch statutory provisions may apply in certain cases. Furthermore, security over Dutch assets must be granted by means of security rights valid under Dutch law.

An exemption may apply to the pledge of receivables. According to Dutch law, the creation of a security interest over Dutch receivables must be done in accordance with the procedure applicable in the law governing the legal instrument that carries the obligation to create this security interest. This title could be a foreign legal instrument; consequently, foreign law would govern the creation of the security interest over the Dutch receivables.

3.3 Real estate investment trusts (REITs) available

The Dutch vehicle most similar to a REIT is the *fiscale beleggingsinstelling*, which is usually referred to by its acronym FBI. An FBI is subject to a corporate income tax rate of zero per cent. One of the requirements of the FBI regime is that the investment is done in a 'passive manner', which includes real estate investment. The FBI is common in the Netherlands.

Another way of investing in real estate in the Netherlands is a tax-transparent entity combined with a Dutch BV or co-op.

4. FINANCING AN ACQUISITION

4.1 Financing corporate property transactions

In the past, property acquisitions were normally financed with a debt/equity ratio of 60 per cent to 90 per cent. However, the current ratio is hovering at around 60-70 per cent.

Straightforward non-recourse loans are not common in the Netherlands. Non-recourse loans are used only in specific situations. However, it has been increasingly common to grant loans to special purpose vehicles. In most cases, additional security has been given only in the form of a limited parent company guarantee. Therefore, in practical terms, a lot of *de facto* non-recourse loans have been made.

4.2 Property as a means of raising finance
In addition to straightforward mortgage-backed financing strengthening the balance position, sale-and-lease-back transactions frequently occur in the Netherlands. The owner of property sells and transfers the property to an investor. Simultaneously, the owner enters into a long-term lease agreement with the investor to lease back the property. The transaction makes cash immediately available to the current owner of the property, and for an investor creates an investment opportunity that includes a lessee that fully knows the property.

4.3 Common forms of security granted over real estate
The security rights system is a closed one. A security right on property is created in the form of a 'mortgage' (*hypotheekrecht*). A security right on movable assets or receivables is created in the form of a 'pledge' (*pandrecht*). The concepts of security assignment, floating charge and trust are unknown in Dutch law.

Security may be granted for existing and future payment obligations. Security rights may be granted only to the beneficiary of a party's payment obligation. In certain situations, the parties agree on a parallel debt mechanism so that one security trustee can hold all security rights. In principle, the wording of the security document determines which obligations are actually secured by the security document at any given time.

As a general principle, a Dutch company is allowed to grant security rights for its obligations. Some limitations may apply because of the principle of corporate benefit (*ultra vires*), especially when providing security for the obligations of third parties. This concept boils down to a formal test (ie, the wording of the written objects clause in the company's articles of association) and a material test (ie, whether the act is in the corporate interests of the company).

If a Dutch company carries out a 'juridical act' (ie, an act having legal consequences under Dutch law) and that juridical act is considered to be *ultra vires* (eg, not in its corporate interest), the company may apply to the court to have that juridical act annulled. If the company is in the bankruptcy process, the bankruptcy trustee (*curator*) may do the same.

4.3.1 Mortgage
The mortgage is the most important security right in Dutch property financing. Mortgage falls into the category of 'limited property right' (*beperkt recht*) in Dutch property law. If a debtor defaults on a mortgage-secured payment obligation, the mortgagee may immediately foreclose on the mortgage, sell the property and take recourse from the sale proceeds. A mortgage is a very strong security right to which almost no exceptions apply. Mortgages and pledges are 'bankruptcy proof'. Nevertheless, a bankruptcy

trustee (curator) may request a cooling-off period for a maximum of four months. During the cooling-off period, the mortgagee (or pledgee) may not enforce its security right.

A mortgage is created by execution of a notarial deed, followed by registration of the mortgage at the Land Registry (*kadaster*). The validity of a mortgage is based on registration of the mortgage. A mortgage given in advance on future property is not possible in the Dutch system, although a mortgage automatically includes new buildings or other structures built on the mortgaged land.

4.3.2 Pledge

A pledge is another type of 'limited property right' (*beperkt recht*), but one that applies to assets and receivables. As is the case with a mortgage, a pledgee may immediately sell the pledged collateral if the pledgor defaults on the payment obligations secured by the pledge and may then take recourse from the proceeds of the sale (or in an earlier stage, collection of receivables, as the case may be).

A pledge may be either 'disclosed' or 'undisclosed'. A pledge of movable assets may be 'possessory' or 'non-possessory'. The following are typical pledges:
- a non-possessory pledge (*bezitloos pandrecht*) of movable assets;
- a disclosed pledge of receivables (*openbaar pandrecht*) under insurance policies and, if applicable, a disclosed pledge of claims under a purchase agreement and a disclosed pledge of claims against a land owner in the case of the mortgage of a ground lease (*erfpacht*, which is similar in some ways to a leasehold); and
- an undisclosed pledge (*stil pandrecht*) of other receivables, such as rental income.

It is possible in an existing legal relationship to pledge future receivables in advance, eg, the rent payable under a lease. To further secure the pledge of other future receivables in a future legal relationship, an agreement to pledge receivables normally includes a provision stating that the pledgor must pledge future receivables as soon as a new legal relationship comes into existence. To further secure the position of the pledgee, the pledgor grants an irrevocable power of attorney to the pledgee to make the pledge on its behalf.

In the case of a disclosed pledge, future receivables arising out of an existing legal relationship or a future legal relationship can be pledged in advance, because the debtor is known in advance and notified of the pledge.

Movable assets are pledged:
- in the case of a possessory pledge (*vuistpand*): by bringing the assets under the control of the pledgee; or
- in the case of a non-possessory pledge in which the pledgee does not have possession of the pledged assets (*bezitloos pandrecht*): by the pledgor and the pledgee entering into a written agreement and that agreement being either registered with the Dutch tax authorities or prepared and executed in the form of a notarial deed (to fix the date of the agreement).

A pledgee may require that the pledged assets be brought under its control if the pledgor does not fulfil its obligations towards the pledgee or if there is a legitimate expectation that the pledgor will not fulfil its obligations.

Receivables are pledged:
- in the case of a disclosed right of pledge (*openbaar pandrecht*): by the pledgor and the pledgee entering into an agreement and notifying the relevant debtors of the pledge; or
- in the case of an undisclosed right of pledge (*stil pandrecht*): by the pledgor and the pledgee entering into a written agreement and that agreement being either registered with the Dutch tax authorities or prepared and executed in the form of a notarial deed (to fix the date of the agreement).

If a pledgor does not fulfil its obligations towards the pledgee, or if there is legitimate expectation that the pledgor will not fulfil its obligations, the pledgee may notify the debtor of the pledge. The parties may also agree in advance that the pledgee is permitted to notify the debtor in other situations. On giving notice, the pledgee is entitled to collect the claim; from that point on, the pledgor cannot collect the claim unless it has the approval of the pledgee or the court.

4.3.3 Share pledge

A financier may require a pledge of shares in the borrower holding property. As part of the pledge, the financier may require that the voting rights pertaining to these shares are transferred to the pledgee and this transfer may be subject to certain conditions.

In practice, foreclosing on a share pledge is cumbersome. The pledgee may have to comply with applicable financial market regulations, such as preparing a prospectus. Furthermore, the purchase of shares in a company comes with the risk of assuming the hidden liabilities of the company. Normally, a pledgee will not consider giving any guarantee to a buyer of such shares. It is doubtful whether a public auction of the shares without sufficient guarantees would attract serious bids. Furthermore, the pledgee acquiring voting rights on shares may trigger consolidation issues.

Therefore, a foreclosure sale of pledged shares is rarely seen in the Netherlands. Nevertheless, this instrument can be used for purposes of control.

4.3.4 Guarantee

In certain cases, a financier may request a guarantee from a parent company of the borrower or another third party. The term 'guarantee' (*garantie*) does not have a fixed meaning under Dutch law. In fact, it may even effectively be a limitation of liability, depending on the actual wording. Therefore, the actual wording of a guarantee agreement is essential in determining a guarantor's obligations.

There may be discussion about whether a specific guarantee should in fact be considered to be a surety (*borgtocht*). If so, certain specific statutory provisions relating to sureties apply to the guarantee. In the case of a surety in which 'professional parties' are involved, the parties are entitled to agree to depart from the statutory provisions. In the case of a surety with an individual or 'non-professional party' (*particuliere borgtocht*), the statutory provisions protecting the guarantor (ie, the surety) are mandatory. When dealing with a guarantor (ie, surety) who is an individual or non-professional party, the assistance of a professional adviser is particularly called for in order to avoid the pitfalls.

4.3.5 Step-in rights
A mortgage deed typically includes a provision pursuant to which the mortgagor may take over the management (*beheer*) of the property. The mortgagor is allowed to do so if the debtor is in serious default of its obligations towards the mortgagee and court approval has been given. The management provision (*beheerbeding*) is an effective way for a mortgagee to take charge of the property.

With regard to contractual step-in rights, a financier may request step-in rights for the borrower's key contracts with third parties. In construction financing situations in particular, a financier would like to be able to step into key contracts, such as the agreements with the contractor and the architect. Normally, such agreements do not provide automatically for a financier's step-in right. To establish a step-in right, the borrower, the financier and the contractor/architect would have to enter into a separate, specific agreement to that effect. Although not seen in daily practice, it is becoming increasingly common to specifically arrange for such contractual step-in rights.

4.4 Real estate mortgage securitisation
Securitisation of mortgage loans in the Netherlands has frequently occurred over the past few years. Large Dutch banks have repeatedly sold bundled mortgage loans to free up capital for new activities.

5. MANAGING THE ACQUISITION PROCESS
5.1 Minimum formalities for the sale and purchase of property
Under Dutch law, an oral agreement is binding. Basically, an agreement becomes legally valid if an offer by a party is accepted by the other party. No separate delivery of some kind is necessary. Only in specific cases is a written agreement or notarial deed required.

An agreement for the sale and purchase of a property by professional parties can be entered into orally. A purchase agreement pertaining to residential property with a natural person as the buyer (ie, that person not acting in the exercise of a profession or as part of a business) must be in written form to be valid. In this case, the buyer has a right to cancel the purchase agreement without further explanation within a period of up to three business days after the date of the purchase agreement. The statutory provisions granting this right are mandatory, so the parties cannot contract out of them.

A purchase agreement may be registered in the public registers. Registration of the purchase agreement is not mandatory, but registration provides the buyer with certain protection. For example, the bankruptcy of the seller could not block the transfer of the property to the buyer. The buyer is protected for a six-month period after registration of the purchase agreement. A subsequent registration of the same purchase agreement after the expiry of the six-month period is not possible until six months have elapsed since that time.

5.2 Main legal documents required to transfer a property or grant a lease

The purchase agreement constitutes the obligation of: (i) the seller to transfer the property to the buyer; and (ii) the buyer to pay the purchase price to the seller. The actual transfer of the title to the property is affected by means of execution of a notarial deed of transfer to that effect, followed by registration of the transfer deed with the public registers. Registration of the transfer deed is required for the transfer to be valid. It is possible to combine the purchase agreement and the transfer into a single notarial deed.

A lease agreement can be entered into orally, but in practice leases are usually in writing. A standard model called the ROZ model is often used.

A ground lease (*erfpacht*) is created by a notarial deed to that effect, followed by registration of the deed with the public registers. Registration is required for the ground lease to be valid.

5.3 Property transaction costs

As a general rule, the buyer will bear the notarial costs of a sale, purchase and transfer of property (as well as the transfer tax and VAT). Professional parties normally pay for their own advisers. Of course, the parties are free to agree otherwise. As stated above, transfer tax is in principle payable by the buyer. However, it is possible for a seller to offer to pay the transfer tax as part of the sale offer.

5.4 Does the seller warrant its ownership of the property?

A seller will warrant its ownership of the property and, consequently, that it transfers full legal title to the property to the buyer. It is no problem for a seller to give this warranty. The Dutch system of registration of property provides for a high level of certainty about the seller's title to the property. Furthermore, the civil law notary handling the transfer of the property will satisfy himself that the seller has full legal title to the property. Otherwise, the civil law notary would not be willing to cooperate with execution of the transfer deed.

5.5 Warranties a seller usually gives to a buyer

There is a certain reliance on standard representations and warranties. These representations and warranties pertain to public law matters, the condition of the property (ground water and the use of asbestos) and technical installations, and a few other factual circumstances. In commercial contracts, specific warranties and/or indemnifications are usually implemented in view of the outcome of the buyer's due diligence. Furthermore, warranties relating to existing lease agreements are usually more elaborate.

5.6 Purpose of warranties in the purchase agreement

As a general rule, a seller of property must inform the buyer of all relevant aspects of the property known to the seller. On the other hand, the buyer has a duty to investigate the property and other particulars to determine whether the property will satisfy the buyer's needs. Commercial parties usually try to agree on a specific balance between these two obligations.

In principle, the due diligence process is mainly meant to provide information to the buyer on specific issues and risks. Once identified, the issues and risks can be included in the purchase agreement by incorporating specific warranties, disclaimers and/or indemnifications. Therefore, in essence, the due diligence process serves to provide information to both the seller and the buyer, and also provides the background for agreeing on specific warranties in the purchase agreement. The warranties provide for an allocation of risk in the purchase agreement, especially when warranties are very specific.

5.7 Owners/occupiers' liability for matters relating to the property which occurred before they bought or occupied

In principle, the buyer/occupier of property is not liable for obligations that arose in the past. However, this may not be the case for environmental pollution. Furthermore, in some cases the law provides for the limited joint and several liability of the seller and the buyer for certain charges owed to a third party. This could be the case on transfer of a ground lease (*erfpacht*), a right of superficies or an apartment right.

5.8 Notarisation

As stated above, actual transfer of title to the property requires a notarial deed of transfer to that effect, followed by registration of the transfer deed in the public registers. Therefore, notarisation of the transfer deed is always required. The purchase agreement does not have to be notarised.

5.9 Formalities for a contract becoming a legally binding obligation

In the Netherlands, negotiating parties may become subject to obligations in the pre-contractual phase of the negotiations. In the case law the courts have identified three phases:
- in phase 1, a party may terminate negotiations without any consequences;
- in phase 2, a party may terminate negotiations but not without paying certain costs incurred by the other party; and
- in phase 3, the parties are very close to reaching an agreement and no party can terminate the negotiations without paying compensation, and in some situations, the court may even order the parties to continue negotiations to reach final agreement.

For this reason, when entering into negotiations, it is vital to reiterate the applicable conditions, eg that final board approval is required.

In practice, commercial negotiations usually start with a letter of intent describing the main elements of agreement and the procedure for diligence and further negotiations. It is noted that a letter of intent can be binding on parties as a rudimentary purchase agreement. Therefore, caution is warranted when entering into a letter of intent.

5.10 Point at which the parties become legally bound

As stated above, an agreement becomes legally valid if a party accepts the other party's offer. In certain situations, the agreement is required to be in written form for the parties to be legally bound. Furthermore, obligations may arise in the pre-contractual phase.

5.11 Transfer of title
As stated above, actual transfer of title to the property requires a notarial deed of transfer to that effect, followed by registration of the transfer deed in the public registers. Registration of the transfer deed is required for a valid transfer.

5.12 Insurance of the property if there is delay between agreeing terms and actual sale
Parties usually agree that:
- the seller will keep the property insured until the moment of transfer; and
- the buyer will not bear the expense and risk of the property until the very moment of execution of the transfer deed.

6. REAL ESTATE BASICS
6.1 Main sources of laws that govern property
The main sources of Dutch law are statutory law and case law. Custom may be relevant in the process of foreclosure by public auction. Other than that, the whole of the Netherlands is subject to the same legislation and case law. The Netherlands Antilles has its own legal system, which is not covered in this investment overview.

6.2 Types of tenure
The main types of tenure are ownership (*eigendom*), ground lease (*erfpacht*), right of superficies (*recht van opstal*) and apartment right (*appartementsrecht*).

Ownership is the most complete property right.

Ground lease (which is perhaps comparable in some ways to leasehold in the common law system) provides the ground lessee with the right to use the property as if the ground lessee were the owner. Ground lease can be held in perpetuity or temporarily. Usually, the land owner and ground lessee agree on general and/or specific ground lease conditions that are applicable to the ground lease. Furthermore, it is common to agree on a ground rent (canon), payable in advance or periodically. Ground lease provisions may provide that transfer of the ground lease requires the approval of the land owner.

A right of superficies provides for the right of a superficiary to hold and maintain a building, structure or works in full ownership on someone else's property. Right of superficies allows parties to depart from the otherwise mandatory rule that the owner of a parcel of land is also the owner of the buildings, structures and works on or in the ground of this parcel of land. Most statutory provisions applicable to a ground lease apply accordingly. The right of superficies can be 'independent' (*zelfstandig*) or 'dependent' (*afhankelijk*), eg, dependent on the existence of a lease agreement pertaining to the property. A dependent right of superficies cannot be mortgaged independently.

Property may be split into apartment rights. An apartment right gives the holder of the right an undivided share in the jointly held property and an exclusive right of use of a certain part of it. The holder of an apartment right will automatically and mandatorily become a member of the 'association of owners' (*vereniging van eigenaars*).

6.3 Must land be registered?
In the Netherlands, all land is registered in the Land Registry. When this registry was first created in 1838, any land not registered specifically in someone's name was registered in the name of a government authority.

6.4 Public land register
In the Netherlands, certain facts relating to the property are registered in the public registers. The Land Registry (*kadaster*) is charged with maintaining these public registers. The public registers are a 'negative' system, ie, the content of the public registers does not constitute conclusive evidence of title to property. Not all relevant facts are automatically recorded in the public registers (eg, matters of inheritance and marital law). As such, the public registers form a register of transactions and other documents. Nevertheless, certain parties relying on the contents of the public registers may enjoy specific protection from the law.

Increasingly, there are efforts to connect public databases to each other. This will increase the amount and reliability of the information contained in the public registers.

6.5 Land not covered by a public land register
As stated above, all land and waters in the Netherlands have been recorded in the public registers.

6.6 State guarantee of title and categories of documents and information that are registered
There is no state guarantee of title. There is only the specific statutory liability of the land registry for not correctly maintaining the public registers.

The usual types of property transactions are recorded in the public registers. Categories of documents registered are:
- transfer deeds;
- deeds creating a limited property right (*beperkt recht*); and
- termination of a limited property right.

Specific types of information may not necessarily be recorded in the public registers, such as:
- matters of inheritance;
- matters of marital law;
- insolvency matters; and
- statute of limitations (*verjaring*).

Nevertheless, within certain limits, a party that was able to correct or supplement information contained in the public registers but has not done so, cannot rely on the incorrectness or incompleteness of the information in the public registers against the acquirer of a property.

Northern Ireland

Tughans David McDonnell & Phyllis Agnew

1. INVESTMENT PURCHASE OVERVIEW

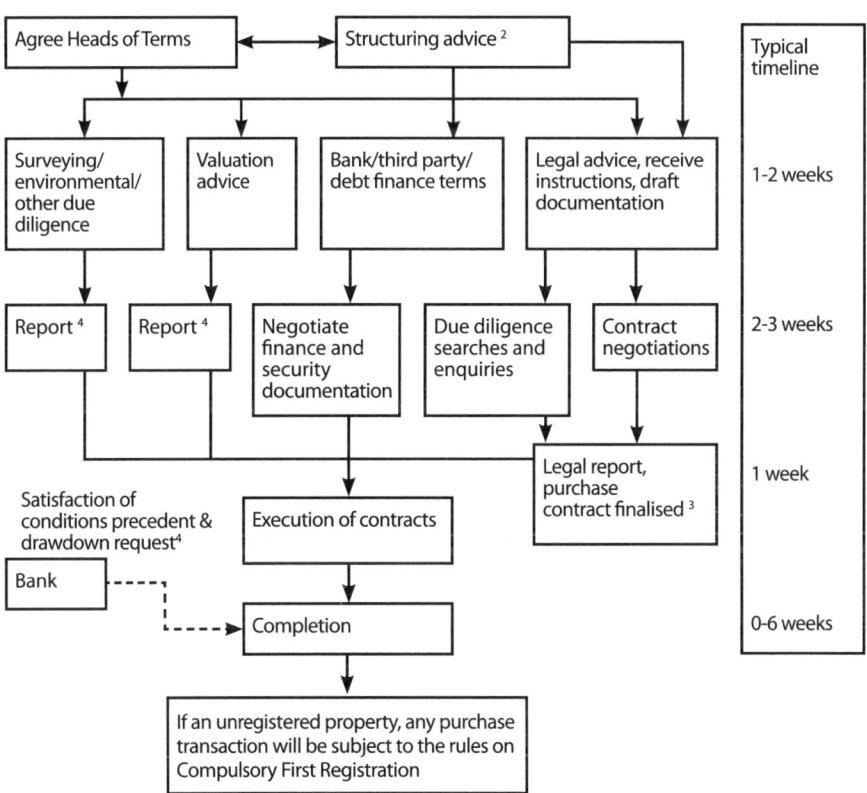

1. Often subject to compression, timescales may differ considerably, exchange and completion may be simultaneous.
2. Establishing an acquisition structure for tax and financial planning is an important early stage which may significantly influence other stages such as the banking arrangements and the purchase contract.
3. Each report will be addressed to the purchaser and bank (if any), a valuation report will be necessary if there is third party debt provided and otherwise is optional.
4. Before exchanging contracts it is advisable to ensure that all conditions precedent are capable of satisfaction.

2. TAX CONSIDERATIONS
2.1 Value added tax (VAT)

The VAT regime is identical to England and Wales and VAT is payable on the sale or purchase of real estate by the purchaser where the seller has elected

Northern Ireland

to waive the VAT exemption on the property (ie, it elects to charge VAT on the sale price.) After the purchase, the buyer must also elect to waive the VAT exemption in order to recover any VAT that it has paid on the purchase price. The current rate is 17.5 per cent and it has been this rate since 1 January 2010. VAT is not payable where: the landlord/seller has not elected to waive the exemption from VAT on the property; or the property is zero rated. Exempt supplies including any property-related supplies and financial services.

2.2 Stamp duty/transfer tax
Stamp Duty Land Tax (SDLT) is payable on property transactions. All property transactions are subject to SDLT (unless benefiting from a specified relief). The amount of SDLT payable will depend on the purchase price. The percentages for commercial property are:
- Not more than £150,000: zero per cent
- More than £150,000, but not more than £250,000: one per cent
- More than £250,000, but not more than £500,000: three per cent
- More than £500,000: four per cent.

There are special rules for calculating the SDLT chargeable in respect of rent payable under leases and the above rates apply to non rental consideration.

Stamp duty instead of SDLT is payable on a transfer of a company. The stamp duty rate is 0.5 per cent, however where an intra-group transfer has taken place in the past three years and SDLT relief was claimed, that relief will be lost and SDLT will be payable on the corporate transfer instead of stamp duty.

Both SDLT and stamp duty are payable within the 30 days of the effective date of the relevant transfer. Generally it is the purchaser who pays. There are exemptions to SDLT and the most notable exemptions in commercial property transactions include sale and lease back transactions, group relief, acquisition relief and reconstruction relief.

2.3 Tax issues for overseas investors investing in real estate
Currently the same tax regime applies in Northern Ireland as in the rest of the UK and therefore the issues are the same as in England and Wales.

3. INVESTMENT VEHICLE CHOICE
3.1 Structures used to purchase property
Properties can be purchased directly, but are more often purchased through a company. It is possible for arrangements to be put in place so that different companies within the same group of companies spread liabilities (eg the payment of SDLT).

3.2 Restrictions on foreign ownership or occupation of property or on foreign guarantees or security
There are no restrictions. Any foreign guarantees or security should be registered on the Slavenburg Register at Companies House.

3.3 Real estate investment trusts (REITS)
REITS tend to be UK based and property in Northern Ireland has been acquired by UK REITS.

4. FINANCING AN ACQUISITION
4.1 Financing of corporate real estate transactions
Generally corporate real estate transactions are financed through bank funding, usually through a mix of debt and equity although in recent times and as elsewhere in the UK bank funding has been significantly restricted and the higher value transactions are being driven by pension and property funds.

4.2 Real estate as a means of raising finance
The bank lends a proportion of the purchase price by way of debt to the buyer in return for security and commonly the most valuable piece of security will be a fixed charge over the particular property and/or other properties owned by the borrower.

4.3 Common forms of security granted over real estate
- Fixed security over the property to be purchased ('legal mortgage'). In the event that other assets are to be charged by way of security a legal charge might well be incorporated within a debenture.
- A debenture (if the buyer is a corporate, and the bank is to take security over all of its assets). The debenture comprises a fixed and floating charge over all the buyers' assets with a 'fixed charge' operating to charge the property on the date the debenture is taken. A 'floating charge' does not attach to any one particular asset and the buyer is free to deal with any assets subject to a floating charge until the bank crystallises the floating charge. At crystallisation, the buyer will be unable to dispose of the assets then charged without the bank's consent. Crystallisation usually occurs where the buyer defaults under the loan conditions or becomes insolvent.
- An assignment of rent received from occupational tenants is standard practice for investment property and the assignment is usually included within the debenture or legal mortgage.
- A charge over shares, (if a borrower is a special purchase vehicle).
- Assignment of benefit of any major contract, where the acquisition includes a development phase for the property to be funded.
- Loan/facility agreement setting out the terms upon which the facility is made available to the corporate will also be reviewed and negotiated.

Where the borrower and/or a third party, such as a parent company or guarantor, is providing security in connection with the financing and it is not incorporated in Northern Ireland, there will be capacity issues to be dealt with and legal opinions will be required from the relevant jurisdictions where the particular entity is incorporated.

Any security taken by the bank must be presented for registration at Companies House within 21 days of the dates of its creation. Failure to do so may mean that the security is void against any subsequent liquidator or administrator or other third party creditor, although it is possible to make applications to court where the 21 day period has not been adhered to but the security remains at risk until such time as the court agrees to registration and involves increased costs for the borrower or bank.

The bank will usually expect first ranking security over the property which is to be secured for the debt due from the borrower. If this is over unregistered land, the security document will be registered in the Registry of Deeds and if over registered land this will be registered at the Land Registry. Registration is critical to ensure the lending institution has priority over any subsequent dealings relating to the title. It is possible to register a restriction against the title at the Land Registry, whereby the borrower cannot make any disposition without the bank's consent.

4.4 Real estate mortgage securitisation
This has been used in Northern Ireland, although most commonly as part of a UK-wide portfolio.

5. MANAGING THE ACQUISITION PROCESS
5.1 Minimum formalities for the sale and purchase of property
For a contract for a sale of an interest in property to be valid it must be in writing, incorporate all agreed terms and be signed by or on behalf of each property.

5.2 Main legal documents required to transfer property or grant a lease
- Freehold purchase – a sale contract and the transfer document.
- Grant of a lease – the lease and any necessary consents from any superior landlord or mortgagee. For some transactions, an agreement preceding the grant of a lease is required which provides for a lease to be granted once works have been completed or other conditions (eg planning) have been satisfied.

5.3 Property transaction costs
The buyer typically pays:
- its own surveyors fee and legal costs, plus value added tax (VAT); (including Registry of Deeds (in the case of unregistered property) where applicable) and Companies House registration fees;
- Stamp Duty Land Tax (SDLT); and
- any environmental or survey report fees required to satisfy its bank.

The seller typically pays:
- the cost of all searches carried out which it is required to supply to the borrower, including Energy Performance Certificates and Asbestos Audit (if applicable);
- its own surveyors fees and legal costs (VAT is charged on both); and
- the costs of preparing certificates of title for the property (if applicable).

5.4 Does the seller warrant its ownership of the property?
No, it is the buyer's responsibility to make full enquiries and research the title to the property thoroughly.

5.5 Warranties a seller usually gives to a buyer
The seller gives only the warranties that are necessary in the standard replies to pre-contract enquiries which are mainly in relation to information which the seller has about the property which cannot be obtained from inspecting the title deeds or usual searches.

5.6 Purpose of warranties in the purchase agreement
It depends on the approach taken by the buyer and the seller. Where the buyer conducts its own full due diligence, it will receive limited or no warranties in the sale agreement.

Where the buyer conducts limited due diligence (for cost or time purposes) the seller might be prepared to provide full warranties.

The third alternative is that the seller's solicitor could provide a certificate of title containing detailed representations made by the seller about the property.

5.7 Owners/occupiers' liability for matters relating to the property which occurred before the above owner occupied
Generally owners/occupiers are not liable for matters relating to the property before they occupied it, although there are some exceptions, including the following:
- leases generally provide that the tenant is required to comply with legislation affecting the use of the property and is to indemnify the landlord against breach;
- persons who cause or knowingly permit contamination of property are liable to clean it up. However, if the person who caused the contamination cannot be found after reasonable enquiry, then the current owner can become liable;
- in a share acquisition of a company, all liabilities pass to the buyer; and
- in an asset acquisition of a company, only those liabilities that have been agreed pass to the buyer.

5.8 Notarisation
Notarisation is not required.

5.9 Formalities for a contract to become a legally binding obligation
The contracts must be in writing and signed by each of the contracting parties. In Northern Ireland a contract is embodied in a single document which is signed by both parties. However, where one particular signatory is overseas, or to speed up exchange in commercial transactions, the contract may be prepared in two identical parts. This means that both parts can be sent out for signature at the same time, with one part being signed by the seller and the other part being signed by the buyer. The parties then agree

to date the contract and it then becomes legally binding and subsequently physical exchange of the respective parts occurs so that each party retains the part duly signed by the other. Exchange of contracts creates a binding contract between the parties, after which neither party will ordinarily be able to withdraw from the transaction without incurring liability for breach.

5.10 Point at which the parties become legally bound
Where embodied in one single document, the parties become legally bound when the seller executes and dates the contract or in the case of two identical parts on the date exchanged between the contracting parties.

5.11 Transfer of title
Legal title to the property passes to the buyer when the transfer is completed, usually this occurs upon payment of the balance of the purchase price and when the executed transfer document is released to the buyer.

5.12 Insurance of the property if there is a delay between agreeing terms and actual sale
This will be specified in the contract, generally it is the seller who continues to insure up to completion.

6. REAL ESTATE BASICS
6.1 Main sources of laws that govern real estate
The main source of law is a combination of legislation and common laws.

6.2 Types of tenure
The following types of ownership exist:
- Freehold: fee simple;
- Freehold: fee farm grant – this allows covenants and an obligation for nominal rent to be imposed on the owner of the freehold; and
- Leasehold.

6.3 Must land be registered?
Northern Ireland has both registered and unregistered land. Any transfers of unregistered property are now subject to compulsory first registration with the Land Registry. On the transfer of any unregistered land the transfer will be registered at the Registry of Deeds ahead of registration of the Land Registry.

6.4 Public land register
There are two public land registers in Northern Ireland. The Land Registry is a register of title and the Registry of Deeds is a register of transactions.

6.5 Land not covered by a public land register
If the land has not been registered at the Land Registry it will be unregistered and it will be evidenced by the chain of title documentation noted at the Registry of Deeds.

6.6 State guarantee of title and categories of documents and information registered

The entries on the public register are conclusive evidence of the ownership of the registered interest (but not of the matters affecting that interest).

With compulsory first registration, solicitors are required to certify title to the Land Registry. Therefore, in addition to relying on the land certificate issued by the Land Registry it is prudent to check the previous title as well.

The Land Certificate details:
- whether the property is leasehold or freehold (if leasehold, brief details of the lease) includes a description of the property and a land registry plan;
- the class of title that is registered (absolute, good fee farm grant, possessory, qualified or good leasehold;
- any restrictions on the owner's ability to deal with the property;
- the purchase price paid for the property;
- any financial charges affecting the property; and
- any encumbrance, easement or covenant affecting the property (although some rights affect the property without registration, but these should be revealed through the enquiries raised with the seller's solicitors).

Republic of Ireland

Matheson Ormsby Prentice Ronan McLoughlin

1. INVESTMENT PURCHASE OVERVIEW
Please see page 261.

2. TAX CONSIDERATIONS
Anyone looking to invest in Irish property should obtain tax advice at the time of acquisition. The comments below are general comments and in no way represent the full picture of an area which is more complex and the treatment of which would take considerably more than the chapter of this book (and possibly even the entire book) to consider in sufficient detail.

The main taxes to be considered in the acquisition of Irish property are stamp duty and value added tax (VAT).

2.1 Stamp duty
Stamp duty is payable by a purchaser or tenant on written instruments that are executed in Ireland or any written instrument relating to Irish property. The rate of stamp duty varies. Generally the transfer of shares attracts a one per cent rate of stamp duty while transfers of commercial lands and buildings attracts stamp duty on a sliding scale up to a maximum of six per cent for properties valued in excess of €150,000. There are significant reliefs from stamp duty on the transfer of assets intra group and in mergers/reconstruction situations. Residential property attracts stamp duty on a sliding scale up to a maximum rate of nine per cent.

2.2 Value added tax
The VAT regime in respect of property was changed completely on 1 July 2008. The amount of VAT recovery available is a material factor in considering the VAT implications of buying and renting property in Ireland.

If acquiring a freehold interest in property, the age of the building, its history in terms of occupation and development, and the VAT status of any lettings, are all factors which may go to determining whether VAT is payable on acquiring a freehold interest. Even if VAT exempt, both parties may jointly opt to charge VAT on the transaction, currently at the rate of 13.5 per cent. If VAT is not charged on the transaction this may result in an inability to recover any of the VAT incurred when acquiring, developing or maintaining or refurbishing the property and the VAT will become an irrecoverable cost. VAT planning is of particular importance and relevance when, as landlord, leasing a premises to a company that has no or limited VAT recovery such as for example banks, insurance companies or similar financial institutions.

VAT is payable by a purchaser or tenant as appropriate and is to be paid on completion on a correct VAT invoice being produced.

All leases granted after 1 July 2008 may attract VAT on the rental payments at the current rate of 21 per cent. The landlord has the option as to whether or not to charge VAT on the rent but must do so in writing.

2.3 Latent capital gains tax in share purchase

In the case of acquisitions by way of share purchase, it is important to be aware for capital gains purposes that the company's history with the asset is of relevance. As such any base cost of acquiring the asset is the base cost at the time that the company acquired the asset and not the date on which the shares in the company were acquired. This would historically have given rise to a significant chance of a capital gain. Where the asset has been acquired within the last 5 to 10 years, given the current state of the property market, it is possible that this may now give rise to a loss which may be of use to the company in a taxation context.

2.4 General taxation

A non-resident company, if trading in real estate in Ireland, may decide to establish and register a branch in Ireland rather than incorporating a separate legal entity. If trading losses are likely to rise following the initial establishment in Ireland such losses may be capable of being offset against profits of the parent company in the parent company's home jurisdiction. On the operation becoming profitable it may then be preferable to establish an Irish company to avail of comparatively low corporation tax rates. Dealings in development land may however be subject to taxation at the rate of 25 per cent.

It is possible that dividends received by an Irish holding company from EU resident companies and companies resident in jurisdictions which have a tax treaty with Ireland may be taxed at a lower rate rather than 25 per cent where such dividends are paid out of trading profits. Ireland operates a self-assessment system for various taxes including corporation tax, however, it is possible to request an opinion from the Irish Revenue Commissioners of the tax consequences of a particular transaction in advance of the transaction taking place. Opinions given by the Revenue are not legally binding and it is open to Revenue officials to review the position when a transaction is complete and all the facts are known.

It should be noted that companies which are resident in Ireland for tax purposes are subject to corporation tax on worldwide income and gains, and non-resident companies chargeable to corporation tax on profits arising from a business conducted through a branch or agency in Ireland. For companies which are not incorporated in Ireland, tax residence is determined by reference to the place where the central management and control of the company abides. In order to benefit from Ireland's tax treaties, companies must in general be resident in Ireland within the meaning of the relevant treaty.

It is possible that tax losses of the company which forms part of a tax group can be offset against taxable profits of another group company. For these purposes a group can include EU resident companies. Losses may also be surrendered between branches of EU companies and Irish subsidiaries.

For parties acquiring property in their individual capacity, any non-domicile person should note the potential exposure to capital acquisitions tax which is a tax imposed on gifts and inheritances in Ireland. It is currently charged at the rate of 25 per cent. It is a beneficiary based tax and is imposed on any Irish situated assets comprised in a gift or inheritance and where, at the time of the gift or inheritance, either the donor or beneficiary is resident in Ireland. There are certain reliefs for non-domiciled individuals provided they have not been resident for five consecutive tax years at the relevant time.

3. INVESTMENT VEHICLE CHOICE

The most common means of acquiring property in Ireland are by either direct acquisition or company acquisition. There are no restrictions on foreign ownership or occupation of property or on foreign guarantees or security save, in respect of the latter, for concerns regarding capacity which will need to be addressed by an opinion letter produced by a lawyer practising in the jurisdiction in which the entity is situated.

Real Estate Investment Trusts (REITs) are not available in Ireland at this stage although certain commentators have called for their introduction.

The choice of structure is primarily driven by tax considerations but allied to this are issues regarding, as mentioned above, control and decision making and the location of the management team. Generally, when determining who exercises the central management and control of a company, the courts place considerable emphasis on meetings of the board of directors. The reason for this is that in general the business of companies is managed by the directors and such management is normally conducted at meetings of the board of directors. If meetings of the directors, who actually manage the company's business in this manner are held in Ireland, the company would generally be regarded as centrally managed and controlled in Ireland.

The number of assets to be acquired may also determine the structuring. If the acquisition is a one-off acquisition then it may make sense to hold the asset directly and it may make sense to establish a single purpose vehicle to acquire the asset on the basis that that company may then be a more attractive proposition when it comes to sell the asset. It is also possible that each asset could be owned by separate companies within a group on the basis that the group or separate assets could be sold by way of share sale at a date in the future. Again tax and corporate considerations need to be borne in mind, particularly if establishing a group of companies in terms of the administrative burden which will be placed on the group.

Limited partnerships are rare in Ireland. As stated above, generally property would be owned either by individuals or by corporate entities either incorporated in Ireland or abroad.

4. FINANCING AND ACQUISITION

Ireland has a sophisticated real estate financing market and real estate financing is usually a good mix of debt and equity. In the current climate the level of equity required is significantly higher than would have been the case up to 2007/2008. Currently the market is very fragile but it is likely that buyers would be required to bring equity of between 30 and 50 per cent as opposed to 0-20 per cent previously.

In return for the bank loan, the bank generally looks for:
- Fixed security over the property to be purchased (a legal mortgage). This is generally by way of a first fixed charge over the property. It may be comprised in a standalone mortgage deed. Where other assets are also to be charged by way of security, a legal charge may be incorporated within a debenture.
- A debenture (if the borrower is a corporate entity and the bank is to take security over all of that company's assets) comprises a fixed and floating charge over all the buyers' assets. A fixed charge operates the charge of the property whereas a floating charge does not attach to any one asset in particular. The borrower is as such free to deal with any assets subject to the floating charge until a lender freezes the charge ie the floating charge crystallises. On crystallisation the floating charge becomes a fixed charge over all assets subject to the floating charge. On crystallisation the borrower will then be unable to dispose of any assets without the lender's consent. Generally, however, crystallisation only occurs in the event of default or on insolvency of the borrower.

In relation to investment property producing a rental income the bank will also look for all rental income and the right to receive rental income to be assigned and the mortgage to the bank as security.

The bank may also look for a charge over shares, particularly for example where the borrower is a single purpose vehicle and may require assignment of the benefit of any major contracts generally in connection with significant development of the property. Such contracts would be construction and project team contracts.

There will be a number of finance documents namely facility agreement and security documents mentioned above, which would need to be negotiated. Banks may also appoint their own lawyers to either carry out a full investigation of title or to negotiate a certificate of title to be provided by the borrower's lawyers.

Generally where security is granted over assets those assets cannot be disposed of without first obtaining the bank's consent. This includes the granting of any leases in respect of those assets. In addition the borrower would be prevented from borrowing from or granting security to other parties ('negative pledge'). In case of a company, a charge when created is required to be registered in the Companies Office within 21 days of creation. In respect of property the bank will want to ensure that it is registered in the Land Registry or Registry of Deeds as appropriate and that no other charges rank in priority to it. As such any existing charges will need to be redeemed and deeds of release or discharge registered.

5. MANAGING THE ACQUISITION PROCESS
In Ireland the terms on which commercial property can be bought and sold

are relatively standardised. They seek to isolate the usual terms that would apply to a sale and purchase of a commercial property asset. If the property is to be acquired by way of share purchase then different terms would apply.

Set out below is the position based on a direct acquisition of commercial property.

5.1 Terms and binding contracts

In Ireland neither the vendor nor the purchaser are bound the sell or buy the property until a note or memorandum, usually in the form of a contract for sale, has been signed by both parties and exchanged.

Prior to this stage, and on a subject to contract basis, the parties, through their agents, normally will agree the commercial terms and set these out in the heads of terms or term sheet. On the basis of the heads of terms the vendor's solicitor will then prepare a contract for sale and furnish a draft of the contract together with all copy title to the buyer's solicitor.

In relation to second hand property, the doctrine of *caveat emptor* or 'buyer beware' applies and the purchaser will be deemed to have carried out all of its due diligence in advance of signing the contract. The contract is generally unconditional and normally the buyer will be bound to complete within a period of up to four weeks after exchange. A completion date however is generally set by agreement between the parties. The vendor would not agree generally to contracts being conditional upon the buyer arranging finance and as such the buyer should have finance in place prior to signing the contract.

There are no legal protections regarding exclusivities and normally parties, if such an arrangement is required, will enter into a formal exclusivity or lock out agreement during negotiation of commercial terms and until the execution of contracts to ensure that the negotiations remain exclusive until formal contracts are exchanged and the parties become bound to the transaction.

5.2 The contract document

The contract for sale is generally in the form of the Law Society standard general conditions of sale. The vendor's solicitor will draft the memorandum of sale and special conditions which apply to the particular transaction, which will contain additional terms, varying the general conditions. The sale contract will include all of the commercial terms and technical legal requirements to bind the parties and will generally be stated to represent the entire of the agreement between the parties such that the purchaser may not rely on any representations made prior to execution of the contract. Where the purchaser seeks to rely on such representations then they should be reflected in the contract for sale.

5.3 Contract terms

The first page of the contract generally sets out the parties to the contract, the purchase price, the completion date, the rate of interest and the amount of the deposit to be paid on signing the contracts (normally 10 per cent of the purchase price). All of these provisions will reflect the agreement reached between the parties.

The contract then recites the particulars and tenure of the property, namely the description of the asset and the title to the property. The contract will then set out the documents vouching the vendor's title and relating to ancillary matters such as planning and development and other documents which the purchaser would be deemed to be on notice.

Then there will be special conditions attaching to the contract for sale, which can address a wide variety of issues regarding the agreement.

What may happen is, where a sale has been negotiated between agencies, that a booking deposit (normally enough to cover the agent's fees) is paid to the agent and is fully refundable until a contract for sale comes into existence and the parties are bound to the transaction, at which stage the auctioneer holds the deposit as stakeholder. Normally, after completion, the auctioneer's fees are deducted from the booking deposit and the balance of the booking deposit paid to the vendor.

The remainder of the deposit ie, the difference between the booking deposit and the sum representing 10 per cent of the purchase price is payable on signing the contract and is generally held by the vendor's solicitor as stakeholder pending completion of the sale. In the event that the purchaser does not complete the sale within the time frame mentioned, and in accordance with the general conditions, the purchaser may end up forfeiting the deposit and may also be liable to the vendor for damages for additional losses and a reduction in value of the property.

Interest will be stated to be payable at the specified rate in the event the contract does not complete on the specified completion date. The general conditions provide that the vendor must close sale without prejudice to any claim that it has for interest. Vendors are now looking to vary this general condition by the inclusion of a special condition to the effect that all interest must be paid on or prior to completion.

In relation to price, in the case of acquisition of a fully occupied property producing a rental income, all payments will be apportioned as of the completion date, which may result in a variation of the actual amount payable on completion.

Generally, apportionment is on a daily rate.

The position regarding the time between exchange and completion is that the seller would normally continue to insure the property, although it can be advisable for a buyer to insure from exchange because the beneficial interest in the property has then passed to the buyer. The buyer will be required to complete the purchase even if the property is substantially damaged between exchange and completion.

It is also possible, in certain circumstances, for parties who wish to do so to have a confidentiality clause inserted in the contract for sale. However the purchase deed must reflect the amount paid for the property and must then be registered with the Land Registry and the Registry of Deeds which are public registries.

After completion of the sale the purchaser must stamp its purchase deed and pay all stamp duty within a period of 30 days of completion. In the event that the acquisition is being funded, the bank will require to have the funds on completion in respect of all stamp duty and registration fees.

Registration can only occur after the deeds have been stamped and in the case of registered property, the transfer deeds and charge must be registered in the Land Registry. In the case of unregistered property it must be registered in the Registry of Deeds. The mortgage charge document where granted by a corporate entity, must be registered in the Companies Registration Office within 21 days of being created. Failure to do so may render the deed void.

Generally the purchaser cannot assign the benefit of the contract for sale although the vendor may, at its absolute discretion, agree to do so. It is however rare.

6. REAL ESTATE BASICS

Under Irish law there are two types of property ownership, freehold and leasehold. The Act under which property law is primarily governed now is The Land and Conveyancing Law Reform Act 2009, which repealed and restated significant late 19th and early 20th century UK statutes. The main act governing landlord and tenant matters is the 1980 Landlord and Tenant Act. Certain sections have been amended by statute subsequently but it is the primary point of reference.

A freehold interest offers the owner absolute ownership of the property to the exclusion of all others and to the land and all buildings and structures on it. The best title a freehold owner can obtain is freehold absolute title.

It relates solely to ownership and does not grant the owner freedom to deal with the property to the exclusion of all other statutory constraints for example those in relation to planning and development of the property.

A leasehold interest is an interest created out of a freehold interest and it gives the right to a tenant (the occupier) to possession on payment of a rent to the holder of the freehold interest (the landlord). A lease may be in respect of land, land and buildings, or a lease of a part only of a building. One property can have freehold and leasehold interest and indeed can have a number of leasehold interests. Leases may be granted for long or short periods. Title leases would normally be leases granted at an amount equivalent to the market value of the freehold, granting an interest in the property to the tenant for a period of 500 or more commonly 999 years, subject to a requirement to comply with certain covenants and to the payment of a nominal amount by way of rent ie 5 cent/€1 per annum.

An occupational leasehold interest is generally in the region of 20 to 25 years, with five yearly rent reviews. Normally they do not involve the payment of a premium but instead reserve a market rent in favour of the landlord, normally payable quarterly in advance. An occupational lease would also contain more onerous covenants and obligations on the tenants' part in order to preserve the integrity and value of the landlord's investment. Leases for under five years do not entitle the tenant to renew the lease on the expiration of the term and are normally construed as short term lettings entered into for the temporary convenience of both landlord and tenant. It will reserve

Republic of Ireland

a market rent but the covenants will generally be slightly less onerous than those contained in the full 20 or 25 year occupational lease. The market now operates on the basis that all short-term occupational tenants will renounce any rights they would have to a new lease where they remain in occupation for upwards of five years and meet certain statutory requirements. This means that if they stay for more than five years the landlord does not have to pay compensation for disturbance where the landlord does not grant a new lease.

There are other means of occupation of a property such as a licence, however a licence does not grant proprietary interest in the property and is effectively a contract between the parties which in the normal course would be capable of revocation in accordance with its terms. It does not offer any security of continuous occupation.

Title to property is registered either in the Land Registry or the Registry of Deeds, both of which are part of the Property Registration Authority. It is proposed that in the near future all titles will have to be registered in the Land Registry. Currently where property is 'unregistered' ie Register of Deeds property and is sold, in 24 of the 26 counties (Dublin and Cork are excluded) the ownership of that property must be registered ie is subject to compulsory registration in the Land Registry. It is proposed that Dublin and Cork be subject to compulsory registration within the next year or two.

The Land Registry offers a state guarantee to the title of the property. The Registry of Deeds simply contains a register of deeds which relate to a property sale. It does not guarantee the title to the property but is of significant relevance in terms of priorities and in particular a priority of interest or claim to a particular property.

On completion of a sale of registered property the deed of transfer, having been stamped, is lodged in the Land Registry. Registration is not automatic and in the case of the transfer of an entire freehold folio can be completed within a relatively short time period. However in the case of a more complicated registration of part of a folio or a first registration, the timeframe for registration may be considerably longer. The Property Registration Authority is moving towards electronic conveyancing and transfer of title but it will be some years before the project is completed.

Title registered in the Land Registry is registered in a document called a 'folio'. The folio is broken into three parts. Part 1 section 1 recites the description of the property and the reference to the property on an ordnance survey map. Part B section 1 will show any elements or areas of the lands comprised in that folio which have been transferred (generally by way of sale of portion of the land) and are now registered under different folios.

Part 2 will confirm whether or not the title to the property is absolute title, possessory title or, in the case of leasehold, good leasehold title. It will show the registered owner of the property. Part 3 will disclose all burdens affecting the property such as easements and charges.

The Land Registry has recently completed a full digitisation of its mapping registry and each folio or plot forming part of a folio is now referenced by a seed point which can be accessed through the Land Registry electronic access system.

Republic of Ireland

Property identified		
Commercial terms agreed		
Structuring agreed		
Property acquisition		**Corporate acquisition**
Due diligence: (a) Title due diligence; and (b) Property due diligence Structural/ground survey Environmental survey	**Arranging finance**	Due diligence: (a) Title due diligence; (b) Financial due diligence; (c) Taxation due diligence – corporate due diligence
Negotiation of contract for sale		**A) Negotiation of share purchase agreement to include all warranties and indemnities required**
Execution of contract for sale	Negotiation of loan facility	Capital gains tax clearance certificate
Requisitions on title	Attending to financing conditions precedent to drawdown	Completion – execution of share transfer
Capital gains tax clearance certificate	Negotiation of security documentation and ancillary documents	Post completion registration
Drafting the deed of assurance	Execution of security documentation and compliance with all other security requirements	Change of directors/ secretary in companies registration office
Ancillary completion documentation	Registration of security on title registries and companies office (if applicable)	Registration of charge in companies registration office
Completion		**B) Asset purchase agreement and warranties**
Post completion registration (a) Title – Land Registry; (b) Security – Land Registry and Companies Registration Office		Capital gains tax clearance certificate
		Completion – execution of share transfer
		Post completion registration
		Change of directors/ secretary in companies registration office
		Registration of charge in companies registration office
		Drafting deed of assurance and other pre-completion matters
		Completion
		Post completion registration in the Land Registry: (a) Registration in the Land Registry (b) Registration in the Companies Office

Russia

Goltsblat BLP Elena Barinova, Andrey Shpak, Matvey Kaploukhiy & Svetlana Savina

1. INVESTMENT PURCHASE OVERVIEW

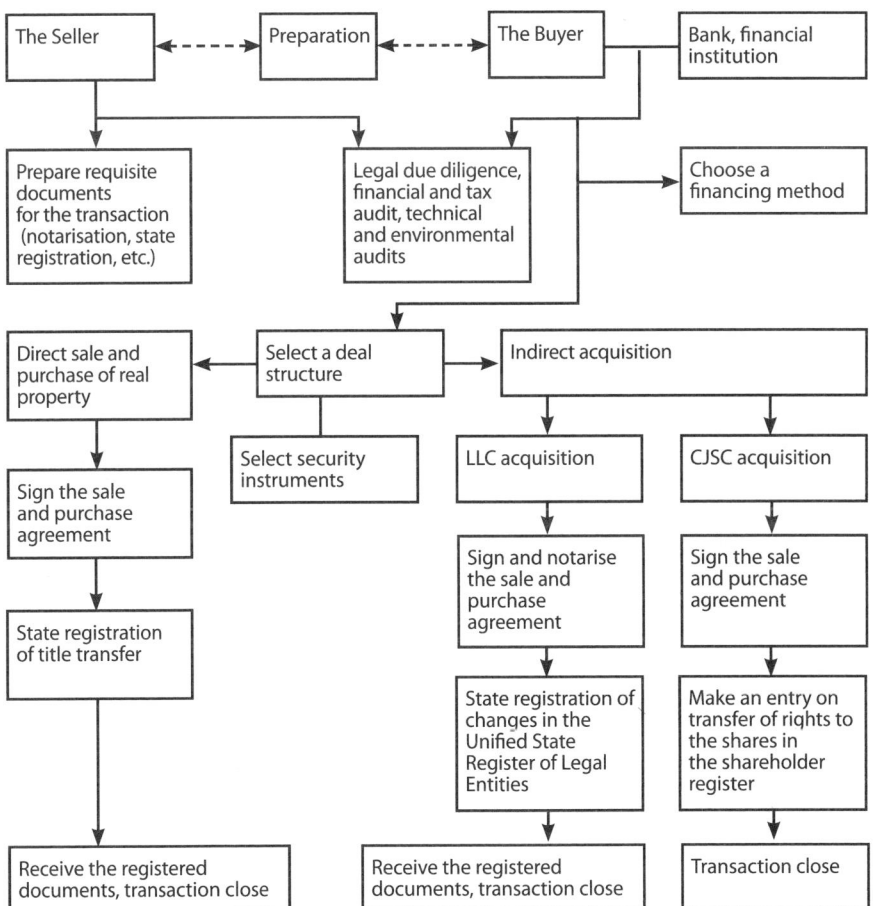

2. TAX CONSIDERATIONS
2.1 Value added tax (VAT)
As a general rule, the sale of a building (or other real estate) is subject to VAT at a rate of 18 per cent. Yet the sale of land, as well as apartments for individuals, is exempt from VAT.

Russia operates a VAT system that is largely similar to the EU system, (although various deviations exist – especially in terms of interpretation and practical application of the rules): eg, the seller charges the buyer VAT based on a VAT invoice and the buyer subsequently recovers the input VAT against its VATable supplies.

An important feature of the Russian VAT system in practice is that the Russian tax authorities are generally reluctant to refund net VAT receivable in cash, preferring the taxpayer to recover input VAT against future VATable supplies. Refunding net VAT receivable in cash typically requires lengthy court litigation, which exerts a significant effect on the timing of such recovery. Investors need to take this into account when planning cash flow models for development projects.

2.2 Typical sale structures
It is typical for sale of real estate in Russian practice to be structured in the form of a sale of shares in the company that owns such real estate by a foreign owner (typically based in Cyprus due to its favourable tax regime applicable to capital gains and dividends and good double tax treaty). In addition to various legal advantages, this allows the seller to avoid Russian profits tax on the capital gains realised on the sale (otherwise taxable at 20 per cent). The advantage for the buyer is that such a sale of shares allows it to avoid VAT and thus potential problems with recovering it.

2.3 Stamp duty
Russia does not levy any material stamp duty in connection with sale or purchase of real estate – although there are various fees for performing different types of registration, though these are not substantial (eg, the registration fee for registering real estate is 15,000 roubles (about €375).

2.4 Other key tax and accounting considerations relevant for investing in Russian real estate
Russia levies property tax at a rate of up to 2.2 per cent on the fixed assets of Russian legal entities and permanent establishments and on real estate owned by foreign companies with no permanent establishment (the specific rate is set at the regional level).

Interest deduction for loans in a foreign currency is currently limited to 15 per cent and for loans in roubles – to twice the Central Bank rate (ie, effectively 16 per cent as of 20 May 2010), which is to be reduced to 1.1 times the Central Bank rate after 30 June 2010.

Russia also has thin capitalisation rules that limit deduction of interest on loans received by a Russian company with direct or indirect foreign ownership exceeding 20 per cent of capital from:
(i) its direct or indirect foreign parent;
(ii) Russian affiliated companies of such parent; and
(iii) guaranteed by such parent or such Russian affiliated companies.

Deduction is limited to loans of up to three times the capital. The current legislation includes a loophole that exempts loans from foreign 'sister' companies (ie, those not in the direct or indirect ownership chain) from thin capitalisation rules. It is not clear, however, when this loophole will be closed. Also, some double tax treaties signed by Russia appear to provide protection against thin capitalisation rules by allowing companies owned by residents of the particular treaty country to deduct such interest in full (eg, such exemptions are contained in Protocols to the Germany-Russia and Netherlands-Russia treaties).

Russian corporate and accounting rules allow dividends to be paid only out of statutory Russian profits. Distributing reserves (in some cases of the initial charter capital) is not, as a general rule, allowed. For this reason, getting proper leverage into a property development company is often important not only for tax reasons but also in order to ensure that the cash is not trapped in the Russian property development company.

Recently, we have seen an increasing number of cases of investors who intend to operate the building after the initial construction and development using a closed investment fund (the Russian equivalent of a unit trust). Although such a structure is subject to onerous compliance and registration requirements, it currently offers substantial tax advantages (some of which are, however, based on interpretation rather than on the explicit wording of the law). For example, it exempts real estate from property tax; received rent is also not subject to profits tax until it is distributed to the owner of the shares in the fund; even upon distribution, it is often possible to obtain a favourable tax rate under a relevant double tax treaty.

3. INVESTMENT VEHICLE CHOICE
3.1 Rights of foreigners to real estate

As a general rule, foreign citizens enjoy the same rights and bear the same obligations in the Russian Federation as Russian citizens do. Even so, the legislation stipulates certain specific features with respect to the rights of foreign commercial entities to real estate.

For instance, foreign citizens are not allowed to own land plots in border regions or other territories subject to a special regime, in particular, territories accommodating strategic and military facilities.

Foreign citizens and legal entities are granted ownership of state or municipally owned land plots only for a consideration. Individual categories of Russian citizen and legal entity listed in the law may be granted ownership of plots free of charge.

Agricultural land cannot be owned by foreigners. Foreign citizens and legal entities, as well as legal entities in the authorised (joint) capital of which foreign citizens or foreign legal entities hold a more than 50 per cent ownership interest, may hold agricultural land only on lease.

The given restrictions also apply to water bodies located on such land plots.

3.2 Assets vs. shares deal

As already noted, in practice it is not the real estate as such that constitutes the subject of the transaction, but ownership interests or shares in the legal entities owning this real estate. Control over the real estate is thus acquired through corporate mechanisms without the special alienation procedures and the restrictions set for real estate. When a company is purchased, the new owner acquires all the rights and obligations of the purchased legal entity, including all of its assets.

As a rule, this method is used when major assets or a whole investment project in the real estate sphere is acquired (for example, a complete class 'A' office complex or a logistics complex construction project, including transfer of all the relations involved in the given construction). An average of about 80 per cent of all such major deals are carried out through acquisition of a legal entity. This is also connected with the fact that such a method precludes the need to re-execute permission documentation and agreements with third parties concluded in relation to the investment project. At the same time, let us note once more that, in the majority of cases, it is participation not in the Russian legal entity owning the assets that is sold, but in the foreign parent company of the said owner (most often registered in Cyprus).

The main advantage of acquiring real estate through a legal entity is the absence of any need for state registration of transfer of title to the assets, which is mandatory on acquisition of real estate (this being particularly important in cases when, within the scope of a single transaction, a multitude of different properties is acquired). This helps:

(i) to exclude potential difficulties in state registration (for example, if there are inaccuracies in the entitling documents that might hamper registration);
(ii) to avoid formalities associated with specifics of acquisition of the facility (if, for example, construction in progress is acquired and the contractor agreement has to be terminated for state registration purposes); and
(iii) to save time (by law, state registration takes one month, but the process may be suspended and may, in the worst case scenario, last for six months).

In addition to the advantages indicated above, acquisition of a foreign legal entity allows the purchase relations to be subordinated to foreign law and foreign legal instruments to be used (eg, those of English law), this not being the case, by express virtue of law, when real estate as such is purchased.

Moreover, as already mentioned, purchase of a legal entity is more beneficial than purchase of real estate from the tax point of view, since it is not subject to VAT and enjoys a series of other tax benefits.

At the same time, it should be noted that such a deal structure should not be used exclusively for tax optimisation purposes. Individual judicial acts have recently started appearing that interpret sale of a stake in a legal entity that owns real estate as sale of the actual real estate from a tax point of view.

In addition, use of the given method for acquiring real estate is not always possible, primarily because the seller does not always have a special purpose vehicle (SPV) that owns only the real estate of interest to the purchaser: for example, the seller's business is not diversified and all of its assets are concentrated in a single legal entity, whereas the buyer is interested only in one of the assets. The creation of and transfer of assets to a separate design company or SPV specifically for the transaction (by setting up a new company, reorganising or otherwise) involves its own complications and requires additional time and money. And even when the asset of interest is the only property of the seller's company, purchase of an existing company also involves purchase of its debts, thus requiring a detailed due diligence.

3.3 Alternative instruments
Russian law does not allow for the structuring of a trust in the traditional understanding. Even so, instruments have quite recently appeared in Russia that are similar in nature to a trust, such as mutual investment funds and mortgage participation certificates, and active use is being made of these.

A mutual investment fund (MIF) is a separate set of assets consisting of property handed over by the fund management founder to a management company for fund management and of property received in the process of fund management, shares in the title to which are certified by a security issued by the management company. An MIF is not a legal entity. The legal relations associated with management of the fund arise between the founders of the fund management (unit holders) and the management company, which issues units for raising funds to be placed in financial assets.

Mortgage participation certificates are securities whose owners acquire common shared ownership to mortgage coverage (that is, claims for repayment of a debt and interest under credit agreements and other obligations secured by mortgage). This mortgage coverage is under trust management by the issuer of the mortgage participation certificates. The owner of a mortgage participation certificate has the right to purchase the debt and to receive the proceeds from discharge of the obligations the claims on which constitute the mortgage coverage. Mortgage participation certificates may be issued only by commercial organisations licensed to manage investment funds, mutual investment funds and non-state pension funds.

Mortgage participation certificates are not emissive securities and may be issued only in uncertified form. These securities do not have a face value and are traded freely, without any restrictions. This description of a mortgage certificate largely coincides with the legal description of an investment unit, which is also a non-emissive, registered security without a face value that is traded freely on the market once the unit investment fund has been set up.

4. FINANCING AN ACQUISITION
4.1 Choice of financing
Before the crisis, a large proportion of major real estate projects were financed by borrowings. Specifically by virtue of its dependence on outside financing, the real estate sector has been among those that have suffered most from the crisis, during which credit interest rates for developers rose substantially, resulting in many of them mothballing a considerable share of projects and focusing on the most liquid of them. Banks and other professional investors now mainly extend credits only for facilities that are most attractive from the market point of view and are close to completion and, as a rule, for collateral exceeding the value of the loan. At the same

time, far more significance is now attached to the quality of the collateral. Currently, it is, in the main, only major production companies that are using their own funds to purchase and build real estate assets for developing their core business.

4.2 Mortgage as an institution
Mortgage transactions at the moment predominate in Russia mainly in crediting of legal entities. Mortgage of real estate is viewed, as a rule, as priority collateral.

4.3 Securitisation
The institution of securitisation is currently becoming established and developing in Russia and a relevant market is taking shape. A law on securitisation is at the stage of being considered by the State Duma of the Russian Federation. Adoption of the law should be accompanied by a change in other regulatory and legal acts relating to securitisation, in particular the law on bankruptcy. First of all, mortgage deals, car loans, consumer credits and others might become subject to securitisation. Existing Russian securitisation transactions are concluded, as a rule, overseas, with the participation of foreign partners. The main problem, however, for development of securitisation in Russia is, at the moment, a shortage of investors.

5. MANAGING THE ACQUISITION PROCESS
5.1 Introduction
The requirements stipulated by law on real estate sale and purchase transactions, as well as the procedure for concluding such deals, are different depending on the structure of the deal (sale and purchase of real estate or sale of a legal entity holding a real estate title).

5.2 Direct sale and purchase of real estate
5.2.1 Minimum formalities and the required agreement format
A real estate sale and purchase agreement must be concluded in writing in the form of a single document signed by the parties, at which time, as a general rule, the agreement comes into effect and becomes binding on the parties. The real estate sale and purchase agreement itself is not subject to state registration and does not have to be notarised.

Transfer of the real estate title from the seller to the buyer is, however, subject to state registration, after which the buyer becomes the owner of the real estate in the eyes of third parties. This also applies when the seller and the buyer have fulfilled their contractual obligations long before state registration.

One exception is an agreement on sale of a house, apartment, or part of a house or apartment, which is subject to state registration itself and is considered concluded from this time.

If the parties so wish, a real estate sale and purchase agreement may be notarised, though this is not required by law. In practice, such agreements are notarised very rarely, mainly by individuals.

5.2.2 Fundamental terms of real estate sale and purchase
A real estate sale and purchase agreement must indicate fundamental terms, otherwise it will not be deemed concluded. By law, the fundamental terms of a real estate sale and purchase agreement are the subject of the agreement and its price. In addition, each of the parties is entitled to class as fundamental other terms requiring mutual agreement.

5.2.3 Subject of the agreement
A real estate sale and purchase agreement must give details making it possible to identify the real estate to be transferred to the buyer under the agreement, including its location on the relevant land plot or within other real estate. In the absence of such information in the agreement, the condition regarding the real estate subject to transfer is deemed not to have been agreed by the parties and the real estate sale agreement not to be concluded.

The specific real estate is identified in the sale and purchase agreement in accordance with the entitling and title-confirming documents of the seller (certificate of state registration of the seller's title, excerpt from the Realty Register, etc), the technical documentation relating to the real estate (technical data sheet), as well as information regarding the real estate contained in the State Real Estate Cadastre (cadastral passport, cadastral excerpt).

5.2.4 Price
The real estate sale agreement must set the price of the property. If the agreement lacks a written condition on the price of the real estate agreed by the parties, it is deemed not to be concluded.

The general rule is that the price set by the agreement for a building, structure or other real estate located on a land plot includes the price of the part of the land plot transferred together with the real estate or of the rights to it.

5.2.5 Rights to land on sale of real estate
Under a sale agreement for a building, structure or other real estate, together with the title to the given real estate, the buyer also receives the rights to the land plot accommodating it and required for its use. The nature of these rights depends on whether the seller of the real estate is the owner of the relevant land plot.

If the seller owns the land plot occupied by the real estate and necessary for its use, the title to it is transferred to the buyer.

If the seller of the real estate does not own the land plot on which it stands, the buyer acquires the right to use the land plot on the same conditions as the seller. It should be borne in mind that sale of such real estate located on a plot that does not belong to the owner of the real estate is permitted without the consent of the land plot owner only provided this does not contravene the terms for use of the plot established by law and the relevant agreement.

If the building or structure and the land on which it stands belong to one and the same person, the land plot may not be sold without the building or structure located on it.

5.2.6 Seller's warranties and obligations

Russian law lacks the institution of 'warranties' in the traditional understanding. At the same time, the rule established in Russian legislation puts several obligations on the seller for the purpose of achieving the same goals as those pursued by 'warranties' in English law – such obligations as transfer of the real estate free from any third party rights, of due quality, etc.

5.2.7 Obligation to transfer the real estate free from any third party rights

By law, the seller is required to warn the buyer of all third party rights in relation to the given real estate (with the exception of encumbrances of which the buyer is aware or should be aware). At the same time, the seller is only entitled to transfer goods encumbered by third party rights to the buyer if the buyer accepts the goods with the encumbrances.

In the event of sale of a facility encumbered by third party rights, the buyer is entitled to demand a reduction in the price or cancellation of the sale and purchase agreement, unless it can be proved that the buyer was aware or should have been aware of the third party rights to the item.

If an item is seized from the buyer by third parties on grounds arising before fulfilment of the sale and purchase agreement, the seller is required to reimburse the buyer for its losses, unless it can prove that the buyer was aware or should have been aware of these grounds.

5.2.8 Conditions regarding quality and quality guarantees

Requirements relating to the quality of a facility for transfer (its technical characteristics, connection to utilities, etc) are usually indicated in the real estate sale and purchase agreement. In turn, the seller has to provide the buyer with goods of the quality indicated in the sale and purchase agreement.

If the real estate has any defects, the seller must, by law, agree on them with the buyer, otherwise a buyer that receives a substandard facility is entitled, at its own discretion, to demand from the seller a proportionate reduction in the purchase price, elimination of the defects free of charge within a reasonable time, or reimbursement for its own outlays on eliminating the said defects. In the event of a material violation of the quality requirements (identification of irremediable defects, defects that will cost a disproportionate amount or take too long to remedy, or defects identified repeatedly or reappearing after being eliminated, and so on), the buyer is entitled to withdraw from the sale and purchase agreement and claim return of any monies paid.

The general rule is that the seller is responsible for any defects in the real estate if the buyer can prove that they arose before the facility was handed over or for reasons arising before that time. With respect to goods the quality of which has been guaranteed by the seller, the latter is liable for any defects unless it can prove that they arose after transfer of the goods to the buyer, as a result of misuse by the buyer, actions of third parties or force majeure.

It should be borne in mind that, after a facility has been purchased, the responsibility for maintaining it in due condition (in compliance with the fire

Russia

safety, sanitation and environmental requirements, absence of any threat to life and limb of third parties, etc) transfers to the new owner, so if the relevant rules and regulations are violated, it is the new owner, not the seller, who will be held administratively or criminally liable. In turn, in cases envisaged by law or the agreement, the buyer will be entitled to lodge relevant claims (for instance, for reimbursement of fines paid, etc) against the seller in accordance with the civil law relations between them.

5.2.9 Seller's rights to the alienated property
In most cases, the seller of real estate is its owner.

Russian legislation does not yet determine definitively whether a seller who, at the time a transaction is concluded, is not the owner of the alienated property, can conclude a relevant sale and purchase agreement. This applies primarily to cases when, at the time the transaction is concluded, the seller has not yet acquired the real estate or when the seller wants to dispose of a facility that has not yet been built (sale of a future item). In Russian judicial doctrine and practice, such transactions are assessed differently. The main difficulty consists in answering whether an effective transaction can be conducted if the seller does not hold the registered title to the property at the time it is concluded. As noted, no position has yet been formulated in this respect.

In the instances when the property is subsequently seized from the buyer by the proper owner, the legislatively envisaged liability of the seller that was not entitled to sell the property and sold the facility to the buyer comes down to the obligation to reimburse the buyer for its losses.

Sellers may also be legal entities to which state or municipally owned property belongs by special proprietary right – by right of economic management or operational administration. Such disposal usually requires the consent of the owner (the state or municipality).

5.2.10 State registration of title transfer
As noted, under Russian legislation, transfer of real estate title is subject to state registration in the realty register. State registration constitutes the only proof of the existence of a registered right and a registered real estate title can be disputed only in a court of law.

The documents submitted for state registration may differ depending on the specifics of the transactions and the requirements of the relevant registration authority. As a rule, in addition to the sale and purchase agreement and application for state registration, for title registration purposes the real estate cadastral passport, the cadastral passport of the land plot on which the real estate facility is located, and documents confirming the legal capacity of the parties (constituent documents, certificates of state registration of a legal entity, etc) are submitted.

In accordance with Russian legislation, the standard time required for state registration of transfer of title is one month. Even so, the state registration procedure may be suspended if the registrar finds any mistakes in the documents provided/requests additional documents. In the worst case scenario, state registration may take six months.

A state fee of 15,000 roubles (about €375) is paid for state registration of title transfer. The costs of paying the state fee are distributed between the parties by mutual agreement and may differ depending on the situation.

5.3 Indirect purchase of real estate (purchase of legal entity)
5.3.1 Choice of organisational and legal form of a legal entity sold

On indirect purchase of real estate (ie, through a legal entity), the most two common types of Russian legal entity used are a limited liability company (LLC) and a joint-stock company (JSC). A company incorporated in either form enjoys separate legal identity. Apart from special, very limited situations, participants in LLCs and shareholders in JSCs assume no legal liability for the company's actions or obligations and incur the risk of losses in connection with the company's activities within the value of the interest/shares they own. Neither LLCs nor JSCs can be wholly owned by a single participant/shareholder, if the participant/shareholder is, in turn, wholly owned by another individual or legal person. Though it is argued that this restriction may not be applicable to foreign shareholders, our recommendation is to observe it.

Until recently, the LLC structure was the most popular form of legal entity for real estate transactions. Its establishment is less onerous and time-consuming than that of a JSC, as there is no legal requirement for LLCs to issue and register shares. It is also a more flexible option if a participant decides to increase its authorised capital, which is one financing instrument. Since LLCs are private companies, they have more room for manoeuvre and are less regulated in terms of corporate governance and financing. All these made the LLC very attractive for both the seller and the buyer. Owing to recent amendments to the law, however, any transfer of participatory shares in LLCs has become subject to certification by a Russian notary. In practice, this means that the sale of participatory shares in an LLC has become a complicated procedure with lots of practical and legal inconveniences.
For example, Russian notaries are reluctant to notarise long share sale and purchase agreements. It is also almost not possible, in current practice, to sign an LLC share sale and purchase agreement governed by foreign law. Thus, an LLC is likely to be the last choice if the parties structure the deal through purchase of a Russian legal entity. Conversely, it still might be chosen if the buyer purchases a foreign entity with a 100 per cent Russian subsidiary-owner of the real estate.

JSCs can be 'open' (OJSC) or 'closed' (CJSC), the former being similar to a public company and the latter resembling certain provisions of LLCs. OJSCs are rarely used for real estate transactions.

All Russian companies are included in the Unified State Register of Legal Entities, with the basic information about the company being publicly available: company name, legal address, amount of authorised capital, list of participants in LLCs or the holder of the shareholders' register of JSCs, corporate governance, the General Director (or external manager or management company), licenses, tax registration and certain other information.

5.3.2 Share sale and purchase agreement
The sale of a Russian legal entity is executed in the format of a share sale and purchase agreement. For an LLC, the share sale and purchase agreement must be notarised. The buyer obtains legal title to the participation shares in an LLC as soon as the share sale and purchase agreement is signed and notarised; to the shares in a JSC – as soon as an entry is made in the shareholder's register, which may be maintained by the company itself or by an independent registrar. Such an entry is made on the basis of an instrument of transfer executed by the seller in accordance with the terms of the share sale and purchase agreement. In the event of sale of participatory shares in an LLC, no instrument of transfer is executed; transfer of title is made solely on the grounds of the executed share sale and purchase agreement.

The parties become legally bound as soon as the share sale and purchase agreement is signed, unless it is conditional upon specific external events (conditions precedent). It should be noted, however, that it is currently difficult to execute a conditional share sale and purchase agreement for participation shares in an LLC owing to the ambiguity of current Russian legislation.

Sale of a Russian legal entity is not associated with any significant transactional costs.

5.3.3 Application of foreign law
In structuring a transaction through purchase of a JSC, as a rule, the parties apply foreign law to the share sale and purchase agreement (usually English law). In this case, the seller provides a standard set of representations and warranties, ie, in relation to the company's status, rights to shares, rights to real estate, etc.

With respect to sale of participatory shares in an LLC, as mentioned above, the choice of foreign law is problematical since Russian notaries refuse to certify a contract governed by foreign law. For this reason, inclusion of representations and warranties in a Russian law governed share sale and purchase agreement is also problematic, since, as mentioned, these institutions are not recognised by the Russian legal system (at least to the extent that these institutions are developed in common law jurisdictions).

5.4 Sale of an enterprise as a set of assets and liabilities
Russian legislation also allows for the possibility of selling an enterprise as a set of assets and liabilities. In the given case, the enterprise is considered as a particular type of real estate (set of assets), for which a special legal regime is established, this being connected, in particular, with confirmation of the composition of the enterprise, its transfer, securing of creditors' rights, etc.

The enterprise is composed of all the types of property intended for its operations, including land plots, buildings, structures, tools, raw materials, output, receivables, debts, and rights to designations individualising the enterprise, its output, work and services (corporate name, trade marks and service marks), as well as other exclusive rights.

Such a sale of an enterprise should not be confused with sale of a legal entity since, in the given case, the subject of the deal is the actual set of assets, and not participation in the legal entity (ownership interest/share).

In contrast to an ordinary real estate sale and purchase agreement, a sale and purchase agreement for an enterprise is subject to state registration and is considered concluded from that time on. In addition, the transfer to the buyer of title to the enterprise is also subject to state registration, this being carried out as a separate act from registration of the enterprise sale agreement.

The institution of enterprise sale is not properly regulated in Russia, so practical difficulties inevitably arise in connection with its complexity, meaning that sale of an enterprise is used in practice very rarely.

6. REAL ESTATE BASICS
6.1 Legal regulation of real estate relations
Relations involving real estate are complicated, being regulated by a variety of legal acts.

The basic act determining the grounds and procedure for emergence of title and other rights to real estate and regulating contractual and other obligations in relation to real estate, as well as the procedure for exercising proprietary and other rights, is the Civil Code of the Russian Federation. Relations involved in protection and use of land are regulated by the Land Code of the Russian Federation. Relations in the sphere of territorial planning and urban zoning with respect to location and use of real estate are determined by the Town-planning Code of the Russian Federation, and the state fees for performance of real estate transactions are set by the Tax Code of the Russian Federation.

The main rules on state registration are set out in the Federal Law 'on state registration of real estate rights and transactions'. The fundamentals of maintenance of the state real estate cadastre are regulated by the Federal Law 'on the state real estate cadastre'. The mortgage rules are contained in the Federal Law 'on mortgage (pledge of real estate)'. The fire safety requirements during construction and operation of buildings are envisaged by the Federal Law 'technical regulation of fire safety requirements'. Real estate relations are also regulated by other federal laws and subordinate legislation (resolutions of the Government of the Russian Federation, Decrees of the President of the Russian Federation, acts of federal executive authorities).

With respect to real estate relations, the legislation on which, in accordance with the Russian Constitution, lies outside the jurisdiction of the Russian Federation or under joint jurisdiction, the relevant relations may also be regulated by the legislation of the constituent entities of the Russian Federation and regulatory acts of a local government body (for instance, the procedure for setting the sales price of land plots by state or local government authorities).

In Russia, judicial acts are not a source of law. At the same time, some acts (interpretations, clarifications) issued by higher courts are binding (such as interpretations by the Constitutional Court of the Russian Federation, which are binding on all state and local government authorities, organisations and individuals; resolutions of the Plenum of the Supreme Arbitration Court, which are binding on state arbitration courts, etc).

Moreover, there has been a recent tendency towards an increase in the role of court practice within the legal system in Russia and the possibility of introducing precedent into the relevant legislation is under discussion.

6.2 Types of property rights
Most often, in the Russian Federation, real estate is held by title or on lease.

At the same time, the legislation envisages a broad range of real estate rights, such as the right of economic jurisdiction, the right of operational management, easement, the right of permanent (termless) use of a land plot, the right of lifetime inheritable possession of a land plot, the right of fixed-term, gratuitous use of a land plot, etc.

6.3 State Cadastre and State Register
Russian legislation envisages creation of a Unified State Real Estate Cadastre (the Cadastre), into which information about all real estate should be entered, together with the technical characteristics and location. The Cadastre is currently maintained only in relation to land plots but it is planned that, by 2013, the Cadastre will also contain information about other real estate: buildings, structures and premises.

In addition, a Unified State Register of Real Estate Rights and Transactions (the Realty Register) is also maintained in Russia. In contrast to the Cadastre, which includes mainly technical details, the Realty Register contains information on rights to real estate and their transactions.

By law, state registration of rights and transactions in the Realty Register constitutes a legal act of recognition and confirmation by the state of the emergence of, restriction (encumbrance) on, transfer or termination of rights to real estate. Under the law, the relevant state registration authorities are responsible for timely, full and accurate performance of their obligations, as well as the completeness and veracity of the information submitted regarding the registered real estate rights and transactions, though this legal provision is mostly declarative in nature.

A title registered in the Realty Register is certified by a Certificate of State Registration of Title and when a transaction undergoes state registration, a relevant mark is made on the agreement to this effect.

The information in the Realty Register and the Cadastre is public and may be provided to anyone. The payment for an excerpt from the Realty Register is 300 roubles (about €7.5) for organisations. No charge has yet been established for obtaining information from the Cadastre and such information is provided free of charge, but it is planned to set a relevant fee in the near future.

Scotland

Brodies LLP Dale Strachan & Alistair Campbell

1. INVESTMENT PURCHASE OVERVIEW

The Scottish legal system differs from that of England and Wales, however, the commercial and practical considerations for a buyer contemplating an investment purchase are virtually the same as those applicable to England and Wales as illustrated on the diagram (see next page).

Essentially, broken down into four stages, structuring, due diligence, contract/finance negotiation, and completion, Scotland offers the investor a mature, established market in all sectors.

Deals are usually brokered through commercial surveyors, who will generally assist in the sourcing of suitable property for investment, working closely with the client's other professional advisers to negotiate heads of terms.

Early advice on structuring is key to successful investment, invariably tax-driven, and/or to take into account investor-specific requirements such as equity participation, debt structuring and exit strategy.

Synchronisation and co-ordination of the activities of all members of the client's professional advisers, including, suitably experienced commercial property solicitors, valuation surveyors, building surveyors and, where appropriate, specialists in tax, are also critical to a successful investment purchase. The commercial property solicitor will usually lead the team for buyer, or seller, as appropriate.

In Scotland the system of conveyancing differs from that in England/Wales, as does the law of landlord and tenant. The main features of interest to an investor are outlined on the diagram on next page.

A typical investment purchase in Scotland may take from six to 10 weeks, but may be much shorter depending upon circumstances.

Typical investment purchase in Scotland

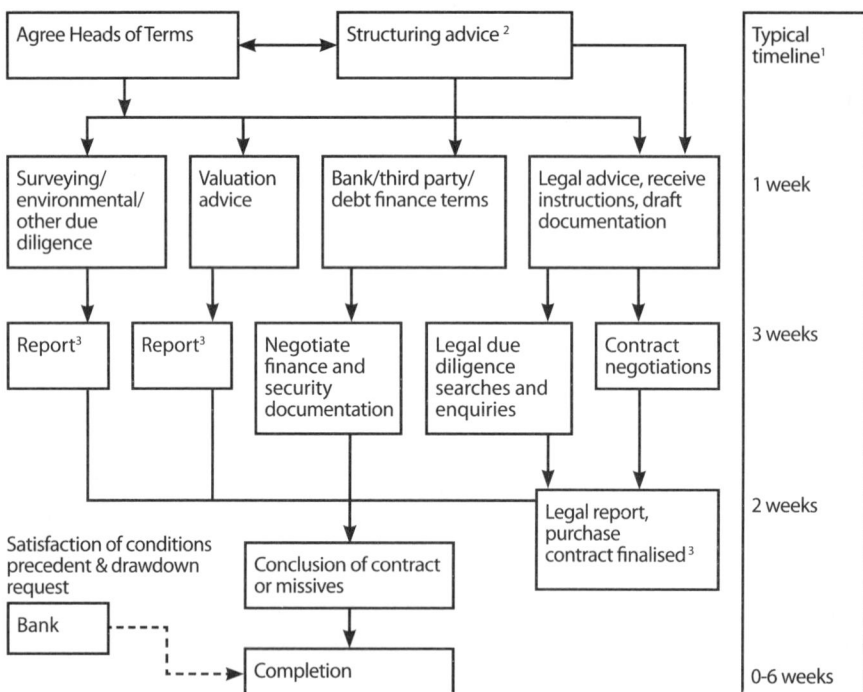

1 Often subject to compression, timescales may differ considerably, conclusion of contract and completion may be simultaneous.
2 Establishing an acquisition structure for tax and financial planning is an important early stage which may significantly influence other stages such as the banking arrangements and the purchase contract.
3 Each report will also be addressed to the bank (if any), a valuation report will be necessary if there is a third party debt provided and otherwise is optional.
4 Before concluding a contract it is advisable to ensure that all conditions precedent are capable of satisfaction.

2. TAX CONSIDERATIONS
2.1 Value added tax (VAT)
VAT will usually be chargeable on the acquisition of commercial real estate. The rate is 17.5 per cent and the VAT is payable by the buyer to the seller. If the property is let, then a sale may be treated as a transfer of a going concern, provided certain conditions are met. In that situation no VAT will be payable, reducing funding costs and stamp duty land tax (SDLT) payable.

Owners of UK commercial real estate are not automatically required to charge VAT on the rents or sale price. It depends upon whether they have opted to charge VAT. However, if a landlord does not 'opt to tax' in this way, they will not generally be able to recover any of the VAT payable when acquiring the property, maintaining or refurbishing it etc and the VAT will become an absolute cost. It is generally only worth a landlord not 'opting to tax' if it can charge more rent as a result and the extra rent makes up for the lost VAT.

Scotland

Different VAT rules apply to property for residential or charitable use. Specific advice should be obtained on the facts where appropriate.

2.2 Stamp duty/transfer tax
SDLT is tax payable on the purchase of land in Scotland. SDLT is payable whether or not the transaction has been committed to writing and whether or not the buyer is resident or non-resident in the UK. Every land transaction is subject to SDLT unless is it exempted in terms of the legislation or benefits from reliefs which include transfers between related companies (subject to clawback conditions). The buyer or tenant is liable to pay SDLT.

SDLT is charged as a percentage of the total chargeable consideration (including any VAT). The rates are as follows:

Purchase price/lease premium or transfer value (non-residential or mixed use)	SDLT rate
Up to £150,000 - annual rent is under £1,000	Zero
Up to £150,000 - annual rent is £1,000 or more	1 per cent
Over £150,000 to £250,000	1 per cent
Over £250,000 to £500,000	3 per cent
Over £500,000	4 per cent

For leasehold properties, SDLT is payable on the net present value (NPV) of the lease which is a factored calculation based on the rental value of the property. The rate chargeable on the NPV is one per cent of the value that exceeds £150,000. SDLT is also payable at the fixed rates above on any premium paid for the grant of the lease or assignation of a lease.

Currently the tax rules in relation to property are the same in Scotland as in the rest of the UK except for some minor differences caused by the different property law and conveyancing practice in Scotland. The Scottish parliament only has power to raise local taxes (eg business rates).

2.3 Tax issues for overseas investors investing in real estate
See section 2 in UK chapter.

3. INVESTMENT VEHICLE CHOICE
3.1 Most commonly used structures to purchase property
It is more common to invest in property in Scotland or elsewhere in the UK indirectly. This section considers some of the most popular vehicles that can be used. This is not an exhaustive list and any potential investor should seek legal and tax advice in the light of its particular circumstances.

3.1.1 Issues affecting the type of vehicle/structuring when making an indirect investment

- Control and decision making – certain vehicles prohibit investors from managing or controlling the assets held by the vehicle. Others are more flexible.
- Cost – investing indirectly is generally more expensive at the point of set up than acquiring an asset directly. There will be ongoing running costs and potential regulatory costs.
- Size and number of assets – where an investor is proposing to hold only one or two assets it can be more efficient to hold them directly. Where there are multiple assets, it is common to hold these through a single vehicle.
- Location of the management team – an asset manager may be required if the management team is not based in Scotland or elsewhere in the UK. Indeed, sometimes this is necessary to ensure that the investors retain offshore tax status.
- Liability of investors – some vehicles afford limited liability to investors; others do not.
- Objectives – whether the assets are to be held for investment purposes or for trading will affect the choice of investment vehicle.
- Regulatory compliance – some structures are more heavily regulated than others; some have more onerous publicity and filing requirements. The UK's Financial Services Authority (FSA) regulates 'collective investment schemes' and requires an FSA authorised person to operate and manage them. This may require the investors to appoint a third party to provide this service to the vehicle. The degree of regulation may impact on the type of investors that can invest and the activities of the vehicle.
- Multiple vehicles – a combination of vehicles may be required for a particular funds structure eg to maximise the tax efficiency of the structure as well as the investors' exit options. Funds structures may involve a 'feeder' vehicle through which the investor invests into the main 'holding' vehicle.
- Taxation of the vehicle – the summary below considers some of the tax issues affecting different structures. In particular, the SDLT position will need to be considered, as this could be the main set-up or transactional cost. On-going tax will also be relevant and may depend on the likely level of the investor's involvement.
- Liquidity – some types of vehicles have established markets for the trading of interests (eg, REITs). Some funds will attempt to create an informal market where potential sellers and buyers are matched.
- Investor-specific requirements – does each investor's constitution permit investment in the vehicle? How does its jurisdiction treat the vehicle? Do the various aspects of the vehicle meet its objectives (whether long term or short term where liquidity may be a particular issue)?

3.1.2 Types of vehicle
The most common vehicles used for indirect investment in property in Scotland are:
- Scottish limited partnerships;
- limited liability partnerships; and
- companies.

Less common are 'general' partnerships and real estate investment trusts (REITs) which will be touched on only briefly.

Scottish limited partnerships (SLPs)
An SLP must have at least one general partner and at least one limited partner. The general partner has control over the management of the partnership and unlimited liability for the debts and obligations of the partnership. The limited partners are the passive investors and their liability is limited to their capital contribution as long as they are not involved in management of the limited partnership.

In a simple funds structure, the fund manager will be the general partner and receive directly the management and incentive fees. To mitigate the risks associated with his having unlimited liability: (i) it is common to set up a separate legal entity specifically to be the general partner – this protects other assets of the funds manager; and (ii) the legal entity is often a limited liability vehicle (such as a company limited by shares).

The relationship between the general partner and the limited partners, and between the limited partners themselves, is set out in a partnership agreement. Limited partnership agreements can vary widely in their scope and level of detail. It will depend on the number of investors, their requirements, and the complexity of the commercial arrangements.

Key features
- Separate legal personality – this is a unique trait of an SLP which is not enjoyed by limited partnerships registered elsewhere in the UK. The SLP itself can own assets, enter into contracts, sue or be sued, own property, borrow money and grant certain types of security.
- Tax transparency – SLPs are tax transparent for direct tax purposes, enabling different types of investor to invest together, but to be taxed according to their individual status.

Typical uses
The hybrid status of separate legal personality coupled with tax transparency and the fact that it is not a body corporate makes the SLP one of the most popular vehicles for indirect real estate investment in the UK. SLPs enable different types of investor to invest together but to be taxed according to their individual status. They offer flexibility for a variety of investment structures because they have separate legal personality.

An SLP can either be a main funds vehicle or – because it has separate legal personality – it can be a participant within a funds structure where 'persons' are required to be members eg, the use of an SLP as a carried interest partner.

SLPs are sometimes used in conjunction with offshore vehicles to enable day to day management of the property assets to take place onshore without prejudicing the general tax status.

Tax
SLPs are tax transparent, and no tax is chargeable at the partnership level. Instead partners pay tax on their share of the partnership profits.

SDLT is chargeable on transactions involving partnerships. Contribution of property to a partnership and a transfer of a partnership interest may trigger a four per cent charge on the gross underlying asset value of the interest acquired or transferred. The SDLT rules relating to partnerships are complex, and expert advice must be taken on SDLT, VAT and other tax issues.

Marketability of interests
Interests in an SLP would be classified as units in an unregulated collective investment scheme and could not generally be marketed to private individuals.

Regulatory
SLPs must be registered at Companies House. There are minimal formalities and ongoing filing requirements. Generally, an SLP set up as an investment vehicle requires an FSA authorised operator.

Limited liability partnership (LLP)
Investors in an LLP are known as members. An LLP must have at least two members. There is no distinction between types of members. Unlike SLPs, the member can be involved in the day-to-day management without jeopardising its limited liability status.

Each investor has an undivided share in the assets of the LLP and will be taxed on their share of the LLP's profits.

An LLP offers great flexibility with regard to its organisation and management. The LLP agreement regulates the relationship between the members, their contributions and profit-sharing arrangements, and the day-to-day management of the LLP's affairs.

Key features
An LLP is a body corporate with separate legal personality. All investors in an LLP have limited liability ie, they are protected from personal liability for the LLP's debts and liabilities. LLPs are tax transparent provided they are carrying on a business (which can include an investment business).

Typical uses
An LLP is popular where some or all of the investors wish to be involved in the management of the vehicle. It is therefore more suitable for a relatively small number of investors (say, fewer than 10).

Tax
Where an LLP is a property investment partnership, tax exemption on income and gains is denied to exempt funds, life funds and certain other bodies (but not charities). Accordingly, this is not likely to be a suitable investment vehicle where entities of this type may become investors or otherwise acquire an interest.

Contribution of the property to and transfer of an interest in an LLP would carry the same SDLT liabilities as outlined above for an ELP.

Marketability of interests
Provided it is structured so that it is not a collective investment scheme, a member's interest in the LLP could be freely marketed. The LLP agreement may contain restrictions on transfer and the market may not be particularly liquid.

Regulatory
LLPs are incorporated easily by the filing of certain forms at Companies House. They are subject to many of the requirements of UK company law such as the filing of accounts and annual returns.

Subject to investors' requirements, it is possible to structure an LLP so that it is not a collective investment scheme and therefore would not require an FSA authorised operator.

General partnerships
A general partnership requires at least two people to carry on business in common with a view of profit. Relations between partners can be set out in a partnership agreement.

Key features
A general partnership is an unincorporated entity. Nevertheless, a general partnership formed in Scotland – unlike its English equivalent – has separate legal personality. A general partnership is generally tax transparent but this status may be lost if the structure amounts to a collective investment scheme.

Partners in a general partnership are jointly and severally liable, without limit, for the debts and obligations of the partnership. Each partner can bind the partnership.

Typical uses
Because of the unlimited liability of partners, this vehicle is not often chosen for indirect investment purposes. It is generally only useful for risk-free investments with no gearing where the number of investors is very small (eg some family investments).

Tax
Again, the SDLT charges outlined above for SLPs would apply, and may render this vehicle unsuitable if a liquid investment is sought.

Marketability of interests
An interest in a general partnership fund is not particularly marketable.

Regulatory
General partnerships do not have to be registered. There are few statutory or filing requirements. An FSA authorised operator would not be required if all the investors were involved in the day-to-day control and management of the property assets.

3.1.3 Partnership agreements
Whatever the type of partnership, the affairs of the partners can be governed by a partnership agreement. All forms of partnership have great flexibility in the way in which they can be set up. This can be contrasted with the structure and procedures associated with companies. Also, unlike the constitutional documents of companies, partnership agreements are private documents which do not have to be filed at Companies House.

Company
A company structure is very flexible. One or more persons can incorporate a company. Shares can be issued to investors in return for their investment, and can be issued with different rights attaching to them eg, rights to share in profits, rights to participate in management, etc. Those who manage the company are called directors. The directors can be – but need not necessarily be – the same people as the shareholders.

The company must file its constitutional documents with Companies House. These set out how the company will be managed and the respective powers and responsibilities of the shareholders and the directors. Shareholders can, if they wish, enter into a separate private shareholders' agreement detailing how their relationship is to be managed.

Key features
A company is a body corporate with separate legal personality. The investors in a company are known as shareholders. They have limited liability ie, they are protected from personal liability for the company's debts and liabilities. Companies are not, however, tax transparent.

Typical uses
Use of a company as the principal investment vehicle is less common because of the tax position (see below). Companies are, however, often used in funds structures to be the holders of individual assets. This can assist with alternative exit strategies.

The asset to be acquired is often already held by a UK-incorporated company. This enables investors to acquire the asset either directly from the company (using one of the vehicles mentioned in this chapter) or indirectly by acquiring the shares in the company. Which method is chosen will depend largely on the tax position. Acquisition of a company holding real estate is more common where the asset is held in a 'single purpose vehicle' which has

Scotland

been established solely to hold the relevant asset. If this is not the case then extensive due diligence should be undertaken before acquiring the company.

Tax
Companies are not tax transparent. There can be an element of double taxation as the company is taxed on its profits at rates of up to 28 per cent, and any distribution to its shareholders will also be taxable in the hands of the shareholders.

Further, companies do not provide exempt investment returns for charities, exempt funds, UK individuals and offshore investors. The transfer of properties to a company can also trigger a four per cent SDLT charge.

Marketability
Shares are transferable instruments but there may be restrictions on transfer in the company's articles of association (eg, rights of pre-emption for other shareholders) and there may not be a market for the shares – particularly where a private company is concerned. Shares in a private company cannot be offered to the public.

Shares in a public company can be offered to the public. A prospectus may be required which can be costly. Public companies can apply for a listing on the London Stock Exchange if they can meet the trading history requirements. Listing widens the potential investor base. Listed companies are suitable for investors who are ISAs, self invested personal pensions and small self-administered schemes which may make them more attractive to retail investors.

Regulatory
Companies are subject to UK company law which includes certain publicity and filing requirements. Directors are subject to statutory and common law duties. Listed companies are subject to additional regulatory and corporate governance requirements.

A company would not usually qualify as a 'collective investment scheme' and so an FSA authorised operator would not be required.

3.2 Restrictions on foreign ownership or occupation of property
There are no such restrictions.

3.3 Real estate investment trusts (REITs)
The UK REIT regime enables qualifying quoted companies and groups to elect to be treated as a REIT for accounting periods beginning on or after 1 January 2007. A company or group which becomes a REIT will be exempt from UK corporation tax on the profits and gains of its qualifying property rental business as long as various conditions are met.

Due to large upfront costs (including an entry charge of approximately two per cent of the market value of the relevant properties) and the conditions which have to be met to qualify for REIT status, REITs are only used by the largest quoted real estate investment companies.

4. FINANCING AN ACQUISITION

4.1 Financing corporate real estate transactions and how real estate is commonly used to raise finance

A sophisticated real estate financing market operates throughout the UK, including Scotland. Real estate financing traditionally comprises a mix of debt and equity. A lending institution, conventionally a bank, will lend a proportion of the purchase price for real estate by way of debt. In the recent past, loan to value ratios could be as high as 90-95 per cent, but in the current climate closer to 50 per cent where available at all.

4.2 Common forms of security granted over real estate to raise finance

Where the debt is funding an asset purchase the lender will expect to receive security, being all or some of the following:

- fixed security over the property to be purchased. In Scotland this may only take the form of a 'standard security' in prescribed statutory form. A fixed legal charge may not be incorporated within a debenture in Scotland;
- a floating charge (if the buyer is a corporate). The floating charge will be taken over all of the buyer's assets. A 'floating charge' does not, unlike a fixed charge, attach to any one asset in particular; the borrower is accordingly free to deal with any assets subject to a floating charge until the charge freezes ('crystallises'). On crystallisation the borrower will then be unable to dispose of assets subject to that crystallised charge. A floating charge crystallises, usually, on the appointment of an administrator or receiver or on the commencement of the winding up of the borrower;
- an assignation of the right to receive rents from occupational tenants at the property to be mortgaged (in the case of investment property). This assignation is usually documented separately from any floating charge and is critical from the lender's point of view as it will be used to service the debt repayments;
- a charge over shares (if a borrower is an SPV for example); or
- assignation of the benefit of any major contracts (eg, in connection with recent development of the property). Again these assignations will usually be separate from the floating charge itself.

Where the borrower (or a third party, such as a parent company) giving security in connection with the financing is not incorporated in the UK, legal opinions will have to be taken from local counsel as to the good standing of the party concerned and the legal enforceability of any obligations undertaken by it.

The lender will usually expect first ranking security over the property which is to be secured. Fixed charges over land in Scotland must be registered in the Land Register of Scotland or the Register of Sasines (as applicable) in order to be effective.

A security taken by a lender must be presented for registration at Companies House, within 21 days of the date of its creation. A standard security is deemed to have been created upon the date of registration in the

Land Register of Scotland. A floating charge is deemed to have been created on the date of signature by the borrower. Failure to register any charge timeously may cause the security to be void against any liquidator or administrator or other third party creditor.

4.3 Has real estate mortgage securitisation been used in your country?
Scottish residential and commercial mortgage-backed loans (and rental streams) have been securitised with the main activity commencing in the mid-90s. Assets include prime and sub-prime residential mortgages (pre- and post-mortgage regulation), care homes, pubs, shopping centres, petrol stations and telecommunications assets. The Scottish assets have generally formed part of much larger UK-wide portfolios and as such, English equity-based securitisation structures have been adapted for use in respect of such Scottish assets. Established techniques are now used regarding such assets.

5. MANAGING THE ACQUISITION PROCESS
5.1 Minimum formalities for the sale and purchase of property. Formalities for a contract becoming a legally binding obligation and point at which parties become legally bound
In Scotland the process by which a commercial property is bought and sold is relatively standardised, however the contractual terms used may vary from transaction to transaction. This section explains how contracts for the sale and purchase of a commercial property investment are negotiated, concluded and implemented.

If the property is to be acquired by purchase of the corporate vehicle that currently owns the property, different terms would apply. Auction sales also have their own procedural rules.

5.1.1 Agreeing terms and binding contracts
Heads of terms containing principal intended contractual terms are usually adjusted by commercial surveyors. The seller's solicitor will co-ordinate the provision of due diligence information, and the buyer's solicitor will draft the purchase contract although it is increasingly common in larger investment sales for the seller's solicitors to prepare a contract for sale.

Purchase contracts are commonly adjusted in draft and formalised immediately prior to completion (financial close), frequently on the same day. This is generally at the insistence of the buyer, particularly where the purchase is being partly funded by debt and the buyer requires all elements of conditionality of the offer of the loan to be satisfied prior to entering into a binding legal commitment to purchase.

Care must be taken in Scotland to avoid conclusion of a binding contract where not intended – the expression 'subject to contract' having a quite different (opposite!) meaning to that in the rest of the UK. In Scotland a written offer to buy or sell, containing key provisions, will upon written acceptance, form a binding legal contract subject only to its express terms. Any written exchanges not intended to create contractual relationships should clearly so state.

The seller and buyer are not legally bound to sell or buy property until a written contract has been signed and delivered by the parties. Where extensive due diligence is required, or where market conditions are volatile, a buyer may seek an early contractual commitment from a seller in the form of a lock-out or exclusivity agreement.

In Scotland, contracts are commonly signed by solicitors acting as agents for their respective clients, but only where duly authorised to do so.

Scottish solicitors are bound by a code of professional conduct designed to ensure that negotiations can occur with only one party at a time, unless appropriate disclosure is made. Strict rules apply regulating the conduct of solicitors in circumstances giving rise to conflicts of interest, and to protect client confidentiality. These rules are, however, subject to overriding statutory duties to the state where money laundering is suspected, criminal activity is involved or the proceeds of crime are used to fund property acquisition.

5.1.2 Completing the purchase/sale

Conventionally a target completion date (financial close) will be fixed between 10 and 20 working days after conclusion of the contract. Increasingly, however, contracts will be adjusted in draft and formalised simultaneously at completion.

Completion monies are usually under the control of the buyer's solicitors and transferred electronically within banking hours on the day of completion, in sufficient time to allow for same day transfer in cleared funds. Where the seller has secured lending on the property it is quite normal to split the completion monies at source so as to allow for the immediate delivery at completion of any relevant discharge of security.

The amount payable at completion will be the contractually agreed price, adjusted by:
(i) an apportionment of entitlement to rents;
(ii) an accounting for any rental deposits held; and
(iii) possibly VAT, although that is not usually payable on commercial property investments.

Where applicable, service charge reconciliations and accounting will require to be provided for, although this usually forms a post-completion item to allow time for preparation of closing accounts.

Occupational rents are usually apportioned on a daily rate basis, but care must be taken in Scotland to ensure a fair basis of apportionment on an annual basis where the usual quarterly payment intervals may be of unequal duration.

If there are arrears of occupational rents at completion the contract will usually defer apportionment unless and until the arrears are recovered from the tenant. Any VAT paid on the rents are not apportioned, but accounted for by the primary recipient.

5.2 Main legal documents required to transfer a property or grant a lease?

A disposition signed by or on behalf of the seller is granted to transfer a heritable interest, ie, ownership of a property.

A lease of a property is granted by the signing of a lease by or on behalf of the landlord and the tenant. In Scotland, it is common for the lease to be signed after the date of entry in terms of the lease. The parties will conclude a contract to lease the property which will oblige the parties to sign the agreed lease within a specified period after conclusion of the contract and to comply with the terms and conditions of the agreed lease pending and after full signature of the lease.

5.3 Property transaction costs
Each party usually meets their own costs for the transaction. A buyer in Scotland is not usually required to pay a deposit upon conclusion of contracts.

VAT (if applicable) and SDLT are payable by the buyer. The buyer must pay the SDLT to the tax authority within 30 days after completion. Any VAT payable on the price will be paid to the seller who will account for it to the tax authority.

5.4 Does the seller warrant its ownership of the property?
The seller when granting a disposition of property for value will grant warrandice, that is, a guarantee that it owns the property and that the buyer will be entitled to occupy the whole of the property. The buyer will still demand searches from the property registers to confirm that the seller owns the property.

Warrandice will be qualified if there are any tenants in the property or any rights affecting the property which would prevent the buyer from occupying the whole of the property.

5.5 Warranties a seller usually gives to a buyer. Purpose of warranties in the purchase agreement
The principle of 'buyer-beware' (*caveat emptor*) applies throughout the UK. There are no standard contracts in Scotland and so care must be taken to ensure an appropriate allocation of risk as between buyer and seller.

The contract will generally contain all of the commercial terms and any relevant warranties. It is rare for warranties to be given as to the condition of the property by the seller.

The buyer will generally undertake all due diligence prior to concluding a purchase contract at the buyer's risk and cost and without recourse against a seller who withdraws from negotiations before a contract is concluded.

The required due diligence may vary widely depending upon whether the seller's title is a land certificate (which will normally carry a state-backed guarantee of title) or where the land registration process is incomplete or not yet initiated.

The form which due diligence takes may also vary. In certain circumstances, the buyer may be invited to rely upon certificates of title (and relative lease reports) prepared by the solicitors for the seller, but it is more usual for the buyer to instruct its own solicitors to carry out all necessary due diligence. The benefit of the relevant reports is often extended to any secured lenders/debt providers funding the purchase.

Particular attention must be given to environmental warranties and the allocation of responsibilities for environmental liabilities which may arise. The onus is generally upon the investment buyer to satisfy itself by its own enquiries and investigations prior to contract.

5.6 Owners/occupiers' liability for matters relating to the property which occurred before they bought or occupied

They can be liable for such matters so due diligence is essential. At completion the contract will usually provide for delivery of good title to the buyer unburdened of secured debt, and the buyer's solicitor will supervise the registration of appropriate discharges.

5.7 Insurance of the property if there is delay between agreeing terms and actual sale

The seller remains in control of the property and will administer all leases etc, until completion. The contract will usually oblige the seller to conduct all management in the normal course of business and to consult the buyer on discretionary matters such as outstanding rent reviews.

The allocation of risk of destruction or damage passes under common law to the buyer at the contract stage, but this is invariably amended by contract to defer passing of risk to the contractual completion date. Usually the contract will oblige the seller to maintain the insurance in accordance with the lease provisions, and entitle the buyer to have the benefit of any relevant insurance proceeds derived from any claim arising prior to completion.
A materiality test often is provided for entitling a buyer to terminate the purchase contract if the property is destroyed or materially damaged prior to completion, leaving all insurance monies in the hands of the seller.

5.8 Notarisation

Dispositions and leases do not require to be notarised.

5.9 Transfer of title

The title to the property transfers on the date of registration of the title in the Land Register of Scotland. It is in the interests of a buyer to register its title at the earliest opportunity.

There is a delay between delivery of the buyer's title and the date of registration of its title called the 'registration gap'. The seller's solicitor will undertake searches to the last completed date of the relevant registers to ensure that there are no competing interests which might be prejudicial to the registration of the buyer's interest.

By convention the seller's solicitor will also grant a contractual undertaking to clear the registers of any competing title claims which arise within a period (not exceeding 21 days) following the date of the last available search. The solicitor's undertaking is backed by insurance under the Law Society of Scotland Master Policy.

Scotland

6. REAL ESTATE BASICS
6.1 Main sources of laws that govern real estate
The sale and purchase of property is now governed partly by the following statutes:
- Conveyancing and Feudal Reform (Scotland) Act 1970 – introduced the standard security, the only form of fixed charge over real estate.
- Land Registration (Scotland) Act 1979 – introduced the concept of land registration by way of a map based system.
- Abolition of Feudal Tenure etc (Scotland) Act 2000 – abolished the superiority level of ownership of land which entitled superiors to retain control over what could and could not be done on the land by way of title conditions. Some control has been retained by reallocation of the right to enforce title conditions for the benefit of adjoining land.
- Title Conditions (Scotland) Act 2003 – codified the law relating to title conditions including how they may be created, varied, discharged and enforced and stipulated who has the power to do the aforesaid.
- Tenements (Scotland) Act 2004 – provided a default set of rules for the management and maintenance of properties which are part of a tenement, that is, a building divided horizontally in ownership. The rules apply where the title deeds contain no equivalent or similar provision.

The common law plays an important role in expanding on and interpreting the legislation and in establishing the rules for the practice of real estate law.

With regard to leasehold property, there are very few statutory rules which apply and the common law plays an even larger role in defining practice.

6.2 Types of tenure
Heritable title
Under Scottish law there is only one type of property ownership in the true sense which is ownership of the heritable interest in land. A title to the land is unlimited in time and automatically carries with it title to buildings/structures erected on that land. Heritable title is the equivalent of the English 'freehold' title.

The heritable title is not restricted to land alone, but may be specific to parts of that land. For example, it is possible to have a building where particular floors of a building, or parts of such a floor, may be owned by different proprietors. The title deeds will usually provide for a management and maintenance regime in relation to common parts used by two or more owners.

Leasehold title
In Scotland property may also be held on lease however, unlike in England/Wales, this is not strictly regarded as a form of property ownership. A lease in Scotland may only be validly created by the owner of the heritable title, or by the tenant under an existing lease which is itself valid.

Sub-leases are competent, subject to compliance with any restrictions upon sub-letting contained in superior leases. A sub-lease is and remains vulnerable

Scotland

to termination or forfeiture of any lease which is superior to it in the lease chain. A sub-tenant can mitigate such risks by entering into a 'forfeiture protection agreement' by which the parties, including any superior landlords, undertake to enter into new leasehold arrangements in the event of forfeiture (irritancy) of a superior lease.

A lease or sub-lease, once validly constituted and (where applicable) registered, confers upon the tenant or sub-tenant as the case may be the right to possession of the property on payment of a rent to the holder of the immediate landlord's interest.

Land in Scotland, as in the rest of the UK, may be subject to a series of leases where different parties may hold leases of differing durations, and relating to different properties within the same building. See the diagram below by way of illustration.

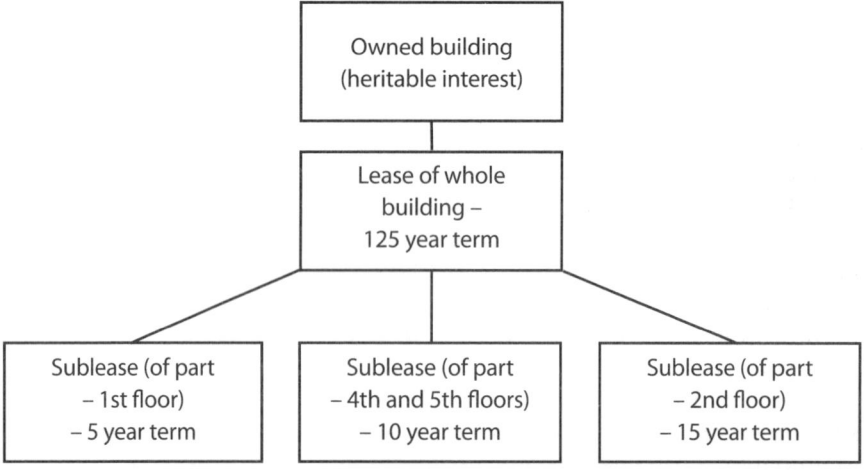

Lease structures are flexible in Scotland. An owner may grant a lease of its entire interest in land to one tenant for a particular duration, and may subsequently grant a further lease of the same property to a different tenant (the latter lease being known as an 'interposed' lease). This can be a useful device when structuring so-called side by side, or rent sharing leases, by which different interests may be created out of the same property.

The investment market in Scotland, is structured to take advantage of the rental income received by landlords (the investors) from their tenants under so-called occupational leases, typically for a term of 25 years (for older leases) but now more commonly 15 or 10 years, often subject to break options in favour of the tenant.

Leases in Scotland for a term exceeding 20 years (known as 'long leases') are registrable and may be the subject of the grant of fixed security. For current leases, registration is mandatory in order to secure a real right to the tenant, ie a right of possession valid against successors in title to the landlord's interest. Where the lease or sub-lease is registered, the tenant's interest under the lease will normally be subject to a state-backed guarantee

Scotland

of title similar to that which applies to outright ownership (as above).

Leases of commercial property may not exceed 175 years duration without specific enabling legislation. Leases of long duration are commonly granted in return for a premium similar to that which would be charged on the sale of the land itself and a nominal rent. A common example of a long lease is a 'geared lease', typically granted for a 99 (or more) year term at a rent which is a proportion of the income which the tenant in the head lease itself receives from its sub-tenants.

The law of landlord and tenant in Scotland is quite different from that applied in the rest of the UK and appropriate legal advice should be taken.

6.3 Must land be registered?
Scotland has been subject to a system of land registration for around 400 years. All land in Scotland is registered either in the Register of Sasines or in the Land Register of Scotland. Both are public registers. Registration in either register creates what is known as a 'real right' in land ie, title good against the world.

6.4 Public land register and land not covered by a public land register. State guarantee of title and what categories of documents and information are registered

6.4.1 Register of Sasines
This is a register of deeds rather than of title interests and is gradually being phased out. Searching facilities are available and copies of all recorded titles may be obtained upon application and payment of a fee. Similar details to those available in the Land Register and noted below may be obtained. However, plans may not be available in relation to older titles.

Titles recorded in the Register of Sasines do not have the benefit of a state-backed guarantee of title. Quality of title may only be established by examination of title by a suitably qualified solicitor. Many defects in title may be cured by appropriate possession over time, usually 10 years (20 for servitudes, wayleaves or leases) following the recording of a suitable deed. There is no equivalent in Scotland to possessory title.

6.4.2 Land registration
Title to all land bought for valuable consideration is now subject to compulsory registration in the Land Register of Scotland. This map-based register of interests has a computerised searching facility and is open to public scrutiny. Following completion of the registration of the interest, details may be obtained of the following:
- a description of the property including plans;
- identity of the owner;
- certain rights affecting the property and other matters benefiting the property;
- any burdens affecting the title;
- any financial charges affecting the property;
- copies of any registered leases (noting that not all leases need be so registered); and

- the price paid by the current owner.

Even if there is no trigger for compulsory registration it is still possible for the owner of land not yet registered in the Land Register of Scotland to apply voluntarily for its registration. Registration does afford some additional protections for a landowner, and may be particularly useful where development of that land is contemplated.

The proprietor of land interests which have been registered in the Land Register of Scotland will, in most cases, have a title fortified by a state-backed title guarantee evidenced by the issuing of a Land Certificate. This guarantee is subject to certain inherent limitations, for example it does not guarantee title to underlying minerals or the enforceability of servitude rights (easements) disclosed in the title. In some cases the guarantee may be subject to express exclusions, for example where there is known to be a competing title to a particular area of land.

Slovak Republic

Havel & Holásek Jan Holásek & Pavol Polácek

1. INVESTMENT PURCHASE OVERVIEW
The acquisition of commercial property in the Slovak Republic typically includes the following recommended legal steps:
- execution of a letter of intent;
- execution of a future purchase agreement (may be agreed prior to the commencement of due diligence, instead of a letter of intent, or after the due diligence process is completed);
- review of the site (land plots to be purchased) as to future use and taking into consideration the current valid municipal zoning plan;
- ownership title due diligence investigation;
- due diligence investigation of encumbrances over the property as registered in the Cadastral Register;
- due diligence investigation of other agreements and contracts and possible encumbrances (rights and obligations) relating to the property that are not registered in the Cadastral Register;
- legal review of the statutory provisions that govern the purchase and development of the property binding on the seller, the purchaser and attached to the property;
- tax and legal structuring of the acquisition respecting the purchaser's and seller's specifications, character of the property and legal and other defects detected during the due diligence process;
- property (or special purpose vehicle (SPV)'s shareholding) purchase agreement which includes: (i) the purchase price; (ii) warranties to be provided by the seller to the purchaser and vice versa; (iii) termination of the currently valid and effective contracts concluded with suppliers or tenants; (iv) payment of the fee to be paid for registration in the Cadastral Register;
- executing an application for registration of the new owner in the Cadastral Register (if an asset deal) and filing the application and purchase agreements (with attachments required by Slovak laws) with the relevant Slovak Cadastral Register;
- payment of the purchase price only after the purchaser receives approval from the Cadastral Register that the purchaser has become the legal and beneficial owner of the property – the reason for delaying the payment of the purchase price is that title is formally transferred after registration which typically takes between two and four weeks.

2. TAX CONSIDERATIONS

2.1 Acquisition of a Slovak company
There are no connected taxes with respect to the acquisition of a Slovak company. The acquisition of a share in the company is VAT exempt.

2.2 Acquisition of real estate
2.2.1 General
A building is not part of a land plot and *vice versa*. Land and buildings have separate legal statuses and consequently their own tax regimes.

This, *inter alia*, suggests that if a total price is agreed for land and a building, the price should be split.

2.2.2 Real estate transfer tax
No transfer tax duty will be payable on the transfer of real estate. However, administrative or notary fees may be payable, for example, in relation to perfecting the transfer contract and registering it in the real estate register. However, such fees are negligible.

2.3 Value added tax (VAT)
2.3.1 VAT – acquisition of land
The acquisition of land from a person registered for VAT may be subject to VAT. In general the transfer of land is VAT exempt. However, the transfer of building land is subject to 19 per cent VAT.

2.3.2 VAT – acquisition of a building
The transfer of a building is exempt from VAT if the building is transferred five years after the first approval of the building or a part thereof based on which the building or a part thereof was approved for use, or five years from the day when the building or a part thereof was put in use for the first time.

2.4 Construction of a building
2.4.1 VAT deduction from construction costs
A VAT payer who receives goods and services may deduct the input VAT, provided that it uses them for business purposes. The full input VAT deduction is allowed when the received supplies are used for taxable or other specified supplies. Otherwise, the tax payer cannot deduct the whole input VAT or may only deduct it partially.

If a building is sold within five years after the first approval of the building or a part of it based on which the building or a part of it was approved for use, or five years from the day when the building or a part of it was put in use for the first time, the sale is a taxable supply and VAT should be applied. In other cases the sale of a building is VAT exempt.

Full VAT deduction is also possible if the building is leased and VAT is applied to the rent. If the building or its part is leased without VAT for 10 years following completion of the building, it would be necessary to return the VAT deduction (fully or partially). If the building is sold within 10 years following the completion of the building and the sale is VAT exempt, it would be necessary to return the VAT deduction (fully or partially).

2.4.2 VAT rates at construction
The standard VAT rate amounts to 19 per cent.

2.4.3 Corporate income tax – tax loss
A tax loss incurred during construction can be utilised in seven consecutive tax periods if the general conditions of the Income Taxes Act are met. This is a general loss carry-forward period; no loss carry-back is possible in the Slovak Republic.

2.5 Holding real estate
2.5.1 Corporate income tax
Depreciation
Buildings (administrative) and engineering buildings are depreciated for tax purposes over 20 years. Movable assets are depreciated over four, six, or 12 years. One can opt for an accelerated or straight-line method.

Fit-outs and other improvements
Fit-outs and other improvements not having the character of repairs and maintenance (fit-outs) increase the acquisition price of the building and also the base for tax depreciation.

Dividends
According to the Slovak Commercial Code, a company can pay dividends if the retained profit exceeds the retained losses and if a statutory reserve fund was created.

According to the Slovak Income Taxes Act, the dividends are outside the scope of corporate income tax.

2.5.2 VAT
VAT on rent
Rent (leasing or subleasing all or part of immovable property) is generally VAT exempt, except for:
- letting or subletting accommodation facilities (for example, a hotel, motel, guesthouse, or hostel);
- letting or subletting premises and sites for parking vehicles;
- letting or subletting permanently installed equipment and machinery; and
- hiring safes.

The VAT payer who lets immovable property or a part of it to a taxable person can decide not to apply the VAT exemption to the lease or sublease of such immovable property. In such a case, the standard rate of 19 per cent is applicable.

Condition for VAT deduction
Generally, a person registered for VAT in the Slovak Republic (VAT payer)

is allowed to deduct an input VAT if it uses the supply of goods or services for taxable output or a supply that is exempt from VAT with the right of deduction.

If a VAT payer uses the supplies of goods and services only for an output that is VAT exempt without the right of deduction (for example the lease of premises to non-VAT payers or to VAT payers when VAT is not applied to the lease), it has no right to deduct the VAT related to the inputs.

If the inputs are used for both taxable and exempt outputs, a partial deduction can be claimed.

2.5.3 Real estate tax
The rate of real estate tax depends of the type and use of the land/building, location, number of stories and the local coefficent. Real estate tax is not significant.

2.6 Limitations on acquisitions
2.6.1 Acquisition of real estate by EU citizens and citizens of other countries
Since 1 May 2004, citizens from EU and other countries have not been limited in the nature and scope of acquiring real estate in the Slovak Republic (except for land which forms part of the agricultural land fund located outside the border of the built-up area of a municipality, land which forms part of the forest land fund located outside the border of a built-up area of a municipality, and certain plots of land whose acquisition is restricted by separate regulations). The abovementioned restriction regarding the acquisition of land which forms part of the agricultural land fund or part of the forest land fund shall not apply to a non-resident who inherits the property or to a non-resident who is: (i) a citizen of the Slovak Republic or (ii) a citizen of a member state of the European Union who has the right to temporary residence on the basis of registration, in the case of the acquisition of ownership rights to land which forms part of the agricultural land fund and which it has been managing for at least three years following the date of the validity of the treaty on the accession of the Slovak Republic to the European Union. The same process of real estate acquisition by Slovak citizens applies to foreigners, and is, in principle, based on two fundamental steps: firstly, a contract such as a purchase, donation or barter contract must be entered into between contracting parties; secondly, the acquisition process must be completed by registration of the ownership in the Cadastral Register.

2.6.2 Acquisition of public land: tendering requirements
Acquisition from the Slovak Republic
The Slovak Republic may transfer its real estate only if the country does not need it for performance of its functions anymore and it must, as a rule, be approved by the Ministry of Finance of Slovak Republic.

Acquisition from municipalities or regions
Municipal or regional authorities may transfer their real estate in public

commercial tender, in public auction, or in direct sale at least for a price in the amount of general assets' value stipulated by special regulation. The intent of a municipality or region to transfer its real estate shall be published on the website of the municipality or region, on the official board of the municipality or region, and in the regional press. The transfer shall be approved by the Assembly of the Municipality or by the Regional Council.

Acquisition from the Slovak Land Fund
The sale of real estate by the state or other public authorities (such as municipalities and regions) does not fall within the scope of public procurement in accordance with the EC directives or other specific tender procedures, with the exception of the sale of state real estate administered by the Slovak Land Fund.

The state real estate administered by the Slovak Land Fund, with regard to which the entitled persons (eg entitled persons under restitution laws, municipalities, etc) have not shown interest, is sold in public commercial auctions with the prior written consent of the Ministry of Agriculture, Environment and Regional Development of the Slovak Republic, which shall stipulate the conditions of such public commercial auction.

3. INVESTMENT VEHICLE CHOICE
3.1 Most commonly used structures to purchase property
The two most common methods for conducting real estate acquisition transactions are asset deals and share deals. However, there are several modifications to these schemes, for example, a merger; a second SPV; or the sale of the business or its part. Therefore, the structure of the transaction should always be set out with respect to the particular project and the investor's needs and should also reflect the results of due diligence investigations.

3.1.1 Asset deal
If the real property is transferred by an asset deal, the agreement on purchase of the real estate is concluded. However, the applicable tax consequences arising from such purchase must always be considered. (For example, the position of the seller with respect to the sale of an asset may not be advantageous because: (i) corporate/personal income tax shall be paid with respect to the sale of the asset; and (ii) 19 per cent per cent value added tax (VAT) might be applicable. For more details please refer to section 2 of this chapter.

3.1.2 Share deal
In general practice, SPVs are established for the development of projects in the form of either a limited liability company or a joint stock company. Since the majority of SPVs are established in the form of a limited liability company, we will summarise briefly below the way of transferring the ownership interest in such a company through a share deal.

The shares in a Slovak limited liability company (ie, ownership interests, *obchodné podiely*) can be acquired on the basis of an ownership interest transfer agreement. Such agreement must be in writing and signed by all participants and a notary must verify the signatures. As a rule, the general meeting of the company (provided that the company has more than one shareholder) shall approve the transfer prior to concluding the agreement on transfer of the entire ownership interest.

The change of the shareholders must be registered in the Commercial Register of the company in question. However, the registration does not affect the effectiveness of the ownership interest transfer, which becomes effective upon signing of the ownership interest transfer agreement and delivery of this agreement to the company, or later upon the fulfilment of the conditions precedent, if applicable.

3.2 Other possibilities after acquisition
3.2.1 Financial leasing

Financial leasing is a *sui generis* contract, not regulated in the Civil Code or Commercial Code. The applicable rules are based on civil law, commercial law, banking law, and tax law. Financial leasing is a lease under the terms of which a leasing company acquires, pursuant to an investor's request, real property in order to lease the real property to an investor for a certain term. The investor pays for all the expenses incurred in the acquisition and lease transaction in exchange for the use and undisturbed enjoyment of the real property. Upon expiry of the lease, the investor has the option to acquire the real property.

3.2.2 Operating a lease without the option to purchase

Operating leases are also *sui generis* contracts, similar to financial leasing. The main difference is that a tenant of an operating lease agreement will not purchase the real property at the end of the lease period. The real property needs to be physically returned to the landlord who owns the real property during the entire lease period.

3.3 Sale
3.3.1 Sale of an SPV

In general, the sale of an SPV does not have any VAT consequences.

Gains from the sale of shares are taxed within the general corporate income tax base at the rate of 19 per cent. However, this provision may be overruled by an applicable tax treaty.

3.3.2 Sale of a real estate
Corporate income tax

Gains from the sale of assets including real estate are taxed within the general corporate income tax base, ie, there is no separate tax basket for capital gains. For more details please see section 2. As a rule, a general corporate income tax base is calculated from the accounting profit based on Slovak accounting standards.

At sale the acquisition value of the land or tax residual value (for real

estate disclosed as a fixed asset) can be applied as a cost.
The current corporate income tax rate is 19 per cent.

VAT
The sale of a building or its part, including sale of land on which a building is built is subject to VAT if the sale is realised within five years after the first approval of the building or a part of it based on which the building or a part of it was approved for use, or five years from the day when the building or a part of it was put in use for the first time; otherwise it is exempt from VAT.

The sale of land, except for building land, is exempt from VAT. The sale of building land is subject to VAT. As long as the land is supplied along with the building, the sale of the land shall abide by the regime mentioned above for a building.

The standard rate of 19 per cent is applicable.

The taxpayer can decide not to apply the VAT exemption to the sale of the abovementioned immovable property.

Real estate transfer tax
No transfer tax will be payable on the transfer of real estate. However, administrative or notary fees may be payable, for example, in relation to perfecting the transfer contract and registering it in the real estate register. However, such fees are negligible.

3.4 Obligation to report to the Slovak National Bank
Please note that a Slovak company has to report certain transactions (eg, a loan granted from foreign entities) to the Slovak National Bank for statistical purposes.

4. FINANCING AN ACQUISITION
4.1 Common forms of security
Since an investor often requires a credit facility from the bank to finance the purchase of land for the project or the completed projects, summarised below are the most common forms of security provided to ensure repayment of the provided credit.

The Credit Facility Agreement must be carefully drafted and must contain:
(i) the amount of the loan and its currency;
(ii) the terms of drawing the credit;
(iii) terms of repayment of the credit;
(iv) the interest and fees to be paid to the bank;
(v) the security provided; and
(vi) the terms and conditions of termination of the agreement.

The practice of banks usually does not differ very much, and apart from the abovementioned elementary terms of the bank loan, the established practice for providing bank loans includes:
(i) the bank's rights and the lender's obligations;
(ii) specification of the event of default;
(iii) the obligation of the lender to replenish the security if the provided

security loses its value;
(iv) change of control clause; or
(v) contractual penalties.

Therefore, the Credit Facility Agreement should be carefully negotiated with the bank if possible.

4.2 Pledge
Under Slovak law, *záložné právo* is used as a term to describe security rights referring to a 'mortgage' as an encumbrance over real estate and a 'pledge' as an encumbrance over any other type of asset. All mortgages and pledges are governed by general rules contained in the Civil Code, as well as by specific laws.

Both mortgages and pledges are used to secure monetary or non-monetary receivables. Slovak law allows one receivable to be secured by several mortgages or pledges and a secured receivable to be used for securing another receivable.

4.2.1 Mortgage
In general, a mortgage right is a real right that encumbers the mortgaged real estate property and applies to any subsequent owner of the real property that is encumbered by the mortgage. A mortgage has two important functions: (i) as a security of the receivable; and (ii) in case the receivable is not duly fulfilled, the creditor is entitled to satisfaction from the receivable by means of encashment of yield of the mortgaged real property.

Under Slovak law the mortgage applies not only to the relevant real property but also to its parts, accessories, accruements, and proceeds (provided that they have not yet been separated from the real property) unless the Mortgage Agreement stipulates otherwise. Slovak law also enables securing of the credit by mortgage over several individual real properties (ie, a collective mortgage). The law allows more than one mortgage to be established on the same real property. For satisfaction, the rank of such mortgage rights is crucial. The secured receivables shall be satisfied in sequence according to the time when the mortgage was established.

The mortgage may be established upon:
(i) a written agreement (the Mortgage Agreement);
(ii) an inheritance settlement agreement approved by a decision of a court;
(iii) a decision of the court or an administrative authority; or
(iv) by law.

A mortgage over real property established under the Mortgage Agreement that is subject to registration in the Cadastral Register and over apartments and non-residential premises is established by the registration of a mortgage right in the Cadastral Register.

A mortgage over real property established under the Mortgage Agreement that is not subject to registration in the Cadastral Register is established as of the date of its registration in the Central Notary Register of Pledges maintained by the Notary Chamber of the Slovak Republic (the Register of Pledges).

4.2.2 Pledges
A pledge is an encumbrance over any type of asset other than real estate. A pledge over a movable asset (eg, a production unit) is effective either: (i) upon delivery of the asset to the pledgee or to a third party on its behalf; or (ii) upon registration of the pledge in the Register of Pledges, which is a public register.

If the pledge is established by registration in the Register of Pledges, the pledge agreement must be executed in writing. Slovak law distinguishes different pledges as such:
- Pledge over receivables – under Slovak law, current and future receivables may also be subject to a pledge, provided that they are clearly specified. A pledge over receivables must be registered in the Register of Pledges.
- Pledges over ownership interests in Slovak limited liability companies – such a pledge requires registration with the Commercial Register.
- Pledges over the shares in Slovak joint stock companies require registration in the register of pledges administered by the Central Securities Depository of the Slovak Republic.
- Pledges over trade marks – a pledge over a trade mark requires registration with the Industrial Property Office of the Slovak Republic.
- Pledge over enterprise – the enterprise shall be understood as the sum of all property owned by an entrepreneur and used for entrepreneurial activity. The pledge must be registered in the Register of Pledges; however if the enterprise contains property the pledge over which is to be registered in a special register, separate registration of the pledge over this property is required as well.

4.2.3 Assignment of receivables as collateral security agreement
The Civil Code allows the securing of obligations by assignment of a right (including ownership rights) and assignment of receivables.

The receivables of the bank may also be secured by the transfer of a right of the borrower. The right is temporarily transferred to the lender; however, in the event of default the lender is not entitled to keep the right, as the execution of the security transfer of the right similar to the execution of a mortgage or pledge must be performed, ie the lender is entitled to transfer the right to a third party and satisfy itself by means of encashment of the yield of the sold right. The contract for the assignment of the right must be in writing.

Receivables may also be secured by a security assignment of receivables of either the debtor or of another party (the security provider) to the holder of the security.

4.2.4 Bank guarantee
The bank guarantee is based upon a written declaration in which the bank (the security provider) undertakes to satisfy the entitled person up to the amount stated therein if the debtor fails to satisfy its obligations or if other conditions are met. The bank guarantee is also often used for the purpose of

securing the rent and service charge payments with respect to the lease of non-residential premises.

4.2.5 Notary deed on direct enforcement
A notary deed on the approval of direct enforceability is an agreement witnessed by a notary public and concluded in the notary deed, under which the debtor undertakes to satisfy the creditor's receivable and provides consent for direct execution of payment of the receivable in case the debtor does not fulfil its obligation – in such case the receivable may be directly enforced without taking any further action.

4.2.6 Promissory notes
Promissory notes are securities binding the issuer (either the debtor or another person) to pay a certain amount to a creditor. Promissory notes are usually issued blank. The creditor and the issuer conclude an agreement on the creditor's right to fill in the promissory note in case of the debtor's default.

4.2.7 Guarantee
This security is created by a declaration of the guarantor in which the guarantor undertakes to be bound to fulfil an obligation of the debtor in case the debtor fails to do so, though having been so requested by the creditor. The guarantee must be provided in writing. The creditor is obliged to inform the guarantor, upon request and without undue delay, of the current amount of the secured receivable. If the secured receivable is assigned, the guarantor must fulfil its obligations towards the new creditor only if it was notified about the assignment by the assignor or the assignment has been evidenced to it by the assignee. Once the guarantor repaid the debtor's obligation towards the creditor, the guarantor has a right to recourse against the debtor.

5. MANAGING THE ACQUISITION PROCESS
5.1 Minimum formalities for the sale and purchase of property
Before the investor signs a contract to purchase plots of land, there are various enquiries that should be made regarding the target property and its owners. First of all, the property should be inspected to establish whether the property suits the investor's business plans. An inspection can also serve to identify potential legal problems. The investor or investor's advisors should also contact local authorities to examine issues such as the ownership of roads, sewers, and other infrastructure affecting the property; tree preservation orders; historical architecture orders; and planning issues.

Please note that under Slovak law, a construction/building is not a part of the land. Therefore, the owner of the land is not automatically the owner of any construction that is built on the land.

5.2 Legal documents required for transfer
5.2.1 Letter of intent
There are several documents that are usually signed before any transfer of property. The first document that can be concluded by the parties is a letter of intent, which is a proposal of the main elements and aims of the contract that will be concluded subsequently. The letter of intent specifies the parties to the contract, the subject of the contract, the price and conditions for sale. It is up to the parties whether they wish to be legally bound by the letter of intent and what sanctions they set for not meeting the stipulated requirements. However, the letter of intent is most commonly considered as a non-binding document.

5.2.2 Agreement to conclude the future agreement
According to Slovak law, it is possible to conclude an agreement to conclude a future agreement (the AFA) that is to be understood as an agreement between the parties, ie, the future seller and the future purchaser, to conclude, within a specified period of time, a future agreement with specific content. The AFA is usually used in cases in which the future seller is not the owner of the relevant real estate at the date of signing the agreement on the future purchase agreement.

5.2.3 An AFA for business purposes must be concluded in writing.
If the obliged party fails to meet its obligation to conclude the future agreement, the other party may demand that the court (or a person specified in the agreement) determine the content of the agreement, or it may claim compensation for damages caused by a breach of the obligation to conclude the agreement.

5.2.4 Purchase agreement
If the real property is transferred by an asset deal, the agreement on purchase of the real estate is concluded. Any agreement relating to the transfer of real property must be concluded in writing and the signature of the seller must be notarised. The agreement on transfer may be also concluded in the form of a notary deed or authorised by an attorney-at-law. In such a case, the registration proceeding is shorter and the registration fee is decreased by €15.

In addition to the plots of lands and the buildings, the buildings under construction may also be transferred. Such buildings can be registered in the Cadastral Register as buildings under construction. Since Slovak law recognises buildings separately from land, the owner of the building may differ from the owner of the land.

The purchase agreement for purchase of an apartment can be concluded if the apartment is completed, ie, was approved for use by the relevant Building Office. The agreement on purchase of the apartment shall be concluded if the purchase agreement is governed by the provisions of the Act on the Ownership of Apartments and Non-residential Premises. The law requires that more essential elements be fulfilled in the case of an agreement on purchase of an apartment than the purchase agreement on other real estate. The same applies to sale of non-residential premises.

5.3 Property transaction costs
5.3.1 Purchase price
The price is one of the essential elements of any purchase contract. The purchase price must be agreed by parties in accordance with generally binding legal regulations, otherwise the purchase contract will be declared null and void.

5.3.2 Registration fee for Cadastral Register
The fee for the registration of the ownership and other rights in the Cadastral Register is €66 for each filing; in such a case the registration shall be performed within 30 days. The fee for a faster proceeding, in which the registration shall be performed within 15 days, is €265.50. The fee is lower if the petition for registration is filed electronically and also if the agreement on transfer is concluded in the form of a notary deed or authorised by an attorney-at-law. The fee is paid by the party that submits the petition for registration (either the seller or the purchaser).

5.4 Creating a legally binding obligation
The parties become legally bound when the contract becomes effective. The effectiveness of the contract arises at the moment when the contract is signed by the parties. Agreements on transfer of real estate property must be concluded in writing. The obligatory written form of an agreement is kept if a written offer is accepted in writing. As for an agreement on transfer of real estate property, the expressions of the participants must be on the same document. The signatures of the seller or its authorised representatives have to be notarised. As mentioned above, the agreement on transfer of real estate property may be concluded in the form of a notary deed or authorised by an attorney-at-law.

5.5 Transfer of ownership
Ownership of real property that is subject to registration in the Cadastral Register is acquired (if transferred by agreement) upon its registration in the Cadastral Register. The ownership transfer is deemed effective from the date of legal effectiveness of the decision on registration issued by the Cadastral Office.

Ownership of certain real property (typically minor constructions) is not subject to registration in the Cadastral Register, its ownership (if it is transferred by agreement) is acquired on the effective date of the relevant agreement.

6. REAL ESTATE BASIS
6.1 Main sources of law
Different types of real estate are governed by different acts. Our purpose here is to give a general overview of the legal framework and therefore we do not intend to include all acts related to real estate in this summary.

The transfer and lease of the building and plot are governed by the Civil Code.

Referring to purchase of apartments and non-residential premises, the Act on Ownership of Apartments and Non-residential Premises is used. The lease of apartments is governed by the Civil Code and when the subject of the lease is a non-residential premises, the Act on Lease and Sublease of Non-residential Premises will be applied.

The Commercial Code governs relations between businessmen in the course of their business.

The Building Code regulates the procedures for zone planning, regulatory plans, building permits, occupancy permits, and all the procedures connected with these decisions.

The Cadastral Act relates to the real estate enlisted in the Cadastral Register. It governs the procedures of registration of property transfer, registration of other rights related to real property (eg easements or mortgages) or registration of newly built real estate.

Last but not least is the Act on Local Taxes. The rate of real estate tax depends of the size of the land/building, location, and the local coefficient. Real estate tax is not significant.

6.2 What types of tenure exist?
Under Slovak law there are several typical types of property ownership. The most common are the freehold and leasehold of the property.

6.2.1 Freehold
Within the limits of law, the owner shall be entitled to hold the subject of its ownership, use it, consume its proceeds and dispose of it. The ownership is protected by law; however, it is not absolute. The owner of a thing (real estate) must eliminate anything that disturbs another person or that seriously jeopardises the exercise of its rights. Another limitation is that the owner of a thing must permit use of such thing in a state of distress or in an urgent situation regarding public interest for the necessary time and to the necessary extent and for reimbursement unless the purpose of the use cannot be achieved otherwise.

6.2.2 Leasehold
Leasehold is limited in time. It gives the right to the occupier (the tenant) to possession against payment of a rent to the holder of the freehold interest (the landlord). A leasehold interest may be made in respect of land and buildings or the lease of only part of a building, for example a single floor.

6.2.3 Co-ownership
The property may be co-owned by multiple owners. The share specifies the extent to which an individual co-owner may take part in the rights and duties following from the co-ownership of the common thing. If not agreed by the co-owners or stipulated otherwise by law, the shares are equal. All co-owners shall be jointly and severally entitled and obliged to legal acts concerning the

common property. If the share is transferred, the co-owners shall have a pre-emptive right unless the share is transferred to a close person.

6.2.4 Joint property of spouses
Joint property may arise only between spouses. It consists of property acquired by any of the spouses or by both of them during the marriage and obligations arise on one spouse or jointly on them both during the marriage. The Civil Code defines exceptions from the property and obligations that are not included in the joint property of spouses.

6.2.5 Ownership of a unit
In buildings with at least two apartments or two non-residential premises or one apartment and one non-residential premises and subject to further conditions, it is possible to divide ownership of the apartments or non-residential premises into units. In such a case, a co-ownership share of the common part is automatically connected with the ownership of the relevant unit. The co-ownership share is calculated as the share of the area of the unit against the total area of all the units. The co-ownership share is transferred automatically once the ownership right to the unit is transferred. If the owner of the unit is also the co-owner of the land on which the building of units is situated, the unit may be transferred only together with the transfer of the ownership share to the land.

6.2.6 Easement
Easements represent a specific set of real rights permitting their beneficiary a repeated or lasting use of another person's real property, and thus are distinguished from other real rights, such as the right of pre-emption or mortgage. Easements limit the use of such property by its rightful owner, who is obliged, under the easement to suffer the specified usage of its property by the beneficiary, to refrain from a specified use of the property itself and/or from acting in a certain way in relation to the real property.

6.3 The Cadastral Register
6.3.1 Acquisition of ownership
Real property registered in the Cadastral Register
The Slovak Republic does not dispose of the register of transactions. The Cadastral Register only contains information about property by title. The subject of registration in the Cadastral Register is always land in the form of plots of land, buildings built directly on the land and apartments and non-residential premises. Minor constructions, as well as roads and engineering structures, are not subject to registration.

Ownership of real property that is subject to registration in the Cadastral Register is acquired (if transferred by agreement) upon its registration in the Cadastral Register.

Even though the Cadastral Register as a public register enjoys a state guarantee of title, the ownership rights may be challenged. If previous transfers were not valid for any reason, later purchasers of the real property will not become the legal owners even though they are evidenced as the owners in the Cadastral Register. In such case, the ownership title to real property may only be acquired by positive prescription, ie, good faith possession of the property for a period of at least 10 years. Good faith possession of the real property by previous owners is included in the calculation of the 10-year period. As such, it is recommended to investigate the acquisition titles, which basically involves tracing the chain of ownership back 10 or more years to help guarantee that there are no hidden problems and establish that the current owner has legally acquired the real estate.

The registration process itself may take a long time. Although the Cadastral Offices are required to complete the registration procedure within 30 days (or within 15 days if the fee for faster proceeding was paid), in practice it may take even longer to register the ownership transfer. Therefore, for purchase of real property, it is recommended to credit the purchase price to an escrow account and instruct the escrow agent to release it to the seller only after the Cadastral Register has issued the extract evidencing the transfer. However, when acquiring apartments for private use, this practice has often not been respected by developers due to high demand in the real estate market. However, this business principle may again be established in the market if demand decreases.

Real property not registered in the Cadastral Register
If the real property is not subject to registration in the Cadastral Register, the ownership is acquired on the effective date of the relevant agreement, if it is transferred by agreement.

6.3.2 Extract from the Cadastral Register
The key information related to particular real estate registered in the Cadastral Register is shown in the extract from the Cadastral Register. Such extract specifies who owns the land or building, as well as most of the third party rights that may encumber the land (eg, easements, mortgages, pre-emption rights of a real nature).

As stated above, Slovak law distinguishes between the land and the buildings or other constructions on the land. This distinction can cause problems because while all land must be registered, not all constructions require registration with the Cadastral Register. It is important to emphasise that the Cadastral Register records are only presumed to be correct and evidence to the contrary can still override the records.

Spain

Cuatrecasas Gonçalves Pereira Jordi Sagrera,
Bernat Mullerat, Iñigo Rubio, Meritxell Yus, Iñigo de Luisa,
Victoria González & Silvia Alcoverro

1. INVESTMENT PURCHASE OVERVIEW

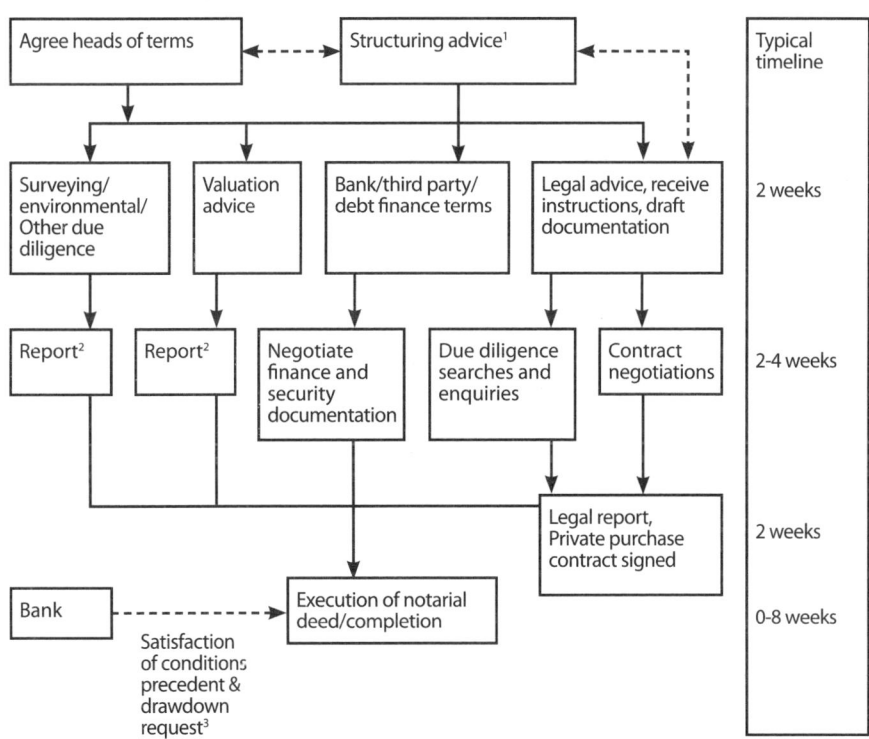

[1] Mainly to consider tax issues as well as a ring-fenced structure for the vendors.
[2] Each report will also be addressed to the bank (if any), a valuation report will be necessary if there is third party debt provided and otherwise is optional.
[3] Including the purchase deed and the granting of all the security over the property, mainly the mortgage.
Timeline may differ depending on each specific case.

2. TAX CONSIDERATIONS

The acquisition of real estate assets located in Spain will levy either VAT or transfer tax, depending on the legal and material features of the real estate to be transferred and on whether the seller is a VAT taxpayer or not.

The main difference between both taxes is that in certain circumstances

Spain

VAT is a neutral tax whereas transfer tax is always a final tax. Depending on the business activities carried out by the purchaser, VAT paid in the acquisition of a real estate may be recovered either by offsetting it against VAT charged in other transactions, or by directly claiming a refund from the tax authorities.

2.1 Value added tax (VAT)
If the seller is a VAT taxpayer (a company or an individual) and the transaction constitutes a business activity, as a general rule the transfer will be subject to VAT (unless the transaction involves an autonomous business branch) although in certain circumstances an exemption may be applicable:
- Transfer of land:
  (i) The transfer of non-developed land or land not suitable for construction is exempt from VAT.
  (ii) The transfer of developed land or land in the process of being developed for building purposes is not exempt from VAT (the VAT rate is 16 per cent; 18 per cent from 1 July 2010).
- Transfer of a building:
  (i) As a general rule, the first transfer of buildings by the developer is not exempt from VAT. The general VAT rate is 16 per cent (18 per cent from 1 July 2010); seven per cent (eight per cent from 1 July 2010) for residential real estate, and four per cent for certain public protected residences and for transfer of residential real estate to Housing Companies. If the developer has rented the building or used it for its own business for more than two years the transfer of the building will be exempt from VAT (with some exceptions).
  (ii) The second or subsequent transfer of buildings is exempt from VAT unless the purchaser intends to demolish or restore it, provided certain requirements are met.

VAT exemption may be waived by the seller if the purchaser has the right to deduct all the VAT invoiced by the seller in the transfer of that real estate, depending on the business carried out by the purchaser.

The general rule is that VAT accrues at the time of the transfer of the real estate property. If payments are made in advanced, VAT on those payments will accrue at the time of the payment.

A transfer of real estate subject to VAT in a public deed, will be levied with stamp duty as set out below.

2.2 Transfer tax
When VAT is not applicable (that is, when the transfer of the real estate is either not subject or subject but VAT exempt), transfer tax shall be paid by the purchaser, on the actual value of the real estate.

As a general rule, transfer tax rate is between six and eight per cent; different rates and exemptions may be applicable depending on the autonomous community were the property is located and the property specific features (a 95 per cent reduction of Transfer Tax/Stamp Duty is applicable on the acquisition of land for housing development or on the acquisition of housing by RECIV and SOCIMI, provided certain requirements are met).

If the transaction is subject to transfer tax, no stamp duty is accrued.

If acquisition of real estate is done through a share deal, the transfer of shares is normally exempted from VAT and transfer tax, although there is a relevant exception: under certain circumstances transfer tax at rate between six and eight per cent shall apply when acquiring (or increasing) control of an entity having more than 50 per cent of its assets in real estate.

2.3 Stamp duty
When VAT is applicable, the purchaser will have to pay stamp duty on the public deed documenting the transfer of the real estate.

As a general rule, stamp duty rate is between one and two per cent; different rates and exemptions may be applicable depending on the autonomous community were the property is located, and the property's specific features. It is common that the stamp duty rate is higher in those real estate transactions exempt from VAT when the seller has waived this exemption.

2.4 Other tax relevant issues
2.4.1 Tax on increase in value of urban land
The seller of an urban land (regardless of whether there are buildings on it) will have to pay a municipal tax for the increase of its cadastral value (the amount payable is determined in accordance with the cadastral value of the land and the number of years the property has been held by the seller).

2.4.2 Tax due diligence
Real estate properties are liable for certain taxes that previous owners should have paid; when acquiring a property it is advisable to check these possible contingencies.

3. INVESTMENT VEHICLES
This section describes the most popular investment vehicles, with an indication of their main advantages and disadvantages. This is not an exhaustive list, the most efficient vehicle needs to be decided on a case by case basis.

Non-residents can easily invest in Spain, as there is no restriction on ownership, occupation of property or guarantees granted over Spanish land for the benefit of non residents. Accordingly, most asset transactions are only subject to reporting requirements for: (i) statistical and tax purposes; and (ii) compliance with money laundering regulations. Investment in shares or quotas of Spanish entities is also liberalised except if the company undertakes activities in a restricted sector. Under certain circumstances, investments originating in a tax haven shall require prior declaration.

3.1 Types of vehicles
Investment in Spanish real estate directly by a non-resident through an overseas vehicle, without a permanent establishment in Spain, has the following direct tax consequences (indirect taxation being common for national and overseas purchasers):

- in general, gross income (net income for EU residents) obtained in Spain will be taxed at a 24 per cent rate and capital gains at a 19 per cent rate;
- when selling a real estate property, the purchaser shall withhold three per cent of the price to be paid on account of the seller's due tax for the capital gain;
- a special tax of three per cent of the real estate cadastral value shall be paid annually, if held by overseas vehicle, with some exceptions.

The main Spanish vehicles to invest in real estate properties are set out below. Depending on the type of investor, and the specific characteristics of the investment, foreign investors may decide:

(i) to set up a Spanish subsidiary through a limited liability company;
(ii) to open a branch of the foreign company, with no separate legal entity;
(iii) to form a 'temporary business association' for a specific project (usually construction); or
(iv) to invest through a real estate collective investment vehicle.

3.1.1 Spanish company: limited liability companies

Most commonly, investors in real estate decide to set up a Spanish subsidiary choosing a limited liability company, because its shareholders or partners are not personally liable. There are two types of limited liability companies, the private limited liability company (*Sociedad de Responsabilidad Limitada* or SL) and the public limited liability company (*Sociedad Anónima* or SA). Since it is possible to have one founding member, foreign investment trend is to set up a Spanish subsidiary whose foundation shareholder is the foreign entity investing in Spain.

Incorporation of limited liability companies must be granted into public deed and must be filed with the Commercial Registry of the place where they have their registered office. The share capital is divided into units (*participaciones*) in SLs or shares (*acciones*) in the case of SAs. One of the main differences between them is that the minimum share capital requirement of SLs is considerably lower (€3,006) than in SAs (€60,101.21). However, in the case of SLs the share capital must be totally paid up upon incorporation, while only 25 per cent is to be paid up upon incorporation of SAs. Units of SLs must be subject to transfer restrictions and may not be traded on a public stock exchange, while no such limitations apply to SAs. SLs may not issue bonds or other negotiable instruments, whereas SAs are entitled to issue debt instruments.

There are other differences between SLs and SAs. However, in general terms SLs are intended to serve as more 'closed' enterprises than SAs, since their regulations are less formal and more flexible.

From a tax perspective, both SAs and SLs will be taxed under the Corporate Income Tax (CIT) at a 30 per cent rate (General Companies). Some reduced rates are foreseen for small sized companies. Provided certain reinvestment requirements are met, capital gains may be taxed at an effective 18 per cent reduced rate.

A special CIT regime is applicable to companies devoted to the renting of housing that fulfill certain requirements (the Housing Companies). Profits from renting are taxed at an effective 4.5 per cent CIT rate.

Dividends received from General Companies or Housing Companies by non-resident shareholders without a permanent establishment in Spain shall be subject to a 19 per cent withholding tax; reduced rates may be applicable depending on the applicable tax treaty. When the parent-subsidiary directive is applicable these dividends are exempt in Spain.

In general, capital gains on transfer of shares are be taxed at a 19 per cent rate; under certain tax treaties the capital gain shall not be taxed in Spain.

Capital tax at a one per cent rate shall be paid on the capital invested in these companies (share capital plus share premium if any).

3.1.2 Spanish branch of foreign companies

A branch is deemed as a secondary establishment operating permanently as representative in Spain without being a different legal entity from its parent company but having a certain degree of independence to manage its own operations, through which all or part of that company's business activities are carried out.

The parent company is liable for the debts of the branch. Therefore investors often choose a Spanish company so that the liability of the shareholders/partners is limited to the capital subscribed.

The establishment of a branch must be set up in a public deed and must be recorded with the Commercial Registry of the place where the branch is located.

The Commercial Registry will require the accounts of the foreign company to be deposited yearly. In addition, if no equivalent accounting rules apply in the foreign company jurisdiction, the parent company will be obliged to prepare the accounts of the business activity of the branch and place them for record with the Commercial Registry.

From a tax perspective, as a general rule Spanish branches of foreign companies are also subject to income tax under similar conditions to General Companies, although some special rules apply to determine the taxable profit. The transfer overseas of profits obtained by the Spanish branch will not be additionally taxed, with some exceptions.

Capital invested by an overseas investor may be subject to one per cent capital tax depending on the location of their headquarters.

3.1.3 Temporary business associations (*Uniones Temporales de Empresa* – UTE)

UTEs are temporary associations of companies which do not constitute a separate legal entity. The main characteristic is that members have joint and several unlimited liability for the debts of the UTE. This type of vehicle is used for carrying out limited duration projects, such as constructions in the public-private sector.

From a tax perspective, UTEs registered in a special register will be taxed under the CIT as general companies for the part of their taxable profit corresponding to their non-resident members, while their Spanish resident members will be taxed in their own CIT for their proportional part of the taxable profit.

Spain

Provided certain requirements are met, no capital tax shall be paid on the capital invested by their members to the UTE.

3.1.4 Real estate collective investment vehicles (RECIV): funds or companies.

The most common RECIVs are: (i) Real Estate Investment Funds (REIF) (*Fondos de Inversión Inmobiliaria*); and (ii) Real Estate Investment Companies (REIC) – (*Sociedades de Inversión Inmobiliaria*) – and the newly created Real Estate Listed Investment Public Limited Liability Company – (*Sociedades Anónimas Cotizadas de Inversión en el Mercado Inmobiliario* or SOCIMIS).

Funds do not have legal capacity. REICs and SOCIMIs, which are in fact public limited liability companies, do have such capacity, and they are regulated vehicles supervised by the Spanish public supervisor in charge of security markets (*Comisión Nacional del Mercado de Valores* or CNMV). All of them must be incorporated in a public deed before a notary public, be registered with the Commercial Registry for companies and with a public registry in charge of the CNMV.

Legislation on RECIVs aims both to subject these structures to a high degree of regulation and to foster long term investment in property (buildings to be exploited through lease), by granting tax benefits.

From a tax perspective for REIFs and REICs, provided they fulfil certain requirements, the CIT rate applicable will be a reduced rate of one per cent. These structures are not allowed to distribute dividends. Capital gains obtained by their non-resident shareholders without a permanent establishment in Spain will be taxed, in general, at a 19 per cent rate. Under certain tax treaties, the capital gain shall not be taxed in Spain.

We would like to make a specific mention about SOCIMIs, a structure created in 2009, which are the Spanish equivalent of Real Estate Investment Trusts (REITs) (although its taxation is different). Its main advantages are tax-related (see chart below).

The main requirements for SOCIMIs are the following:
- the corporate object must be the acquisition and development of urban real estate for lease and the holding of stakes of capital stock of companies with similar corporate object;
- SOCIMI shares must be of the same class and must be listed on a regulated market; and
- SOCIMIs must pay to its shareholders a minimum dividend each year.

From a tax perspective, SOCIMIs are taxed at a 19 per cent CIT rate (with some specialties and provided certain requirements are met). Dividends received by non-resident shareholders (without a permanent establishment in Spain), and capital gains up to a quantitative limit are not taxed in Spain.

As a general rule neither REIFs or REICs or SOCIMIs shall pay capital tax.

In general terms (with some specialties and exceptions), taxation of these investment vehicles and its non-resident shareholders is as follows:

Spain

Vehicle	General company	Housing company	RECIV	SOCIMI
CIT (1) – Income from renting	30 per cent (2)	4.5 per cent (2)	1 per cent	19 per cent
CIT – Capital gains	30 per cent (2)(3)	30 per cent (2)(3)	1 per cent	19 per cent (4)
Transfer, stamp duty and capital tax	No specific exemptions	No specific exemptions	Certain exemptions and reductions	Certain exemptions and reductions
Non-resident Shareholder (without permanent establishment in Spain)				
Dividends	19 - 0 per cent (5)	19 -0 per cent (5)	–	0 per cent
Capital gains	19 per cent (6)	19 per cent (6)	19 per cent (6)	0 per cent

(1) CIT: Corporate Income Tax
(2) Reduced CIT rates for small sized companies
(3) 18 per cent effective rate if reinvestment with certain requirements
(4) 6.5 per cent effective rate if reinvestment with certain requirements
(5) Reduced rates depending on the applicable tax treaty
    Potential application of the parent subsidiary directive
(6) Certain exceptions depending on the applicable tax treaty.

4. FINANCING AN ACQUISITION

Financing of real estate acquisitions has been extremely active and booming in Spain during the past decade due to inexpensive financing and to significant asset value appreciation every year; however, since 2007 it has suffered the effects of both the financial liquidity crisis and the explosion of the Spanish real estate bubble.

Notwithstanding the above, the structuring of current transactions remains very similar to the booming years and it has hit more the percentage of the amount financed by the lenders (loan-to-value ratios down from 75-90 per cent to 55-65 per cent) than the structure itself. Borrowers are required to have higher equity contributions than earlier years (with the additional effect of reducing the number of transactions) and with additional security and guarantees. It should be noted that financing is not a regulated or restricted activity in Spain so no authorisation is required.

Transactions are generally structured through special purpose vehicles (SPV) in order to establish a ring-fenced scheme to the lenders and follow very similar procedures to other jurisdictions, where the asset acquired will be considered as the main security for the financing. In case the borrower is allowed to request a return of the VAT accrued on the acquisition, lenders tend to grant a separate VAT facility with limited security that will be repaid with the reimbursement of the VAT by the Spanish tax administration.

Spain

The security generally requested by lenders includes:
- a mortgage over the acquired property asset, which by law covers: (i) the plot of land and the buildings on it; (ii) the proceeds from the insurance policies insuring such property; and (iii) the improvement works carried out on the property and natural accretions. Generally, by agreement among the parties, the mortgage also extends to: (i) movable assets located permanently in the mortgaged property; (ii) proceeds (legal or natural) of the mortgaged property; and (iii) any outstanding rent payable on the charged property when payment of the secured obligations is demanded.
- a pledge over the shares, in case the property is acquired through an SPV;
- a pledge over the receivables (credit rights and rentals from commercial contracts and lease agreements);
- a pledge over the credit rights of any relevant contracts, including the insurance policies (including the designation as beneficiaries of the insurance policies);
- a pledge over the bank accounts where the income is credited;
- an undertaking to pledge any future asset or credit rights to be held by the borrower;
- for the VAT facilities, a pledge over the credit right of the reimbursement from the tax authorities, together with a pledge over the account where the reimbursement is to be credited.

There have also been several real estate transactions in the Spanish market structured as 'sale and lease backs' in similar structures and terms as others executed in the international market. Particularly active have been Spanish financial institutions using this structure to transfer their premises and offices to foreign investors. Other large companies have followed this trend, including offices and even supermarkets. In some cases these structures have been combined with securitisation schemes in order to issue bonds for investors.

It is important to mention that with the enactment of the Mortgage Market Reform Act, one single mortgage can now secure several obligations, provided that the secured obligations are specified or specifiable and the procedure for settling each obligation is established (the principle of determination, one of the basics of Spanish mortgage law). These so-called 'variable security' mortgages (*hipotecas flotantes*) are set up for finance companies or governments. Such mortgages secure one or more obligations of any type and may combine existing and future obligations (for finance companies) or tax or social security credits (for governments), with no need for a renewal and amendment agreement. In this case, the principle of determination is satisfied, as it is not necessary to identify the secured obligations and a 'general description of the basic transactions that may give rise to the secured obligations in future' is sufficient. In the case of finance companies, the privilege of agreeing that the creditor finance company may make the final settlement as stipulated by the parties in the deed is also allowed.

With regard to formalities, Spanish law provides for a requirement for granting mortgages and pledges before a notary public by means of a public document (*póliza o escritura*), and in the case of the mortgage, it has to be granted by means of a deed (*escritura*) that has to be filed and registered at the applicable land registry.

Lastly, it is worth mentioning the impact that the securitisation has had in allowing banks to grant mortgage loans. Act 2/1981, of 25 March, regulating the mortgage market and the financial institutions (banks, saving banks, the Spanish Confederation of savings banks, credit cooperatives and financial credit establishments) referred to in that Act, can grant mortgage loans and issue the securities necessary to fund them subject to the requirements and objectives established therein. Spanish financial entities have been among the major issuers of securitisation bonds over the past few years in Europe.

The abovementioned institutions can offer third parties the opportunity to participate in all, or a part of, one or several mortgage credits in their portfolio, through the issue of securities named 'mortgage participations' (*participaciones hipotecarias*), if the loans comply with the requirements established on Section II of Law 2/1981, or by means of the issuance of 'mortgage transfer certificates' (*certificados de transmission de hipoteca*). Those securities should be subscribed by securitisations funds (mortgage or asset securitisations funds) or by professional investors.

5. MANAGING THE ACQUISITION PROCESS
5.1 Introduction
The process of selling and purchasing commercial real estate is relatively standardised in Spain. This section explains the usual terms that apply to a sale and purchase of commercial property. If the property is to be acquired through a corporate vehicle owning the property, different terms would apply.

For the purposes of this section, we assume that the transaction involves the acquisition of commercial property.

5.2 Agreeing terms and binding contracts
Under Spanish law, transfer of title to a property requires either: (a) execution of a private contract, provided possession of the property is transferred to the purchaser; or (b) granting of a notarial deed which, unless otherwise agreed, is deemed to constitute transfer of possession. Only contracts executed through a notarial deed can be registered at the Land Registry. Therefore, if a private contract (ie, not notarised) has been entered into, and possession has been delivered to the buyer, the buyer may require the seller to notarise the transfer through a notarial deed, so that the buyer can register the acquisition with the Land Registry.

From a practical point of view, once the parties have reached an agreement on the main commercial terms and a letter of intent has been entered into, the purchaser may have a period of approximately 30 days to undertake due diligence, and afterwards a private contract would be entered into between the parties. This private contract, which does not usually imply transfer of title or possession, sets out the main terms and conditions of the transaction (essentially price, guarantees and representations and warranties) and binds the parties to grant the corresponding deed of sale and purchase within the agreed term.

The deed is usually granted within a period of two months, to enable the purchaser to obtain financing. These days, it is not rare to see private purchase contracts subject to the purchaser being able to obtain sufficient and satisfactory financing.

Upon execution of the private purchase contract, a deposit is usually given to the seller. This private contract can allow either of the parties to pull out of the transaction (by losing or paying the deposit), or otherwise the Civil Code shall apply, and therefore if one of the parties breaches the obligation to grant the notarial deed of purchase, the other can either request specific performance or termination, in both cases with a penalty for damages.

Costs of the transaction are usually allocated as follows: purchaser pays notary and Land Registry fees, taxes related to the transaction (transfer tax/ stamp duty or VAT), and the seller pays the municipal value added tax.

5.3 The contract documents

Contractual documents usually consist of the private sale and purchase contract, and the transfer deed. As mentioned before, transfer of the property usually takes place through the granting of the notarial deed.

The deed, to be granted before a notary and having access to the Land Registry, contains the commercial covenants which were already agreed by the parties in the private contract.

If the property is let to tenants, other documents may be executed, such as notifications to tenants, notifications to the public entities holding the mandatory bonds of the leases, notifications to lenders (if applicable), assignment of licences, etc.

5.4 Typical contract terms

The following is a summary of typical sale contract terms:

5.4.1 Private sale and purchase contract: deposit and possibility to pull out of the transaction

Usually, upon signing the private sale and purchase contract a percentage of the total price (approximately 10 per cent) is paid to the seller although the payment of such percentage by the buyer is not compulsory for the validity of the private contract. The rest of the price is then usually paid upon granting of the notarial deed of transfer.

The advanced payment on account of the total purchase price is delivered to the seller (and not to the lawyer). If the seller fails to grant the sale and purchase deed on the agreed date and on the agreed conditions, usually it is obliged to reimburse the deposit, and pay an additional amount as a penalty (this can be an amount equivalent to the deposit, or an even higher amount). To cover the risk of the seller not reimbursing the deposit, the parties can agree that the seller issues a bank guarantee. If the purchaser fails to grant the sale and purchase deed on the agreed date and on the agreed conditions, usually the seller can keep the deposit as a penalty, and is free to sell the property to any third party, or may alternatively seek specific performance.

5.4.2 Representations and warranties
The seller must provide the buyer with copy of the title documents, in order to ascertain its ownership of the property. In case this is not possible, this can be ascertained through the Land Registry.

The seller usually provides warranties related to:
(i) title;
(ii) absence of any liens and encumbrances over the property other than those disclosed to the seller;
(iii) absence of outstanding amounts regarding charges, expenses and/or taxes;
(iv) absence of any outstanding proceedings and/or claims in relation to the property;
(v) planning and licensing compliance; and
(vi) absence of contamination.

In a case where the affected plot refers to a property on which a construction exists or an activity is being carried out, the seller may also give a warranty in relation to the licenses granted to the construction works and/or the activity. For those properties in condominium, the seller shall also give a warranty regarding the fulfilment of the by-laws of the owners' community. For leased properties, representations and warranties related to fulfilment of existing leases and absence of debts are also usual. It is also usual to include a warranty related to the information provided to the buyer during the negotiations.

By granting the representations and warranties the seller is bound by their contents, and therefore in the event that they are false or inaccurate the buyer would have grounds for a claim against the seller (in the case of negligence or wilful misconduct). Therefore these warranties have not only an informative purpose, but also decrease the risks for the buyer due to the fact they exclude their liability.

Representations and warranties are usually included in the private sale and purchase contract, and reproduced in the sale and purchase deed. They normally cover issues detected through the due diligence process.

In addition to what the parties may agree through representations and warranties, unless otherwise agreed by the parties, the seller is subject to good title and hidden defects and charges liabilities (see section 6 below).

5.4.3 Price and adjustment of price
The price needs to be determined or determinable (for example, by agreeing a price per square metre).

Price can be adjusted depending, for example, on:
(i) town planning rights which are not determined upon execution of the deed;
(ii) retentions of the price made by the purchaser to cover any sellers' liability such as payment of mortgages or taxes, or undertaking of certain agreed works at the property;
(iii) if the property is let, the daily rents corresponding to the days remaining until the end of the month of execution of the transfer deed;

(iv) *pro rata* of the amount corresponding to the real estate tax; and
(v) other taxes.

5.5 Managing the property between execution of the private sale and purchase contract and the transfer deed

The seller remains as owner of the property until possession of the property is transferred to the purchaser (by the physical transfer of possession or, most commonly, by the granting of the notarial deed). Therefore, it is usual to establish specific obligations in relation to the property in the private sale and purchase contract.

If the property is insured (under Spanish law this is not a legal obligation), the property will be insured by the seller until the transfer is completed. On completion, the seller must inform the insurance company of the transfer, and within a period of 15 days after the sale, both the insurer and the buyer can decide to terminate the insurance contract.

If this property is occupied by tenants, the purchaser will normally require that no contract or amendment is entered into without its express approval. This would include rent reviews, entering into new contracts, etc. Apportionment of rents as well as service charges and other expenses is also provided.

6. REAL ESTATE BASICS
6.1 Main sources of law governing real estate

Spain is a civil law country; its main local sources of law, apart from international treaties and European regulation, are statutes enacted by the National Parliament or the Regional Parliaments (called *Comunidades Autónomas*). Real estate in Spain is governed by statutory law. The *Comunidades Autónomas* have legislative power in matters relating to dwelling and planning matters, as well as civil matters in those that had historically developed civil laws. Furthermore, the state, regional and local governments may enact rules and regulations relating to real estate matters. Therefore, location of real estate shall determine the applicable law, resulting sometimes in a complex amalgam of rules and regulations from different sources.

6.2 Property rights

The main property rights under Spanish law are the following (taking into account that some specifics apply to different *Comunidades Autónomas*):
- Absolute freehold (*plena propiedad*): this is the right to fully and exclusively own, dispose, use and benefit from the property (both the land and the buildings on it). In principle, an owner of a property enjoys all rights over the property. However, these rights may be limited legally (by the application of planning restrictions or the existence of legal encumbrances such as easements or legal mortgages) or contractually.
- Surface right (*derecho de superficie*): which is the right to build on someone else's land and to have a separate ownership of the building for a period of time while the owner of the land retains ownership over the

Spain

land. When such right expires, the landowner becomes the owner of the building. Surface rights shall be granted by public deed and, in general, surface rights exist upon registration with the Land Registry (registration is constitutive).
- A beneficial interest (*derecho de usufructo*): which is the right of a person (*usufructuario*) to temporarily use and benefit from someone else's (*nudo propietario*) property. This right is temporary but the *usufructurario* may convey its own limited right to third parties, unless otherwise agreed. The right holder usually is not entitled to make alteration to the property.
- Right of use (*derecho de uso y habitación*): is the right to use and profit from dwelling premises. It is not common anymore.
- Condominium (*comunidad de propietarios*): each co-owner owns in a building a separate piece of property (usually a flat) and a quota over common areas (adjacent and serving the private units, such as lobby, corridors, elevator, roof, gardens, etc). The condominium is managed by the assembly of all co-owners that aside from approving the annual expenses budget, must elect a chairman and a secretary (often an independent professional is appointed for this post). The co-owners may draft by-laws ruling down, among other things, the use of the common elements, stating the necessary quorum and majorities for passing resolutions (which at all events shall respect the mandatory provisions of the law). By disposing of the private unit, the title over its quota over common areas shall pass to the acquiring party automatically.
- Common ownership (*comunidad de bienes*): is a type of tenure according to which each co-owner owns a share of the whole (a quota). This share may be transferred and encumbered. All the co-owners have equal rights to use the whole of the property, but the tenure of a quota does not give to each co-owner the right to use and dispose fully or exclusively of a particular part of the property (except if the common ownership is set up for parking lots and the constitutional regime attributes to each quota the use of a certain parking lot). The co-owners must contribute to all necessary expenses in proportion to their quota. Co-owners have a pre-emption right over the quotas of the other co-owners in the event of transfer.

In principle, management of common ownership is carried out by a decision of the majority of the co-owners. However, alterations of the property shall require the approval of all co-owners, which sometimes makes this type of tenure unmanageable.
- Timesharing (*aprovechamiento por turno*): is the right granted to use a tourist accommodation for a number weeks each year in a building composed of several accommodations.
- Easements: is a limited right, which confers on the owner of the dominant plots rights over another person's land (denominated servient plot). Easements may be negative (forbidding the owner of the servient plot from doing something on its land) or positive (allowing the owner of the dominant plot to do something on the servient plot), and

Spain

apparent or non-apparent. Easements may be imposed by law or as a result of an agreement.
- Leases: leases are personal rights giving the tenant the right to use a property (and not a property interest). Although leases are not under Spanish law, rights *in rem*, they may be registered with the Land Registry if granted in public deed. With some exceptions, and unless such right has been waived by the tenant (which is quite common), tenants of urban properties hold first refusal and preemption rights in the event of transfer of the leased property.

6.3 Property title
Under Spanish law there is only one class of title. The main difference between different property titles is whether they have been registered or not at the Land Registry as explained above.

Title insurance to cover possible defects in title is very unusual. However, the Spanish Civil Code sets forth two guarantees for the buyer that protect it from title defects up to a certain extent and for a limited period:
- Good title liability (*Responsabilidad por evicción*). Should the buyer of a property be deprived of it by a third party with a preferential right which is previous to the sale and purchase, the seller must compensate the buyer.
- Hidden defects and charges liability (*Responsabilidad por vicios y gravámenes ocultos*). The seller of a property is liable under certain circumstances, during the six-month (in the case of defects) and 24-month term (in the case of charges), following handover of the property, for all hidden defects and charges.

6.4 Land registration
In Spain there is a public Land Registry, which is a register of titles (not of transactions). The general rule is that registration has declarative effects, limited to gathering in the Land Registry previous legal and factual situations. Exceptionally, registration has constitutive effects; this is the case for mortgages and surface rights, in general.

Documents which may be registered include:
- the public deeds transferring or declaring titles of property or rights *in rem* related to them;
- the titles incorporating, recognising, transferring, amending or extinguishing beneficial interest rights, rights of use, *emphyteusis*, mortgage, ground rents (*censo*), easements and any other right *in rem*;
- the acts and contracts allocating properties or rights *in rem*;
- judicial resolutions regarding the alteration of civil capacity of persons in relation to the free disposal of their goods; and
- leases, as well as subleases, assignments and subrogation of leases.

Only public documents (public deeds, judicial orders or certificates issued by public authorities) may be registered with the Land Registry.

Although registration is not compulsory, it is commonplace, as it protects the registered landowner. Failure to record the sale and purchase deed with the Land Registry implies that the purchase cannot affect *bona fide* third parties who have acquired onerously the property. As a general principle, the party who records its ownership right with the Land Registry first has a prevailing right on that over any other party which registers it later, even if it purchased it beforehand.

The risk of the 'registration gap' (the gap between the day on which the public deed is granted and the day on which the purchaser becomes the registered owner) is nowadays covered by the co-operation between the notary and the registrar and the implementation of the technical means in the correspondence between them. On the day of the transfer, the notary must inform the parties on the title and charges of the property registered at the Land Registry, and therefore, it shall consult by electronic means the books of the Land Registry immediately before the transfer or warn the parties that it was not able to carry it out. Furthermore, on the day of granting the deed, the notary shall inform the Land Registrar of the transaction made and the parties may even request the notary to file the transfer deed directly for registration.

6.5 Unregistered land
If the property is not registered it could have access to the Land Registry by different means:
(i) a court decision following a judicial procedure;
(ii) a public title of acquisition with an attested affidavit; and
(iii) an administrative certificate when it refers to publicly held land.
Excess of surface may be registered, under certain conditions, with a certificate issued by the cadastral register.

Sweden

Gernandt & Danielsson Advokatbyrå KB
Bob Johanson, Carolina Hertzen & Sara Edström

The Swedish real estate market was to a great extent affected by the global financial crisis during 2008 and 2009. The market, which during previous years had grown significantly, was subject to a general decline in the number and size of both domestic and international transactions. Instead focus has been on reconstruction of property companies and portfolios. As in many other countries, one of the major reasons for the decline in transactional activity has been the difficulties in the financial market which has made it significantly harder to obtain financing for real estate transactions on acceptable terms and conditions. At this point, in 2010, the market seems to be recovering slowly and both Swedish and international investors see new possibilities for investments in Swedish real estate.

1. INVESTMENT PURCHASE OVERVIEW
Typical investment purchase in Sweden

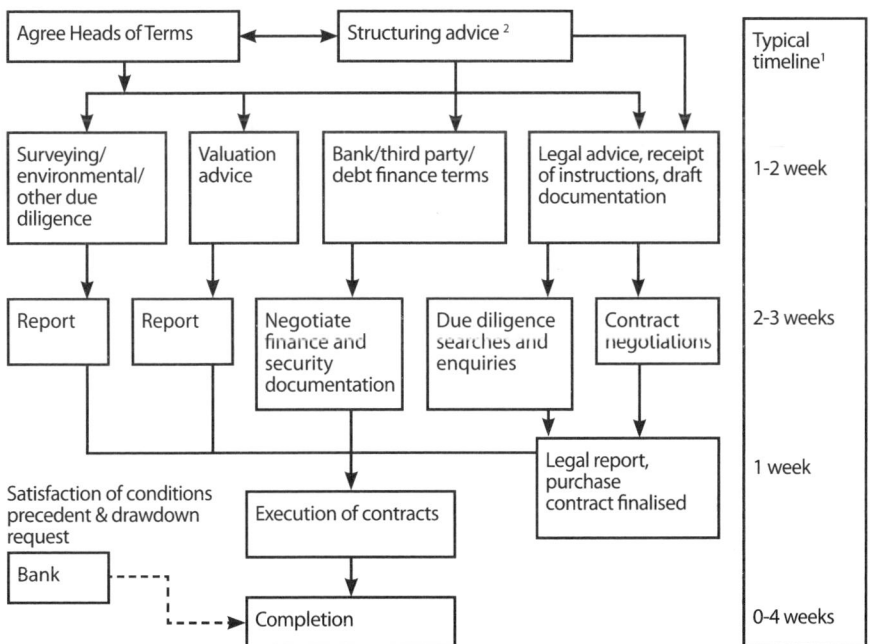

1. Often subject to compression, timescale may differ considerably, exchange and completion may be simultaneous.
2. Establishing an acquistion structure for tax and financial planning is an important early stage which may significantly influence other stages such as the banking arrangements and the purchase structure.

2. TAX CONSIDERATIONS
2.1 Value added tax (VAT)
The legal rules governing real estate-related VAT in Sweden are complex and, therefore, VAT issues may arise in connection with real estate transactions. In general, VAT is not payable on the actual sale of real estate but VAT may, however, be payable on the sale of other assets which may be included in the transaction. Furthermore, various types of work performed on a real estate as well as rental income etc are under certain circumstances subject to VAT.

2.2 Stamp duty
Acquisition of real estate (and site leasehold rights, see further below) are, with some exceptions that are normally not available to commercial purchasers, subject to stamp duty payable by the purchaser. The rate is 1.5 per cent of the value of the real estate if the purchaser is a natural person and three per cent if the purchaser is a legal entity. According to a new proposal, the rate will be 4.25 per cent as of 1 January 2011. In this context, the value of the real estate is the higher amount of the purchase price and the tax value of the real estate in question. Stamp duty is the only tax paid on the actual sale of real estate. In this context, it could be noted that no stamp duty or similar taxes are payable in respect of the transfer of shares in a company, even if that company's only asset is real estate (see section 3.2 regarding indirect purchase).

3. INVESTMENT VEHICLE CHOICE
3.1 Direct purchase
Generally, direct purchase refers to the situation where real estate is acquired directly by the purchaser from another entity or natural person. As further described below, certain other rules apply to a direct purchase than those that apply to an indirect purchase and indirect purchases of real estate will therefore be addressed separately.

3.2 Indirect purchase
Further, an indirect purchase normally refers to the acquisition of shares in a corporation which in turn owns real estate. This is by far the most common procedure for acquisitions of real estate in Sweden, due to the fact that stamp duty is not payable on the transfer of shares as opposed to a direct purchase of real estate.

The limited liability company (*aktiebolag*) is undoubtedly the most common corporation in Sweden and is regulated in the Swedish Company's Act. However, as investment vehicle choice in real estate transactions, limited partnerships (*kommanditbolag*) and trading partnerships (*handelsbolag*) are more frequently used, due to tax reasons (see section 2 regarding tax considerations). A short description of common Swedish corporations is presented below.

Sweden

3.2.1 Limited partnership
The limited partnership has historically been a popular vehicle for real estate investments, mainly due to tax reasons. However, given recent judgments from Swedish tax courts, the potential tax benefits of using limited partnership seem to have been reduced. The limited partnership requires at least one limited partner and one general partner. The limited partner does not participate in the management of the partnership and is only liable up to its initial investment in the partnership as opposed to the general partner who manages the partnership and has an unlimited responsibility for the partnership's obligations.

3.2.2 Trading partnership
The trading partnership may also be used for real estate investments. The trading partnership is similar to the limited partnership except that there are no limited partners. Instead all partners are jointly and severally liable for the partnership's obligations. There need to be at least two partners to form a trading partnership.

3.2.3 Limited liability company
The limited liability company does not need more than one shareholder and can, depending on the circumstances, also be an appropriate vehicle for real estate investments. The limited liability company must have a board of directors and the shareholders are not refrained from being members of the board.

3.3 Real Estate Investment Trusts
Real estate investment trusts (REITs) are not recognised by Swedish law and there are no similar forms of entity. However, Swedish law does not prevent foreign real estate investment trusts from acquiring real estate in Sweden.

3.4 Real estate funds
There is no form of direct joint ownership of real estate created for taxation purposes under Swedish law. The only form of joint ownership of real estate recognised by Swedish law (*samäganderätt*) is described below under section 6. Indirect joint ownership of real estate can be obtained through owning shares in a real estate holding company, or through investing in real estate funds, ie, share investment funds where real estate is the investment object.

4. FINANCING AN ACQUISITION
4.1 Real estate mortgage securitisation
When financing a real estate acquisition a lender would normally require a mortgage over the real estate as security for the loan. In relation to an indirect purchase, a pledge of the shares in the company owning the real estate is often required. The Swedish registered mortgage system for real estate (including site-leaseholds) operates in a manner that differs from the corresponding systems of many countries. The loan documentation is not submitted for registration with a mortgage register or similar. Instead, the

real estate owner requests a mortgage registration (*inteckning*) from the Land Registration Authority for a particular amount (in Swedish crowns) in the real estate. Such a registration also entails a stamp duty of the registered mortgage amount of 1.5 per cent of the real estate value for natural persons and three per cent for legal entities. The real estate owner then receives a mortgage certificate (*pantbrev*) evidencing the registration and may thereafter pledge the mortgage certificate as security for a debt. Mortgage certificates can be either in physical (paper) or electronic form. Upon redemption of the loan, the lender will release the mortgage certificate to the real estate owner or to a new lender, as applicable. Where a lender takes a legal mortgage over the specific real estate it will register this at the Land Register. In this way no other creditors can have a prior claim over the real estate asset to the lender.

The holder of a mortgage certificate may, but is under no obligation to, register itself as holder of the certificate with the Land Register. Such registration has no legal effect but will facilitate the notification process in the event of an enforced sale.

4.2 Pledge of shares in the real estate holding company
As mentioned above, in respect of indirect purchases of real estate, the shares in the real estate holding company are often pledged as security for financing the acquisition. As opposed to a pledge over real estate, a pledge over shares does not require a mortgage registration. Normally, a share pledge agreement is entered into and the pledge is perfected by the creditor's receipt of the share certificates.

4.3 Floating charges
According to the Swedish Floating Charges Act (2008:990), floating charges (*företagshypotek*) can be granted to a certain amount in all real estate owned by the applicant. Evidence of registration is referred to as a floating charge certificate. In cases where a company grants security in respect of a claim by delivering a floating charge certificate regarding its real estate, the creditor obtains priority in respect of the payment of its claim up to the amount specified in the certificate. Right of priority refers to a creditors' right of priority in the event of execution of a debt or bankruptcy, or insolvent liquidation. Since mortgages generally are the preferred security for lenders regarding real estate transactions, the limited floating charges are sparsely used in this context.

4.4 Financial assistance restrictions
It should be noted that there are certain restrictions with regard to financial assistance for the acquisition of limited liability companies.

A limited liability company may not lend funds to, nor provide security for loans to its shareholders and certain parties with a close relationship to the company or its shareholders. An important exception is that the restriction does not apply to loans to or security for companies within the same group.

The most important restriction is the so-called acquisition loan prohibition (*förvärvslåneförbudet*) which applies to the actual acquisition. The acquisition loan prohibition restricts the limited liability company from lending funds, providing security or giving guarantees to be used for the acquisition of its own shares, or shares in another company in the same group, meaning, *inter alia*, that the real estate owned by the target company cannot be used as security for the financing of the acquisition. There is no general exception to the acquisition loan prohibition for loans to or security for companies within the same group as there is for the general prohibition on loans. There is one exception, though, pursuant to which a parent company may grant loans or provide security for the acquisition of a subsidiary.

5. MANAGING THE ACQUISITION PROCESS
5.1 Introduction
Detailed below are the minimum formalities, main legal documents and other relevant factors when acquiring real estate through direct and indirect purchases including the typical and most important factors and documents affecting, or used in a real estate transaction, but it is not exhaustive as to all possible relevant factors and documents.

5.1.1 Direct purchase
When acquiring real estate in Sweden through a direct purchase, there are formal requirements to observe in order to acquire the real estate with good title. The legal provisions governing such a purchase are found in the Land Code. The minimum formalities are:
- the sale and purchase agreement must be in writing and signed by both the seller and the purchaser;
- the sale and purchase agreement must contain information regarding which real estate the purchase refers to, the purchase price and a declaration of transfer of the real estate from the seller to the purchaser; and
- the seller's signature should be certified by two witnesses, in order to avoid a (six month) delay in receiving the registered ownership (see below).

It should be noted that, due to the aforementioned formal requirements, an option to purchase or sell real estate is in principle never binding.

5.1.2 Indirect purchase
An indirect purchase may be conducted in various ways. The most common method is the so-called portfolio purchase, carried out either by acquiring the shares in a limited liability company which in turn owns the real estate or by acquiring the shares in a limited partnership (or a trading partnership) which in turn owns the real estate. As mentioned, there has to be at least one limited partner and one general partner in a limited partnership (or two partners for the trading partnership) at all times, which means that the buyer must have one additional partner (which, for instance, can be a subsidiary of the buyer).

For indirect purchases, no specific formal requirements apply for entering into share purchase agreements regarding the shares of the target company, instead the general statutory provisions regarding sale of goods applies.

However, regarding both direct and indirect purchases certain rules need to be observed in some cases (see below).

For the limited liability company, share certificates evidencing the ownership of the real estate holding company are normally handed over from the seller to the buyer at close of the transaction. Further, the share register of the limited liability company has to be updated with the new shareholder's details.

5.2 Main legal documents
5.2.1 Direct purchase
A direct purchase of real estate normally involves at least two different documents: the sale and purchase agreement and the deed of purchase. The sale and purchase agreement is the only required document and is used to regulate the parties' obligations in relation to the transaction, while the deed of purchase, if used, often serves as a receipt for the payment of the purchase sum. Normally, the purchase agreement contains customary representations and warranties with respect to the real estate. If a deed of purchase is used, the same formalities apply as for the sale and purchase agreement. Also, conditions precedent to the consummation of the transaction need to be repeated in the deed of purchase in order to remain valid and binding.

When closing under the sale and purchase agreement has occurred, the buyer must file an application for registration of ownership with the Swedish Land Register in order to acquire good title to the real estate.

5.2.2 Indirect purchase
An indirect purchase normally involves a share purchase agreement regarding the shares in the vehicle owning the real estate. The indirect purchase of real estate has many resemblances with a normal M&A transaction. The agreements usually contain customary representation and warranties with respect to the company as well as representation and warranties in respect of the real estate.

Several other documents are usually drawn up in order to comply with the Swedish Company's Act and to clarify the obligations of the parties, eg closing agendas, authorisation documents, board minutes and general power of attorneys.

5.3 Transaction costs
The buyer typically pays its own legal costs (plus VAT), Land Register fees, stamp duty and any valuation fees.

The seller typically pays its own legal costs (plus VAT).

5.4 Warranties
5.4.1 Direct purchase
By operation of law, the rights and obligations of the parties are regulated in the Land Code. Therefore, certain representations and warranties are implied by the Land Code of which some can be waived. In addition, a sale and

purchase agreement contains specific representations and warranties with respect to the real estate.

5.4.2 Indirect purchase
One purpose of warranties in this context is to allocate the risk of unknown defects between the parties.

The seller usually warrants its ownership of the shares in the company as well as the company's ownership of the real estate. Further, a number of different warranties can be given, eg, regarding the company's compliance with law, the absence of mortgages, the correctness of the balance sheet, the absence of change of control clauses in material lease agreements and the absence of environmental contamination.

It should be noted that the articles of association and the articles of partnership often contain a pre-emption clause which needs to be waived by the seller before the sale of the shares.

5.5 Liability for the purchaser due to matters prior to the transaction/ transfer
5.5.1 Environmental liability
There is a risk that the real estate owner might be held liable for contamination on the real estate. Such risk can be neutralised or mitigated through warranties from the seller of the real estate in the sale and purchase agreement or the share purchase agreement. Any decontamination or other corrective measures ordered by relevant environmental authorities would however be issued towards the real estate owner.

5.5.2 Direct purchase
Persons or entities that may become liable to clean up environmental damage may be divided into two categories: (i) operators (ie, persons conducting activities); and (ii) persons who acquired the real estate after 31 December 1998 and at the time of the acquisition were aware, or should then have discovered, the contamination. Operators are primarily liable and real estate owners are secondarily liable. Only where a primarily liable operator capable of bearing the cost of clean-up cannot be identified does the real estate owner become liable.

It is important to note that a real estate owner may be deemed to carry out activities which render it primarily liable as an operator pursuant to the Swedish Environmental Code merely by storing used waste or chemicals in barrels, cisterns and wells or similar on the real estate. This well established principle applies regardless of whether a third party has generated the waste and deposited eg, the barrels on the real estate.

Secondary liability means that the real estate owner is responsible only where liability cannot be imposed on any of the current or previous operators. However, there is one exception: the owner of real estate which has been cleaned up can always be required to bear the costs corresponding to the increase in value of the real estate resulting from the clean-up. This rule is intended to prevent real estate owners from making an undue profit from the clean-up borne by a third party, eg, in cases where a real estate company owns contaminated real estate in attractive locations.

An important limitation on the real estate owner's liability for clean-up is, according to transitional legislation, that such liability applies only to persons who acquire the real estate after the entry into force of the Swedish Environmental Code, ie, after 31 December 1998. The liability rule does not apply to acquisitions prior to that date.

An additional requirement is that the owner, at the time of the acquisition, was aware, or should have discovered, the contamination. This means that the purchaser of real estate on which there is suspected contamination (typically all industrial real estate) should exercise care and conduct enquiries regarding previous use and investigate the areas in which contamination is suspected. The scope of this 'duty to investigate' is determined on a case by case basis.

5.5.3 Indirect purchase
The liability of a real estate owner applies only to those persons or entities that acquire a real estate (or site leasehold rights). At present it is unclear whether liability may be imposed also on parties who, after 31 December 1998, acquire shares or ownership interests in companies which own real estate or merge with a company which owns real estate. However, where the company in respect of which shares or ownership interests are purchased has acquired real estate after 31 December 1998, liability can be imposed on such company in its capacity as real estate owner. This should be taken into account where an acquisition of shares or participations in a company owning, eg, industrial real estate is contemplated.

5.5.4 Undertakings towards tenants
Another possible liability which can arise and affect the purchaser is the sellers' undertakings towards tenants, eg, for restorations or refurbishments of the apartments.

5.5.5 Easements and other registered rights
The real estate may also be encumbered by easements and other registered and unregistered rights which can affect the buyer in various ways, eg, obligations regarding maintenance of roads crossing the real estate or potential restraints in the owner's disposition of the real estate.

5.5.6 Injunctions from authorities
Should injunctions, for instance to alter the premises, have been issued by an authority; the buyer can be obligated to adjust the matter, resulting in costs for the buyer. Any liability with respect to such injunctions should therefore be regulated in the sale and purchase agreement.

5.5.7 Mandatory ventilation control
Due to the potential costs involved, mandatory ventilation control (*Obligatorisk ventilationskontroll* (OVK)) can become a critical issue in an acquisition of real estate. Should the results of such controls not meet the

requirements set out by the authorities, the buyer could be obligated to reconstruct the ventilation systems. This is often very costly. Hence, this issue should be thoroughly regulated in the sale and purchase agreement.

5.6 Notarisation
5.6.1 Direct and indirect purchase
None of the documentation in a direct or indirect purchase needs to be notarised to be valid or binding. However, see section 5.1 above in which we recommend the witnessing of the seller's signature in the sale and purchase agreement regarding direct purchases. This can, however, be done by any person and notarisation is not needed.

5.7 Legally binding contract and transfer of the title to the real estate
5.7.1 Direct purchase
By operation of law, the parties are bound when signing the sale and purchase agreement. However, the ownership of the real estate is transferred gradually in mainly four separate steps:
(i) when the sale and purchase agreement is signed;
(ii) when the deed of purchase, if any, is signed;
(iii) when application for registration of ownership is filed with the Land Register; and
(iv) upon registration of new ownership.

Each of these four steps has certain legal consequences for the transfer of ownership and the transfer is in principal final upon registration.

5.7.2 Indirect purchase
The parties are bound when signing the share purchase agreement and the transfer of ownership is complete when the share certificates, if any, are handed over. Should share certificates not have been issued in the real estate holding company, such certificates should be issued by the seller prior to completion of the transaction. It is customary that the bank requires share certificates to perfect the pledge over the shares and as a security for financing the acquisition.

5.8 Insurance between signing and closing
5.8.1 Direct and indirect purchase
Generally, the sale and purchase agreement or the share purchase agreement regulates the admission day and the seller is normally required to have insurance for the real estate until this day. Hence, the purchaser should be insured from the closing date.

6. REAL ESTATE BASICS
6.1 Real estate legislation
Swedish real estate legislation is divided into two main parts; general real estate law and specialised real estate law. The general real estate law is primarily governed by the Land Code (1970:994) which is divided into two main sections. The first section defines real estate and its boundaries and

stipulates the types of real estate that are deemed to be fixtures to real estate or an actual part of a real estate unit. Furthermore, it contains regulations regarding the legal relation between neighbours, real estate transactions, grounds for invalidity of such transactions, security interests in real estate and the various types of user rights. The second section covers registration of ownership, user rights and security interests as well as the rights following from such registrations.

The specialised real estate law is divided into environmental law, governed by the Environmental Act (1998:808), and land use law, governed by a number of specific acts, such as the Real Estate Formation Act (1970:988), Planning and Building Act (1987:10), Joint Facilities Act (1973:1149), Utility Easements Act (1973:1149), Expropriation Act (1972:719) and the Acquisition of Rental Real Estate Act (1975:1132).

Normally, general real estate law affects the legal relations between private entities, such as a buyer and a seller of real estate or a landlord and a tenant, whilst specialised real estate law is applicable to situations where a public authority affects the ownership or use of real estate exercised by private entities.

6.1.2 Real estate units
The Land Code defines real estate as land. It is further stated that land is divided into real estate units. This division can only be carried out by the National Land Survey (*Lantmäteriet*) subject to the Real Estate Formation Act. A real estate unit is usually delimited vertically on the ground, but can also be delimited horizontally. According to the Real Estate Formation Act, three dimensional real estate units, which were introduced in 2004, can only be created if deemed to be the most appropriate solution.

6.2 Real estate ownership and user rights
6.2.1 Ownership of real estate
As described above under section 5, transactions involving real estate are subject to certain mandatory form requirements. Ultimately, to complete a transfer of ownership, the purchaser must apply for ownership registration. Once the ownership is approved and registered in the Land Register the owner is protected from competing ownership claims. The Real Estate Register will be further described below.

Real estate may be owned individually by one person or legal entity or jointly by several persons or legal entities. Joint ownership is subject to the Co-ownership Act (1904:48) whereby all owners have an equal right to the entirety of the real estate, provided that the owners have not agreed otherwise. Other forms of joint ownership are not recognised by Swedish law.

6.2.2 Ownership rights and limitations
An ownership of real estate entails the right to freely dispose of the comprised land and buildings for an unlimited period of time, although subject to certain limitations. One fundamental limitation is the right to public access, which is established in the Instrument of Government and

grants every person the right to access any real estate (referring to land, not buildings) without permission from the owner. Furthermore, the Land Code establishes that every person in their use of real estate, to which the person or someone else is the owner, must show reasonable consideration in respect of the surrounding neighbourhood. Reference shall also be made to the Environmental Code according to which precautionary measures must be taken to prevent damage to humans and the environment or nuisance for surrounding neighbours when performing *inter alia* construction or excavation work. Further, erection of buildings is generally subject to restrictions and permit requirements following from the Planning and Building Act. In some cases, the opinion of neighbours is part of the process of obtaining a building permit.

According to the Expropriation Act, ownership or user rights to real estate may be claimed by the state or a municipality, under certain conditions, with the purpose of facilitating residential buildings, public transportation, power supply or military purposes etc. An expropriation may not be carried out if there is any other option which satisfies the relevant purpose. If the expropriation is carried out, the owner is entitled to compensation subject to a decision of an expropriation court.

6.2.3 Site leasehold
Real estate owned by the state or a municipality or otherwise owned by the public can be held with site leasehold. Out of the user rights governed by the Land Code, site leasehold most resembles ownership as the site lessee may dispose of the real estate in almost the same manner as an owner, except for putting it up for sale (the user right itself may however be transferred). Consequently, the lessee may convey user rights, erect and maintain buildings and use the real estate as security for mortgages etc.

The Land Code defines site leasehold as a user right to real estate for an indefinite period of time for a certain purpose against an annual fee. The purpose behind this construction was originally to enable the municipalities to provide land for residential building for a reasonable price and at the same time, through an annual fee which is normally regulated every 10 years, to some extent profit from the increase in value of the real estate. The minimum term for a site leasehold is 60 years if the land is used primarily for residential purposes. In other cases, the minimum term is 20 years. The site leasehold can only be terminated by the land owner and only if it is essential that the land is used for a different purpose. The lessee is the owner of the buildings on the real estate and shall be compensated for the value of the buildings if the site leasehold is terminated.

6.2.4 Tenancy
As defined in the Land Code, tenancy entails a right to dispose of buildings or part of buildings for residential or commercial purposes. A lease agreement can be valid for a certain period of time or indefinitely until further notice. Generally, an agreement with a fixed term will be prolonged until further notice if not terminated in accordance with the agreement or

if the tenant continues to use the premises after the term of the agreement has expired (without the landlord requiring the tenant to vacate). Notice on termination regarding an agreement with an indefinite term must be given subject to certain minimum time periods depending on the total duration of the lease. As opposed to residential tenants, a tenant of a commercial lease has no general right of prolongation ie, direct legal protection of tenancy (*direkt besittningsskydd*). The commercial tenant is, however, generally entitled to compensation if the landlord refuses to prolong the agreement or if the agreement is terminated by the tenant due to new conditions imposed by the landlord, which the tenant finds unacceptable, ie indirect legal protection of tenancy (*indirekt besittningsskydd*). A commercial lease agreement may be transferred by the tenant, or subleased, subject to the landlord's consent or, if such consent is not obtained, subject to a decision by the regional rent tribunal.

6.2.5 Land leases

A land lease is a right to dispose of land, including any buildings, on a real estate unit. There are four types of land leases governed by the Land Code, categorised based upon whether the land is used for agricultural, residential, commercial or general purposes.

The agricultural land lease includes agricultural land and in some cases also residential buildings (the lessee may be entitled to reside on the real estate). Typical for the agricultural lease is that the real estate owner owns all buildings on the real estate.

The residential land lease is, as evident from its name, lease of land for residential purposes. As opposed to the agricultural land lease, the buildings are typically owned by the lessee. This is also the case regarding commercial land lease where the lessee normally is the owner of the buildings (such as offices or industrial facilities). Consequently, an agreement regarding residential or commercial land leases usually includes a right for the lessee to erect and maintain buildings on the real estate. This means that such buildings are not deemed to be fixtures to the real estate unit but instead considered as separable personal property (*lös egendom*) owned by the lessee, as opposed to buildings owned by the land owner.

The general land lease includes all leases of land that do not fall under any of the other categories, such as parking spaces, storing space, sport grounds etc. The general lease is only governed by general provisions and the parties may to a great extent decide on the conditions of the lease agreement.

The term of a residential, commercial or general land lease agreement may not be longer than 25 years for land subject to a detailed development plan (*detaljplan*), otherwise 50 years or as long as the lessee is alive. The term of an agricultural land lease may not be longer than 25 years. However, land leases where the real estate is owned by the state are exempted from these time limitations.

Similar to the provisions regarding tenancy, residential land leases, and agricultural land leases where the lessee is entitled to reside on the premises, are subject to a right equivalent to the direct legal protection of tenancy and the commercial land lease is subject to a right equivalent to the indirect legal protection of tenancy, as defined above.

Further, lessees of residential land leases and agricultural land leases, where the lessee is entitled to reside on the premises, are under certain circumstances entitled to purchase the real estate which is subject to the lease.

6.3 Land registration
All owned real estate units in Sweden are registered in the Land Register and each real estate unit is subject to a unique registration designation. The Land Register is managed by the National Land Survey which is the national land registration authority. The National Land Survey handles about a million transactions per year.

The registration of land in the Land Register is an important public function since it ensures security for the real estate owners as well as other interest holders. The Land Register, *inter alia*, contains information regarding current and previous ownership, including the date and the purchase price for each transaction, information on whether the real estate unit is held by site leasehold and in that case current and previous holdings, easements and other encumbrances, previous and ongoing real estate formation procedures, security interests and information relating to tax assessment.

UK

Berwin Leighton Paisner Graham Lloyd-Brunt & Annabel Pyke

1. INVESTMENT PURCHASE OVERVIEW
Typical investment purchase in England and Wales[1]

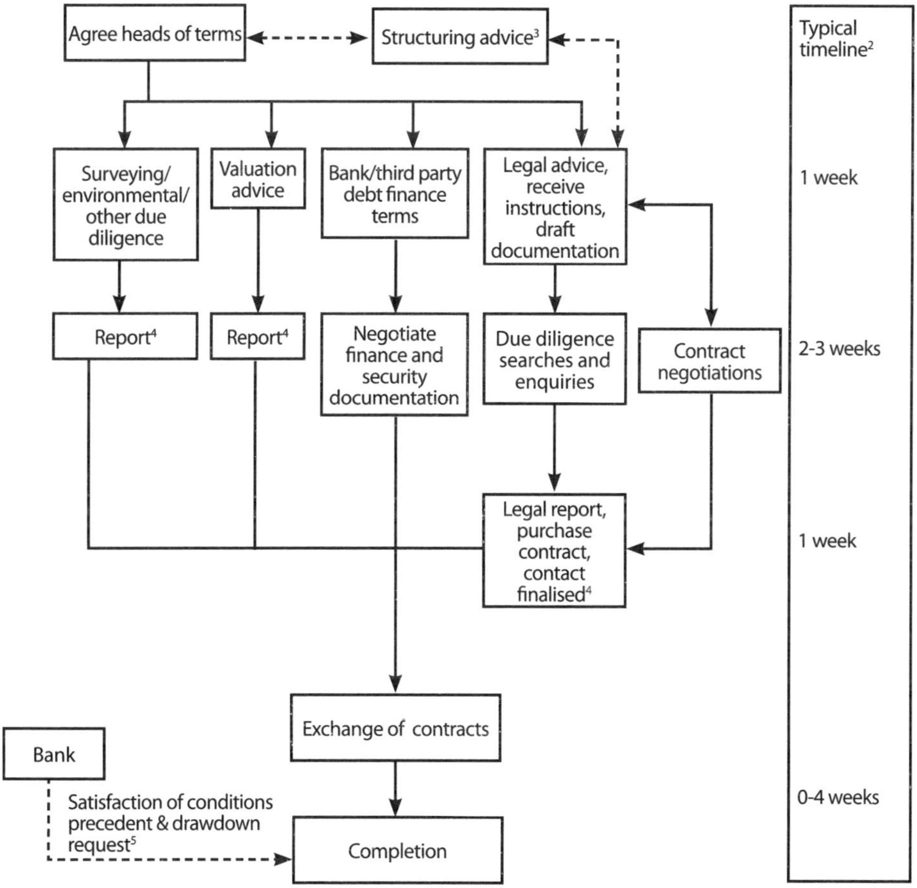

```
Agree heads of terms ◄------► Structuring advice[3] ◄----┐
        │                              │                   │
   ┌────┼──────┬──────────┬────────────┤                   │
   ▼    ▼      ▼          ▼            ▼                   │
Surveying/  Valuation  Bank/third  Legal advice,           │
environmental/ advice  party debt  receive                 │
other due              finance     instructions, ◄─────┐   │
diligence              terms       draft               │   │
   │        │          │           documentation       │   │
   ▼        ▼          ▼            ▼                  │   │
Report[4] Report[4]  Negotiate   Due diligence     Contract
                    finance and  searches and    negotiations
                    security     enquiries
                    documentation   │
                         │          ▼
                         │      Legal report,
                         │      purchase
                         │      contract,
                         │      contact
                         │      finalised[4]
                         │          │
                         ▼          ▼
                    Exchange of contracts
Bank                       │
  Satisfaction of conditions
  precedent & drawdown
  request[5] -----------►  Completion

Typical timeline[2]
1 week
2-3 weeks
1 week
0-4 weeks
```

[1] The legal system in Scotland differs.
[2] Often subject to compression, timescales may differ considerably. Exchange and completion may be simultaneous.
[3] Establishing an acquisition structure for tax and financial planning is an important early stage which may significantly influence other stages such as the banking arrangements (eg using Islamic financing structures) and the purchase contract.
[4] Each report will be addressed to the buyer and its funders.
[5] Before exchanging contracts it is advisable to ensure that all conditions precedent are capable of satisfaction.

2. TAX CONSIDERATIONS
This section is a general guide to some of the main UK tax considerations for a non-UK resident looking to acquire UK real estate as an investment.

UK

Tailored advice should be sought to confirm the precise UK tax implications and ensure the right acquisition structure.

2.1 Typical non-resident structure
A non-UK company is historically a popular vehicle for non-UK residents to hold UK real estate, as it offers the following advantages:

2.1.1 Rent taxed at 20 per cent
UK companies are generally taxed at 28 per cent on their net rental income. However, non-UK tax resident companies holding the property as an investment only pay tax at 20 per cent on income from UK real estate. This rate does not depend upon a tax treaty, so it applies irrespective of where the non-UK company is resident.

The UK operates a system for withholding this 20 per cent tax from rent before it is paid to non-residents. However, it is possible to obtain a prior clearance from the UK tax authorities for rent to be paid gross, pending eventual settlement of the appropriate tax due at the tax payment point (31 January in the year after 5 April).

2.1.2 Generous deductions for interest expenses
The UK has generous rules that allow the amount of rent that is taxed to be reduced by the interest paid on third party finance taken out to acquire the UK real estate. Interest on shareholder debt may also be deductible, subject to the UK transfer pricing rules. The UK generally withholds 20 per cent tax from interest paid to non-residents, though this will depend on the precise structure of the debt and/or any available tax treaty relief.

2.1.3 No UK tax on gains when investment property sold
Non-UK residents holding property as an investment are not generally subject to UK capital gains tax. Therefore, any gain realised when a non-UK company sells UK real estate should not be taxed in the UK. The non-UK company can also generally be sold without triggering UK tax on the gain, or any UK transfer taxes.

2.1.4 Capital allowances available
Non-UK residents can claim capital allowances, which will reduce the amount of rent that is subject to UK tax. Capital allowances are a form of depreciation allowances on plant and machinery, and can be very valuable. Broadly, if available, they can be claimed on a reducing basis at either 10 per cent or 20 per cent per year, depending upon the type of plant and machinery. Agreements should be drafted to optimise these, where possible.

2.1.5 Minimises transfer taxes
Stamp duty land tax (SDLT) is payable by the purchaser of UK real estate generally at a rate of four per cent of the purchase price. The sale of shares in a non-UK company that owns UK real estate is not generally subject to SDLT or any other UK transfer taxes.

UK

2.2 Points to bear in mind
The acquisition of UK real estate can be complex and there are a number of issues that need to be carefully considered and planned around to reduce exposure to UK tax and ensure that the structure is practical to run on a day-to-day basis. Below are just some of the other more significant issues that need to be considered (in addition to the points above) when acquiring UK real estate. As always, it is vital to get appropriate professional advice.

2.2.1 Residence
The offshore entity must be managed and controlled outside the UK to maintain non-UK tax resident status. In the case of a company, this generally requires that a majority of the directors (or equivalents) are non-UK tax resident and that all board meetings are held outside the UK.

2.2.2 Investment vs trading
The tax treatment outlined above assumes that the non-UK resident company will own the UK real estate as an investment. If it is developing or trading in UK real estate, then the profits may be taxed differently. The distinction between trading and investment is important – if a non-UK resident company is treated as trading in UK property, it may become subject to UK corporation tax at 28 per cent on all of its profits from that trade carried on in the UK, including any gain on the disposal. This can be a particular issue if the real estate is sold soon after acquisition or development. Alternative structuring may be possible if trading is intended. Non-UK developers also need to watch out for anti-avoidance legislation, which can bring gains into the charge to UK tax.

2.2.3 Value added tax (VAT)
VAT will usually be chargeable on the acquisition of UK commercial real estate. The rate is 17.5 per cent rising to 20 per cent with effect from 4 January 2011. If the property is let, then a sale may be treated as a transfer of a going concern, provided certain conditions are met. In that situation no VAT will be payable, reducing funding costs and SDLT payable.

Similarly, VAT is usually charged on the rents paid by tenants. Owners of UK commercial real estate do not automatically have to charge VAT on the rents or sale price. It depends upon whether they have opted to charge VAT. However, if a landlord does not 'opt to tax' in this way, it will not generally be able to recover any of the VAT it pays when acquiring, maintaining or refurbishing the property and that VAT will become an absolute cost. It is generally only worth a landlord not 'opting to tax' if it can charge more rent as a result and the extra rent makes up for the lost VAT.

Different VAT rules apply to property for residential or charitable use. Specific advice should be obtained on the facts where appropriate.

2.2.4 Offshore unit trusts
Many investors in UK real estate structure their holdings via an offshore property unit trust. The main difference between an offshore unit trust and

a non-UK company is that the unit trust is generally treated as transparent for UK income tax purposes. The investors in the unit trust will, therefore, be taxed as if they received their share of the rents directly. These vehicles are particularly attractive to UK tax exempt investors because they can receive the rent tax free. These investors prefer not to hold UK real estate via a non-UK company because they cannot reclaim the 20 per cent tax it pays on the rent.

2.2.5 Due diligence
Where an interest in the UK real estate is acquired indirectly (via shares or units) there is always a risk that the vehicle has pre-existing tax or other liabilities. Appropriate due diligence should be carried out so that any such can be identified and quantified and accounted for in the transaction.

3. INVESTMENT VEHICLE CHOICE
This section briefly considers below some of the factors which may influence the type of vehicle or structure to be used when you decide to invest in the UK. This section additionally summarises a few of the more popular vehicles, together with their primary advantages and disadvantages, the majority of which are tax related. However, this is not an exhaustive list and, clearly, does not address the requirements of all potential investors, which would need to be considered on the facts.

3.1 Issues affecting the type of vehicle/structure when making an indirect investment
3.1.1 Control and decision making
Certain vehicles, in order to protect the efficacy of their structure, prohibit investors controlling the assets held by the vehicle. This is true of English Limited Partnerships (ELPs). If an investor is looking to make day-to-day decisions in relation to its assets then these vehicles may not be suitable.

3.1.2 Cost
Investing indirectly is generally more expensive at the point of set up than acquiring an asset directly. There are the ongoing running costs of the vehicle and in addition potential regulatory costs to factor in.

3.1.3 Size and number of assets
Where an investor is only proposing to hold one or two assets it may be more efficient to hold them directly. Where there are multiple assets there is merit in establishing an umbrella vehicle which can allow central management and increase the options on the future sale of the assets.

3.1.4 Location of the management team
If the management team is not based in the UK, how the asset will be managed on a day-to-day basis within the vehicle must be considered. Typically an asset manager is appointed to undertake this task to ensure efficiency and in some cases to ensure that the investors may retain their offshore tax status.

UK

3.1.5 Long term objectives
Is the intention to hold the assets for investment purposes or for trading? The answer to this question will affect the type of vehicle chosen. ELPs for example are most commonly used for investment type assets while limited liability partnerships or companies are often used for trading assets.

3.1.6 Other investor requirements
Certain vehicles are more or less attractive to different types of investors. Some investors have restrictions within their own constitutions which prohibit their investment into certain vehicles. Equally certain jurisdictions do not recognise all the alternative vehicles available in the UK.

3.1.7 Regulatory compliance
Certain vehicles have additional regulatory compliance requirements. For example, the ELP is governed by the Financial Services Authority (FSA) and requires an 'authorised person' to operate and manage it. If there is no authorised vehicle within the group a contract with a third party will be needed to provide this service to the vehicle. Some structures are more heavily regulated than others. The degree of regulation may impact on the type of investors that can invest and the activities of the vehicle.

3.1.8 Multiple vehicles
Often investors hold their assets through a series of vehicles in order to maximise both the tax efficiency of the structure and also the exit options for the investors. This may involve a combination of vehicles. Equally certain investors may require a feeder vehicle through which to invest into the main holding vehicle.

3.1.9 Investment strategy
If the investor is to retain the investment for any length of time, it will wish to ensure that the tax, control and regulatory aspects of the investment vehicle conform to its requirements. Equally, if it is intended to hold the investment for a short time only, it will be necessary to ensure that these characteristics do not prejudice liquidity.

3.1.10 Taxation of the vehicle
The summary below looks at some of the tax issues affecting different structures. In particular, the stamp duty land tax position will need to be considered, as this could be the main set-up or transactional cost. Ongoing tax will also be relevant and may depend on the likely level of the investor's involvement.

3.1.11 Term, exit and liquidity
Some types of vehicles have established markets for the trading of interests, others may be more limited.

In some cases a combination of the structures described below may be needed to achieve the requirements of all anticipated investors.

3.2 Types of vehicle
3.2.1 English Limited Partnership (ELP)
ELPs have traditionally been popular vehicles for indirect real estate investment, because they are tax transparent for direct tax purposes, enabling different types of investor to invest together, but to be taxed according to their individual status.

ELPs offer limited liability to investors provided that they are not involved directly in management. Investors in an ELP are known as limited partners. All ELPs have at least one limited partner and must have one general partner. The general partner has control over the management of the partnership and unlimited liability for the debts and obligations of the partnership.

SDLT has, however, recently been imposed on transactions involving partnerships. Contribution of property to a partnership and a transfer of a partnership interest would trigger a four per cent charge on the gross underlying asset value of the interest acquired or transferred. If liquidity is sought, an ELP would not be an ideal option for this reason, but it may still be an appropriate investment vehicle where a long-term investment is anticipated, there is limited gearing or where the property is in a disadvantaged area.

ELPs are sometimes used in conjunction with offshore vehicles to enable day-to-day management of the property assets to take place onshore, without prejudicing the general tax status.

Interests in an ELP would be classified as units in an unregulated Collective Investment Scheme, and could not generally be marketed to private individuals.

Generally, an ELP requires an FSA authorised operator. This can add to the cost of using this vehicle. However, the ELP remains one of the most popular vehicles for indirect investment in the UK.

3.2.2 English limited liability partnership (LLP)
An LLP is popular where all partners wish to be involved in management of the vehicle and in such a case can avoid the need for an FSA authorised operator.

An LLP is a body corporate with, generally speaking, limited liability and which is treated as transparent for UK income and capital gains tax purposes.

Investors in an LLP are known as members. Each member has an undivided share in the assets of the LLP and is involved in the day to day management of the vehicle.

However, where an LLP is a property investment partnership, tax exemption on income and gains is denied to exempt funds, life funds and certain other bodies (but not charities). Accordingly, this is not likely to be a suitable investment vehicle where entities of this type may become investors or otherwise acquire an interest.

Contribution of the property to and transfer of an interest in an LLP would carry the same SDLT liabilities as outlined above for an ELP.

Depending on the length of the commitment period and the redemption method, an LLP could be structured so that it is not a collective investment scheme.

3.2.3 UK general partnership
A general partnership is generally tax transparent, but this status may be lost if the structure amounts to a collective investment scheme.

Again, the SDLT charges outlined above for ELPs would apply, and may render this vehicle unsuitable if a liquid investment is sought.

Partners in a general partnership are jointly and severally liable, and each investor can bind the partnership.

3.2.4 UK corporate vehicle
A UK resident company is commonly used by investors as the asset they are acquiring is often already held by a company. However, generally, companies are unattractive as indirect vehicles as they are not tax transparent and do not provide exempt investment returns for charities, exempt funds, UK individuals and offshore investors. The company is potentially liable to tax at 30 per cent on its income and chargeable gains, while the transfer of the contribution of the properties to the company would trigger a four per cent SDLT charge.

While transfers of the shares in the company would attract only 0.5 per cent stamp duty as opposed to four per cent on a land transfer, a share purchase may not be attractive to corporate investors either if there are historic capital gains in the company, which would be subject to charge on realisation. Acquisition of companies is, however, more palatable where the asset is held in a single purpose vehicle which has been established solely to hold the relevant asset. If this is not the case then extensive due diligence should be undertaken before acquiring the company.

Companies are often used below ELPs to hold individual assets to assist with alternative exit strategies.

A UK listed company has clear advantages in terms of its wide potential investor base, but trading history requirements often make listing impractical.

Listed companies are suitable for investors who are ISAs, Self Invested Personal Pensions (SIPPs) and Small Self-Administered Schemes (SSAS) which may make them more attractive to retail investors.

3.3 Use of partnerships
Partnerships are frequently used as key components in the structuring of indirect investments. The benefits of partnerships include the following:
- flow-through tax treatment;
- flexible remuneration arrangements for general partners; and
- flexible internal governance and control.

As partnerships are generally treated by fiscal authorities in the UK and the US as tax transparent for purposes of direct taxes, partners are treated as having invested directly in the underlying assets held by the partnership. Direct tax at the partnership level is generally either minimal or non-existent.

3.4 Types of partner
A limited partnership has two categories of partner:
- general partners, who have control over the management of the partnership and unlimited liability for the debts and obligations of the partnership; and
- limited partners, who are passive investors in the activities of the partnership and whose liability to the partnership is limited to their contributed capital.

The partnership agreement will allocate costs between the limited partners and the general partner. Those expenses related to the initial structuring, the ongoing operation and the investment activities of the partnership will be the responsibility of the limited partnership. The general partner will traditionally cover its own internal costs of operation. However, where fund expenses may have placed an unnecessary drag on fund performance, especially in the early years, a fund manager may cap the amount payable by the fund and cover the remaining amount itself.

A partner's interest in a partnership will be based on its capital account, which rises and falls in two ways:
- due to contributions and withdrawals of capital by a partner; and
- due to profits or losses of the partnership allocated to the partner.

The manner in which allocations of realised and unrealised gains and losses, together with income and expenses, are made will be governed by the partnership agreement.

Every limited partnership must have a general partner. In some respects the need to nominate or establish an entity to serve in this role has been a drawback to using partnerships. The rise of limited liability companies in the United States and LLPs in the United Kingdom reflects an attempt by legislatures to provide a vehicle with the flexibility of a traditional limited partnership, but without the formal requirement for a general partner.

A general partner may be either an individual or, more commonly in funds, a legal entity, which may be specifically organised for this purpose. The domicile, tax status and internal structure of the fund manager will frequently drive the choice of general partner.

At its simplest, the fund manager will itself serve as general partner, with the management and incentive fees earned flowing directly into the fund manager. The price for this simplicity is that the fund manager accepts unlimited liability for the debts and obligations of the partnership, therefore putting at risk, at least in theory, any other assets or revenue streams which the fund manager may possess or be entitled to in connection with other funds or clients.

Limited partners may lose the benefit of their limited liability if they participate in the management of the partnership. Where this line is ultimately drawn varies significantly from jurisdiction to jurisdiction.

3.5 Partnership agreements
The affairs of the partners are governed by the partnership agreement, the scope and contents of which are negotiated by the general and limited

partners. This flexibility is one of the principal attractions of partnerships, as opposed to the mandated structure and procedures associated with companies.

The partnership agreement constitutes the partnership and establishes the parameters of the relationships among the limited partners and between the limited partners and the general partner. These agreements can vary widely in their level of detail and breadth of subject matter, depending on the number of investors, any special needs or requirements of particular investors and the complexity of the commercial arrangements involving the general partner and its remuneration.

4. FINANCING AN ACQUISITION

A sophisticated real estate financing market operates in the UK.

Recent trends, particularly for corporate occupiers, have included so-called 'sale and lease backs' whereby property (often a portfolio they own and occupy) is sold to a third party investor, to unlock capital value to the owner for use in its business, followed immediately by a lease back to the owner to occupy, often for a 25 year term, at market rent (often subject to annual fixed rental uplift increases, by reference to a UK price inflation index). The investor obviously gains real estate assets, on purchase, and an income stream from a (usually) strong tenant covenant under the lease.

Real estate financing is usually by a mix of debt and equity. A bank loans a proportion of the purchase costs by way of debt (in the current 'credit crunch' climate, this will be limited to between 60 per cent and 70 per cent; previously much more highly leverage deals were being seen, of up to 90-95 per cent) to the buyer in return for:

- Fixed security over the property to be purchased (a legal mortgage). This may be comprised in a standalone legal mortgage deed. Alternatively, where, as is usual, other assets are to be charged by way of security (see below) the legal charge may be incorporated within a debenture.
- A debenture (if the buyer is a corporate, and the bank is to take security over all assets). A debenture comprises a fixed and floating charge over all the buyer's assets. A 'fixed charge' is one which operates to charge the property on the date it is taken. This will be over all real estate owned by the buyer (or subsequently acquired by it), and goodwill, for example. A 'floating charge' does not, unlike a fixed charge, attach to any one asset in particular; the buyer is therefore free to deal with any assets subject to a floating charge until the lender freezes (crystallises) the charge. On crystallisation, the buyer will then be unable to dispose of assets then charged by that crystallised charge without the lender's consent. A floating charge crystallises, usually, on an event of default under the loan or the insolvency of the buyer.
- An assignment of the right to receive rents from occupational tenants at the property to be mortgaged as security for the loan (standard practice for investment property). This assignment is usually also included within the debenture. The assignment of the rental stream is critical from the lender's point of view; it will be used to service the debt repayments.

- A charge over shares (if a borrower is a special purpose vehicle (SPV) for example);
- Assignment of the benefit of any major contracts (eg in connection with recent development of the property to be funded) (again this will usually be within the debenture).

There will be a number of finance documents, in addition to those mentioned above (not least the loan/facility agreement) to be negotiated.

Where the borrower (or a third party, such as a parent company) giving security in connection with the financing is not incorporated in England and Wales, there are capacity issues to be dealt with.

In the package of rights granted to the lender will be a series of restrictions on the activities a borrower can undertake. In particular, it will be unable to dispose of the assets forming part of the security package without first obtaining the lender's consent. In practice this will only be given where the lender is to receive the payment proceeds, usually, to repay the debt. In addition, the borrower will be prevented from borrowing from or granting security to other parties (the so-called 'negative pledge' provision).

The lender will usually expect first ranking security over the property which is to be secured for the debt due from the borrower. If this is over unregistered land, that will trigger the requirement to register that land at the Land Registry. If over registered land, this must also be registered at the Land Registry. Registration is critical to ensure that the bank has priority over any subsequent dealings relating to the title. In the commercial lending context, the security is almost always accompanied by a restriction registered against the title at the Land Registry, to support the obligations undertaken by the borrower (namely that it will make no disposition without the lender's consent).

There is an additional perfection requirement in relation to security taken by a lender. It must be presented for registration at Companies House, which deals with all corporate related filings, within 21 days of the date of its creation. Failure to do so may mean that the security is void against any subsequent liquidator or administrator (two types of insolvency practitioner appointed where a company become subject to a corporate insolvency procedure) or other third party creditor.

5. ACQUISITION TERMS
5.1 Introduction
In the UK the process and terms on which commercial property is bought and sold is relatively standardised. This section explains the usual terms that apply to a sale and purchase of a commercial property asset. If the property is to be acquired by the purchase of the corporate vehicle that currently owns the property different terms would apply.

For the purposes of this section we assume that the transaction is the purchase of a commercial property that is already let to tenants.

5.2 Agreeing terms and binding contracts
In England and Wales the seller and buyer are not legally bound to sell

or buy property until a written contract has been signed and exchanged by both parties. The parties will usually, through their agents, agree the commercial terms and set those out in a heads of terms or term sheet. The seller's solicitor will then prepare the sale contract and provide the due diligence information about the property to the buyer's solicitor.

A sale contract for a commercial property is usually unconditional so the buyer is bound to complete usually two to four weeks after exchange. All due diligence and all finance arrangements will, therefore, have to be in place before exchange. It is rare for contracts to be conditional upon the buyer arranging finance.

After agreeing the heads of terms if either party wishes to pull-out of the transaction they can do so, usually without any penalty or compensation payable to the other party. Each party normally covers their own costs for the transaction.

The seller's solicitors are bound by professional conduct rules which prohibit the solicitor from dealing with more than one buyer without each of those buyers being informed. It is these conduct rules which the UK real estate market relies upon to ensure exclusivity applies but they only apply from the point at which solicitors are instructed which usually only occurs after the commercial terms are agreed. Occasionally parties will enter into a formal exclusivity or lock-out agreement to ensure negotiations remain exclusive until formal contracts are exchanged.

Substantially different arrangements apply to auctions sales and transactions involving property in Scotland.

5.3 The contract documents

Some contract terms have been standardised in a nationally recognised document called the Standard Commercial Property Conditions (SCPC). These are almost universally used by solicitors in the UK and they are considered to be unbiased towards either party. In addition the seller's solicitor will draft the written agreement that contains additional terms and terms that slightly adjust the SCPC arrangements.

The sale contract will include all of the commercial terms and the technical legal requirements to bind the parties. On completion the parties will also enter into a transfer document which effects the legal transfer of the property interest. There may also be other subsidiary documents, such as assignments of building contracts, depending on the circumstances.

5.4 Typical contract terms

The following is a summary of typical sale contract terms:

5.4.1 Completion

It is common practice to have approximately 20 working days between exchange and completion but the parties can exchange and complete simultaneously. Equally a period of several months or even years could be agreed if required. The completion monies are usually sent by the buyer to its solicitor in the morning of completion. They will transfer completion monies to the seller's solicitors and completion is usually required to occur before 2pm on the scheduled date. This gives the seller's solicitors time to transmit the completion monies to the seller's lender and/or the seller within UK banking hours on the day of completion.

5.4.2 Deposit
Where there is a period between exchange and completion the buyer normally pays a deposit of 10 per cent of the price on exchange. Large pension funds and some other institutions often avoid paying any deposit. It is generally accepted that a deposit of greater than 10 per cent is not enforceable. A buyer may pay a deposit of more than 10 per cent, but if it does the seller may not be able to keep more than 10 per cent of the price if the buyer later fails to complete. The buyer can be liable to pay damages for the seller's additional losses if the buyer fails to complete.

The deposit is usually held by the seller's solicitors in their client account pending completion. Interest accrues to the seller but this point may be negotiated. If the buyer fails to complete the seller can keep the deposit and terminate the contract.

5.4.3 Price
The actual amount payable on completion will, of course, be the agreed price (being an amount fixed at exchange) but adjusted by: (i) apportioned rents received by the seller in advance referable to the period after completion – normally this will reduce the amount payable; and (ii) possibly VAT although for commercial property investments this is often not payable at completion. SDLT is payable by the buyer to the tax authority within 30 days after completion.

Occupational rents are usually apportioned on a daily rate basis (whether the rents are paid quarterly or monthly) up to the scheduled date for completion. If completion is delayed by the buyer the seller can choose to keep the income until the actual day of completion.

If there are arrears of occupational rents remaining at completion the contract will require that arrears are not apportioned unless and until the arrears are actually paid by the tenant after completion. If the arrears are substantial bespoke arrangements can be agreed.

5.4.4 Conditions precedent and due diligence
It is common practice for the buyer to undertake all due diligence before exchanging contracts. The main risk for a buyer is that it will have to cover the whole cost of that due diligence usually without any legally binding agreement for a seller to sell or otherwise refund the cost.

There are usually no conditions precedent so the buyer should have the results of all due diligence reports (legal reports, surveys etc) and all funding arrangements committed prior to exchange. It is likely, therefore, for exchange of contracts to be several weeks after agreeing heads of terms. The principle of 'buyer-beware' (*caveat emptor*) applies. It is very rare for the seller to give any warranties and although the seller may make representations that are relied upon by the buyer during the due diligence process it is also rare for a buyer to claim against a seller if there are problems with the property discovered after completion. If the buyer becomes aware of new information between exchange and completion it has six working days within which to raise the issue with the seller so the buyer must act quickly.

If the seller has debt secured against the property this is usually discharged at completion and the buyer acquires the property free of financial encumbrances.

5.5 Managing the property between exchange and completion
The seller remains in direct control of the property and will have to deal with the tenants until completion. The contract will require the seller to deal with the property and the tenants appropriately and often require the consent of the buyer before undertaking anything that could affect the property. Examples include the following:

5.5.1 Insurance
The seller will usually continue to insure the property. It can be advisable for a buyer to insure from exchange because the contract will pass the risk of damage occurring to the property to the buyer. The buyer will be required to complete the purchase even if the property is substantially damaged between exchange and completion.

5.5.2 Outstanding rent reviews
Under the occupational leases there can be a rent review that takes effect prior to the completion date but has not been finalised. The seller can continue dealing with that rent review up to completion after which the buyer will take control. Any uplift in the rent whether agreed before or after completion of the sale will be apportioned between the seller and the buyer. There are, therefore, arrangements in the sale contract to regulate the conduct of the seller and buyer in relation to rent reviews.

5.6 Confidentiality
For a straightforward acquisition it is rare for the parties to agree to keep the terms of the sale confidential. In any event, following registration of transfer of the property after completion at the Land Registry (HMLR) the price paid will be noted on the title and made available to the public. The details of the legal owner are also a matter of public record.

5.7 Assignment of the contract
The buyer cannot assign the benefit of the sale contract – the buyer will have to complete the transaction.

6. REAL ESTATE LAW BASICS
Under English law there are two main types of property ownership:
- freehold; and
- leasehold.

UK

A freehold interest offers the owner of that interest absolute ownership, unlimited in time, both to the land and buildings/structures on it. 'Absolute' does not mean that the land may be used free from any restriction, planning restrictions may apply. Due to the system of land registration, the best class of title a freehold owner can obtain is 'freehold title absolute'; it is a state guarantee of title.

A leasehold interest, limited in time, is created out of a freehold interest; it gives the right to an occupier (the tenant) to possession on payment of a rent to the holder of the freehold interest (the landlord). Due to the system of land registration, the best class of title a leasehold owner can obtain is 'leasehold title absolute'; it is a state guarantee of title. A leasehold interest may be in respect of land and buildings (a lease of whole) or a lease of part of a building only, for example a single floor (a lease of part).

Land can be subject to both freehold and leasehold interests (for example where it is owned by one entity, and leased to another to occupy for a specified period). See the diagram below by way of illustration:

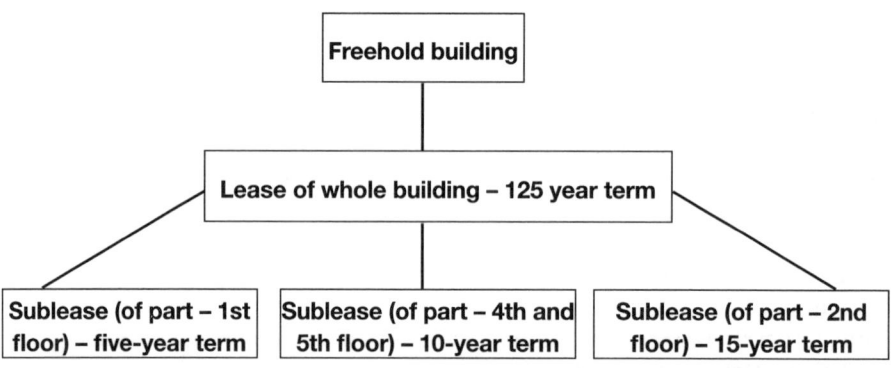

Leases may be granted for long or short periods, as this diagram indicates.

The UK investment market is built around rental income received by landlords (the investors) from their tenants under so-called occupational leases, typically for a term of 25 years or less.

Leases of 99 years and over are known as 'long leases'. A lease may be granted to last a period of up to 999 years (sometimes referred to as a 'virtual freehold', since the fruits of ownership are effectively passed to the tenant for several lifetimes). This will usually be in return for a premium akin to that which would be charged on the sale of the freehold. In consequence, however, the rent then payable under that lease will be nominal only. Not all long leases will be granted at a premium, with only nominal rent. There is another type of lease, commonly referred to as a 'geared lease', typically granted for a 99 (or more) year term which will usually require the rent to be paid up to the landlord to be a proportion of the income (expressed as a percentage) which the tenant itself receives from its sub-tenants (the tenant being the tenant under the 125 year headlease in the diagram above, for example).

Commonhold is, strictly, a species of freehold interest, it is akin to condominium ownership. It is a relatively new means by which a

UK

(residential, usually) development may be split into individual units, sold to so-called 'unit-holders' who will in turn then make up the 'commonhold association' to which the common parts will be transferred for ongoing maintenance of the estate as a whole. It has been little used, to date.

It is possible to occupy property under a licence, though this is a personal right and not a type of property interest. Since it is revocable in accordance with its terms it offers, of itself, no security of continued occupation.

6.1 Land registration

England and Wales has been subject to a system of land registration for over 150 years. There are more than 20 million registered properties in England and Wales, currently, so it is an increasingly comprehensive (and public) record of ownership. A separate title number identifies each piece of real estate registered. There does remain a significant portion of land which is unregistered.

There is a delay between the date on which the buyer actually purchases land, and the date on which the buyer becomes registered at the Land Registry as the legal owner of that land. This is called the 'registration gap'. The availability of a 'priority search' against the (registered) title to be acquired, undertaken to protect a buyer immediately before it completes the property purchase, offers some protection in this respect, since it ensures no competing applications can, usually, take priority to the buyer's purchase. The 'registration gap' can have consequences for a buyer, particularly in relation to ongoing management issues where land is registered.

6.1.2 Land which is registered

Copies of title can be obtained from the Land Registry. These are records of title, rather than particular transactions.

Title matters are set out in an official register of title, known as an 'official copy'. It includes:
- a description of the property (by reference to a title plan);
- the type of title (and whether freehold or leasehold);
- identity of the owner;
- certain rights affecting the property and other matters benefitting the property;
- any financial charges affecting the property;
- (if leasehold) brief details of the lease under which the property is held;
- the price paid by the current owner on its purchase of the property (this is not yet uniform across all titles);
- any restrictions on the owner's ability to sell the property; and
- brief details of occupational leases to which the property is subject (note that this is not comprehensive in all cases), namely the duration, tenant and initial rent payable.

Mention has been made of the quality of title with which a property may be registered. These are, in order of desirability:
- **Title absolute** (this may be given to both freehold or leasehold property). It is a state guarantee of title, incapable of defeat by anybody

claiming a superior interest. The title will be subject to the matters shown on the entries for that title and other matters revealed by due diligence.
- **Qualified title** (this may be given to both freehold or leasehold property). It is very rarely encountered in practice. It is given when there is some specific defect that has been identified, and is stated in the title entries of what would otherwise be a 'title absolute'. The state guarantee of title will not extend to cover that identified defect.
- **Good leasehold title** (only relevant to leasehold property). This is granted where the landlord's title to grant the lease to the tenant has not been shown. It is therefore vulnerable if it can subsequently be shown that the landlord did not have title to grant the lease. It is possible to upgrade the title to leasehold title absolute if the landlord's title is subsequently provided to Land Registry to evidence its right to grant the lease (often where the landlord's title is subsequently registered). Good leasehold title is not that uncommon; often tenants taking leases for shorter periods do not wish to go to the trouble and expense of having solicitors look over the landlord's title, so there is an element of risk allocation.
- **Possessory title** This is the most vulnerable class of title, since it is capable of being defeated by someone who can show a better title to the land. It is awarded to someone who can demonstrate they have occupied land for 12 years or more either without any formal right to do so (otherwise known as adverse possession) or where they are the legal owners but the title deeds have been lost. It is therefore given where the owner is not able to show documentary title to the property. It is possible to upgrade 'possessory title' to 'title absolute' once the owner has been registered with possessory title for 12 years or (at any time) they can then show documentary title – usually because the title deeds are found. Registration with possessory title means that the title is subject to all adverse matters affecting the property on registration of which it may have no actual knowledge; a note will be made to this effect on the title. This is because the documentary title is not of course available to otherwise specify what these may be.

The vulnerabilities of the various classes of title may be offset by insurance in most cases, though the cost/terms/limitations will vary, as will the number of insurers willing to offer particular types of insurance.

6.1.2 Land which is unregistered
If land is unregistered, information pertaining to its title must be supplied by the owner or its solicitors. This will usually comprise a collection of deeds and documents recording the seller's right to the property, and other matters affecting it. These copy deeds/documents are usually supplied in a so-called 'Epitome of Title' or 'Abstract of Title', which demonstrates a complete chain of ownership going back at least 15 years and ends with the sale to the current owner.

Most transactions will now trigger the requirement to register land.

Failure to register title, when one of these 'triggers' occurs, has serious consequences; after a given period title reverts to the seller (albeit to hold on trust for the buyer, the value in the property having been paid over by the buyer on completion).

Even if there is no trigger for compulsory registration it is still possible for the owner of unregistered land to apply voluntarily for its registration. Registration does afford some additional protections for a landowner.

Contact details

GENERAL EDITOR
Graham Lloyd-Brunt
Berwin Leighton Paisner
Adelaide House
London Bridge
London
EC4R 9HA
UK
T: +44 20 3400 1000
E: graham.lloyd-brunt@blplaw.com
www.blplaw.com

AUSTRALIA
David Turner & David Sharpe
DibbsBarker
Level 8 123 Pitt Street
Sydney
NSW 2000
T: +61 2 8233 9713
F: +61 2 8233 9555
E: david.turner@dibbsbarker.com
   david.sharpe@dibbsbarker.com
www.dibbsbarker.com

BELGIUM
Yves Delacroix (Real Estate) & Henk Verstraete (Tax)
Liedekerke Wolters Waelbroeck Kirkpatrick
Boulevard de l'Empereur, 3
Brussels
Belgium
1000
T: +32 (0) 2 551 14 18,
   +32 (0) 2 551 15 72
F: +32 (0) 2 551 15 54
E: y.delacroix@liedekerke-com
   h.verstraete@liedekerke.com
www.liedekerke.com

BULGARIA
Nickolay Nickolov & Iva Miteva
Borislav Boyanov & Co
82 Patriarch Evtimii Blvd
Sofia
Bulgaria
1463
T: +359 2 8 055 055
F: +359 2 8 055 000
E: mail@boyanov.com
www.boyanov.com

CANADA
Heather McKean, assisted by Jack Silverson & Brian Donnelly
Osler Hoskin & Harcourt LLP
100 King Street West,
1 First Canadian Place
Suite 6100, PO Box 50
Toronto
Ontario
Canada
M5X 1B8
T: +1 416 862 6612
   +1 416 862 5678
   +1 416 862 4247
F: +1 416 862 6666
E: hmckean@osler.com
   jsilverson@osler.com
   bdonnelly@osler.com
www.osler.com

CZECH REPUBLIC
Jan Holásek & Daniela Kozakova
Havel & Holásek s.r.o.
Attorneys at Law
Tyn 1049/3
Prague 1
Czech Republic
110 00
T: +420 224 895 950
F: +420 224 895 980
E: jan.holasek@havelholasek.cz
   daniela.kozakova@havelholasek.cz
www.havelholasek.cz

Contact details

DENMARK
Henrik Groos, Partner/Advokat/
Attorney-at-Law
Accura Advokatpartnerselskab
Tuborg Boulevard 1
DK-2900 Hellerup
Copenhagen
Denmark
T: +45 3945 2800
F: +45 3945 2801
E: henrik.groos@accura.dk
www.accura.dk

FRANCE
Mathieu Finaz, Véronique Lagarde &
Antonia Raccat
Lefèvre Pelletier & Associés
136, avenue des Champs Elysees
Paris
France 75008
T: +33 1 53 93 30 03
F: +33 1 53 93 30 51
E: mfinaz@lpalaw.com
   vlagarde@lpalaw.com
   araccat@lpalaw.com,
www.lpalaw.com

GERMANY
Dr. Axel Schilder & Dr. Nicole Kadel
Beiten Burkhardt
Westhafentower
Westhafenplatz 1
Frankfurt am Main
Germany
60327
T: +49 69 756095 276
   +49 69 756095 0
F: +49 69 756095 518
   +49 69 756095 512
E: Axel.Schilder@bblaw.com
   Nicole.Kadel@bblaw.com
www.beitenburkhardt.com

GREECE
Eliana Paschalides, Spyros Foulias &
Alexandria Mitsokali
V & P Law Firm
15 Filikis Eterias Sq.
Athens
Greece 106 73
T: +30 210 7206900
F: +30 210 7231462
E: mail@vplaw.gr
www.vplaw.gr

GUERNSEY
Aimee Curzon & Paul Nettleship
Collas Day
PO Box 140
Manor Place
St Peter Port
Guernsey
GY1 4EW
T: +44 1481 723191
F: +44 1481 711880
E: property@collasday.com
www.collasday.com

HUNGARY
Péter Berethalmi & Balázs Karsai
Nagy és Trócsányi
Ugocsa utca 4/B.
Budapest
Hungary
1126
T: +36 (1) 4878712
F: +36 (1) 4878701
E: berethalmi.peter@nt.hu
www.nt.hu

INDIA
Sudip Mullick (Partner) &
Sirish Vardhan (Associate)
Khaitan & Co
One Indiabulls Centre, Tower One,
13th Floor
841 Senapati Bapat Marg,
Elphinstone Road
Mumbai (Bombay)
Maharashtra
India
400 013
T: +91 22 6636 5000
F: +91 22 6636 5050

E: mumbai@khaitanco.com
www.khaitanco.com

ITALY
Avv. Umberto Borzi (Partner)
Chiomenti Studio Legale
Via XXIV Maggio 43
Rome
Italy 187
T: +39 06 46622 376
F: +39 06 46622 626
E: umberto.borzi@chiomenti.net
www.chiomenti.net

JERSEY
Christopher Philpott (Advocate and Partner) & Will Whitehead (Associate)
Carey Olsen
47 Esplanade
St. Helier
Jersey
JE1 0BD
T: +44 (0) 1534 822311
F: +44 (0) 1534 887744
www.careyolsen.com

LUXEMBOURG
Eric Fort & Claude Niedner
Arendt & Medernach
n 14, rue Erasme
Luxembourg
L-2082
T: +352 40 78 78 306
F: +352 40 78 04 633
E: eric.fort@arendt.com
www.arendt.com

NETHERLANDS
Aart Barkey Wolf & Wouter Ekkelkamp
Houthoff Buruma
Gustav Mahlerplein 50
Amsterdam
Netherlands
1082 MA
T: +31 20 605 6103
   +31 20 605 6943
F: +31 20 605 6700
E: a.barkey.wolf@houthoff.com
   w.ekkelkamp@houthoff.com
www.houthoff.com

NORTHERN IRELAND
Phyllis Agnew & David McDonnell
Tughans
30 Victoria Street
Belfast
Northern Ireland
BT1 3GG
T: +44 28 90553300
E: Phyllis.agnew@tughans.com
   David.McDonnell@tughans.com
www.tughans.com

REPUBLIC OF IRELAND
Ronan McLoughlin
Matheson Ormsby Prentice
70 Sir John Rogerson's Quay
Dublin 2
Ireland
D: +353 1 2322374
T: +353 1 2322000
F: +353 1 2323333
E: ronan.mcloughlin@mop.ie
www.mop.ie

RUSSIA
Elena Barinova, Andrey Shpak, Svetlana Savina, Matvey Kaploukhiy
Goltsblat BLP
Capital City Complex Moscow City Business Centre
8, Presnenskaya Nab., Bldg.1,
Moscow
Russia
123100
T: +7 (495) 287 4444
F: +7 (495) 287 4445
E: elena.barinova@gblplaw.com
   andrey.shpak@gblplaw.com
   svetlana.savina@gblplaw.com
   matvey.kaploukhiy@gblplaw.com
www.gblplaw.com

Contact details

SCOTLAND
Dale Strachan & Alistair Campbell
Brodies LLP
15 Atholl Crescent
Edinburgh
Scotland
EH3 8HA
T: +44 131 228 3777
F: +44 141 228 3878
E: dale.strachan@brodies.com
    alistair.campbell@brodies.com
www.brodies.com

SLOVAK REPUBLIC
Jan Holásek & Pavol Poláček
Havel & Holásek s.r.o.
Apollo Business Center II
Mlynské Nivy 49
Bratislava
Slovak Republic
821 09
T: +421 2 32 113 902
F: +421 910 822 593
E: pavol.polacek@havelholasek.sk
    jan.holasek@havelholasek.cz
www.havelholasek.sk

SPAIN
Jordi Sagrera
Cuatrecasas Gonçalves Pereira
Velázquez 63
Madrid
28001
T: +34 915 247 824
F: +34 915 247 164
E: jordi.sagrera@cuatrecasas.com
www.cuatrecasas.com

Bernat Mullerat
Cuatrecasas Gonçalves Pereira
VPº de Gracia 111
Barcelona
08008
T: +34 932 905 500
F: +34 932 905 567
E: bernat.mullerat@cuatrecasas.com
www.cuatrecasas.com

SWEDEN
Bob Johanson, Carolina Hertzen
& Sara Edström
Gernandt & Danielsson Advokatbyrå Kb
Hamngatan 2
Box 5747
Stockholm
Se-114 87
T: +46 8 670 66 00
F: +46 8 662 61 01
E: Bob.Johanson@gda.se
    Sara.Edstrom@gda.se
    carolina.hertzen@gda.se
www.gda.se

UK
Graham Lloyd-Brunt
& Annabel Pyke
Berwin Leighton Paisner
Adelaide House
London Bridge
London
EC4R 9HA
T: +44 20 3400 1000
E: graham.lloyd-brunt@blplaw.com
    annabel.pyke@blplaw.com
www.blplaw.com